Beyond Market and Hierarchy

Beyond Market and Hierarchy

Interactive Governance And Social Complexity

Edited by
Ash Amin
University of Durham, UK
and
Jerzy Hausner
Cracow Academy of Economics, Poland

Edward Elgar
Cheltenham, UK • Lyme, US

Published by
Edward Elgar Publishing Limited
8 Lansdown Place
Cheltenham
Glos GL50 2HU
UK

Edward Elgar Publishing Company
1 Pinnacle Hill Road
Lyme
NH 03768
US

A catalogue record for this book is available from the British Library

Library of Congress Cataloguing in Publication Data
Beyond market and hierarchy : interactive governance and social complexity / edited by Ash Amin, Jerzy Hausner.
'Derives from the Seventh Annual Conference of the European Association for Evolutionary Political Economy (EAEPE) held in Kraków in October 1995'—Pref.
Includes bibliographical references.
1. Institutional economics—Congresses. 2. Policy sciences—Congresses. 3. Social systems—Congresses. I. Amin. Ash. II. Hausner, Jerzy. III. Conference of EAEPE (10th : 1995 : Kraków, Poland) HB99.5.B49 1997
330—dc21 96–39589
CIP

ISBN 1 85898 482 3

Printed and bound in Great Britain by
Biddles Limited, Guildford and King's Lynn

Contents

List of Figures

List of Tables

List of Contributors

ASH AMIN is Professor of Geography at the University of Durham. Recently, he has edited *Post-Fordism: A Reader* (1994), *Globalization, Institutions and Regional Development in Europe* – with N. Thrift (1994) and *Behind the Myth of European Union: Prospects for Cohesion* – with J. Tomaney (1995).

JØRN ANDERSEN is registered for a Ph.D. at Roskilde University and currently employed as a National Expert in DGIII of the European Commission. He is author (with Michael Kluth) of 'Pooling the technology base – Europe's Research and Technology Organisations', in Michie, J. And J. Howells (eds) *Technology, Innovation and Competitiveness* (forthcoming).

BERNARD CHAVANCE is a Professor of Economics at the University of Paris 7. He is known for his work on the systemic change in post-socialist economies. His major publications include *Les Figures de L'Irréversibilité en Économie* – with B. Boyer and O. Godard (1991), *The Transformation of Communist Systems: Economic Reforms since the 1950s* (1994) and *La Fin des Systèmes Socialistes: Crise, Réforme et Transformation* (1994).

ROBERT DELORME is a professor at the University of Versailles and CEPREMAP (Centre d'études prospectives d'économie mathématique appliquées à la planification), Paris. He is known for his work on public economics, theory of state-economy interactions and theory of complexity. His major publications include *L'État et L'Économie* – with C. André (1983), 'Economic Intervention in the History of the French and Other European States: A Comparative Study' (1992), and 'The Case for Controlled Pluralism: A Bottom-up Approach'.

JERZY HAUSNER is the Head of Department of Public Economy and Administration at Cracow Academy of Economics. He is known for his work on regional industrial restructuring, industrial relations, transformation processes in Eastern Europe, and interest representation. His major publications include *Markets, Politics and the Negotiated*

Economy. Scandinavian and Post-Socialist Perspectives – with B. Jessop and K. Nielsen (1991), *The Protracted Death-Agony of Socialism: Political Mechanisms of Societal Life in Poland in the 1980s* – with T. Klementewicz (1993), *Financial Crisis of a State in Transformation. The Polish Case* – with S. Owsiak (1992), *Populist Threat in the Transformation of Socialist Society* (1992) and *Institutional Frameworks of Market Economies* – with B. Jessop and K. Nielsen (1993).

Bob Jessop is Professor of Sociology at Lancaster University. He is best known for his work on state theory, the regulation approach, and the political economy of postwar Britain. Most recently he has been involved in research projects on regional economic strategies in post-socialism and on local economic governance in Britain. His most important publications are: *The Capitalist State* (1982), *Nicos Poulantzas* (1985), *Thatcherism: a Tale of Two Nations* (1988) and *State Theory* (1990). He is currently working on a book on regulation theory.

Michael Kluth is Assistant Professor in the Department of Social Sciences at Roskilde University. His work is on industrial strategy, national systems of innovation and continental trading blocs. He is author (with Jørn Andersen) of 'Globalisation and financial diversity: the making of venture capital markets in France, Germany and the UK', in D. Archibugi, J. Howells, and J. Michie (eds) *National Systems of Innovation or the Globalisation of Technology* (forthcoming).

Riitta Kosonen is a senior researcher in Economics in the Department of Marketing, Helsinki School of Economics and Business Administration. She is currently involved in a research programme on Russian and East European studies financed by the Academy of Finland. Her recent work includes: 'Boundary, Institutions, and Indigenous Development: The Case of Vyborg' (1996).

Jürgen Lange-von Kulessa studied at the universities of Berlin and Freiburg where he received a Master's degree in Economics. At the moment he is preparing his Ph.D. thesis on models of collective learning processes and cultural evolution. He works at the Walter-Eucken-Institute in Freiburg. His main research interests are methodology and philosophy of economics, Austrian, evolutionary and institutional economics. He has co-edited a book on constitutional aspects of European integration.

Eric Magnin is a teaching and research assistant at the University of

Paris 1. He is known for his work on complexity and national trajectories of transformation. His publications include *La Trajectoire Tchèque de Transformation Économique Post-socialiste* (1996).

MAGALI ORILLARD is Professor of Economics at University of Aix-Marseille III and member of the Groupe de Recherche sur l'Adaptation, la Systématique et la Complexité Economique (GRASCE) (CNRS, Aix-en-Provence). For some years, her research has been in the area of modelling self-organizing socio-economic systems through cognitive networks. A recent publication is 'Stratégies de groupes et coordination des activités economiques', *Revue d'Economie Politique*, 105(1). She is a member of the 'Enterprise' committee of the French Commissariat General du Plan and of the boards of ADSE (Association pour le développement de la socio-économie) and of the European Program of Complexity Modelling (AEMCX).

WINFRIED RUIGROK is Professor of International Management at the University of St Gallen Research Institute for International Management. He is currently involved in research on the internationalization processes of large and medium-sized firms. He is the co-author with Rob van Tulder of *The Logic of International Restructuring* (1995) and of a forthcoming book on restructuring strategies in the world car industry (also with Rob van Tulder).

SILKE STAHL is a senior researcher at the Max-Planck-Institute for Research into Economic Systems. Her research interests include evolutionary-oriented explanations of the transition process in post-socialist states, long-run socio-economic change and property-rights theory.

NGAI-LING SUM is Alex Horsley Research Fellow at the Political Economy Research Centre, University of Sheffield. She has research interests in the political economy of newly-industrializing countries, cross-border regions, and the relationship between political economy and identity politics. Her most recent publications include an article on identity politics in Hong Kong in *Economy and Society*, and book chapters on the global-regional-local dynamics of 'Greater China' and identities of East Asian newly-industrializing countries. She is currently working on a book which examines the nature of capitalism in these countries from a regulationist perspective.

ROB VAN TULDER is Associate Professor of International Business,

Erasmus University, Rotterdam. His research interests include the strategies of multinational corporations, small industrial countries, competitiveness, technology and industrial policies. His most recent major publications include: *Dealing with Dilemmas: Case Studies on Information Technology and Strategy* (1995); *The Logic of International Restructuring* (1995) – with Winfried Ruigrok; and *Skill Sheets* (1996).

Preface

This book derives from the seventh annual conference of the European Association for Evolutionary Political Economy (EAEPE), held in Crakow in October 1995. The theme of the conference was 'Transforming Economies and Societies: Towards an Institutional Theory of Economic Change'. More than a hundred papers were presented at the conference, covering a wide spectrum of research areas, from analysis of economic transformation in East and Central Europe, to contributions on diverse aspects of theory and methodology in institutional economics. The practice of the Association is to publish a book from each of its annual conferences, with the objective of developing the profile of the Association, and more importantly, advancing evolutionary and institutional economics.

Originally, our aim as editors of this volume, was to produce a book representing approaches to economic transformation that would go beyond the limits of the orthodox alternative between market or hierarchy. We were spoilt for choice in finding excellent papers which fulfilled this criterion. In the course of reading the papers, however, it became clear that there were strong complementarities between the papers for final selection. This gave us the opportunity to go beyond the usual edited post-conference volume, and to produce a book with conceptual and empirical integrity, a strong line of argument and considerable novelty. But, to use this opportunity, our task as editors became much more ambitious. The thrust of the book shifted away from simply representing non-orthodox papers on economic transformation, towards articulating the conceptual framework of a novel institutionalist approach to economic change. It occurred to us that at the core of such a framework lay two basic concepts: social complexity and interactive governance.

The first concept signals the need to recognize that modern economy and society are driven by a variety of actors and rationalities, and as such, they are not only complex ontologies, but demand a non-reductionist epistemology that finds unity of causation and influence among structure, agency, action and cognition. For us, social complexity is ontologically and epistemologically constituted in parallel, through the recursive feedback between observer and observed. This feedback is not only a mechanism for reconciling theory and practice, but also the foundation for governance in a complex social world. Thus, the second concept stresses both the existence of networks of social organization and governance that cannot be reduced to purely spontaneous order (market) or deliberately constructed order (plan), and the requirement for a multiplex and interactive mode of governance. The combination of these two concepts allows us to properly grasp the relation between the governance of complexity and the complexity of governance. As a result, the framework we propose for making sense of social and economic change is non-reductionist, non-essentialist, non-teleological and post-rationalist. As such, this is a framework that, beyond substantial or even procedural rationality, recognizes the significance of a recursive procedural rationality – defined as the logic of reflexive thought and action by subjects in a complex and dynamic social setting.

In one way or another, the chapters in this book articulate this framework, or empirically illustrate its usefulness. In particular, the first five chapters develop the ontological, epistemological and theoretical foundations for dealing with social complexity, economic governance and change. The remaining six chapters describe the failures and successes of different governance set-ups in different cultural and institutional contexts. In so doing, they lend strong support to our argument stressing the significance of social context and of path-dependence, and the need for multiplex and interactive governance strategies in managing economic change.

Only the reader can judge whether this book achieves the coherence and ambition that we desire from it. Whatever this judgement, we wish to thank the authors for agreeing to embark on such a project and for their willing responsiveness to our suggestions for revision. In addition, we are enormously grateful to Jasper Tilbury and Anna Szczepanik for their editorial assistance.

Ash Amin and Jerzy Hausner

1. Interactive governance and social complexity

Ash Amin and Jerzy Hausner

1. INTRODUCTION

The ambitious question addressed in this book is how to comprehend, and act, in a complex world. The history of modernity has been that of increasing complexity in the patterns of social and economic organization, defiant of singular or all-embracing solutions (Sayer and Walker 1992, Luhmann 1979, Beck et al. 1994, Misztal 1996). Yet, in much of our thinking, we continue to believe that society can somehow be governed or steered. Alternatively, at the other extreme, individual-centred or 'geneticist' approaches hypothesize that market selection or autopoesis is the best you can hope for. This book tries to break free from the dualist logic that either nothing or everything can be achieved by collective action, by starting from the assumption that what exists (social ontology) and knowledge of what exists (epistemology) are not reducible to rationalist logics of abstraction or action. It assumes that both society and social knowledge are regenerated interactively and procedurally. Thus it discusses collective agency, in the context of social complexity, as the capacity to guide and shape existing networks through reflexive interaction and strategic guidance.

The practical significance of a root and branch reappraisal of issues of agency in a complex world cannot be over-emphasized. In the area of economic governance, for example, it is clear that without such an effort, it may not be possible to systematically imagine alternatives to the major policy orthodoxies of the latter part of this century, all of which are now under question. The crisis in Eastern Europe has thrown into sharp relief the problems of inefficiency and inequity associated with state-centred solutions. In the West, the problem of reconciling

We are very grateful to Bob Jessop for his perceptive remarks on an earlier draft. In addition, we wish to acknowledge the support of the EU's PHARE-ACE Programme, which provided the fellowship that allowed Jerzy Hausner to be based in the Department of Geography at Durham University in order to work on this chapter.

economic efficiency with social equity has returned to the political agenda in the wake of dogmatically pursued neo-liberal programmes, which have created social divisions on a scale that threatens economic efficiency and competitiveness. Elsewhere, the historic alternative to neo-liberalism, in the form of the Scandinavian welfare state model or the German social market economy, has come up against the limits of state provision owing to the scale of cost for their maintenance. Further afield, the East Asian developmental state, though without doubt a source of rapid economic modernization, is under scrutiny because of its weak political legitimacy. The dominant models of economic governance as we know them are increasingly threatened by their own internal contradictions.

These models have come under the strain also of a changing global economic environment. Neither states nor markets are capable on their own of making the continuous structural adjustments demanded by the process of globalization (Hirst and Thompson 1996, Ruigrok and van Tulder 1995). The pervasive integration of local, regional and national markets into a global market has exposed all economic agents to international forces that cannot be fully regulated (Amin 1996, Cox 1993, Jessop 1995). Markets, more than ever before, are actively contested in a perilous context of rapid product obsolescence and technological innovation; factors are increasingly mobile and interchangeable; communications reach all corners of the world; production and financial systems have become globally integrated; and so on. These are aspects of permanent instability and uncertainty which challenge the assumption of regulated competition presupposed by the majority of postwar models of economic governance. The models were designed to manage relative stability and reach equilibrium, while the present context requires models that are able to govern change and promote economic adjustment.

To a degree, these deficiencies of economic practice are the product of methodological reductionism within the social sciences. One problem is that much of the debate on methodology in the social sciences continues to be framed by dualist oppositions of ontology and epistemology. Against structure is posed agency, against holism is thrown individualism, against rational actors are cast behaviourally conditioned actors, against teleology is opposed historical contingency, and against constructivism is pitted spontaneity. Through such simple oppositions, heterodoxy on either side has been turned into orthodoxy, offering a one-sighted perspective on complex and changing social phenomena.

This said, there are liminal signs of a breakthrough across the social sciences, constitutive of methodologies that transgress these dualist oppositions. In sociology, for example, Anthony Giddens has developed the concept of 'reflexivity' to add a cognitive dimension to his earlier effort to reconcile structure and agency via the concept of structuration (Giddens 1991). In economic sociology, the work of Mark Granovetter, Richard Swedberg and others has sought to show how the economy is embedded in networks of interpersonal relationships, and how agents are locked into institutional and social networks (Granovetter 1985, Smelser and Swedberg 1994, Sabel 1994). Some sociologists see mutual interdependencies such as trust and reciprocity as important intermediaries for societal cohesion (Misztal 1996).

The latest advances in the behaviourial and cognitive sciences are grappling with the simultaneity and mutual reinforcement of different sorts of rationalities, from substantive and procedural, to reflexive rationality (see chapters in this book by Delorme and Orillard). Similarly, realist philosophy of science has made major advances in bringing closer structure and contingency through such intermediate concepts as 'contingent necessity' (see chapter by Jessop). In addition, the hermeneutic tradition that has been rediscovered around the work of Jürgen Habermas, together with what has come to be known as 'actor-network' theory in organizational sociology (Morgan 1986, Callon 1986), helps us grasp how individual and collective identities are forged through language, and the human and technological architecture of interaction and communication (Latour 1993). In economics, the rediscovery and advancement of old institutionalist thought had done much to stress the role of formal rules, institutions, and informal conventions such as habits, norms and values, in bridging the divide between individual agency and structured behaviour, and between historical continuity and change (Hodgson 1988, Hodgson et al. 1994, Mulberg 1995).

This catalogue of innovation in the social sciences is by no means exhaustive. What it does indicate, however, is an undercurrent of desire to develop new concepts and approaches that transgress the boundaries and restrictions of existing paradigms. At the simplest level, this might amount to a transdisciplinarity of approach that breaks with the artificial divisions imposed by containerization of the social sciences into separate subject disciplines. More fundamentally, however, the consensus appears to be for a non-reductionist social science that is capable of grasping the complexity of social systems without recourse to a purely rationalist and teleological logic. In addition, there is a discernible effort to conceptualize properly the dialectic between structure and agency, and between individual and collective, in explaining the nature of social relationships in advanced societies. These explorations do not as yet amount to a coherent, post-rationalist, social theory. Much more conceptual refinement, confrontation and systematization is required, but the explorations are indicative of an irrepressible foundational change in the social sciences.

The task of this chapter, and the volume in general, is to contribute to this process of rethinking the social sciences. More specifically, the chapter focuses on the issue of social complexity, by linking its epistemological and ontological dimensions with its policy-making dimension. In forging this link the aim is to discuss issues concerning the governance of complexity, both conceptually and practically. We use the concept of recursive procedural rationality as the intellectual and cognitive basis for dealing with complexity. The concept, we contend, helps to explain in a novel way the failures and successes of different economic governance systems, and to discuss the practicalities of governing complexity in various national and cultural settings. The argument we advance is that the successful governance of complex economic systems in the contemporary global environment requires a strategic interactive approach. Such an approach can be summarized as one combining central strategic guidance with decentralized associative governance. Our aim, to be clear, is not to propose a new magic formula of universal applicability – this would contradict the essence of our approach. Instead, the aim is to outline an agenda in which the principles of action are clear, but where their implementation has to be decided by specific actors in specific settings.

2. GRASPING SOCIAL COMPLEXITY

What do we mean by social complexity? First, and restricting our analysis to the economy, an evolutionary and institutionalist approach would argue that economic life is the product of multiple determinations, since the economy is socially and culturally embedded, as well as time- and space-bound (see opening sections of Jessop's chapter). Economic activity is seen to be neither solely driven by abstract universal laws, nor by economic agents behaving identically (e.g. *homo oeconomicus*). Instead, the social intermediation of the general necessities of economic reproduction (e.g. the wage relation, property rights, exchange regulations, etc.), together with time- and place-specific patterns of economic behaviour, constitute a multiple set of non-universal determinants of economic activity. Bob Jessop refers to this dialectic as 'contingent necessity', to allude to the interaction of different necessary 'rules of the game' and contextual influences in shaping economic behaviour. Thus, ontologically, economic complexity presupposes variety and multi-layering of influence.

A second aspect, thus, of economic complexity is variety and variability. In part, this follows from the recognition in the literature in socio-economics and economic psychology that economic systems are socially and institutionally embedded and that economic behaviour is cognitively and culturally bounded. When we ask, for instance, why global capitalism today is so different from capitalism in the last century, or why contemporary patterns of economic organization in Germany, Britain, the USA, East Asia and Japan are so different, we are forced to concede that the variations might be connected with socio-institutional specificities of time and space. Diachronically, the institutions of economic life and economic regulation one hundred years ago were very different from those today. Firms, markets and financial institutions were less monopolistic, labour institutions were weaker, technologies were more rudimentary, training was less formal and education was less generalized, channels of distribution and exchange were less sophisticated, public coordination of the macro-economy was restricted, and so on. These historical factors – need it be said – undoubtedly help to explain why the economy then was organized differently from today. Synchronically, the same kind of logic applies. Differences in business organization, business cultures, regulatory regimes, training and educational systems, institutionalization of economic life, cooperation and conflict between the major social partners and so on, tell us much about why, for example, the German or Scandinavian economies are more corporatist than the British or US economy.

Variety is generated also by the cognitive and cultural influences on economic behaviour, as hinted above. Everyday societal habits, norms, values, expectations, and codes of behaviour become assimilated by economic agents in different cultural settings as the 'natural' or acceptable way of organizing, interacting and learning (Hodgson 1994). Recognition of such 'soft' institutional parameters takes us a long way in explaining why, for example, some business systems can rely on social solidarity, trust and reciprocity as a basis for organizing the production process and business networks, while others depend on contractual and other formal procedures of negotiation (Whitley 1992, Misztal 1996). In addition, beyond these cultural influences, lie cognitive and behaviourial influences. If we reject the proposition that all economic actors think and behave in the same way (e.g. the utility-maximizing, rational and perfectly knowledgeable actor of neoclassical economics), then we are forced to see economic agents as hedging, reflexive, satisficing and bounded in their cognition of opportunities (see chapters by Delorme and Orillard). Limitations associated with fully knowing the external environment and with one's own mental ability to absorb, process and act on information, play a vital role in shaping individual preferences and choices. In turn, these individual behaviourial differences carry different meanings in different social settings, owing to variations in the cultural assumptions and cultural supports embedding individuals.

The above influences – multiple determination, non-teleological change, cultural and cognitive boundedness, social and institutional embeddedness – all contribute to economic complexity. The empirical outcome is variety and diversity and, within any one economic system, differentiation. The complex economy, consequently, is a microcosm of criss-crossing organizational and institutional forms, logics and rationalities, norms and governance structures. It is difficult to grasp in anything like its entirety by individuals and it escapes the reach of a central organization, but somehow, each economic system does possess a paradoxical 'unity of diversity' that is characteristic of most vital organisms.

How can we grasp and make sense of this kind of complexity? How do real actors and organizations cross the line between thinking and acting in a complex world? How can the researcher develop an understanding of complexity without reducing it to simple abstractions or ideal types? Part of the problem, for both participant and observer, is methodological. It concerns the means of reconciling the clear separation between the ontological and epistemological dimensions of complexity, that is, the divide between complexity as an 'objective' social reality and complexity as a paradigm that helps to make sense of the world as it is. One route is to presuppose that there exist intermediating properties, such as actor reflexiveness and social interaction, and perhaps even trust as Luhmann (1979) has argued, which serve to reconcile the two dimensions of complexity by narrowing the traditional divide between the objective and subjective aspects of the social world. This idea is explored in the rest of the section.

The chapter by Robert Delorme, on how to deal with complexity in economic theorizing, is very helpful in this regard, offering insights that are valid for both thought and action in the social world. Delorme asks how we can explain economic behaviour in complex environments. He draws the distinction between first and second order complexity, ascribing different actor rationalities to each. He defines first order complexity as contextual complexity, in which agents (observers and actors) confront unpredictability, radical uncertainty and the unknown. These are attributes which defy the powers of 'substantive rationality', the tools of which – computation, optimization, algorithmics, decision and result – are better suited to certain and predictable environments (ontological and epistemological). The alternative rationality, through which agents seek to adjust to the complexity of the environment, is Simonian 'procedural rationality', composed of behaviour rooted in deliberation, satisficing, heuristics, and attention to decision-making and the decision-making process.

First order complexity takes us no further than the possibility of bounded behaviour and action in the framework of existing rules. Science (practical and conceptual) and society remained separated, with the former adjusted to the latter. Second order complexity, however, closes the gap between the two, by demanding reflexive knowledge on the part of science and interaction between observer and observed. As such, it potentially allows for rational behaviour not only at the level of interaction between social agents, but also at the level of system-building or rule-changing. What is the logic behind this argument? Delorme argues that reflexive knowledge rests on interaction and feedback between science and society, with the acceptance on the part of the observer that a complex problem is resolved iteratively through communication, cumulative knowledge and continual feedback between deliberation and outcome. There is no implied predefined science or superior mode of behaviour. Thus, second order complexity, through the establishment of a 'recursive loop' between participant and observer, effectively endogenizes the relationship between science and society (Barnes 1996).

The novelty of this approach, which draws centrally on new advances in cybernetics and the cognitive sciences, is to propose that a particular type of actor rationality (rooted in deliberation, design and interaction) is the basis for coping with social complexity. Another challenging proposition is that second order complexity is itself a mode of knowledge – a 'grounded' epistemology and cognitive procedure – that, in being such, is capable of reflexively transforming social systems and rules. Recursive knowledge, therefore, becomes a tool for, at once, understanding and transforming.

3. AGENTS, NETWORKS AND SYSTEMIC UNITY IN A COMPLEX WORLD

In acknowledging social complexity, we accept multiple rationalities and multiple actors. We also assume, however, a measure of systemic unity, or, put negatively, absence of anarchic individualism and incoherence. If we reject as too simple both individualist explanations of coherence centred around games between rational actors as well as essentialist explanations, which stress the powers of hegemonies or hidden laws of history, we are left with the dilemma of understanding how systemic unity is maintained and how individuals come to be locked into shared understandings and common projects.

The preceding discussion provides a partial explanation, through the concepts of contingent necessity and recursive feedback. Both concepts stress the dialectic, respectively, between systemic necessity and historical contingency, and between social rationalities and the social environment. Both reconcile the opposition between system and subjectivity. To this we may add the ideas of contemporary 'old' institutionalists who suggest that social institutions, from actor groups to habits and conventions, are the bridges between individuals and society which help to secure coherence as well as the fine balance between historical continuity and change (Hodgson 1988, 1993). Similarly, insights into long-term, but socially and historically contested regularities of societal behaviour are provided by '*longue durée*' approaches such as regulation theory or world systems theory, which look for recurrent or dominant influences in the arena of economic organization or social regulation.

In general, however, these approaches are relatively silent on the psychological and cognitive aspects of human behaviour that help to bridge the gap between agent and system. Could it be that certain forms of social behaviour, in reconciling subject and object, facilitate, at once, both individual agency and systemic coherence? In Chapter 4, Jürgen Lange-von Kulessa makes an attempt in this direction by reinstating Hayek as a theorist of the interdependencies between the individual and the collective. Kulessa argues, against the grain, that Hayek's methodological individualism is non-reductionist and sensitive to the role of cultures of socialization (learnt or imitated, conscious and unconscious, formal and informal) in helping individuals to frame the world, internalize group cultures and select between competing cultures. However, for us Hayek's 'reconciliation' is ultimately individualist, since social behaviour is seen as the product of diverse aggregates of individuals in relations of interdependence and competition with each other. The schema, therefore, offers a one-sided and rather simple interpretation of the cultural and behaviourial processes which integrate individual agency and social system.

In contrast, the chapter by Magali Orillard draws on cybernetics, cognitive psychology and systems theory to posit *social* rationalities that are neither reducible to the individual nor to the whole. In addition, in identifying different types of rationality, Orillard makes space for differentiating social worlds by their cognitive aspects. Her ideas provide a novel avenue for exploring agency in a complex social setting. From her chapter a distinction can be made between three different types of social actor: reactive, cognitive and creative. Each type of actor is guided by a specific rationality: substantive, procedural and complex (or 'recursive reflexive', as we prefer). These 'triads' can be seen as the ontological equivalents of the triads identified by Delorme in his theory of economic knowledge. Reactive agents lack reflexivity; therefore their rationality is not equipped to adapt to or transform environments. Cognitive agents, in contrast, behave intentionally and knowledgeably, searching for solutions based on perception and conscious design. They respond heuristically and procedurally in satisficing goals. Finally, creative agents are those with ability to shape and transform the environment, owing to their capacity to think and act strategically and multidimensionally. Theirs is a recursive rationality that, at once, draws on the capabilities of autonomy and self-management, together with the strengths of group membership and interaction.

This differentiation between actor-rationalities is helpful in two senses for making sense of agency in a complex world. First, and most obviously, in such a world, different types of actors and different types of rationalities coexist, fulfilling different roles and displaying different potentialities. From a socio-political perspective, as we discuss later, recognizing this can help *ex ante* to develop an understanding of the scope and relevance of different types of policy action, and of the problems associated with mixing incompatible actor-rationalities. Thus, for example, it might help explain why only context-changing policies such as new property laws or macroeconomic adjustments might provoke reactive adjustment, but fall well short of outcomes that presuppose cognitive or strategic adjustment on the part of actors (see chapters by Chavance and Magnin, Kosonen, and Stahl for the limits of 'shock therapy' in Central Europe).

Second, and assuming a minimum degree of systemic coherence in a complex social order, a key problem concerns the way in which the actors and respective rationalities intersect and communicate. The diverse agents and rationalities are not separate and closed orders, but distinctive levels of the same social order. Socialization and societal reproduction, in a context of diverse individual and group rationalities and capabilities, require the presence of mechanisms that provide actors with the possibility of communicating at the meta-level (generating a conceptual framework for communicating and understanding beyond the normal channels). Orillard refers to these mechanisms as coding and supercoding devices, which serve, respectively, to secure intra-group and inter-group interaction. They constitute the glue that holds things in place, and in this regard Orillard suggests that the psycho-social foundations for belonging, interaction and communication play a central role. These foundations may include any number of things, from common goals and shared meanings, to reflexive and hermeneutic communication. The intricate interweaving of codes and supercodes, thus, is the process by which independence of agency and systemic unity in a complex world are reconciled. This observation too has immediate practical implications. For instance, it warns that strategic actions designed to encourage, let us say, social innovation and self-organization, cannot ignore social hermeneutics, nor the imprint of behaviourial and cultural codes on agents, groups and networks.

At the centre of the idea of agency in a complex world lies the assumption that agents are locked into networks of association, and that networking somehow facilitates the governance of complexity (e.g. by reconciling observer and observed, agency and structure, individual and system, etc.). The idea of society as a web of interlocking networks of affiliation and interaction which are structured around a multiplicity of institutions, formal and informal, is a powerful metaphor for grasping the problems of social complexity. For example, affiliation and interaction could be seen as the means by which individuals act rationally in a context of complex and conflicting demands. In addition, relational interaction (networking) might be seen to provide a solution for overcoming the rigidities associated with hierarchy or the complex demands of unmediated market interaction. Finally, institutional webs might be seen as an adaptive way of organizing and interlocking a disparate social order. But such a logic runs the risk of fetishizing networks as an ideal type or a normative panacea. It is important to distinguish between types and qualities of networks, since networks and intermediate organizations could be found to exist everywhere, but not all are the same nor do they fulfil the same purpose.

Let us first focus on the typology of networks, and restrict our attention to four aspects that are particularly relevant to the concerns of this book: behaviourial rationality; contextuality; strength of ties; and power relations. Turning to the first aspect, it is important to acknowledge behaviourial differences associated with the sedimented rationalities of particular networks of belonging and action. Orillard, in her chapter, distinguishes between reactive, cognitive and creative (or adaptive) networks, where the differences in behaviour are associated with differences in rationality – substantive, procedural and complex (or 'recursive reflexive'). Different networks possess different actor-rationalities. Reactive networks tend to be less complex in both scope and arrangement than, say, adaptive networks, since there is far less reflexive interaction and feedback between relatively autonomous actors, and since goals are specified and relatively easy to reach. One normative reason for making such a distinction, as we shall see in the next section, is to warn against expectations that fail to take into consideration the rationality limitations of the networks in question. For example, business or political networks driven by a rationality of fixed and centrally determined rules are not likely to become networks of reciprocity and interchange without pervasive changes in the dominant rationality of the network (from framework rules to individual behaviour).

In emphasizing the significance of behaviours rooted in different rationalities, we are not implying in any way that the latter are innate. We see them as socially constructed rationalities, tied up with the specificities of time and place. Second, therefore, networks differ because they are embedded in different contexts – cultural, institutional, locational and historical. The chapters by Bob Jessop and Ngai-Ling Sum focus on the significance of time-space embeddedness, to add to the growing theoretical emphasis in the socio-economic and geographical literature given to contextuality in explaining difference and trajectory.

Let us take the example of business networks to illustrate this point. It has become fashionable to stress the efficiency advantages of cooperation, reciprocity and trust between and among firms, over relations of hierarchy or market. The concept of embeddedness, however, forces a less universalist interpretation, in drawing attention to the powers of context, and in so doing, cautioning against assumptions of transferability. The expanding research on networking-based business organization distinguishes between a variety of forms: flexibly specialized industrial districts in Italy or in inner city areas (Pyke and Sengenberger 1992); international networks of alliances and subcontracting centred around transnational corporations (Dunning 1994, United Nations 1992, Ruigrok and van Tulder 1995) and business systems in Western Europe or East Asia that draw on distinctive combinations of state-industry links, and inter-firm association (see Chapter 7; Lane 1995, Whitley 1992). Each network form is the product of forces that have matured in the course of time and of relationships that are peculiar to particular contextual circumstances. For example, networks of cooperation among craft industrial districts in Italy draw upon age-long republican forms of civic trust (Putnam 1993) and upon interdependencies associated with task specialization among firms. In contrast, in Japan or Korea, different cultures of social interaction combine with an organizational frame of strong ties between politicians, state and large firms, to forge large-firm business networks with very different rules of reciprocity and trust. These are important factors that generate unique path-dependencies, and as such defy decontextualized or universalist manipulations, as elegantly shown by Bernard Chavance and Eric Magnin in their chapter on variety of patterns of restructuring in Eastern and Central Europe.

Third, networks differ in terms of the strength of their ties (Grabher 1993), and the differences play a significant part in defining both the importance of the network for actors and its adaptive qualities. A network characterized by strong ties of association is very different from one characterized by weak ties. While the former may secure unity of purpose and rapidity of response, as in the case of say, a network of clientelist relations cultivated by a politician or a business boss, it is likely to foster relations of dependence, as actors are deprived of alternative connections as well as the capacity to improvise or innovate. Thus, a network of strong ties risks becoming an inadaptive network if contextual circumstances change. In contrast, a network of loose alliances, such as say, periodic meetings between community organizations working in a similar field, is one that brings together a variety of agendas and rationales, and is probably difficult to mobilize as a single unit. On the other hand, loose alliances in representing variety of capability spread across relatively self-governing actors, are likely to offer a wider pool of possibilities to draw from when circumstances change. Relatedly, and with similar implications, a setting consisting of many networks is not the same as one offering limited options to actors (Bianchi and Miller 1994). If actors are confined in their choice of associative options, there are greater chances of forced loyalty, as exit might represent isolation. In contrast, multiple membership or multiple choice might raise the risk of exit from particular networks, yet simultaneously raise the potential for voice and innovation, owing to the increased bargaining position and multiple experience of particular actors.

Fourth, and finally, networks have to be differentiated in terms of their power dimensions. There is a creeping tendency in the socio-economics literature to privilege the qualities of networks over those of markets and hierarchies. Relations within and across networks are seen to be somehow more reciprocal and more egalitarian, because they rely on interaction. Nothing could be further from the truth. Not all networks are non-hierarchical, mutually beneficial or discursive, therefore it is important to distinguish between different types of power relations within the network form. Rob van Tulder and Winfried Ruigrok in their chapter focus on industrial complexes (networks drawing in firms, suppliers, dealers, workers, financiers and banks), to distinguish one important dimension of power relations. This is the bargaining position of 'partners', which they differentiate in terms of the relations of dependency between actors. They distinguish between five types of relationships, reflecting different links of association with 'core' firms: relations of independence, resulting in cooperation or competition; relations of independence, resulting in compliance; relations of interdependence, resulting in coalition; relations of dependence with core firm influence, resulting in direct control; and relations of dependence without partner influence, resulting in structural control. This example usefully illustrates that the bargaining position of actors differs enormously from one network to another in accordance with the power of individual actors over others. Hence, the usefulness of exploring the *nature* of interaction between actors, beyond simply recognizing the existence of ties.

In constructing a typology of networks, we are forced to acknowledge the quality of networks in shaping outcomes. From Ngai-Ling Sum's chapter, which focuses on Japan-centred East Asian economic governance networks, we can deduce that 'successful' networks are distinguished by at least three features: a high level of self-organization among specialized actor circuits; strong ground rules of governance which bind agents into a common frame of action; and a precarious balance between independence and interpenetration between state and non-state governance structures. Functional flexibility, diffuse reflexivity, strategic orientation and collective adaptability seem to be some of the key qualities of successful networks, allowing a course to be steered between governance by deliberative associations and by strategic leaders. In contrast, Riitta Kosonen's chapter, focusing on the challenges faced by the Russian border town of Vyborg in transforming itself from a culture of 'patient' to that of 'active agent' in the face of market transition, draws attention to pathologies of interaction which privilege reinforcement or resistance, rather than adaptation, in the face of change. The same could be said of networks of criminality or social closure dominated by regressive attachments or fixed goals. Such networks tend to be non-deliberative, hierarchical, centralized, and fixed. Thus, at polar opposites, we can distinguish between regressive and progressive networks, closed and open networks, adaptable and non-adaptable networks, deliberative and non-reflexive networks, and centralized and decentred networks.

The question which follows concerns the nature of the factors which shape the qualities of networks. Part of the answer has already been given in the discussion above on the typology of networks. First, the rationalities of networks will have a direct effect on the cognition, behaviour and capabilities of agents, which, in turn, will have a direct bearing on the reflexive, strategic and adjustment properties of networks. Similarly, the strength of ties within and between networks will influence the degree of openness to new influences, the extent to which ties are a real source of organizational efficiency and cohesion, and the evolutionary or regenerative qualities of networks. The nature of power relations, too, has a bearing on the spread of authority and responsibility across networks, and therefore also the architecture of decision-making. Deliberative networks are likely to be flatter, more discursive and more democratic than command-based networks in which the main role of interaction is to transmit information and orders rather than to share power and duties.

But, what counts also, importantly, is the *institutional set-up* of networks, which we could define as the enduring collective practices and organizations within networks. This includes formal rules and institutions of regulation and governance, as well as the embedded cultural and social practices, and conventions which constitute the reproductive framework of networks. Institutional set-up, thus, defines the enduring qualities of networks, their stability and degree of coherence, their collective efficacy, and above all their overall governance structure. Institutions – hard and soft – constitute the webs and nodes of networks, the channels of collective organization and communication, as well as the points of intersection and encounter. In a sense, they are the architectural frame of networks.

To make sense, therefore, of the logic and effectiveness of different types of networks, we need to examine the institutional set-up of networks. The earlier remarks on the time-space embeddedness of networks go some way towards defining institutional set-up as the broad spatial and temporal context within which networks are located. Indeed, the chapters by Stahl and Kosonen make it perfectly clear that institutionalized socio-cultural legacies, respectively, in Russian agriculture, and in a border town between Finland and Russia that has oscillated between a culture of self-organization and that of dependence, have played a central role in defining the qualities of each context in the face of new challenges associated with the collapse of state socialism.

More specifically, however, the term 'institutional set-up' refers to the governance logics of different types of networks, shaped by the division of authority and responsibility. For example, in the context of business systems, van Tulder and Ruigrok identify at least five governance logics resulting from the interpenetration of particular business and institutional relations. They distinguish between (in their terminology) the Italian small firm model, the Swedish model, the

German model, the US model and the Japanese model, each characterized by different shades of control or dependence between core firms and partners, and different shades of hierarchy or autonomy between institutions (business networks, government, unions, financiers, etc.). Similarly, Kluth and Andersen, in their chapter on national variations in the organization of research and technology, draw on the examples of Italy, the UK, France and Germany, to distinguish between four institutional set-ups to explain variation and relative performance. In the arena of strong formal governance, they draw the distinction between state-centred governance and post-corporatist governance based on inter-institutional discourse, both of which they distinguish from weak arenas consisting of either pluralist competition between elites or clientelist patronage-based governance.

Both examples underscore the significance of the institutional aspects of networks: atomistic or hierarchical networks follow quite a different governance logic to interactive networks. The latter are dense networks of divided responsibilities, relying heavily on specialization and interaction as a basis for collective governance, while the former are more dependent on competition between independent agents or upon a clear hierarchy of command, control and division of tasks. The architecture of governance in interactive networks is made up of many overlapping nodes and webs, probably underpinned by an institutional culture of shared values and responsibilities, while the architecture of atomistic or hierarchical networks lacks institutional density and overlap, and tends to be underpinned by cultures of contract or of command and subordination. Without understanding such differences, there is a danger of underestimating the decisive importance of institutional factors in different settings.

In summary, the nature of agency, interaction, institutional set-up, and governance varies enormously between networks, and it is these differences which shape the character, form and vitality (or not) of patterns of interaction and organization. These differences, as the next section shows, crucially influence governance possibilities in complex social settings.

4. GOVERNING COMPLEXITY

In this section we explore complexity from the point of view of the decision-maker, as an agent who undertakes to somehow 'govern' social complexity. From this perspective, the analytical distinction between complexity in the objective and cognitive sense vanishes. The observer becomes a participant in the social world that he or she seeks to shape, perceiving its complexity in a broader or narrower way.

The governance of complexity is not exclusively an intrinsic factor in the reproduction of social systems; it concerns the endless creation of these systems, through factors which reproduce themselves and adapt to the changing environment. The creation of social systems thus understood is equivalent neither to constructivism, nor to the spontaneous formation of social order. Acknowledging that in practice social order is always contingent and consciously determined, Jessop employs the notion of 'contingent necessity' when he describes the mechanism by which social systems are created. He identifies four key consequences of this mechanism: first, practices which reduce the complexity of the world facing social actors through acts with implications that are both congruent with real world processes and relevant to their own objectives; second, developing the capacity for dynamic social learning about various causal processes and forms of interdependence, attributions of responsibility and capacity for actions, and possibilities of coordination in a complex, turbulent environment; third, building methods for coordinating actions across different social forces with different identities, interests, and meaning systems, over different spatio-temporal horizons and over different domains of action; and fourth, establishing both a common world view for individual action and a system of meta-governance to stabilize key players' orientations, expectations and rules of conduct.

A social order thus formed is not only – as Hayek and many of his followers contest – the result of human action; it is also to some degree the result of design. However, this need not imply, as it usually does, constructivist designing and social engineering. What it implies is interactive social designing, the result of which can never be wholly determined by its various participants, even if some of these participants attempt to impose their own will on others. This is because – as Jessop clearly shows in his chapter – interactive social designing in developed systems occurs simultaneously on three different levels where reciprocal social interdependence becomes crystallized: interpersonal relations; inter-organizational relations; and relations between functionally differentiated institutional orders (subsystems). Jessop's concern echoes the work in regime theory by Clarence Stone (1993), who has analysed the role of state and non-state coalitions and mutual understandings, in securing governance in the context of complex and disparate institutional arrangements in urban politics.

A necessary condition for the evolution of the social system through interactive social designing is the emergence of functionally differentiated institutional structures. Yet this is not a sufficient condition. An important factor is also the sense of community, resulting from a recognition by the system's participants of common norms and values. Silke Stahl cogently illustrates this in her chapter, by discussing the importance of shared values and bolstering social interaction in the evolution of property rights and new forms of governance in Russian agriculture. She contends that the analysis of transaction costs endorsed by the proponents of new institutional economics is clearly insufficient to explain this process.

However, the functional differentiation of subsystems, as well as shared norms and values, are not the only conditions for governance through interactive social designing. Another condition is the infrastructure of discourse and communication, which means, among other things, the evolution within the system of a common framework of meaning. This is what Magali Orillard calls common reference space. Its presence determines social dialogue and the elaboration of compromises.

The final condition we identify for evolution on the path of interactive social designing is strategic guidance, which can only be provided by creative actors (as defined by Orillard in Chapter 3) acting in accordance with the rules of recursive procedural rationality. It is only these types of actors who are able to coordinate the actions of functionally differentiated, autonomous (albeit materially and socially interdependent) institutional structures (subsystems). By influencing their codes and procedures, they facilitate the self-regulation of these structures, and at the same time ensure the regulatory function and development of the entire system.

Our concept of strategic guidance is not the idea of hegemony or leadership as it is traditionally understood. Hegemony means the structural dominance of a certain social group. Leadership implies formally constituted and hierarchical power. Strategic guidance is a mixture of highly diffused and reflexive governance capability resulting in inter-institutional overlap and contact (networking), and forms of leadership in which the main task is not to dominate but to guide, arbitrate and facilitate. Here, leadership is an endogenous quality rather than the preserve of an external authority.

Strategic guidance is not, therefore, possible merely by attaining a high formal status in the social system's hierarchy. It can only be achieved as a result of complex social interaction, in which adaptation, reinforcement and resistance overlap, as Riitta Kosonen shows in her chapter. The axis of interaction thus understood is negotiation which, oriented towards solving specific problems, in the wider sense also enables action-building and articulation, while cutting out exit from the system and building internal loyalty.

Strategic guidance understood as the ability to coordinate multiple governance networks is the quintessence of governing social complexity, which, as we have shown, has procedural and systemic foundations. Governing complexity is thus a function of a particular type of empowerment which is neither universal, nor permanent, but which becomes possible and reproducible under the procedural and systemic conditions outlined above.

This interpretation gives rise to a number of methodologically important questions. An immediate temptation is to ask: is governing complexity possible if not all the systemic and procedural conditions are met? An equally unavoidable question concerns the effectiveness of governing complexity: why is it effective in certain cases and not in others?. To tackle these questions, we need to start by examining the role of the state in the governance of social complexity.

5. THE STATE AND INTERACTIVE GOVERNANCE OF COMPLEXITY

A very interesting example of a system of governance, which in its early phase of development proved effective, but which later lost ground, is the democratic corporatism established in many West European countries after the Second World War. Jessop addresses this issue in greater depth in his chapter; at this juncture, all we wish to stress is that over time West European corporatism proved to be too narrow a solution, and, more importantly, too inflexible and therefore unable to change and adapt. Corporatism was relatively successful in enabling the reconstruction of war-torn economies, ensuring social harmony and macroeconomic stability, without which reconstruction would have been impossible. However, it gradually became a barrier to successive waves of restructuring at the micro- and meso-level, necessitated by the rapidly changing competitive environment and the emergence of many new forms and dimensions of competitiveness. Under these conditions, corporatism, built on the pillar of agreement between three hierarchical and bureaucratic structures – the government administration, the trade unions and employers' organizations – was not able to transform itself effectively, in our view, owing to the absence of the recursive loop which, according to Delorme, turns governing complexity into strategic governance.

This example clearly highlights the risk with which governing complexity is burdened. On the one hand, it enables specific structural problems to be solved and the systemic crises connected with them to be overcome; on the other hand, the institutional order connected with governing complexity creates barriers to gradual adaptation, which may then form the basis of a subsequent crisis. This weakness in governing complexity is greater if the institutional order enabling it is imposed by imperative from above, rather than by way of interactive social designing. In her chapter, Ngai-Ling Sum convincingly argues that the success of the cross-border governance networks in East Asia is owing, among other things, to the fact that they were not established directly by the state, and to a high degree are the result of socially embedded market forces. She adds that the emergence and functioning of these networks cannot be explained in terms of the dichotomies dominant in the European tradition: state versus society; private versus public; external versus internal; central versus peripheral.

On the other hand, Europe has its own positive examples of governing complexity, one of which is the Danish negotiated economy which Jessop perceptively analyses in his chapter. Without glossing over the particular weaknesses of this governance system, Jessop identifies three fundamental preconditions of its effectiveness: first, an approximate symmetry in power relations among the major societal agents; second, no exit alternatives for the latter; and third, a certain measure of cultural homogeneity to make communication and consensus achievable in the first place.

Elsewhere, one of us (Amin and Thomas 1996, p. 257) has argued, following the work of Klaus Nielsen and Ove K. Pedersen (1991) that at the level of decision-making and policy implementation, the negotiated model consists of five discernible aspects:

> The first is a high level of interest representation and organization of public life across economy, politics and society. The second is the considerable spread of decisional authority and autonomy across a system of plural interest representation. Third, and as a consequence, the state plays a distinctive role as arbitrator and facilitator between autonomous organizations, in addition to that of rule-maker and specialized provider of collective services. The fourth aspect concerns the evolution of a dense network of vertical and horizontal channels of representation and communication as the basis for decision-making and policy coordination. The final aspect is the reliance on iterative dialogue for conflict resolution and policy consensus, through a variety of routine organizational devices such as informal policy networks, arbitration councils, multi-interest special committees and co-representation.

The Danish governance system is one of dispersed and interactive governance of the economy. Consequently, this system is not so inflexible as corporatism. Its institutional set-up allows constant innovation, leading to the gradual modification and adaptation of the mode of regulation to the changing competitive environment.

The basic foundational difference between corporatism and the negotiated economy is that the former system of governance became a centralized, and often imperative-based institutional arrangement, while the latter was the result of a long process of evolution, during which the state came to rely consistently on an interactive strategy. In practice, this involved continual effort at maintaining the balance between various decentralized and autonomous subsystems of governance, by creating an infrastructure of communication between them, and by using this balance to agree upon common aims and procedures. The essence of such an approach is to avoid destroying, or even only paralysing or weakening, spontaneously created governance networks characterized by different kinds of rationality; on the contrary, the aim is to influence these networks so that, as they begin to overlap and complement each other, they can form the basis of second order governance complexity. The point – as Jessop makes clear – is to enable the participants of various governance networks to reflect upon and redefine, within certain boundaries, their identity and interests, to evaluate their long-term situation, and consequently to empower themselves – albeit to a limited degree – by way of a recursive procedural rationality.

The advantage of the imperative approach is that institutional homogenization can, in a short period of time, facilitate the adaptation of the social system necessary in a situation of structural crisis. However, there is also a high price to pay: rapid adaptation achieved in this way blocks further adaptation. This is why, from an evolutionary perspective, only the interactive approach, by preserving and bolstering institutional heterogeneity, can create permanent possibilities for adaptation (Grabher, and Stark 1995, p. 2). Of key importance is that – contrary to the imperative approach – 'institutional legacies are not about the persistence of the past but about resources for the future' (ibid.).

In synthesis, the interactive approach may be said to comprise three elements: interaction as a procedure of social change; networks as agents of social change; and strategy as a method of structural problem-solving.

The adoption by the state of interactive strategies in the context of an advanced social system possessing the structural preconditions described in preceding sections, is a question of *political choice.* But, what is to be done in the context of societies where these preconditions, for whatever reason, do not exist? Post-socialist societies are one such example. In this context, it seems reasonable to ask: 'Can interactive mechanisms be set in motion in these societies, and if so how, given that the relevant structures – or at least so it would seem – are not in place?' (Hübner 1995, p. 11).

At first glance, it seems that such a situation precludes the interactive approach; that it would be more appropriate to adopt the imperative approach, or to limit all state intervention and rely on the spontaneous emergence of conditions which in time will make it possible to implement the interactive approach. On reflection, however, it is easy to see the weakness in this line of argument. A total reliance on spontaneous development is possible only in theory. In practice, the state is always forced to act and to undertake some kind of intervention in the economy in response to grass-roots pressure from various social groups. Of course, one can always claim – as did the first non-communist Polish government between 1989 and 1991 – that 'the best industrial policy is no industrial policy', but sooner or later social pressure will force the government to engage at the microeconomic level, which practically implies carrying out some kind of industrial policy, even if undesired and chaotic.

In cases where the state is paralysed not as a result of adopting the free-market doctrine but by actual disintegration (as in many post-Soviet countries) unfettered spontaneous development is also to a large extent illusory, for under such conditions other agents will appropriate some of the regulatory functions of the state. In Russia, for instance, these functions are now performed by huge financial-industrial groups – a result of the 'mafia' taking control of branch corporations formed under the command economy. As Nesterenko (1995, p. 7) rightly points out, the emergence of these groups is a consequence of two conflicting and overlapping tendencies: the striving of branch corporation managements to rebuild ties between the state and economy in order to secure state protection for themselves; and the increasing penetration of these corporations by groups evolving out of the 'free' market. Formed in this way, the financial-industrial groups perpetuate the monopolistic structure of the Russian economy and gradually rebuild the state's dominance within it.

On the other hand, the imperative approach, in practice motivated by the neo-liberal doctrine, is possible under post-socialist conditions – the Czech Republic and Poland are two examples. However, and limiting our assessment to economic consequences, we should stress that the actual economic structures, and the property relations and management mechanisms characteristic of them, are a clear departure from the classical assumptions of neo-liberalism and the notions of the initiators of the imperative approach. Drawing on David Stark (1996), Pavel

Mertlík (1995) has convincingly shown that the Czech path of top-down mass privatization has thus far led to a 'recombinant property' model, in which the main investor is the state, effectively controlling the whole economy through shares in the National Property Funds (NPFs).

The two extreme examples outlined above show that, for the moment, post-socialist economies are – to use Domenico Mario Nuti's (1996) definition – 'mutants' which are inconsistent with either the starting or the target model. Whether such recombinant economies can survive and develop in the highly competitive external environment remains an open question. It seems that, irrespective of the type of transformation method adopted, these societies can only be mutants, for it is impossible to sever ties with the past completely and immediately, as so convincingly shown by Bernard Chavance and Eric Magnin in Chapter 8. Yet this makes it all the more relevant to ask which type of mutation affords the greatest long-term development possibilities. We believe that to answer this question, it is less important to focus on a target model, than on which transformation method is most appropriate. In this respect, and bearing in mind all possible reservations, the interactive approach seems to be the most promising.

The relevance of the interactive approach stems from the fact that in the wake of the sudden collapse of the socialist system, the societies of Central and Eastern Europe have found themselves in a 'systemic vacuum'. To fill this vacuum requires the formation of a state that can implement some kind of strategy (Hausner 1992). One may say that the starting-point for a successful transformation would be to complete the process of 'building up' the state. By this we do not mean the imperative reconstruction of the state apparatus, but rather the emergence of a power bloc (a group of political, intellectual and moral leaders) that can develop an institutional design for meta-governance that will need, in part, implementation through the state. This is what we mean by a state-building project. As a result, the state could achieve sufficient potential for strategic action, and for its economic functions to be defined.

In discussing the relevance of interactive strategies in the context of post-socialism, we have in mind a state-building project, rather than an act of the state itself. Such a project cannot be executed without support from other actors. Therefore, the interactive alternative to the imperative approach implies recognition of the fact that the state is formed in the course of negotiations and agreements between interest representatives. Hence, the negotiations between such representatives have a double significance: on the one hand, they create an institutional framework and market rules, allowing particular economic projects to be realized (the meso- and micro-structural level); and, on the other, they can use the resulting arrangements as a basis for defining and implementing a specific strategy to shape the economic system, thereby 'building up' the state (the macro-structural level).

The examples given above, which pertain equally to post-socialist and developed market economies, allow us to draw some general conclusions about the role of the state in facilitating the governance of social complexity. The first important observation to be made is that the state has to perform a number of functions that other social agents cannot perform. Drawing on the Danish experience, Amin and Thomas (1996) show that one set of functions relates to the state fulfilling the roles of strategy-maker, coordinator, arbitrator and consensus-builder. What is important, however, is that these roles are performed by various semi-autonomous organs of the state, which, as the 'negotiated economy' develops, also become subject to functional differentiation, implying a gradual change in the organization and structure of the state itself.

Another aspect of this process is the formation of non-state public institutions enabling the negotiating parties to communicate with each other and reach agreements. Pedersen (1993) defines them as campaign and discourse institutions – public relations agencies, independent think tanks, academic and research institutions, and so on. These institutions furnish the negotiating parties, but also the public at large, with relevant information, data and 'language' (notions, definitions, categories, etc.). Thanks to this, opposing interests can often reach compromise solutions. These types of supercoding institutions – to use Orillard's term – service all the participants in the negotiation process, including the state. Their establishment, however, would not be possible without the active interest and support of the state.

On this basis, a second important observation can be made. In governing social complexity, the state must basically perform the role of a partner enabling other actor-partners to perform their own roles; and in some cases it might even have to create these roles. Wanting to implement its interactive strategy, the state, in the most general sense, has to act like a facilitator with respect to other actors. We would wish to give this role a broader definition than that used by Wolfgang Streeck (1995) in his analysis of relations between the state and interest groups in Germany. Streeck defines the German state as an 'enabling state', showing how, through an institutionalized mechanism of social partnership, it corrects market forces and provides social protection to given social groups. The German state accords certain functions to selected interest groups, for example, the organization of vocational training. At the same time it grants them a monopoly of representation within a specific area, helping them to overcome the free-rider problems associated with collective goods production, and to reconcile member expectations with public responsibility. Streeck himself adds that the German model derives to an important extent from the slowness, predictability and bargained character of decision-making (ibid., p. 28). What this implies is that the model is stable, but also inflexible and therefore costly. In addition, the state interacts chiefly with traditional peak interest groups (trade unions, employer organizations, chambers of trade and industry, craft associations, etc.), and, by guaranteeing them a monopoly of representation, is less able to support other types of evolving governance networks.

For this reason, whilst recognizing the large overlap in scope, we prefer the concept of 'facilitative state' to that of 'enabling state'. The former encapsulates the role of the state in a more dynamic and multifarious way. It also implies a measure of reflexivity enshrined in the state's role as a facilitator of social interaction. For if it is to manage social complexity effectively, the state must be able to modify the existing public agency structure and set a new agenda for it.

Operating in this way, the state regulates the functioning of the economy and channels its development towards forging an entrepreneurial, networking and governance culture, rather than towards directing or running business activity. It thus becomes, in the Schumpeterian sense, an 'entrepreneurial state'. As Michael Kluth and Jørn Andersen rightly point out (see Chapter 11), Schumpeter neither equated entrepreneurship with the individual, nor the entrepreneur with the owner. Accordingly, in the broad sense, the state can perform an entrepreneurial function to the extent that its activity catalyses social innovation and creativity. Yet this depends above all on how the state carries out its policies, particularly economic policy. It is precisely this issue that we shall address in the next section.

6. REFLEXIVE ECONOMIC POLICY-MAKING

Reflexive economic policy-making is above all linked to overcoming the basic political cycle, which consists in appeals for state intervention in response to market failures and for market regulation in response to governance failures. The periodic shifts along the market-state axis by governments show that the main political forces continue to adhere to traditional doctrines and divisions. Liberal-market orthodoxies are replaced by dirigiste-social-democratic orthodoxies and vice versa. Both leave insufficient space for institutional innovation and social creativity.

Both these dominant orthodoxies systematically redefine and reinvigorate old formulas that are divorced from present realities. These formulas, in turn, determine the rules of government which are chiefly directed towards restoring and maintaining the system's equilibrium. However, a general alternative to mono-centric government oriented towards achieving equilibrium through implementing formulas is for the state to participate in coordination networks that consciously govern change by agreeing upon and determining the aims of these networks and the ways in which they function.

In practice, this type of alternative – interactive and reflexive – approach presupposes the existence of a dense mass of overlapping governance networks intensively exchanging information and resources. That is, it requires a pluralism of networks and institutional set-ups of the sort described earlier, within which the state is one strategic actor. The state can effectively influence the networks and help shape their spatial boundaries and temporal horizon of action. This idea is elaborated by Jessop, who stresses that space and time are not simply external conditions and contexts of action, but can also be transformed and constituted through action. Social practices, organizations, institutions and systems are typically associated with specific structurally inscribed temporal and spatial forms and horizons of action. Hence, the heterogeneity and rationality of economic behaviour can to a certain degree be discursive and materially constituted.

The practical aspect of this problem is addressed by van Tulder and Ruigrok, who describe, on the basis of the experience of various countries, the formation of industrial complexes which due to their complex nature may be termed core governance networks. The deliberative shaping of industrial complexes thus presents the state with a valuable opportunity to influence the structure and direction of economic development. However, the shaping of industrial complexes thus understood is not free of dangers if it is carried out by way of the imperative method.

On this point it is appropriate to return to the excellent paper by Grabher and Stark, who make a fundamental distinction between allocative and dynamic effectiveness (1995, p. 11). The first pertains to the effective use of available resources, while the second is understood as the ability to promote innovation. The first is above all ensured by competition among firms, the second by competition among organizational forms (ibid., p. 16). Simplifying the system helps to achieve allocative effectiveness, while dynamic effectiveness, conversely, requires the internal differentiation of the system, allowing it to respond in an adequate way to the changing environment. Orientation towards both allocative and dynamic effectiveness is connected with the use of governance networks. In the first case, governance networks are treated as property; in the latter case, the properties of governance networks are of particular importance (ibid., p. 30).

Let us then try to imagine what in practice it means to apply, on the one hand, the imperative method of pursuing economic policy, and on the other, the interactive-reflexive policy process. The imperative approach implies that the future will not materialize unless the past is first overcome. What, then, is transformation under the imperative approach? Transformation means adapting society to the new market environment by destroying institutions originating from the previous system. What are these institutions? They are barriers on the path to a new order. What then should we do with them? Destroy them as quickly as possible.

In the case of the interactive approach, the future results from eliminating the restrictions of the past and making use of the resources deriving from it. What, then, is transformation? The issue is how to bolster or even create an ability to reorganize the heterogeneous internal structure of the economy so that it can function effectively in the face of unpredictable future changes in environment. What, from this perspective, are institutions originating from the former system? They are resources for the future which must be used and set in motion. What, then, should we do with them? Above all, we should help them to adapt, encourage their transformation and certainly not destroy them.

The imperative approach implies institutional mimicry, which is socially and economically costly. Even if it brings rapid gains in effectiveness (allocative effectiveness), it undermines the ability to adapt, which becomes a barrier to effectiveness in the longer term (dynamic effectiveness). The incorporation of the eastern regions after German unification reveals very well the illusiveness of the imperative approach. This process has been perceptively analysed by Grabher, who shows that while the adopted approach may have led to the emergence of various new organizational forms in the East German economy, these forms are separated from one another and are not linked by an exchange of resources and information. Hence, their heterogeneity does not yet constitute a 'genetic pool' for the evolution of more effective forms of organizing production and services (Grabher 1994).

This phenomenon is not exclusive to post-socialist economies. History provides numerous examples of relatively effective economic systems which, in simply concentrating on reproducing themselves, have degenerated. The sclerosis of the Swedish political economy in the face of a sudden and all-embracing economic crisis might be seen as one contemporary example. Although these systems managed to achieve high allocative effectiveness, they were not sufficiently able to innovate. In reproducing themselves, they did not develop their institutional structure. Locked into orthodox formulas, they were not predisposed towards reflexive policy-making: the practical dimension of governing social complexity.

7. CONCLUSION: BUILDING INTERACTIVE POWERS

The normative orientation of this chapter has been towards suggesting that socially complex orders defy both centralized and spontaneous forms of governance. The existence of autonomous networks and multiple rationalities, especially in an increasingly globalizing world, sharply limits the powers of a central national authority. Equally, a pluralist bazaar based on the autonomy of even the most articulated and reflexive of networks and associations (Hirst 1994), fails to tackle the qualities which render societies more than a sum of the parts, namely strategic orientation, social cohesion, and societal evolution. Thus, neither holism nor the most sophisticated permutations of individualism will suffice. Instead, we have tried to argue the case for a model of interactive pluralism centred around a strategic state, reflexive policy-making, and associative autonomy.

It is difficult to identify a set of easily applicable policies within such a framework, since it lacks the logic and assumptions of a substantive rationality in pursuit of fixed policy targets. The rationality of interactive governance is that of process and procedure, focusing on building capabilities, securing institutional innovation and adaptability, deriving efficiency through social cohesion and social involvement, and obtaining solutions through interaction, dialogue and confrontation. These are the propensities of a procedural and reflexive rationality, demanding a completely different understanding to the one commonly held concerning the aims and modalities of policy action.

From an orthodox perspective, such a governance framework is easy to dismiss for its lack of pre-established substantive targets and clear policy instruments. If taken seriously however, it suggests the need for a rather fundamental reorientation of policy action in the direction of influencing actor rationalities, expectations and capabilities. Thus, typically, public policy actions would focus on encouraging the formation of reflexive and autonomously run actor networks and communities of fate; on establishing rules and fora for interaction and intermediation; on building voice, capacity and capabilities across economy and society; on decentralizing state power and state duties at the same time as retaining the powers of strategic leadership, arbitration, sanction and resource allocation – in general, on building and empowering society (Amin and Thrift 1995, Amin 1996, Hirst 1994, Cohen and Rogers 1992). Of course, this is not in any way to suggest that substantive targets such as the control of inflation or interest rates, wages and incomes policies, training and education expenditure levels, investment in infrastructure and so on, are eschewed within an interactive framework; only that policy action has to exceed such goals.

The challenges posed to strategic actors, notably the state, are considerable, because interactive governance demands memory and an acute sensitivity to path-specificities. This amounts to much more than a sense of history. The chapters in this book on transition, especially those dealing with change in the post-socialist economies, reveal that path-shaping is possible only when the past is respected by strategic actors. Shock therapy, frankly, has been no therapy, since it has introduced reforms which have been distorted or undermined by the preceding trajectory. Instead, adjustment programmes that have sought to build on past institutional and social legacies have proved to be much more successful, owing to their greater appropriateness to local circumstances and most importantly owing to their reliance on proven social practices of organization, action and learning. In other words, here tradition has been mobilized as a source of innovation, rather than rejected as a historical anachronism or barrier to change. The ability to strike a fine balance between rupture and continuity, in turn, seems to be related to the degree to which strategic and reflexive capabilities are widely diffused through the social and economic fabric. Where change has centred around modernizing or 'expert' elite networks, it has tended to produce a particularly cavalier treatment of the past, in part owing to the absence of organicist alternatives, checks and balances that are available in genuinely pluralist societies.

The ultimate policy challenge, consequently, lies less in the identification or imposition of single sources of competitive survival in an open global economy, than in seeing to an adequate supply that permits a 'competition of forms'. The challenge is less that of building capacity to compete, but capacity to *evolve* in order to compete. This requires nurturing potential locked up in variety, slack and perhaps even redundancy. In labelling an environment complex, we acknowledge the coexistence of diverse forms, as well as rapidity of redundancy and renewal of markets, technologies and organizational structures. Such an environment cannot be reduced to one logic of survival, or to a belief in the endurability of such a logic. The best that public policy can achieve is to help unlock diversity of potential, and potential for continual adjustment and evolution.

REFERENCES

Amin, A. (1996) 'Beyond Associative Democracy'. *New Political Economy*, 1(3): 309–33.

Amin, A. and Thomas, D. (1996) 'The Negotiated Economy: State and Civic Institutions in Denmark'. *Economy and Society* 25 (2): 255–81.

Amin, A. and Thrift, N. (1995) 'Institutional Issues for the European Regions: From Markets and Plans to Socioeconomics and Powers of Association'. *Economy and Society* 24 (1): 41–66.

Amin, S. (1996) 'The Challenge of Globalization'. *Review of International Political Economy* 3 (2): 216–59.

Barnes, T.J. (1996) *Logics of Dislocation: Models, Metaphors, and Meanings of Economic Space*. New York: Guildford.

Beck, U., Giddens, A. and Lash, S. (1994) *Reflexive Modernization: Politics, Tradition and Aesthetics in the Modern Social Order*. Cambridge: Polity.

Bianchi, P. and Miller, L.M. (1994) 'Innovation, Collective Action and Endogenous Growth: An Essay on Institutions and Structural Change', mimeo. Bologna: Nomisma.

Callon, M. (1986) 'Some Elements of a Sociology of Translation' in J. Law (ed.) *Power, Action and Belief*. London: Routledge and Kegan Paul, pp. 196–233.

Cohen, J. and Rogers, J. (1992) 'Secondary Associations and Democratic Governance'. *Politics and Society* 20 (4): 393–472.

Cox, R. (1993) 'Structural Issues of Global Governance: Implications for Europe' in S. Gill (ed.) *Gramsci, Historical Materialism and International Relations*. Cambridge: Cambridge University Press.

Dunning, J. (1994) 'Globalization, Economic Restructuring and Development', mimeo. Department of Economics, University of Reading.

Giddens, A. (1991) *Modernity and Self-Identity*. Cambridge: Polity.

Grabher, G. (ed.) (1993) *The Embedded Firm*. London: Routledge.

Grabher, G. (1994) 'The Disembedded Regional Economy: The Transformation of East German Industrial Complexes into Western Enclaves' in A. Amin and N. Thrift (eds) *Globalization, Institutions and Regional Development in Europe*. Oxford: Oxford University Press.

Grabher, G. and Stark, D. (1995 and 1997) 'Organizing Diversity: Evolutionary Theory, Network Analysis, and Post-Socialist Transformations' in G. Grabher and D. Stark (eds) *Restructuring Networks in Postsocialism: Linkages and Locality*. Oxford: Oxford University Press.

Granovetter, M. (1985) 'Economic Action and Social Structure: The Problem of Embeddedness'. *American Journal of Sociology* 91: 481–510.

Hausner, J. (1992) *The Populist Threat in the Transformation of Socialist Society.* Warsaw: Friedrich Ebert Foundation.
Hirst, P. (1994) *Associative Democracy. New Forms of Economic and Social Governance.* Cambridge: Polity.
Hirst, P. and Thompson, G. (1996) *Globalization in Question.* Cambridge: Polity.
Hodgson, G.M. (1988) *Economics and Institutions.* Cambridge: Polity.
Hodgson, G.M. (1993) *Economics and Evolution.* Cambridge: Polity.
Hodgson, G.M., Samuels, W.J. and Tool, M.R. (eds) (1994) *The Elgar Companion to Institutional and Evolutionary Economics.* Aldershot: Edward Elgar.
Hübner, D. (1995) 'Ekonomia polityczna wzrostu: przypadek "Strategii dla Polski" ' [Political Economy of Growth: The 'Strategy for Poland' Case] in *Procesy Transformacji w Polsce* PBZ-115–01 (24), Warsaw: Instytut Nauk Ekonomicznych PAN (December).
Jessop, B. (1995) 'The Nation-State: Erosion or Reorganization?'. *Lancaster Regionalism Group Working Papers (Governance Series)*, No. 50.
Lane, C. (1995) *Industry and Society in Europe: Stability and Change in Britain, Germany and France.* Aldershot: Edward Elgar.
Latour, B. (1993) *We have never been Modern.* Brighton: Wheatsheaf.
Luhmann, N. (1979) *Trust and Power.* Chichester: Wiley.
Mertlík, P. (1995) 'Czech Privatization: From Public Ownership to Public Ownership in Five Years?'. *Prague Economic Papers* 4 (4): 321–36.
Misztal. B. (1996) *Trust in Modern Societies.* Cambridge: Polity.
Morgan, G. (1986) *Images of Organization.* Beverly Hills: Sage.
Mulberg, J. (1995) *Social Limits to Economic Theory.* London: Routledge.
Nesterenko, A. (1995) 'Creating a Legal Framework for Market Reforms in Russia'. Paper presented to the EAEPE conference on 'Transforming Economies and Societies: Towards an Institutional Theory of Economic Change', Cracow, 19–21October 1995.
Nielsen, K. and Pedersen, O.K. (1991) 'From the Mixed Economy to the Negotiated Economy: The Scandinavian Countries' in R. Coughlin (ed.) *Morality, Rationality and Efficiency: New Perspectives on Socio-economics.* New York: M.E. Sharpe.
Nuti, D.M. (1996) 'Post-Communist Mutations'. *Emergo. Journal of Transforming Economies and Societies* 3 (1): 7–15 (Winter).
Pedersen, O.K. (1993) 'The Institutional History of the Danish Polity: From a Market and Mixed Economy to a Negotiated Economy' in S.-E. Sjöstrand (ed.) *Institutional Change. Theory and Empirical Findings*, New York: M.E. Sharpe, pp. 277–300.
Putnam, R. (1993) *Making Democracy Work.* Princeton: Princeton University Press.
Pyke, F. and Sengenberger W. (1992) *Industrial Districts and Local Economic Regeneration.* Geneva: International Institute for Labour Studies.
Ruigrok, W. and van Tulder, R. (1995) *The Logic of International Restructuring.* London: Routledge.
Sabel, C.F. (1994) 'Learning by Monitoring: The Institutions of Economic Development' in N. Smelser and R. Swedberg (eds) *Handbook of Economic Sociology.* Princeton: Princeton University Press.

Sayer, A. and Walker, R. (1992) *The New Social Economy: Reworking the Division of Labour*. Cambridge, MA: Blackwell.

Smelser, N. and Swedberg, R. (eds) (1994). *Handbook of Economic Sociology*. Princeton: Princeton University Press.

Stark, D. (1996) 'Recombinant Property in East European Capitalism'. *American Journal of Sociology* 101: 993–1027 (January).

Stone, C. (1993) 'Urban Regimes and the Capacity to Govern: A Political Economy Approach'. *Journal of Urban Affairs* 15 (1): 1–28.

Streeck, W. (1995) 'The German Social Market Economy: External Competitiveness and Internal Cohesion'. Contribution to a conference on 'Comparative Study of Systems of Market Economy and Land Ownership in England, France, Germany, Japan, Sweden and the United States', Honolulu: East-West Center (EWC), 9–11 August 1995.

United Nations (1992) *World Investment Report 1992: Transnational Corporations: Engines of Growth*. New York: UN Transnational Corporations and Management Division.

Whitley, R. (ed.) (1992) *European Business Systems*. London: Sage.

2. The foundational bearing of complexity

Robert Delorme

1. INTRODUCTION

This chapter explores how a particular kind of complexity arising out of a case study on the interaction between the state and the economy may have a broader, paradigmatic bearing in economics.[1] This we call self-referential complexity. The term complexity is rather elusive and has become a catch-all fashionable word. Here we defend a restricted use of it and attempt to show how it provides a solution to a particular problem.

Although this chapter deals with method, it is not concerned with either epistemology or methodology. It is primarily concerned with theorizing on a particular subject matter in economics, that is, the interaction between the state and the economy based on empirical investigation. We are looking for a solution to a particular problem arising in this area through the application of a theory of complexity. On the one hand, the very notion of complexity has been developed mainly at the epistemological and methodological levels. There is a wealth of literature in this domain, yet little has been done in the way of associated empirical and theoretical research in economics. Thus, the discourse on complexity is perceived by many economists as essentially programmatic and abstract. On the other hand, research which addresses complexity using chaos theory and non-linear modelling still seems far from being capable of providing a tool for empirically based investigation. Some economists have preferred to take a position whereby complexity is not modelled but, instead, is viewed as a description of the real world. Several theoretical systems have been developed as a consequence of the recognition of the complexity of the economic system. These are the so-called heterodox theories. In this chapter, it

[1] This chapter builds mainly on the first part of Delorme (1997) in which an analysis of self-referential complexity is developed. The author is especially indebted to Jean-Louis Le Moigne and to John Foster. Any remaining errors are the author's sole responsibility.

will be shown that such theories can assist us in understanding state-economy interactions provided that complexity is dealt with in an explicit and specific manner.

Complexity denotes the impossibility of depicting a 'complex' phenomenon in a reduced and simplified way. Thus, the phenomenon can only be depicted in its full form, which is in itself a complex task. The difficulty in dealing in a scientific way with complexity arises from this apparent contradiction. Properties of ignorance, unpredictability and radical uncertainty ensue from complexity. A profound debate currently divides the economics discipline between the majority of economists who refuse to introduce these notions into theoretical work, in order to preserve the predictive goal of theorizing thus conceived, and a growing minority accepting these notions. This divide provides a criterion for differentiating between a standard approach and a heterodox – and heterogenous – one, in which one would find evolutionary, institutionalist, Keynesian, Austrian and Marxist approaches, including their neo and post prefixed variants. Our objective is to show that complexity is not only an obstacle but may also provide a solution in dealing with complex situations. The solution we propose is based on shifting from complexity, commonly understood and practised as object-based and reflexive complexity, to self-referential complexity.

This chapter develops in three sections. The nature of the problem to be solved and the issue of complexity as an obstacle are analysed in the following section. Complexity as a solution to the problem is examined in the next section. In the final section we explore the prospect of extending the solution to a broader, foundational issue.

2. OBJECT-BASED, REFLEXIVE AND SELF-REFERENTIAL COMPLEXITY

2.1. Interactions between the State and the Economy

This chapter is the outcome of research on public spending in France and other industrialized countries which has evolved progressively towards a study of the role of the state in industrialized economies compared at an international level. This research commenced with extensive observation through statistical data and testing the available theoretical explanations concerning the determinants of public spending (Delorme and André 1983, Delorme 1984). Several hypotheses were tested and it was found that most of them had some relevance for particular, local issues under specific and sometimes very limited conditions. An example is the theme of the productivity lag in the public sector. This is viewed by some as a cause of the growth of public expenditure relative to overall economic activity. It was demonstrated that the empirical evidence for this thesis is difficult to establish, even in those cases most applicable to it, such as the provision of services in health, hospital and education. Still more problematic, it leaves wide open the issue of the rationale for projecting this kind of assumption to public expenditure taken as a whole.

Research on international comparisons (Delorme 1992) of the role of the state in market-led economic systems reinforced the discrepancy between what could be reasonably derived from the available theories and what appeared to be features of the subject matter, resembling stylized facts in the Kaldorian, not in the ad hoc sense (Kaldor 1963, Boland 1988, Lawson 1989). The notion of strong diversity, not amenable to the one-sided nature of available theories, was the main finding. Such evidence offered the challenge of capturing both difference and sameness in an articulated, unified, theoretical framework. The notion of characteristic *modes of interaction between the state and the economy* (MISE) was elaborated as an answer to this question. MISEs are plural, since they differ over time and across countries. This was a conjecture. It could be stated only because the decision was taken at some point of the research programme to go ahead without obeying any of the methodological approaches associated with the available theoretical systems, since none of them appeared satisfactory.

It should be emphasized that this is not a question of all or nothing. The problem is that no available theory is capable of articulating the diversity of institutional and organizational patterns of state-economy interactions whose existence is established by careful observation in otherwise market-led economies. Table 2.1 illustrates the difficulties encountered with available theories and Figure 2.1 contains a schematized presentation of the MISE developed in Delorme (1995).

We thus dispose of what can be called a stylized conjecture derived from stylized facts. These stylized facts originate from empirically identified regularities that display strong differences and similarities over time as well as spatially, across countries. Historical and spatial contexts, the institutionalization of key relationships, historical paths and enduring differences in the perceptions of issues form the basis of any attempt to come to grips with the need to elaborate a theoretical representation of the articulation of these features.

Next, we need to show how the problem identified above is in the nature of an object-based complex problem. We examine the tools

Table 2.1. A comparison of theoretical systems on public expenditure evolution

APPROACHES	EXAMPLES	EXPLANATORY PRINCIPLE OF PUBLIC EXPENDITURE GROWTH	STATE BEHAVIOUR
Determinant models	Wagner's law Public goods as superior goods Fiscal barrier Displacement effect Productivity differential	Relation to industrialization Analogy to consumption theory Financing constraint Financing constraint and growth through a threshold effect Growing absorption of resources in sector with lagging productivity	No explicit theoretical conception
Individualistic approach	Collective goods theory	Market failure or no market owing to the very high exclusion costs	Voluntary exchange The state as a benevolent device
	Public choice	Institutional asymmetry, various biases (voting system, logrolling, etc.) Fiscal illusion Bureaucracy Politico-economic interactions	Political market Analogy to the market Pathological state, as a market degradation
Constraint	Exogenous state The industrial state, the corporate state	Arbitrating state State decisions oriented according to the interest of particular groups (ruling class, technostructure, etc.)	The state as a centre of power radically different from the market Either benevolent state (public interest) or partisan state (particular and vested interests)
Marxist approach	SMC (state monopoly capitalism)	Tendency of capitalism towards over-accumulation, depressing the profit rate, with counteraction by the government through expenditure	Instrumental state

Source: Delorme (1984).

Level of interaction	Logic of interaction Coordination Legitimation Coercion
Global: nature of the game Rules of the game: institutional forms Organization of the game: organizational forms Actors	MISE

Figure 2.1. The MISE (mode of interaction between the state and the economy)

available in the economics discipline to deal with this kind of complexity. None of them seems to be helpful at this stage. We are left again with a problem relating to the nature of reflexive radical uncertainty. Reflexivity provides a strong incentive to explore decision theory in the context of radical uncertainty and complexity. Simon's theory of rationality provides such a framework. Finally, the consequences of introducing reflexive complexity in a procedural rationality framework are evoked.

2.2. Object-Based Complexity and Reflexivity

In order to explain public spending, one needs to know why a particular state action takes the form of spending rather than any other qualitative form. In order to explain some particular state action, whatever its concrete form, one must explain why it is public rather than private. There are, thus, varying interrelated levels requiring investigation. Thus, this matter appears to comprise numerous components with strong interdependencies between them, making the subject matter a complex phenomenon and rendering it irreducible to some tractable analytical representation (Weaver 1948, Ashby 1956, von Bertalanffy 1973). In this sense, complexity originates in the properties of the subject matter that the analytical capacities of the scientist cannot reach. This may be called *object-based* complexity since it is considered to be an intrinsic property of the object of study. A broader conception includes the scientist, thus denoting the inevitable relational character of complexity: it is always related to an observer or a scientist's mind. This is a common theme in systems theory. It is akin to unpredictability, radical uncertainty and ignorance.

Unpredictability, radical uncertainty and ignorance play the same roles here. This problem faced by the theoretician is similar to the one evoked by Popper concerning how to predict the growth of theoretical knowledge (Popper 1984, pp. 54–7). Future knowledge cannot be predicted in a probabilistic way. A body of knowledge cannot provide a probabilistic representation of what is, by assumption, unknown. In such a case there seems to be no other solution than to reflect upon what comes before, that is, on the process of reasoning and deciding. Decision theory dealing with complexity is well developed. Our task is to discover which aspects of such theorizing are most useful in our chosen context.

2.3. Procedural Rationality

Procedural rationality is a notion introduced in economics by Simon. Although Simon's theory of decision-making is well known, there is the possibility of some confusion regarding how the types of rationality attached to it can be used. Above all, the potential insights yielded by the notion of procedural rationality have still not been investigated. It has to do with reflexivity. It is our contention that procedural rationality offers a very helpful theoretical framework for investigating the scientist's decision-making process. This implies applying the concept reflexively – the scientist applies it to her/himself and explores the consequences. To the author's knowledge, this is a step about which Simon seems to have remained silent and has tried to avoid.

Part of the difficulty regarding the use of Simon's notions of rationality seems due to the fact that he did not develop these notions in a general unified theory but presented them rather in a plurality of models and contributions pertaining to several disciplines including management, psychology, economics, organization theory and artificial intelligence. However, one cannot but be impressed by the unchanging core of Simon's works since his 1943 dissertation (published in 1947). In the first edition of *Administrative Behaviour*, objective rationality (later understood as substantive rationality) and subjective rationality (later called procedural rationality) are presented. 'Substantive' and 'rational' are related to behaviour and programming. Bounded rationality is introduced in the second edition (1957). It is distinguished from global rationality. The pair – procedural rationality and substantive rationality – appeared in a paper presented in 1973 and published in 1976 (Simon 1976). The notion is presented by Simon under the word 'bounded' solely in the New Palgrave edition (1988) and in *Models of my Life* (1991). Although Simon's indifferent use of the two words is quite consistent in his writings, it may create some ambiguity. It is tempting to consider bounded rationality as a kind of rationality simply intended to supplement complete or substantive rationality, understood as 'the rationality assumption' as J. Elster does (1989, p. 31).

In this case bounded rationality is secondary to the core notion of rationality. It seems to us that this view runs counter to the essence and the very logic of these concepts.

Simon defines these concepts in the following way:

> Behaviour is substantively rational when it is appropriate to the achievement of given goals within the limits imposed by given conditions and constraints. . . . Behaviour is procedurally rational when it is the outcome of appropriate deliberation. Its procedural rationality depends on the process that generated it. (Simon 1976, pp. 130–31)

> [Procedural rationality may be expected in situations that are not] sufficiently simple as to be transparent to [the] mind. [Then] we must expect that the mind will use such imperfect information as it has, will simplify and represent the situation as it can, and will make such calculations as are within its powers. (Simon 1976, p. 144)

Using the correct available algorithm is the usual way to operate in substantive rationality. There is no interference between the decision-maker and the way in which he/she tries to solve a problem. Such a possibility is not, by definition, available when uncertainty, ignorance or complexity prevail. In this case, a decision embodies deliberation, search and the forms of representation the decision-maker prefers. A solution is then constructed through a heuristic process in which it is reasonable to retain 'an alternative that meets or exceeds specified criteria, but that is not guaranteed to be either unique or in any sense the best' which defines *satisficing*, a term introduced by Simon in 1956 (Simon 1988). A situation is satisficing when it is adequate for some aspiration level. This is the essence of procedural rationality.

Simon's theory subverts conventional economics since it makes the case for seriously considering the formation of human preferences as part of the decision problem. It says that it is no longer possible to get rid of deliberation when there is uncertainty, ignorance or complexity. A decision is, so to speak, contaminated by the decision-maker's mind: 'A body of theory for procedural rationality is consistent with a world in which human beings continue to think and continue to invent; a theory of substantive rationality is not' (Simon 1976, p. 146). With satisficing, the utility function is no longer necessarily consistent over time. Learning is acknowledged. The choice made may vary according to the order in which alternatives are considered.

Thus procedural rationality introduces into complexity a situation in which the decision-maker plays a key role. Complexity is not only object-based in the sense of being intrinsic to the observed object, it is also related to the observing subject: it is a cognitive notion; it is perceived complexity. The complexity of an object for an observer depends on the way he/she interacts with it (Klir 1985, Morin 1985, 1992, Le Moigne 1990a, 1991, Segal 1990, Watzlawick 1988). To paraphrase Simon on uncertainty (Simon 1976, p. 437), complexity exists in the eye and mind of the beholder. Complexity thus defined is reflexive and necessarily entails the observer reflecting on how to proceed in dealing with a complex object. Reflexive complexity is a way to express such a concern for method arising out of the perception that the object of enquiry is complex.

The difficulty becomes even greater when the decision-maker does not know how to decide on the procedure or the method. This is the situation from which we started. In this case, the problem of how to deal with a complex object is itself complex. Something new is thus introduced. Until now, we have reasoned on the procedural consequences arising from the complexity of an observed object. Now the concern regarding procedure is explicitly considered as a complex problem for the observer. This we could call self-referential complexity or 'complexity of complexity'.[2] Elsewhere (Delorme 1997) we have shown how this leads to a satisficing solution. The reason for this is that there is no determinate substantive solution because of the presence of a self-referential regressive spiral. Self-referential complexity cannot be solved in the sense of directly reducing it to simplicity. This does not mean, however, that we must abandon the task. Self-referential complexity cannot be solved substantially but it can be dealt with. This is what procedural rationality tells us.

In a complex situation the issue of ignorance over the question of what is a good explanation cannot be solved without relying on procedure. And a satisficing procedure is not the outcome of a deductively determined choice, but of deliberation. This indicates a general starting-point for developing a satisficing strategy, that is, a strategy that is appropriate for the subject matter at hand and for the situation. In this sense, complexity understood as self-referential complexity provides a basis for a solution.

3. COMPLEXITY AS A SOLUTION

Satisficing has no determinate substantive contents. And it may lead to subjectivism. Thus it needs to be controlled by submitting it to an

[2] It is analysed as *second order complexity*, with a more developed argument, in Delorme (1997).

external constraint. This constraint cannot but be related to the environment of the research process. Here, the relevant environment is scientific practice. The constraint consists of making compatible the three dimensions around which our argument has revolved until now: scientific practice, the inclusion of complexity and operationality. They define an aspiration for a level at which it is reasonable to expect general agreement on the following global directives: *do science, embody complexity* and *be operational.* A theory will be appropriate if it meets these three conditions. Let us explore how this can be done.

3.1. Scientific Practice

3.1.1. Definition

At a basic, practical level, what distinguishes doing science from other cognitive or intellectual operations may be learnt from the dictionary definition of science. There seems to be a widely held consensus that doing science entails the combination of three elements. Doing science involves the search for some kind of explanation of a certain reality, and systematically putting it to the test (Granger 1990). It seems reasonable to consider that this definition is the common reference point for all scientific activity. It is the shared vision from which the divide between different conceptions of science arises. This divide comes from the various ways of conceiving explanation, reality and testing.

Explanation is taken here at this stage in a broad sense. It refers to the operation of producing knowledge. It can mean causal explanation in a strict sense, but it can also involve prediction, representation or understanding. For the purpose at hand, the main differentiation is between the goals of causal explanation and prediction in mainstream economics on the one hand, and the emphasis on representation common to most heterodox views on the other. The next divide occurs over the question of what is to be considered as reality. The subject matter of science has a bearing on the real world. It is at this point that opinion is divided into two opposing positions. The first, ontological realism, attempts to know the nature of reality and discover its laws. It thus views reality as objective, independent of the mind, and its goal is to produce statements that are scientific because they depict reality independently from the observer's eye.

According to the second viewpoint, true reality is beyond our reach and we know it only through our experience of phenomena. This is phenomenological realism. Instead of being discovered, laws and other statements are invented. Scientific practice aims more at diminishing our ignorance than at establishing truths. This is a fallibilistic standpoint which accommodates complexity well. It draws on a rich intellectual tradition that for a long time has held a subaltern status owing to the overwhelming pressure and dazzling influence of the analytical, positivist scientific doctrine in science. This tradition is known nowadays as constructivism. Its modern revival has its roots in Piaget's genetic epistemology (Piaget 1968), Simon's model, and the 'construction of reality' perspective offered by Bateson (1972), Morin (1985, 1992), von Foerster (1988, 1992), von Glasersfeld (1988), Watzlawick (1988), among others. Positivism is still pervasive in economics, It finds its strength in the ignorance of constructivism as an alternative, and in the wide unspoken consensus on immunizing stratagems in economics, a practice which destroys the possibility of identifying when a theory is false or irrelevant and which deprives economic theory of the possibility of learning from its errors and of progressing. In this sense, the practical invulnerability of analytical positivist economics is its main weakness.

This brings us to the third feature, namely, testing. This is the principal and most difficult question in economic science, for it lacks a final arbiter. The situation is incomparably better in natural science, where experimentation and controlled observation provide criteria for empirical validation. In so far as we are interested in empirico-theoretic science, not in formal science, a final arbiter rests on controlled protocols of empirical validation. It is not indulging in catastrophism to acknowledge that standard economics is in a disastrous state in this regard. Exceptions can be found in simple, transparent enough problems such as those for which substantive rationality is relevant, at a micro level, or those which are simple enough at the macroeconomic level, thus enabling reasonably reliable predictions. This difficult state of affairs is widely admitted in the literature on economic methodology. Until now one must say that its influence on the way most economists work has been almost nil. Economic theory consists mainly of conversation at a formal and abstract level. As a consequence, a final arbiter is avoided.

3.1.2. How to put scientific knowledge to the test?

There are two other features that are closely linked to scientific practice. They pertain to the manner in which reasoning is conducted and communicated. Scientific practice requires a language. As with any other language, it is made up of signs, symbols and rules. The first feature has to do with the requirement contained in the triad of communicability, systematicity and cumulativeness of science. Communication is the basis for diminishing confusion and establishing systematicity thanks to which some progress and cumulative knowledge may be envisaged. These notions point to the importance of the way scientific knowledge is represented and communicated, which is the essence of the second feature.

At this stage it is necessary to emphasize a feature which still receives only limited attention in economic science. Every science embodies its statements and results in signs. Semiotics, the science of signs, comprises three fields of investigating languages – also termed portions of semiotics (Morris 1971) or levels of communication (Shannon and Weaver 1949): syntax, also called syntactics (Morris) or the technical level (Weaver), pertains to the relations of signs to one another independently of the relations of signs to objects or to interpreters; semantics, which deals with the signification of signs understood as the relation of signs to the objects which they denote; pragmatics, which designates the relation of signs to their interpreters, thus dealing with the origin, the uses and the effects of signs (Morris 1971). Scientific practice may be expressed as necessarily covering these three levels of communication.

Within economics, perspectives can be differentiated according to the relative weights they give to these levels. The formal orientation focuses on syntax while most dissident perspectives emphasize the other two terms. The ideal is a balance. The standard perspective in economics gives priority to syntax. Thus, in the case of radical uncertainty, it is no surprise that primacy will be given to the method over the object of inquiry, that is, to syntax over semantics. Exclusion of radical uncertainty, because it cannot be captured with the analytical tool kit, illustrates this point clearly. The tools are thus taken for granted and applied to situations which are made to adapt to them thanks to ad hoc assumptions. A different approach is to start from problematic situations and empirical facts and try to adjust the method and syntax applied to them, thus putting the bulk of adjustment on the pragmatic and syntactic levels. Yet this procedure does not mean that facts can be taken a priori as granted. They are inevitably arbitrary. However we would find it difficult to express our experience of reality without relying on facts. Thus, it seems reasonable to admit that some adaptation of the facts is inevitable. Of course it does not mean that observation will be modified in order to fit the observer's own preferences! Adjusting facts means making them relevant to the question addressed. In the research reported earlier, we found that it was impossible to address public spending in the long run independently from public finance. And we discovered that it would be quite difficult to investigate public finance over time and in international comparison independently of the other forms, both quantitative and qualitative, of interaction between the state and the economy. Thus, the facts investigated were initially public spending, then public finance, then the quantitative and qualitative dimensions of the public sector (Delorme 1984).

One would expect that in any empirical science consistency prevails not only in the manner in which the signs are used, in the way they are relevant and in the way they combine in syntax, but also in the overall consistency of the semiotic triangle. It is difficult here not to think of the discrepancy which exists in economics between professed and actual method. It is the price paid for preserving formalism. It illustrates how excessive formalism may constrain scientific practice either by preventing the study of empirical situations that do not fit the syntax or by asking the public at large, first, to accept that economics relies mainly on syntax and must be programmatic for the time being and, second, to believe that it will have empirically relevant results at a continually postponed and unknown future date. The alternative approach also has its own price: it is the weakness of its syntax, the evasiveness or the absence of a body of founding logical principles. Here we face once again the ongoing debate over the trade-offs between 'well-derived' and 'empirically relevant' theories.

3.2. Complexity

The choice made in the trade-off discussed above is driven by the condition that it be consistent with the state of radical uncertainty. Complexity comes into the picture here. How can we ensure that a procedure is consistent with complexity? How does it compare with the analytical perspective? A condensed way of answering these questions involves concentrating on the logical bases of each perspective. The contention is that complexity may be related to a set of founding principles which have the same status as those of the analytical perspective. This may answer a criticism often made against heterodoxy, namely that heterodoxy has no chain of basic principles ensuring its internal consistency in a way comparable to orthodoxy, hence the presumed superiority of orthodoxy. That this seems to be no longer true, at least in the case of complexity, can be shown through a comparison of the well-known axioms of classical logic with the progressively emerging axioms of complexity. The latter are naturally much less codified, diffused and known than the former. It may thus make them appear quite abstract and strange. Yet, if we reflect on the rationale of the axioms of classical logic which form the basis of analytical theorizing, we would see that they are no more obvious than the complex ones. It is our habituation to them which makes them appear familiar and self-evident to the point where we never refer to them explicitly, as if they represented some unspoken basic consensus beyond the realm of questioning.

Moreover, there exists a plurality of logical systems. Each one has its own, inevitably arbitrary, basis. A form of logic relevant to the problem of complexity is that of intuitionist logic, developed by Brouwer and Heyting (Heyting, 1980). The number of propositions which may be considered as axiomatic is not fixed. Indeed, it is not without hesitation that these principles or axioms are introduced below since limited space does not allow us to discuss them fully. The presentation made here is inspired to a large extent by Le Moigne (1991).

3.2.1. The axioms of analytical modelling

The reality to be modelled is perceived on the basis of the following three axioms. A and B stand for propositions:

1. Identity: A is A;
2. Non-contradiction: A cannot be simultaneously B and $\bar{B}$ (not-B);
3. Excluded middle: A is either B or $\bar{B}$.

3.2.2. The principles of complex modelling

The phenomena to be modelled are perceived on the basis of the following three principles.

Operationality and intentionality Modelling is the conjunction of the modeller's purpose with her/his environment, differentiating it from analytical disjunction between causes and effects. Action and interaction as opposed to 'things', and the process itself, not the result of that process, are the basic categories.

Irreversibility Action and process take place over time. Time is perceived as irreversible.

Included middle Operation or action is perceived as generating a product. The generating principle and its product are not separable. The product is producing what produces it. This is a situation of recursiveness.

3.3. Operationality

Until now we have remained at the logical and the methodological levels. The next task is to combine what has been said about scientific practice and complexity in an operational way, that is, enabling us to apply these results to actual cases and to compare them with alternative theoretical perspectives. Let us recall our goal of taking into account reflexive radical uncertainty, a task which is incorporated in reflexive complexity.

The satisficing principle has thus hitherto proved effective. Nevertheless, we still need to submit complexity to the test of whether it is adequate to the problem. In this sense complexity becomes controlled complexity. We contend that operational control relies on three rules: consistency, communicability and relevance.

3.3.1. Consistency

Consistency is concerned with avoiding the discrepancy between the professed and the actual method, and an imbalance between the three elements of the semiotic triangle. Although it is difficult to define substantively a balance between these elements, it can be defined procedurally as mutually adjusting semantics and syntax up to the point where the actually practised pragmatics meets the declared pragmatics – that is, the professed method. It may be summarized as: preach what you can do, do what you preach. In the study of a phenomenon perceived as complex, for which there exists no available substantive theory or model, empirical investigation combines with abduction and attempts at theorizing: hence the priority given to the object of study and to the role of the semantics over the syntax in the first step.

3.3.2. Communicability

It may look trivial to insist on *communicability* as a rule. Yet it conditions potential systematicity and cumulativeness. Above all it is a precondition for mutual criticism and the real exercise of control within and outside the scientific community. It implies transparency and voluntary exposure to criticism. It runs opposite to the immunization so often denounced by methodologists in economics (Caldwell 1991). Even if it may seem too idealistic to believe in the elimination of immunization, the least that can be done is to eliminate hidden immunization. This requires that when immunization is introduced, it be made explicit. One finds here an illustration that the proof of the pudding is sometimes more in the making than in the eating. A way to foster transparency is the comparison between theories for a given problem, in a meliorative strategy. It implies that statements be designed in a way that makes comparison possible.

3.3.3. Relevance

In line with the fallibilistic stance of the complex perspective, relevance amounts to reducing ignorance and arbitrariness in theorizing.

Emphasizing the reduction of arbitrariness seems fruitful because of its generality and its capacity to be used as a criterion for comparison and assessment. We express this in the following propositions:

- there is no non-arbitrary way of reasoning. There is no non-arbitrary ultimate foundation;
- there are degrees of arbitrariness. They can be identified through comparison;
- the aim is to reduce the degree of arbitrariness for a given problem.

3.4. Anchored Complexity

These conditions constitute what may be termed ‘anchored complexity’. It provides a solution to the problem of the unifying principle mentioned above: anchored complexity is a leading thread satisfying the conditions enumerated. The plurality of methods is intrinsic to complexity and is bounded by what is admissible for anchored complexity. Moreover, anchored complexity reduces *ipso facto* the degree of arbitrariness in comparison to the analytical approach, since it takes into account radical uncertainty.

Finally, anchored complexity may be considered as a generating principle whose product has stimulated its own production. This sentence simply describes the recursive loop between an initial inference (stylized facts) transformed into a stylized conjecture (a characteristic configuration of the interaction between the state and the economy) and later into a theoretical conjecture (a mode of interaction between the state and the economy: MISE) after having been informed by anchored complexity (symbolized as ACX in Figure 2.2).

It seems reasonable to think at this point that the above development is adequate for the purpose at hand and is thus a satisficing solution. However, it must be recognized that there is no external universal criterion to help assess whether it is true or false. The only way is to expose it to criticism. But here, what is exposed to criticism is more accurate, more specified and more operational for research strategy than what was available at the beginning.

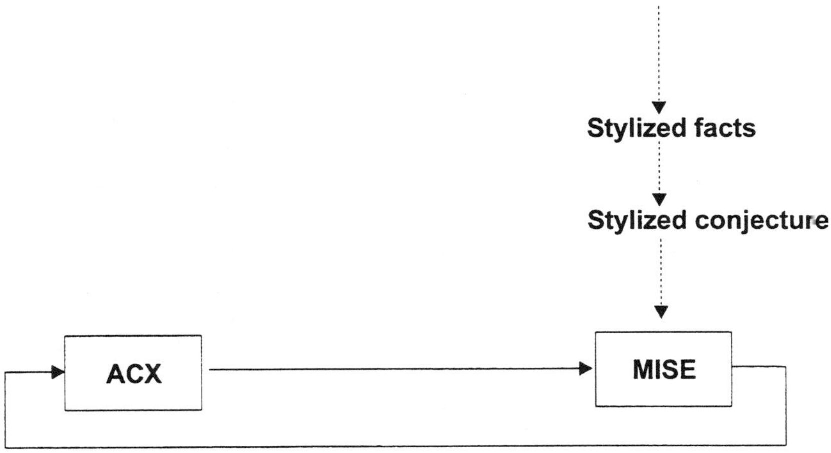

Figure 2.2. Research on the case in point as a recursive loop

4. THE SCOPE FOR EXTENSION

4.1. Complex and Analytical Chains of Reasoning Compared

In view of the progress made in the previous section, it is possible to show how the solution arrived at is also a solution to a broader issue. The arguments which have been incorporated provide a consistent and complete chain of reasoning comparable to the classical, analytical chain of reasoning. Putting together the pieces that have been introduced thus far enables a comparison of the analytical (positivist) and the complex (constructivist) perspectives (see Table 2.2).

The construction proposed here conforms to a hierarchy comprising ten levels. The first level represents the division which occurs between the standard approach and the approach of complexity. We assume that the dictionary definition of scientific practice is considered relevant by proponents of both perspectives. The division occurs over the conception of scientific knowledge and unfolds downwards until it reaches the end-product level.

The terms mentioned in each column indicate the primary focus of each perspective at each level. They do not describe all the ingredients. We simply contend that the terms retained here form the respective starting-points in each approach, and on which the other features are dependent. In light of the previous argument, the items in Table 2.2

Table 2.2. The analytical and the complex perspectives compared

	ANALYSIS	COMPLEXITY
1. General definition of scientific practice	Common to both perspectives: some kind of explanation of reality, systematically put to the test	
2. Conception of scientific knowledge	Positivism	Constructivism
3. Mode of reasoning	Analytical	Complex
4. Position of reality	Ontological realism Objective character of reality	Phenomenological realism Constructed character of reality
5. Main purpose of scientific practice	Prediction	Active representation
6. Logical core	Axioms of classical logic	Axioms of complex logic
7. Methodological stance	Deduction Disjunction Discovery Universal norm of truth	Abduction, Investigation Conjunction Design, invention Satisficing
8. Method	Taken as granted: 'The scientific method'	Adjusted according to anchored complexity: built-in controlled pluralism
9. Theoretical perspective and theorizing	x, y, z . . .	a, b, c . . .
10. End product (statements on the real world, policy prescriptions)	x′, y′, z′ . . .	a′, b′, c′ . . .

do not require further explanation, given the scope of this contribution. The only exception concerns the main purpose of scientific practice in the complex perspective at level 5. A common trait of complex reasoning is its representation of a reality that is itself perceived primarily through a process of construction. Representation is then active, not passive. In passive representation, knowledge is viewed as reflecting a world with intrinsic predefined properties leaving the scientist with the task of uncovering some hidden truth 'already there'. In active representation, design and invention play an important part.

A related notion is that of the world view. Having a world view cannot be abolished. It is commonly understood in economics as pertaining to a set of basic statements shared by a scientific community on how the economy functions. Neoclassical, Keynesian, Post-Keynesian, Austrian and Marxian world views, among others, illustrate this definition. Divisions in the discipline are usually understood in terms of these world views. The conceptualization presented here is different. We have attempted to show that introducing complexity changes the issue from one of substantive preferences shared by respective communities to one concerning cognitive procedure. We introduced the conception of scientific knowledge as a basic criterion of choice independently of any preference regarding the question of how the economy should function. Indeed it is only at level 9 that particular theoretical perspectives come into the picture. On the one hand, one may find at this level the theoretical perspectives mentioned at the beginning of this chapter together with the particular form of theorizing derived from them ($x,y,z \ldots$) and the end statements ($x',y',z' \ldots$). On the other hand, the MISE may appear as a, together with other theoretical notions and end statements likely to be developed along the complex lines ($b,c, b',c' \ldots$). The end statements will logically differ from one approach to the next.

In view of the confusion and the limitations attached to the substantive world views in the case of complexity, we think that the cognitive conception developed here clarifies the issue and is more general.

The complex and the analytical perspectives are not symmetrical. At first sight, one might consider that the analytical perspective is warranted whenever we are in a situation of no uncertainty and that the same goes for complexity in cases of uncertainty. However, the analytical approach cannot accommodate uncertainty while the complex approach can accommodate the situations pertaining to the analytical approach. One finds the same asymmetry between substantive and procedural rationality: the former excludes consideration of the latter whereas the inverse is not true since procedural search allows by definition for the possibility of constructing situations locally relevant for substantive rationality (Delorme 1997).

Thus complexity incorporates analysis. The situations relevant for analysis appear as particular cases. Whereas the trademark of analysis is exclusivism, complexity does not exclude a priori the analytical method. It excludes only analytical exclusivism. It incorporates the analytical approach thanks to its greater generality and relevance. It allows for the local relevance of analytical and positivist methods provided their relevance is established on every specific subject matter under consideration. This asymmetry supports the case for arguing that the complex perspective offers a more general methodological stance than the analytical one. However, complexity is not reducible to methodology. We have attempted to show how designing a research strategy and putting it to work as anchored complexity is of utmost importance. The analytical perspective can no longer base its strength on the absence of an alternative perspective which would meet similar standards of consistency and operationality.

4.2. Programmatism, Floating Eclecticism and the Gains from Self-Referential Complexity in Economics

We consider here only those parts of the economics discipline that pertain to complexity. Indeed a closer look at the history of economic thought reveals the importance played by complexity mentioned explicitly or present *de facto*: Veblen, Keynes, Hayek and, naturally, Simon are some examples.

The three notions of complexity introduced above form the basis for mapping complexity, structured around three levels of scientific investigation: epistemological, methodological and theoretical-empirical (see Table 2.3).

We have filled the cells of Table 2.3 with what we consider to be representative notions. The most intriguing case is the bottom right cell. It is empty in the economic discipline. The two ways of arriving at this cell are a vertical top-down one in the extreme right column and in a horizontal direction, from left to right, along the bottom line. These two ways reveal two serious limitations encountered with complexity in economics. The first limitation appears vertically. It is programmatism, meaning that the wealth of developments in self-referential complexity at the epistemological and methodological levels is not prolonged at the theoretical, operational level. Indeed it is even a source of discouragement. Yet nobody can be blamed for this because methodology has its own logic at its own level and cannot provide tailored research strategies adapted to particular research issues at the empirical level. It can provide only broad orientations. Our starting-point illustrates that between a stylized conjecture arrived at through an empirical investigation striving to take care of the many-sidedness of the subject matter, and the general orientation offered by the methodology of complexity, there is a gap, a missing link. Remedying this is the purpose of anchored complexity.

Yet we followed a quite different path for arriving at anchored complexity. We engaged in theoretical problem-solving, from left to right, at the bottom line level, as is in fact demonstrated throughout this chapter. It illustrates why we began by saying that this chapter is about

Table 2.3. Object-based, reflexive and self-referential complexity at three levels of scientific investigation

LEVELS OF SCIENTIFIC INVESTIGA-TION	OBJECT-BASED COMPLEXITY	REFLEXIVE COMPLEXITY	SELF-REFERENTIAL COMPLEXITY
Epistemological	Positivism	Peirce, Dewey, Bachelard, Popper	Second order cybernetics. Piaget, von Foerster, Pask, Atlan, Maturana, Varela, Morin, Dupuy, Bateson, Watzlawick, von Glasersfeld
Methodological	Method taken as granted: 'the' scientific method	Concern for method: Veblen, Keynes, Hayek, Simon Institutionalism First order cybernetics First systemics	Second systemics: Morin, Le Moigne
Theoretical Empirical	Chaos theory	Decision theory (Simon . . .) Keynes, Kaldor Regulation school Evolutionary theory	Empty cell in economics Anchored complexity proposed

theorizing. Programmatism is also a limitation at this level. Chaos theory illustrates this point since it is mainly developed at a syntactic level. Decision theory of the reflexive complexity type is based on a conception of realism. It may have value for well-defined and limited subject matter. The main challenge facing the other theoretical lines in this central column is floating eclecticism. Anchored complexity appears to offer a way of achieving anchored eclecticism.

4.3. The Foundational Bearing of Self-Referential Complexity

We have not devoted space to a discussion of the various conceptions of complexity that exist in science. We have used a simple general definition that appears sufficient for our argument. We introduce a few remarks on this question which we intend to develop at a future date.

It is to be noted first that complexity differs from complication, although these notions are often confused (Atlan 1979). Second, a common trait of complexity is its character of a knowledge relationship. It denotes an irreducible lack of knowledge whose sources pertain to the observer and the observed object. The bounded cognitive capacity and competence of the observer, reflexivity and the permanent creation of meaning in human affairs account for the former. The latter pertains to the intrinsic properties of the object. They range from 'organic interdependence' (Keynes 1921, Carabelli 1988) to 'organized complexity' (Weaver 1948), high variety (Hayek 1967, Ashby 1956), system indecomposability (Simon 1991). Theories based on radical uncertainty and ignorance should also be taken into account here. One would like to dispose of a clear-cut quantitative measure of complexity, such as the ones afforded by algorithmic complexity and the entropy formulations (Shannon in Shannon and Weaver 1949). The latter deal with a very restricted technical notion of complexity in which it is possible to abstract from meaning, from information creation and from the interplay between integrated levels of organization, an example of which is the observer-observed coupling (Atlan 1979).

Two definitions of complexity stand out and have been used throughout this chapter. They both pertain to a conception emphasizing not the components of an 'object' but what an 'object' can do (taken in the broad sense of an acting entity). Then complexity becomes based on the consideration of the interaction between a generating principle and what is generated. We have shown how procedural and substantive rationality accord with this conception. The second conception is von Neumann's intuition about complexity:

> 'complication' on its lower levels is probably degenerative, that is, that every automaton that can produce other automata will only be able to produce less complicated ones. There is, however, a certain minimum level where this degenerative characteristic ceases to be universal. At this point, automata which can reproduce themselves, or even construct higher entities, become possible. This fact, that complication, as well as organization, below a certain minimum level is degenerative, and beyond that level can become self-supporting and even increasing, will, clearly play an important role in any future theory of the subject. (von Neumann 1961, p. 318)

In a simple situation, it is easier to depict the outcome than the generating principle. Complexity appears as the level, or the threshold, beyond which it is much less difficult to depict the generating principle than what is generated. A direct consequence is that the study of a complex situation can hardly be carried out independently of considerations of the generating principle, that is, the cognitive capacity of the scientist. In research not limited thus to a syntactic stance, it seems difficult to proceed as if the generating principle can be neutralized and as if empirical investigation comes 'after'. Hence, not only is it debatable not to include explicitly considerations of what kind of knowledge is produced, but it may well be inconsistent, if we take Simon and von Neumann seriously. At this stage, complexity appears to be even more than a research strategy, it is a *mode of knowledge.*

Under what conditions is it possible to study a complex object independently of self-referential complexity? It seems that such a problem would necessitate a reliable method meeting satisficing requirements. Again, if one sticks to a balance between semantics and syntax, it may be difficult to avoid constructing a procedure. Then, complexity can hardly be *applied* to a given situation. It has to be *constructed.*

The previous discussion provides an answer to what we may call the Pasinetti problem (Pasinetti 1994). Pasinetti contends that an improved theory depends on abstracting from institutional diversity what he calls the 'natural economic system'. Our argument would support the idea of complexity as a foundation for theories addressing institutional diversity. It illustrates the difficulty of basing a theory on complex subject matter through the direct use of substantive categories which bypass an initial procedural phase, as Pasinetti actually seems to do.

Finally, this chapter complements what we wrote in our introduction to *The Political Economy of Diversity* (Delorme 1994) and provides a background for that work. We mentioned historical time, process, change, individual-institutional interaction, radical uncertainty, procedural rationality and methodological pluralism as common basic features of evolutionary perspectives. The common foundation of all these features is that of complexity and anchored pluralism. This may clarify why diversity exists at two levels, substantive and procedural. In complexity, the procedural level receives priority. Theorizing is acceptable if it is appropriate to anchored complexity. This is the reason why diversity envisaged in *The Political Economy of Diversity* is mainly procedural and not limited to studying the consequences of substantive diversity on evolution. We have attempted here to show how 'open ended' and 'complex' do not mean that everything goes. Formal modelling and equilibrium thinking, among others, are acceptable provided that they work. The same goes for non-formal and non-equilibrium discourse. Anchored complexity seems to provide a means of disciplined scientific practice in economics.

REFERENCES

Ashby, W.R. (1956) *An Introduction to Cybernetics*. London: Chapman and Hall.

Atlan, H. (1979) *Entre le cristal et la fumée. Essai sur l'organisation du vivant*. Paris: Seuil.

Bachelard, G. (1934) *Le nouvel esprit scientifique*, Paris: Presses Universitaires de France.

Bateson G. (1972) *Steps to an Ecology of Mind*. New York: Chandler.

Boland, L.A. (1988) *Stylized Facts*. The New Palgrave. Aldershot: Edward Elgar.

Caldwell, B.J. (1991) 'Clarifying Popper'. *Journal of Economic Literature*: 1–33 (March).

Carabelli, A.M. (1988) *On Keynes's Method*. London: Macmillan.

Delorme, R. (1984) 'A New View on the Economic Theory of the State. A Case Study of France'. *Journal of Economic Issues*: 715–44 (September). Repr. in M.R. Tool and W.J. Samuels (eds) (1988) *State, Society and Corporate Power*. New Brunswick: Transaction Publishers.

Delorme R. (1992) 'Economic Intervention in the History of the French and other European States: A Comparative Study' in A.A. Zini Jr (ed.) *The Market and the State in Economic Development in the 1990s*. Amsterdam, North-Holland, Contributions to Economic Analysis, pp. 23–50.

Delorme R. (1994) 'Economic Diversity as Cement and as a Challenge to Evolutionary Perspectives' in R. Delorme and K. Dopfer (eds) *The Political Economy of Diversity. Evolutionary Perspectives on Economic Order and Disorder*. Aldershot: Edward Elgar.

Delorme R. (1995) 'An Alternative Theoretical Framework for State-Economy Interactions in Transforming Economies'. *Emergo. Journal of Transforming Economies and Societies*: 5–24 (Autumn).

Delorme R. (1997) *From First Order to Second Order Complexity in Economic Theorizing*. Paris: CEPREMAP.

Delorme, R. and André, C. (1983) *L'état et l'économie*. Paris: Seuil.

Dewey, J. (1993) *Logique. La théorie de l'enquête* (French translation of Logic: The Theory of Enquiry 1938). Paris: PUF.

Dupuy, J.P. (1988) *Ordres et désordres. Enquête sur un nouveau paradigme*. Paris: Seuil.

Elster, J. (1989) *Solomonic Judgements*. Cambridge and Paris: The Cambridge University Press and Editions de la Maison des Sciences de l'Homme.

Granger, G.G. (1990) *Epistémologie*. Paris: Encyclopaedia Universalis.

Hayek, F.A. (1967) *Studies in Philosophy, Politics and Economics*. Chicago: The University of Chicago Press.

Heyting, A. (1980) *Intuitionism: An Introduction*. Amsterdam: North-Holland.

Kaldor, N. (1963) 'Capital Accumulation and Economic Growth' in F.A. Lutz and D.G. Hague (eds) *The Theory of Capital*. London: Macmillan.

Keynes, J.M. (1921) *A Treatise on Probability*. Collected Writings Vol. 8. D. Moggridge (ed.) (1973). London: Macmillan.

Klir, G.J. (1985) 'The Many Faces of Complexity' in UNU. (1985) *The Science and Praxis of Complexity*. Tokyo: The United Nations University, pp. 81–98.

Lawson, T. (1989) 'Abstraction, Tendencies and Stylized Facts: A Realist Approach to Economic Analysis'. *Cambridge Journal of Economics* 13: 59–78.

Le Moigne, J.L. (1990a) 'Epistémologies constructivistes et sciences de l'organis-

ation' in A.C. Martinet (ed.) *Epistémologie des sciences de gestion*. Paris: Economica, pp. 81–140.
Le Moigne, J.L. (1990b) *La modélisation des systèmes complexes*. Paris: Dunod.
Le Moigne, J.L. (1991) 'Sur les fondements épistémologiques de la science de la cognition: contribution de la systémique aux constructivismes' in E. Andreewsky (ed.) *Systémique et Cognition*. Dunod: Paris, pp. 11–49.
Le Moigne, J.L. (1994) *La Théorie du système général. Théorie de la modélisation*. Paris: PUF.
Morin, E. (1985) 'On the Definition of Complexity' in UNU (1985) *The Science and Praxis of Complexity*. Tokyo: The United Nations University, pp. 62–8.
Morin, E. (1992) 'From the Concept of System to the Paradigm of Complexity'. *Journal of Social and Evolutionary Systems* 15 (4): 371–85.
Morris, C. (1971) *Writings on the General Theory of Signs*. The Hague: Mouton.
Pasinetti, L. (1994) 'Economic Theory and Institutions' in R. Delorme and K. Dopfer (eds) *The Political Economy of Diversity. Evolutionary Perspectives on Economic Order and Disorder*. Aldershot: Edward Elgar.
Pask, G. (1990) 'Different Kinds of Cybernetics'. *Communication and Cognition* 23 (2, 3): 125–40.
Peirce, C.S. (1984) *Textes anticartésiens*, Paris: Aubier Montaigne.
Piaget, J. (ed.) (1968) *Logique et connaissance scientifique*. Encyclopédie de la Pléiade. Paris: Gallimard.
Popper, K. (1984) *L'univers irrésolu. Plaidoyer pour l'indéterminisme*. Paris: Hermann.
Samuels, W. (1990) 'The Self-Referentiability of Thorstein Veblen's Theory of the Preconceptions of Economic Science' *Journal of Economic Issues* 3: 695–718 (September).
Segal, L. (1990) *Le rêve de la réalité*. Paris: Seuil. French edition of *The Dream of Reality*. New York: W.W. Norton & Co., 1986.
Shannon, C.E. and Weaver, W. (1949) *The Mathematical Theory of Communication*. Urbana: The University of Illinois Press.
Simon, H.A. (1976) 'From Substantive to Procedural Rationality' in S. Latsis (ed.) *Method and Appraisal in Economics*. Cambridge: Cambridge University Press, pp. 129–48.
Simon, H.A. (1988) *Satisficing*. J. Eatwell, M. Milgate and P. Newman (eds) The New Palgrave. A Dictionary of Economics, London: Macmillan.
Simon, H.A. (1991) *Sciences des systèmes. Sciences de l'artificiel*. Paris: Dunod.
Simon, H.A. (1991) *Models of my Life*: Basic Books.
Taub, A.H. (ed.) (1961) *John von Neumann: Collected Works*. Vol. 5. Oxford: Pergamon Press.
UNU (1985) *The Science and Praxis of Complexity*. Tokyo: The United Nations University.
Veblen, T. (1919) *The Place of Science in Modern Civilization and Other Essays*, New York: Huebsch.
Von Bertalanffy L. (1973) *Théorie générale des systèmes*. Paris: Dunod.
Von Foerster, H. (1988) 'La construction d'une réalité' in P. Watzlawick (ed.) (1988) *L'invention de la réalité. Contributions au constructivisme*. Paris: Seuil, pp. 45–69.
Von Foerster, H. (1992) 'Ethics and Second Order Cybernetics'. *Cybernetics and Human Knowing* 1 (1): 9–19.
Von Glasersfeld, E. (1988) 'Introduction à un constructivisme radical' in P.

Watzlawick (ed.) (1988) *L'invention de la réalité. Contributions au constructivisme.* Paris: Seuil, pp. 19–43.

Von Neumann, J. (1961) *John von Neumann Collected Works Vol V*, A.H. Taub (ed.) Oxford: Pergamon Press.

Watzlawick, P. (ed.) (1988) *L'Invention de la réalité. Contributions au constructivisme.* Paris: Seuil. French edition of *Die Erfundene Wirklichkeit Wie wissen wir, was wir zu wissen glauben? Beiträge zum Konstruktivismus.* München: R. Piper Co. Verlag, 1981.

Weaver, W. (1948) 'Science and Complexity'. *American Scientist* 36: 536–44.

3. Cognitive networks and self-organization in a complex socio-economic environment

Magali Orillard[1]

The purpose of this chapter is to show how alliance networks can be created and used for strategic aims through their capacity to determine the self-organization of groups and unions. To adopt a general viewpoint, we suppose that the various agents involved in this 'game' are part of a multidimensional world where priority can be given to sociological, economic and ecological variables. First, we shall determine the conditions in which a coding and supercoding mechanism is required in order to take into account the necessarily widely divergent motivations of agents. This can be done if we refer to a complex world where the actors, forms of coordination and representations are of different types (Boltanski and Thévenot 1991, Orillard 1990). Second, we shall study the emergence and strategic management of networks (particularly cognitive networks) connected with the notions of code, supercode, shared or distributed intelligence and self-organizing connexity, so as to finally attempt an analysis of the cognitive processes to which learning mechanisms belong. We justify this approach through the analysis of dynamic transformations of socio-economic systems.

1. AN ATTEMPTED DEFINITION OF A 'SOCIAL GAME' IN A COMPLEX WORLD

1.1. Basic Concepts

We assume that agents belong to a complex world. This means that in particular such an environment must be multidimensional and must

[1] The author thanks the members of GRASCE (Groupe de Recherche sur l'Adaptation, la Systémique et la Complexité Economique – Université d'Aix-Marseille III France) for comments and technical assistance.

involve motivations of various types – economic, sociological, ecological, psychological, and so on (Le Moigne and Orillard 1994). It seems reasonable therefore to consider that different sentiments, motivations and intuitions must be translated according to different codes (defined as a system for the manipulation of symbols) in order to define sets of goals that are by nature intelligible, from the viewpoint of all agents using the same code. This should allow us to describe the different types of cognitive processes and to design socio-economic decision-making mechanisms. If the sets of goals are intelligible, we shall argue that they can be compared and even classified according to different pre-order relations.

By assumption, an agent can make use of one or more codes ${}^{v}C$, ${}^{v'}C$, in order to translate his/her motivations into a set of goals ${}^{v}O$, ${}^{v'}O$, . . ., by using coding mechanisms either in parallel or in series, according to Figure 3.1.

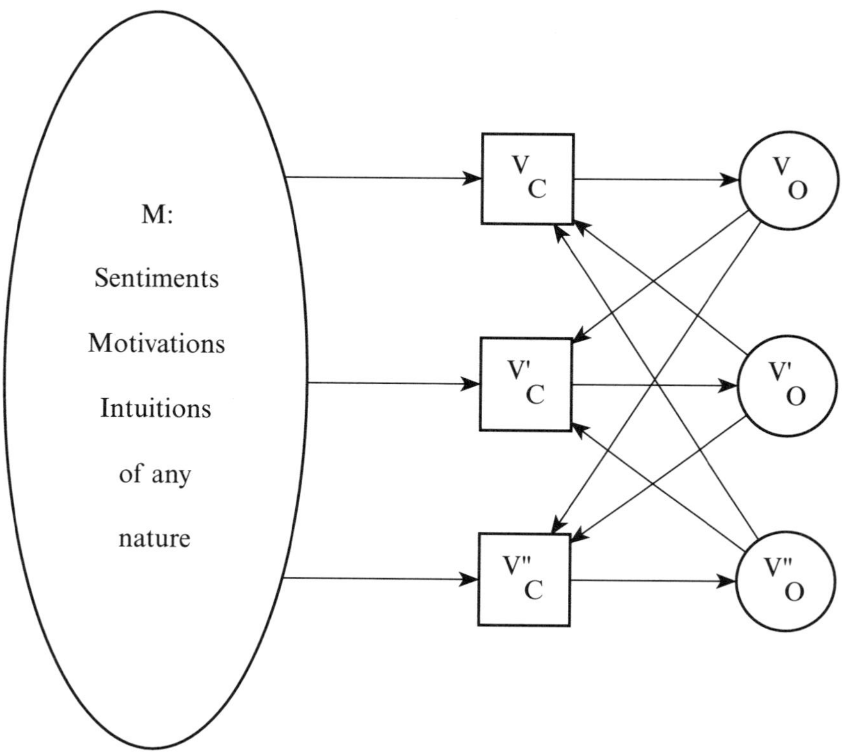

Figure 3.1. Processes to translate motivations, . . .

We shall assume that:

$$^{v}C\ (M) \subseteq {}^{v}O$$
$$^{v'}C \circ {}^{v}C\ (M) \subseteq {}^{v'}O$$
$$^{v'}\ C\ (M) \subseteq {}^{v'}O$$

The explanation is that an identical motivation can be associated with different operational goals inside different sets ^{v}O, $^{v'}O$, . . .

Sets of goals created in this way are defined in a sufficiently broad manner so that any actor using a code can build a pre-order relation on the basis of any set M.

Here we now introduce the supercoding mechanisms. We do this by referring to the manipulation of the codes themselves or to code-to-code reading from which we can obtain, for example:

$$^{v'}C \circ {}^{v}C \circ {}^{v''}C\ (M) \neq {}^{v'}C \circ {}^{v''}C\ (M)$$

Hence an identical motivation can also be translated in several ways within the same set $^{v'}O$, for example.

This is dependent on the connectivity of operators in relation to the self-organizing connexity of actors, in so far as the potential use of one or more codes in different orders allows the actors great flexibility in expressing their motivations and sentiments and thereby in generating and building alliance networks. The only necessary condition for comparing the representations of these motivations is that they must be expressed in the same space – which is the case in the examples below:

$$^{v'}C \circ {}^{v''}C \circ {}^{v}C\ (M) \text{ and } {}^{v'}C \circ {}^{v''}C\ (M)$$

We have thus far presumed that the various actors initially base their actions on motivations evaluated in widely different ways. It is also possible, however, to apply this type of procedure in the same way, for example, to developing projects (P, P′, . . .) in a specific environment involving several socio-economic variables or to building multilateral negotiations, like those described in the final section. In fact, the main objective is to define a space or set of spaces where the different representations – which are for the time being individualized – can be developed and compared, through the cognitive processes of design. The agents can then build binary relations (called first order alliance relations) between each other according to the goals that they wish to defend, and they can join certain groups and unions according to the selected goals, the self-organizing informational structure of the game and the possible aversions. At this point the agents will begin to cooperate on a temporary basis and thus wish to satisfy their primitive motivations. It should be noted that the theory of group emergence to which we refer (Orillard 1990) is not a product of strict methodological individualism (particularly because certain choices can be made selectively or even strategically according to the potentially realizable unions), nor of holism in the sociological sense (since the various agents have individual preferences that they try to satisfy through the alliances they seek to build). Thus, it is more appropriate to refer the concept of 'connectionism' or, even more so, to 'interactionism' (Le Moigne 1990), since the architecture of the relations that are the basis for the construction and identification of groups is determined by the self-organizing interactions between actors.

Therefore, from here on, it seems that we must make the distinction between, on the one hand, a recoding process (where a code is simply used and then another code is used in parallel or in series) and, on the other, the supercoding procedures that are based on the manipulation of codes for either of one of the following two purposes:

- to find a common reference space in order to make discussion possible between two or more agents; or
- to put forward a compromise solution that is intelligible to all participants and that satisfies most of them (in which case, we refer to second order alliance relations).

In relation, for example, to the rules and criteria adopted regarding the choice of projects, this solution can be represented as shown in Figure 3.2. This is a generalization of the first figure (the starting-point is not only the different types of motivations but also the different types of goals, or an initial project P).

All of these objects may be translated and represented through coding and supercoding processes involved in designing other goals or projects.

1.2. Agent Behaviour and Rationality

In a complex world, the actions of agents and the strategies that they develop can have varying degrees of complexity. Here we differentiate between three types of actor and try to demonstrate the criteria of rationality upon which they are generally based. Before doing so, we may begin by referring to the concepts of 'reactive agents' and 'cognitive agents' introduced in certain works on artificial intelligence (Ferber 1994) and also dealt with in sociology. As we shall see, these concepts

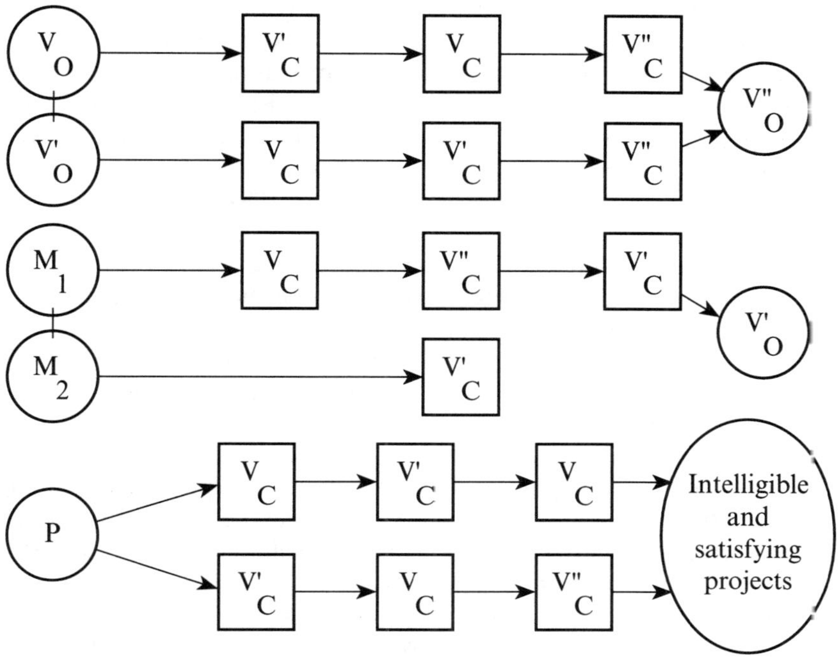

Figure 3.2. Socio-economic decision-making mechanisms

are quite closely related to the questions that we are attempting to resolve in this chapter, and therefore they can be adapted to socio-economic research. We shall try to expand on these concepts and thereby define the concept of 'creative agent'.

Ferber (1994) makes the following assertions concerning 'reactive agents':

- they do not have any explicit representation of either their environment or other agents;
- they do not have any memory of their history;
- they operate according to simple reflex behaviour;
- they communicate with each other in a non-intentional way.

In accordance with decision theory, cognitive science and the works of H. Simon, we can talk about actors of substantive rationality (Simon 1982). For such actors it is often a matter of finding the best solution for a given environment and a goal chosen at the outset. Naturally, the models that involve this type of 'reactive agent' are quite poor; but, often easy to implement in theory, such agents react mechanically and they can accomplish a certain number of tasks in so far as they are sufficiently explicit and do not make use of external elements or new ideas. Here we may refer to routine mechanisms which would take an explicit form and an effective place in the socio-economic activity managing-processes.

The behaviour of 'cognitive agents' (Ferber 1994) is determined by:

- intentional communication procedures;
- representations that agents have of other actors and their areas of competence;
- cooperation through the coordination of actions;
- conflict management based on propositions, evaluations and counter-propositions.

Thus we see the developing outline of the basic principles corresponding to procedural rationality (Simon 1982) in which perceptions of motivations are taken into account, a search for solutions can be heuristic, and the building of possible compromises is attempted.

These ideas are closely related to our approach, since we refer to the intentions of agents, cooperative processes and conflict resolution. However, we can go further and generalize, particularly by introducing the concept of 'creative agents' whose behaviour is determined by a complex rationality principle. This is because the search for compromises may involve supercoding procedures but without making use of the great potential of this type of mechanism. Compromise solutions can be achieved as the result of heuristic searches for possible solutions. The interaction between codes, however, does not seem to play the same essential role, as in design processes; neither does the search for a common frame of reference that makes the actions and projects intelligible for a group of actors. This is where the concept of 'creative agent' arises, particularly if we refer to a supercoder agent, that is, an agent that is able to perform the following functions:

- transform the problem;
- switch from one frame of reference to another;
- guide reflection according to different codes;
- 'invent' new starting-points;
- strategically modify the representations of agents;
- create alliances that can lead to the construction of alternative projects and groups;
- promote the self-organization of multidimensional networks.

For this to be the case, it must be possible to envisage the existence of the following:

- different types of actors (agents, groups, meta-groups, etc.) that have a certain degree of autonomy in the game;
- different types of representations: individual as well as collective;
- different types of coordination (Boltanski and Thévenot 1991) resulting from the self-management of relationships which, in certain situations, induce the actors to cooperate in a specific way;
- different procedures corresponding to the construction of rules of a multidimensional social game;
- different types of strategic behaviour (involving representations, the possibility of introducing biases at informational and relational levels, the possibility of taking any agent aversions into account and making/breaking alliances).

In this context, therefore, we shall refer to complex rationality. Among the points that we consider essential for any perceivable socio-economic analyses, we attribute a special role to the different types of actors that interact in the following manner:

- agents look for allies to defend common goals;
- these agents thereby form groups that have their own independent existence and in which, as a consequence, the actors lose part of their autonomy as the group develops a system of representation with the purpose of participating in the game according to rules formulated inside the group;
- in relation to potential projects, the groups thus formed can connect, coordinate and cooperate in different ways. Furthermore, on the basis of the self-organization of cognitive networks such as those envisaged below, they can use supercoding procedures to generate, for example, new projects and, in other situations (e.g. conflicts), formulate the rules of the game at a meta-level.

2. COGNITIVE NETWORKS AND LEARNING PROCESSES

2.1. An Attempted Definition of Cognitive Networks

We consider that a cognitive network:

- is a multidimensional criss-cross network closely related to the notion of embeddedness (Granovetter 1985);
- is a network whose arcs do not necessarily correspond to concrete flows, but which may correspond to non-material objects such as information, trust and reputation;
- is a network where the nodes are agents that can use a variety of codes in the sense defined above (which is in keeping with the criss-cross character referred to);
- is capable of organizing itself according to different codes in an evolutionary context;
- can be used to adapt to modifications in the relevant environment;
- can be activated when conflicts occur, to generate new solutions not necessarily in an algorithmic, heuristic form, or more spontaneously using the potential activities of supercoding processes;
- can be implemented by agents for specific ends (e.g. by introducing biases).

These last two aspects justify the strategic character of the potential management of these networks. As we have already said, the nodes of these networks may be regarded as equivalent to different agents. Thus the groups correspond to a set of nodes, and their existence depends on a certain number of conditions. According to the problem to be modelled and resolved, these conditions concern the various arcs that connect and structure these sets of agents from a relational, spatial or socio-economic point of view within the same code.

For meta-groups, the above definition must be broadened to include sets of groups or subgroups using different codes, and we must consider the arcs as representing reflections of supercoding procedures that have either already been successful or may be successful.

It is thus easy to imagine the existence of groups within different populations, each using the same code. This results in a strata structure, while, in the case of meta-groups, the structure will be multidimensional, with intra-stratum and inter-strata relations playing a considerable role, as shown in Figure 3.3.

Certain nodes of these multidimensional networks play a special role

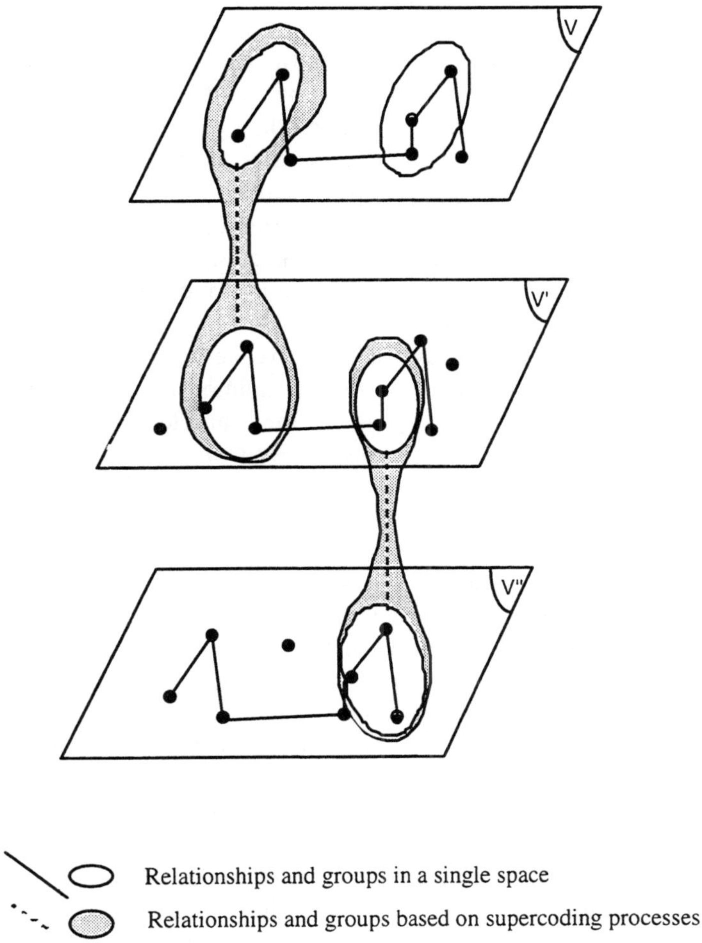

Figure 3.3. Cognitive network

in the game. For example, if we suppose that, in concrete terms, there is an actor (agent, institution or organization) that can act as a supercoder in the self-organizing process, then this actor will represent an attracting node in the cognitive network.

We must now establish the connection between the concepts of 'reactive agent', 'cognitive agent' and 'creative agent', and the formation of groups, meta-groups, and so on, by using the 'rationality argument':

- as regards the formation of groups themselves, we can readily

make use of the reactive character of agents and therefore base our position on the substantive rationality argument;
- as regards the role played by groups in the game (with the agents having lost some of their autonomy by identifying themselves with the groups), particularly if supercoding processes are used, we must assume that we are dealing with cognitive actors whose behaviour is based on procedural rationality;
- in this situation, the interaction between the different groups and the formation of meta-groups are in keeping with the above characteristics (regarding groups and meta-groups, we may refer to 'pseudo collective rationality');
- nevertheless, the strategic use of cognitive networks, the generation of the rules of the game in the multidimensional sense and the emergence of alternative projects, for example, make use of creative actors. Hence, in an evolutionary context, we can confront the cognitive processes of design with the notion of time and rationality.

From a representational viewpoint, it seems useful to refer to the concept of 'mesh', which is traditional in the study of networks, but here perhaps redefined as 'artificial mesh' in a multidimensional socio-economic world. In the model envisaged here, there appear at first sight to be several possible types of meshes, depending on whether we want to represent informational relationships or the existence of common objectives for different agents or the construction of alternative projects (for a formal and mathematical discussion of these elements, see Orillard (1990), based on a pre-topological analysis of the various relations). Another element must be added: regarding the interactive use of different codes and supercoding, it should finally be accepted that in cognitive networks there must usually exist different types of mesh in each plane as well as in each stratum in each dimension. There should also exist multidimensional meshes when we refer to various codes and to supercoding mechanisms, as can be seen in Figure 3.3.

It would then be appropriate to establish the connection between self-organization processes and concepts of shared and distributed intelligence as developed in the field of artificial intelligence, which we can envisage here through the concept of code:

- we can assert that agents using the same code to communicate their motivations, to translate their goals and to describe their

projects, possess a shared intelligence of the game in which they are taking part when we place ourselves at stratum level;
- on the other hand, in groups emerging in different strata, we must refer to the concept of distributed intelligence;
- but the point of this analogy must also reside in the description of the supercoding process. If, at the outset, we consider that we are dealing with agents using different codes but that it is possible to find a common frame of reference so that the goals and projects are intelligible to all, then, on another level, we concur with the characteristics of shared intelligence;
- similarly, if there are different meta-groups (by definition, using different codes) that can generate different types of game rules for building various alternative projects, we may again refer to the concept of distributed intelligence.

The problem of evaluating all the various potential projects in the game – the problem of searching for compromise solutions and the final selection of one of those solutions – then generally requires the involvement of creative actors. This brings us back to the second point discussed above which must be generalized: the role of supercoding actors in the evaluation of the possible results of the various projects is here essential.

Finally, it should be noted that in principle no solution of the multidimensional game can be envisaged or selected by referring only to distributed intelligence, since the actors work in parallel without any mechanism (such as a supercoding procedure) that can effectively connect them together.

2.2. Networks and Learning

At first sight, the concept of learning can be understood in an individual and/or collective sense. As far as we are concerned, we use the existence of groups and meta-groups to analyse these mechanisms on the basis of the idea that the existence of a group arises from the emergence of goals common to its members and that these goals can be formulated within the same reference frame. The existence of meta-groups depends on the possibility of implementing supercoding mechanisms that can generate (through cognitive processes) projects common to the different actors, taking into account the codes used. This is another form of cooperation which is not based on defending a common goal but on designing potential projects.

Thus we can envisage the position of an agent who is a member of at least one group. His/her learning can be informational or relational (in relation to the game's environment and in relation to the members of the groups to which he/she belongs); it can be more generally cognitive in that this individual, in this context, can learn to use his/her information strategically, for example, when selecting first order alliances. At the meta-game level (with the emergence and management of meta-groups) the individuals represented or taking part in this game can learn to use other codes. In both cases, the agent's learning capacity is determined by his/her membership of at least one group. The most interesting point, however, is to discover the extent to which the group itself can learn in its own right. This may be seen in two ways:

- in the common goals that have emerged that determine the group's existence and that can vary when the members change;
- in the meta-game, through the supercoding procedures regarding the potential projects or objectives of other groups. These concern the construction of the rules of the social game involved in the evaluation of projects and in the selection stage.

Naturally, the remarks made here can be generalized as regards meta-groups, through a more general structure.

The strategic nature of cognitive network management can thus be clearly demonstrated since the existence of groups and meta-groups is based on the 'self-organizing connectivity' of these networks. The behaviour of agents as regards communication and selection of alliances is essential in this respect. This enables us to continue our analysis of learning mechanisms by applying the theory of network-meshing on the basis of the concepts of alliances, supercoding processes and so on. It is clear that the multidimensional social game is a criss-cross network in which we can accept that the nodes correspond to the agents. It is also clear that we can differentiate between these individuals and represent the architecture of the groups and meta-groups according to the arcs that form the network's mesh. Therefore, the self-organization and the strategic use of networks that must reflect the behaviour of actors lead to certain modifications of the mesh. For example, we may assert that reactive behaviour reinforces the mesh network in one or more strata and allows for the creation or extension of groups or meta-groups and the number of potential projects. Similarly, we may argue that the characteristic adaptation processes of cognitive networks cause modifications of the mesh on the multidimensional level. Here we come back to the level which concerns evolutionary group choice mechanisms.

2.3. Dynamic Transformations of Socio-economic Systems

We assume that, in order to understand and manage transformations of socio-economic systems in a complex and multidimensional world, we have to take into account these changes in a general way with regard to all their components. We agree with Granovetter's idea (1985) of describing institutions as social constructions. Consequently, we can develop a global analysis of such complex situations.

Cases susceptible to modelling according to the preceding developments – alliance mechanism between consumers, firms, and so on – seem to be particularly interesting. Here, we may refer to Yoshino and Srinivasa Rangan's ideas (1995) on 'globalization and competition' through alliances. For a global analysis of alliance formation, we need to consider first the types of actor motivations: economic motivations, social motivations, cultural motivations, ethical motivations and so on.

Thus, we agree with Orléan (1994) about the incompleteness of pure trading logic in activity analysis.

Concerning the specific modelling process, we refer to the ideas of 'multidimensional network' and 'criss-cross network' (we have seen how these notions may be understood as specific illustrations of what Granovetter (1985) describes through the notion of 'embeddedness'). Our study enables us to connect this modelling process with the management of such non-material goods and actor characteristics as the information, knowledge, experience, trust, dislike, wariness and reputation on which the emergence and dynamics of alliances are based. Similarly, Williamson (1993) speaks of trust – institutional trust – which 'refers to the social and organizational context within which contracts are embedded'. The agents involved in these alliances face uncertainty and strategic risk when selecting projects or making decisions. It is generally assumed that in such a context, they exhibit strategic behaviour and not only routine mechanisms. Therefore, the notions of autonomy, opportunity, reciprocity and manipulation have to be developed through cognitive processes (using coding and supercoding mechanisms), if one wants to explain individual and collective learning processes in an 'economy of the immaterial'.

In this way, we can attempt to model concrete 'search for allies' procedures both between and within various types of populations (firms, consumers, etc.) designed to establish groups and meta-groups in the form of public collectivities, ethnic groups, cultural associations and so on. Thus, it may be possible to analyse real situations, such as goal-building processes, the design of projects, multi-businesses, multilateral negotiations, technological alliances, and research and development procedures used to stabilize socio-economic systems, manage socio-economic development, and resolve conflicts and crises, through agreements, commitments and compromises which are often incomplete and ephemeral. Here we come back to an important question: what are the differences between coordination and cooperation with regard to cognitive processes?

Because of this incompleteness, 'creative actors' can opportunely transform the problem. Such actors aim at linking together certain cooperative agreements in order to coordinate economic activities. Eymard-Duvernay (1989), for example, has studied certain cooperative agreements – agreements of quality (*conventions de qualité*) – in complex industrial systems. Here we have to confront various ways of getting opponents to respect an agreement; coordinating devices being based on personal relations of proximity and temporal faithfulness. We thus find ourselves once more dealing with the notions of immateriality and complexity within project and activity evaluation processes. This is related to what Eymard-Duvernay says about the stress between different principles of coordination (which are simultaneously involved and can threaten the harmonious development of socio-economic activities, inducing crises and conflicts). These crises and conflicts may be resolved through the design and implementation of concertation and deliberation mechanisms – that is to say supercoding processes – in order to set up new projects on an evolutionary basis. Here again, we find the duality existing between self-organizing connexity and alliance dynamic processes.

If we operate the model, we can articulate the evolution of the actors' behaviour and learning processes, and confirm that 'a coordinating process is always going on, brought about in a self-organizing way by individual efforts to find better arrangements' (Witt 1985). Here the central notion is that of self-organizing alliance network. The operational processes used (coding, supercoding processes, goal-building process, partnership elaboration process, etc.) have to translate the flexibility, distortion and rigidity of socio-economic systems, described as 'criss-cross networks' representing family, social, cultural and other relations, and social constructions.

Defining 'social oligopoly' (Lesourne 1981) – here, taken as groups, meta-groups, and so on, – and describing its evolution through the dynamics of the goals and projects which characterize the actors (and the criss-cross networks which determine them), we can explain:

- the impoverishing process or enriching process of alliance networks;

- the stability mechanism or the rupture and dismembering mechanisms which exist among the population.

Finally, we may argue that the modelling tools described here (e.g. coding and supercoding processes, self-organizing connexity), make it possible:

- to model;
- to analyse the evolution of socio-economic phenomena such as loneliness, unemployment, and the internationalization of activities; and
- to develop simultaneous decision-making processes to manage socio-economic changes in complex situations which could be used, for example, in economic policy.

REFERENCES

Binmore, K. (1990) *Essays on the Foundations of Game Theory.* Cambridge, MA: Blackwell.

Boltanski, L. and Thévenot, L. (1991) *De la Justification, les Economies de la Grandeur.* Paris: Gallimard.

Eymard-Duvernay, F. (1989) 'Conventions de Qualité et Formes de Coordination'. *Revue Economique* 40 (2): 329–59.

Ferber, J. (1994) 'La Kénétique: des Systèmes Multi-Agents à une Science de L'Interaction'. *Revue Internationale de Systémique* 8 (1): 13–27.

Frydman, R. (1992) 'Le Territoire de l'Economiste, Marché et Société Marchande'. *Revue Economique* 43 (1): 5–30.

Granovetter, M. (1985) 'Economic Action and Social Structure: The Problem of Embeddedness'. *American Journal of Sociology* 91 (3): 481–510.

Hatchuel, A. (1994) 'Apprentissages Collectifs et Activités de Conception'. *Revue Française de Gestion* 99: 109–20.

Kervern, G.Y. and Rubise, P. (1991) 'L'Archipel du Danger: Introduction aux Cyndyniques'. *Economica.* Paris.

Le Moigne, J.L. (1990) *La Modélisation des Systèmes Complexes.* Paris: Dunod.

Le Moigne, J.L. and Orillard, M. (1994) 'Nearly Uncontrollable Pollution of an Agrarian System: A Socio-economic Case Study' in B. Bürgenmeier (ed.) *Economy, Environment and Technology.* New York: Sharpe Inc., Armonk, pp. 165–74.

Lesourne, J. (1981) *Les Mille Sentiers de l'Avenir.* Paris: Seghers.

Orillard, M. (1990) 'Representation of Decision Making Processes in a Complex Environment'. *Analyse de Systèmes* 16 (4): 5–11.

Orléan, A. (1994) 'Sur le Rôle Respectif de la Confiance et de l'Intérêt dans la Constitution de l'Ordre Marchand'. *Revue du MAUSS* 4: 17–36.

Simon, H. (1982) *Models of Bounded Rationality.* Cambridge, MA: MIT Press.

Williamson, O. (1993) 'Calculativeness, Trust, and Economic Organization'. *Journal of Law and Economics* 36: 453–86 (April).

Witt, U. (1985) 'Coordination of Individual Economic Activities as an Evolving Process of Self-Organization'. *Economie Appliquée* 38 (3–4): 569–95.

Yoshino, M. and Srinivasa Rangan, U. (1995) *Strategic Alliances: An Entrepreneurial Approach to Globalization*. Boston, MA: Harvard Business School Press.

4. Collectivist versus individualist perspectives on the institutional transition process – some methodological remarks[1]

Jürgen Lange-von Kulessa

1. INTRODUCTION

It is now widely accepted that research in the field of economic change, and especially in the transition of economic systems, has to recognize the important role played by institutions. Empirical evidence showing the strong impact institutions have on the welfare of states has created increasing interest in institutional approaches to economics. On the one hand, there are the New Institutional Economics (NIE), which are regarded as a significant addition to neoclassical theories (Eggertsson 1990, Furubotn and Richter 1991, North 1981, 1990). On the other, there are the early contributions of Old Institutionalism, which now serve as the reference point for the revival of the research tradition (Veblen 1899, Mitchell 1936, Commons 1934, Douglas 1987, Hodgson 1993a, 1993b, Mayhew 1987, 1989). In addition, there is now emerging an evolutionary approach to institutional change which draws heavily on Friedrich August von Hayek and his social philosophy of cultural evolution (Hayek 1967, 1973, 1988, Witt 1989, 1991).

Unlike orthodox neoclassical theory, all the above-mentioned approaches share in common the view that rules of behaviour, traditions, and other non-formal and formal institutions are considered important determinants of human action. Institutions are regarded not as neutral but as relevant variables which inevitably have to be included in any economic analysis. There is, however, little agreement as to how to analyse and explain economic change. Rather, a deep-running conflict can be observed in the different philosophical foundations of these

[1] An earlier version of this paper was presented at the research seminar of the Institute for Study of Economic Evolution, University of Freiburg. I wish to thank all participants, in particular Viktor Vanberg and Ulrich Witt for their helpful comments.

approaches and the resulting methodological procedures. On one side of this conflict, individual behaviour is taken as the starting-point for explaining social phenomena – the position of methodological individualism. On the other side, a more collectivist perspective, which focuses on the behaviour of super-individual units as the most significant elements, is chosen as the approach to questions of economic and social change. These methodological positions, already heavily discussed during the 1960s and 1970s (O'Neill 1973, Vanberg 1975), are usually portrayed as mutually exclusive from each other (Boland 1982, 1992, Heijdra et al. 1988, Dorman 1991, Hodgson 1986, 1993a).

In this chapter it will be argued, by contrast, that certain elements of the individualistic and the holistic approaches are compatible. An integration of these elements can be achieved first by acknowledging the legitimate criticism raised against reductionist individualism in theories of rational-actor models (Hodgson 1986, 1993a, 1993b), and second by accounting for this criticism appropriately in an institutional theory founded on individuals. To explain this proposition the ideas of two important advocates of each methodological approach, von Hayek (1948, 1952b, 1988) and Geoff Hodgson (1993a), will be compared. As will be shown, Hayek's work contains an evolutionary theory of institutional change that avoids the reductionism of orthodox individualistic economic theory as criticized in the work of Hodgson. Accordingly, Hayek's position, which in his principle of group selection builds on super-individual selection criteria, should be much more acceptable to scholars favouring a collectivist approach than might appear from Hodgson's writings. The chapter unfolds as follows. Section 2 discusses methodological holism and its criticism of individualistic approaches as reductionist concepts. It will be argued that the criticism is justified in certain areas which have also been attacked by some individualistically oriented scientists. The fact that methodological individualism is by no means a monolithic position is demonstrated in Section 3 where the different characteristics of reductionist individualism, on the one hand, and evolutionary individualism, on the other, will be illustrated. Section 4 briefly looks at Hayek's cognitive theory which serves as the epistemological foundation of his entire social philosophy, including his theory of cultural evolution. It will be argued that without considering his cognitive theory a complete understanding of Hayek's individualism is not possible.

Hayek's theory of cultural evolution is analysed in detail in Section 5. Hayek assigns a decisive role to rules of behaviour and other social institutions in explaining the emergence and evolution of societies. According to him, social scientists can gain insights into collective phenomena by analysing when, how and to what extent such rules are adopted by certain individuals, larger groups or by the population as a whole. Thus, Hayek offers a theory of institutional change based on two different, but interdependent levels of explanation. In order to show how this approach helps to understand the phenomena of institutional transition, Section 6 discusses the theoretical and political relevance of Hayek's duality hypothesis.

In the concluding section it is argued that Hayek's social philosophy offers a methodological approach based on population thinking which in turn thus leads to a theory of institutional evolution. This should complement the more collective-based theoretical framework of Hodgson and his followers. Both lines of thought emphasize the importance of institutions and super-individual processes for changing societies. But Hayek's individually founded population perspective broadens the possibilities for analysing social phenomena. His theory of cultural evolution presents empirically significant hypotheses which are not simply and exclusively focused on the individual, but instead offer an analysis of collective phenomena without excluding *per se* the possibility of tracing them back to behaviourial regularities on the level of the individual.

2. METHODOLOGICAL HOLISM – A SUPER-INDIVIDUAL EXPLANATION OF INSTITUTIONAL CHANGE

Though there is no uniform definition of methodological holism or collectivism, the primacy of the group as the unit of analysis can be seen as a leading idea behind this concept. 'The individual has no importance qua individual, but only inasmuch as he is a member of a particular class' (Heijdra et al. 1988, p. 308). The analysis of social phenomena does not necessarily have to go back to the individual level because super-individual entities have a meaning of their own. The existence of certain institutions and rules of behaviour can be explained by their functions. 'Social wholes are postulated to have purposes or functions that cannot be reduced to the beliefs, attitudes and actions of the individuals that make them up (Blaug 1992, p. 44). As a consequence, the development of social aggregates should be formulated in terms of governing laws – laws which explain how a social entity as a whole has emerged and which allow for predictions of future performance. A theoretical reconstruction of any specific situation can only be provided by a system of socio-cultural laws (Goldstein 1973, p. 274).

From this extreme position, which can be traced back to such collectivist thinkers of the nineteenth century as Comte, Durkheim, and Marx, new holistic concepts have to be distinguished. These new concepts rejected the idea of socio-cultural laws but adhered to a collectivist perspective because they believed that an independent meaning could be applied to super-individual entities. 'Since a group concept refers to a complex pattern of descriptive, empirical relations existing among individuals, there is no reason why the behaviour of this complex should not itself be studied' (Brodbeck 1973, p. 107). And the reason Brodbeck gives for her position is the simple assertion: 'There need be no similarity between the behaviour of a complex and the behaviour of elements of the complex' (ibid.). Another aim of holistically oriented analysis is to demonstrate the legitimacy of macroeconomic theory. Because individualism is seen as a synonym for orthodox neoclassical theory, writers subscribing to the holistic view assume a contradiction *per se* between macroeconomics and individualism. If it is considered desirable to give macroeconomic theory in the Keynesian sense a new stimulus it is no wonder that methodological holism is seen as a necessary condition for achieving this stimulus (Hodgson 1986, 1993a).

Apart from this, holism serves as a general framework for criticism of the empirical weaknesses of reductionist individualism. The assumptions of given preferences and given institutions are considered as the pitfalls of a reductionist position such as that of neoclassical economics, because they do not explain how preferences are moulded and how a certain institutional set-up determines individual actions. Along with the assumption of given individuals is the assumption of given rules of behaviour governing their interaction (Hodgson 1993b, p. 9). Additional criticism focuses on the idea of completely rational individuals who always make optimal choices. This idea is closely connected with the assumption of average behaviour and typological thinking and disregards the diversity of personal characteristics. The consequence is the mechanistic character of the rational-choice models.

A further objection against methodological individualism concerns its claim that individuals represent the primary unit of analysis to which all explanations of complex economic phenomena have to be traced back. For advocates of a holistic perspective there is no reason why the method of reductionism, once it is applied, should stop at the individual level and not go further to the level of genes or even to that of neurons as determinants of human actions. To reduce all complex social phenomena to their basic elements would seem to represent an infinite regress where the question of which unit of explanation is to be chosen remains an arbitrary one. 'For the thoroughgoing reductionist to stop short the process of reduction at any level other than the most elemental subatomic particle currently known to science requires some explanation (Hodgson 1993a, p. 265). Because holism sees no reason why individuals should be the most significant units in the explanation of super-individual phenomena, it advocates social wholes as the autonomous unit of analysis.

Rather than focusing on the impact of individual actions on the social whole, causal relationships in the opposite direction may be considered crucial. This means that the influence of traditions, organizations and other institutions moulding individual aims and actions should be moved to the centre of scientific inquiry. This direction of causality from institutions to individuals finds its evidence, according to the holistic approach, in long-term institutional change. In a long-term perspective, institutions are accounted for as part of a permanent process of variation that changes the institutions themselves and, therefore, the conditions under which the individual acts. An appreciation of the importance of non-formal and formal institutions is almost trivially implied by a holistic view, because it does not take social entities as neutral for individual behaviour. Traditions, patterns of behaviour and other institutions represent certain kinds of collective knowledge and as such part of the cultural endowment of a society that has emerged historically. Collective knowledge, as a super-individual phenomenon, can only be explained from a collective perspective and not as a result of individual actions. An explanation that rejects the idea of collective knowledge as an autonomous phenomenon fails to recognize the unique role played by institutions.

It is thus difficult to detect the existence of culture in individual people. 'Culture and institutions transcend the individuals to whom they relate. By regarding culture as a structured and interactive belief-action system its collective quality can be appreciated' (Hodgson 1993a, p. 174).

As mentioned above, methodological holism criticizes reductionist individualism for leaving unexplained the changes in preferences and institutions. There are non-reductionist variants of methodological individualism, however, to which this criticism obviously does not apply. The sweeping holistic criticism of all social scientists who adhere to the individualist tradition tends to overlook the fact that there are critics of reductionism and advocates of an institutional perspective among individualist thinkers as well. Hayek is a case in point and Hodgson (1993a) fails to do justice to him when he writes: 'In short, according to the methodological individualist, individuals do not evolve. Clearly, assumptions of this type are typical of neoclassical economics, as well as the economics of Hayek' (Hodgson 1993a, p. 153). This statement clearly ignores the fact that Hayek developed his own specific version of individualism which contrasts significantly with the neoclassical one, as I shall explain below.

It was exactly the redefinition of the individualistic conception of man that led Hayek from the early 1930s to formulate his own methodological approach which stands in contrast to general equilibrium theory in economics. His approach deviates from the neoclassical assumptions of stable preferences and mechanistic behaviour (Hayek 1937). The human being is not the perfect calculator who always chooses optimal consumption bundles but a complex actor with only bounded rationality and limited mental capacities. It is from such a perspective that Hayek speaks of constitutional ignorance as the basic human condition and of learning and imitation as the most important strategies in solving problems of knowledge.

Hodgson's erroneous equation of neoclassical individualism with Hayekian individualism seems to be based on a quotation taken from Hayek's article 'Scientism and the Study of Society' published in 1943 in *Economica* and reprinted in *The Counter-Revolution of Science* (1952b). Hodgson (1993a, p. 154) quotes Hayek as follows: 'if conscious action can be explained, he writes, this is a task for psychology but not for economics . . . or any other social science'. This one sentence, however, has to be placed in the context from which it was taken. In *The Counter-Revolution of Science*, Hayek's central aim was to describe the primary task of economics as a social science (Hayek 1952b). This he saw in the explanation of spontaneous orders as complex social phenomena. Because this task was not solved, economists should first concentrate on the open problem he submitted and should not try to solve the problems of psychology at the same time. None the less, Hayek himself tried to offer a solution to both problems, that of spontaneous order (Hayek 1967) and that of epistemics (Hayek 1952a).

Assessing Hayek's individualism as being equally as reductionistic as that of neoclassical economics is a misunderstanding that leads Hodgson to refute methodological individualism *in toto*. In his own, more holistically oriented approach to an institutional theory of economics, Hodgson offers social institutions as units of analysis. He argues that they are more suitable for analysing social phenomena since they are relatively invariant entities in the process of human interaction. Thus, Hodgson tries to explain phenomena at the super-individual level by determining variables of the same level, that is, institutions. The institution, therefore, is 'a socially constructed invariant . . . and institutions can be taken as the units and entities of analysis . . . Accordingly, theories based on aggregates become plausible when based on corresponding social institutions' (Hodgson 1993a, p. 254). From this perspective, super-individual units in the social selection process (in the form of groups, markets, organizations and even entire economic systems) acquire autonomous status as explanatory entities which open up new strategies of analysis. The explanation of institutional change and complex phenomena is supposed to begin directly at the collective level and not be reduced to the level of individuals and individual choices (Hodgson 1993a, p. 176). It remains to be seen whether restricting analysis purely to the collective level is indeed necessary or whether an appropriate, non-reductionist, interpretation of individualism *à la* Hayek can yield additional insights.

3. CHARACTERISTICS OF DIFFERENT INDIVIDUALISTIC POSITIONS

As already discussed above, methodological individualism is far from representing a monolithic school. Rather, within this camp there exist rival positions which appear no less antagonistic than does the wider conflict between holism and individualism. Within the individualist camp the spectrum extends from orthodox neoclassical economics on the one hand, to New Institutional Economics and evolutionary economics (with Hayek as one of its precursors) on the other. The differences between these three schools stem from the most diverse assumptions concerning the skills and abilities of the human being. Rational-actor models of neoclassical economics presume that individuals possess complete knowledge and perfect rationality as well as a consistent system of preferences which remains stable over time. Therefore interest focuses here only on reconstructing optimal choices from a given set of alternatives. Even if the assumption that the actors are in possession of complete information is relaxed, the hypothesis of perfect rationality still causes a mechanistic view of human conduct. Contrasting with this conception of man, which appears reductionistic both from the point of view of holism as well as that of evolutionary economics, an alternative interpretation has been offered within the individualistic tradition. This builds on the following assumptions:

- an individual's rationality is bounded (Simon 1957), and human decision-making is thus characterized by constitutional ignorance (Hayek 1967, pp. 82–95); as a consequence, a subjective interpretation of methodological individualism can be derived which takes into account the factors of missing information and localized knowledge (Witt 1992);

- individuals constantly look for innovations to improve their position in the process of competition; from this results a conception of innovations as endogenous phenomena of market processes;
- analysis in terms of the representative individual is replaced by population thinking; it is no longer typical behaviour which is analysed but frequency distributions of certain classes of actions (Metcalfe 1989).

In the following two sections I will analyse how these elements of an evolutionary concept of methodological individualism are used by Hayek to overcome the problem of reductionism.

4. HAYEK'S EPISTEMOLOGY AS A FOUNDATION OF HIS NON-REDUCTIONISTIC PROGRAMME

The propositions of evolutionary economics mentioned above can partly be found in Hayek's early articles where he aimed at expanding upon mainstream economic theories, especially general equilibrium theory (Hayek 1937, 1952b). The introduction of institutions as explanatory variables is primarily made in his theory of cultural evolution. In the following section I wish to show how Hayek's extensions of general equilibrium theory correspond to the criticisms of neoclassical economics launched by the advocates of holism. In order to assess Hayek's individualist position correctly, a complete consideration of his work is necessary. That is to say, his contribution to theoretical psychology, *The Sensory Order* (1952a), has to be taken into account because it is the epistemological foundation of his entire social philosophy of abstract society. Hayek's methodological assumptions are based on his epistemology. Accordingly, his individualism, which is neither reductionistic nor excludes super-individual phenomena, can only be understood in the broader perspective of his cognitive theory. The starting-point of Hayek's thought is the distinction he draws between the physical and the phenomenological world, that is, the appearance of objects in reality on the one hand, and our perception of them on the other. The perceived characteristics of objects or situations may deviate from their physical characteristics. This is owing to the fact that sensory perception is a form of classification which does not correspond to any known relation between objects in the external world (Hayek 1952b, p. 22). Thus, sensory perception must be regarded as an act of classification where human beings do not perceive the individual characteristics of particular objects, but only the characteristics which these objects have in common with other ones. Perception, therefore, is always a form of interpretation, an assignment of something perceived in particular classes of objects. Sensory perception is based on abstract elements which, Hayek holds, are inherited and which represent classifying devices for sorting between sensory impressions. The abstract elements which make up our mind give us the more or less tacit ability to bring our impressions into a certain order. The capacity to classify is a general characteristic of man. The perceptions of different people therefore operate in similar ways – the reason why some forms of common knowledge shared by different people is possible.

An important result of Hayek's theory of a classifying sensory order is the notion that human beings can only perceive parts of reality. Individual decisions and actions, therefore, are not influenced by all available information but only by parts of it. Knowledge, as Hayek concludes, is always local or subjective knowledge and bound to a certain situation. Because of the limited capacity of human perception, complex phenomena cannot be grasped as a whole. The analysis and explanation of complex processes, therefore, have to start at an accessible level, namely at the level of the elements. 'The consistent use of the intelligible conduct of individuals as the building stones from which to construct models of complex market structures is of course the essence of the method Menger himself described as "atomistic" (or as "composite") and that later came to be known as methodological individualism' (Hayek 1978, p. 276).

According to Hayek's theory, the human mind is limited (Hayek 1946, p. 8). That is why irrationality and misjudgments are as much human characteristics as the ability to make rational choices in certain, limited, situations. Hayek's conception of man thus allows for several dimensions – rational and irrational ones – and cannot be reduced to some homo economicus guided by mere maximizing behaviour. Because of the possibility of misjudgements each individual is dependent on wider social processes, such as that of the market mechanism, which help to reveal and correct the faults of individuals (Hayek 1946, p. 8). This concern with the importance of integrated social relationships explains why Hayek does not consider the individual separately as an optimizing being, but always in relation to an environment which consists of other individuals, groups and institutions. Hayek's individualism starts from men whose entire nature and character is determined by their existence in society, instead of from their existence as isolated or self-contained individuals. Simultaneously, 'there is no other way toward an understanding of social phenomena but through our understanding of individual actions directed towards other people and guided by their expected behavior' (Hayek 1946, p. 6). As a closer look shows, Hayek thus offers an elaborate form of individualism as his methodological principle, one that is carefully founded on an epistemological basis. For Hayek, individualism is not an ad hoc assumption, but a necessary conclusion that follows from his assessment of the cognitive abilities of human beings and their integration within social processes.

5. RULES AND ORDER – THE TWO LEVELS OF EXPLANATION

According to Hayek, the concept of *subjectivism* mentioned above signifies the fact 'that the knowledge and beliefs of different people, while possessing that common structure which makes communication possible, will yet be different and often conflicting in many respects' (Hayek 1952b, p. 29). From this results the dispersion of knowledge as a fundamental condition of human coexistence: 'the concrete knowledge which guides the action of any group of people never exists as a consistent and coherent body. It only exists in the dispersed, incomplete, and inconsistent form in which it appears in many individual minds' (ibid., p. 30).[2] In order to coordinate their local knowledge and their subjective aims, individuals follow particular rules of conduct, traditions and habits as well as laws and other codified rules. These rules emerge during the history of civilization. All rules of conduct taken together, both formal and informal, form the specific institutional infrastructure of a society. People follow the rules of conduct in everyday life usually without being aware of them. When following rules it is not always necessary to examine the whole situation in order to decide on, or react to, recurring events. An implicit reduction of complexity takes place and the individual gains time and the cognitive capacities to solve future problems (Hayek 1973, pp. 17–19).

Most rules and institutions of a society do not develop through intentional action aiming at a specific collective result. Rather, they emerge spontaneously. Institutions are 'results of human action but not of human design' (Hayek 1967, p. 96, referring to Adam Ferguson). This does not rule out the possibility that institutions also come into being

[2] One can see at this point that the basic ideas of Hayek, such as the theories of constitutional ignorance and the dispersion of knowledge, can be traced back to his early articles on scientific theory.

by conscious design in a formal process. Hayek merely wants to point out that our civilization is an abstract society based on a multitude of rules that neither have been consciously created nor exist as explicit knowledge. Obviously, this notion of cultural evolution is incompatible with the idea of a planned and centrally conducted development of society.

The behaviour of each individual is influenced on a conscious, and even more on a subconscious level, by particular rules of conduct. Most of the rules are adopted by simple imitation during the course of socialization because individuals, observing other successful people, try to behave in similar ways.[3] The demonstrated advantages of a certain rule induce more and more individuals to adopt that rule, thus establishing a collectively acknowledged institution.[4] Imitation of observed behaviour is never perfect. Erroneous or conscious variation effect a mutation or recombination of rule-guided behaviour. This means that new rules of conduct, or more generally speaking, innovations, can come into existence by chance. In addition, an institution can be created consciously if an individual tries to achieve a superior position by deviating from habits followed so far. If this new rule proves to be more suitable for a concrete situation, a process of imitation will commence following the pattern described above. Hayek sees the cause of changing preferences and behaviour as a consequence of this permanent process of endogenously induced innovations. Rules of conduct and institutions, respectively, are the traits being adopted, mutated and selected in the transmission of cultural evolution. They are closely connected with individuals as the entities bearing the traits. The transmission of rules between individuals – either in a horizontal direction if the individuals belong to one generation or in a vertical direction if they belong to different generations – takes place through the processes of imitation and learning. Since there are always several individuals who are involved in the transmission, the super-individual character of the rules and, more generally, of cultural evolution is evident. Within groups or societies conventions and rules of cooperation are of special importance. Their relative success in solving economic and political conflicts in a community is decisive for the welfare of a group or society, namely, for the degree of individual satisfaction of needs. The order resulting

[3] A process which is called observational learning in the recent literature of behaviourial psychology (Bandura 1977, 1986).

[4] Hayek takes the rules of conduct as manifestations of collective knowledge. Interaction unintentionally yields collective knowledge. Here a hierarchy of orders turns up which can be found in Hayek's social philosophy. Spontaneous orders result on different levels, from the level of the individual up to group and society level.

from the rule-guided behaviour of the individuals is called in Hayek's theory the spontaneous order of actions. The efficiency of a certain order appears in the fact that the result of individual actions 'will remove the initial stimulus or make inoperative the drive which has been the cause of activity' (Hayek 1967, p. 69). It is the viability or efficiency itself of the rule-based order of actions which is closely connected with Hayek's principle of group selection operating at the collective level. This principle is one of the most important elements in Hayek's theory of cultural evolution though one that has been debated by many critics. The selection of particular rules of conduct within the social process is dependent on the relative efficiency of the resulting order of a group or society. It is true that the viability of an order of actions is based on the rules guiding individual behaviour and their adaptive value in the special situation. But the most decisive fact of cultural selection is not the behaviour of individuals but the efficiency of the whole order. In other words, it is possible for an individual to act according to unsuitable rules without inducing a negative performance of the whole group provided the functioning of the collective is not disturbed by that particular individual behaviour. To clarify this argument consider the problem of the provision of public goods: a public good will be spontaneously provided without central planning as long as a sufficient number of individuals contribute to it. Some individual free-riders do not necessarily prevent the provision of the public good. When free-riding exceeds a certain frequency, however, that is, when a critical number of cooperating individuals does not exist, a viable order of actions cannot be established and the well-known problem of social dilemma occurs. In order to represent Hayek's idea of group selection in an appropriate way two different, though interdependent, levels of explanation have to be distinguished as shown in Figure 4.1.

A viable order of actions develops if a sufficient number of individuals behave according to well-adapted rules. On the other hand, rules of conduct only survive in the selection process if they belong to an efficient order of actions adapted to a given environment. 'This means that the individual with a particular structure and behaviour owes its existence in this form to a society of a particular structure, because only within such a society has it been advantageous to develop some of its peculiar characteristics while the order of society in turn is a result of these regularities of conduct which the individuals have developed in society' (Hayek 1967, p. 76).

Let us have a closer look at the interdependencies between the individual and the collective level. The selection mechanism is in two ways effective at the group level. Groups with more suitable rules of

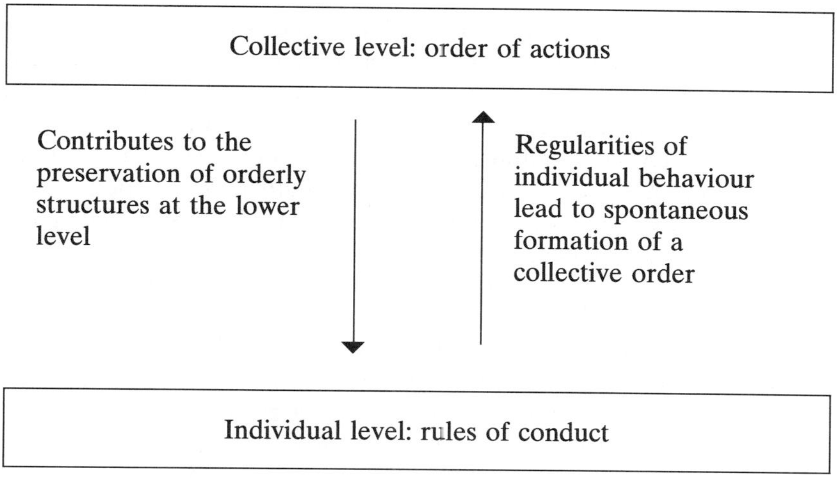

Figure 4.1. Two levels of explanation

conduct yield a greater degree of satisfaction of individual needs and more effectively adapt to the specific environment. This may be attractive to outsiders who try to obtain similar results by imitating the more successful rules they observe. In this way, the relatively better and more adaptable rules of conduct spread throughout the population, or, as Hayek says, the group itself grows (Hayek 1973, p. 17). Such new rules spread not because people regard them as more effective, or because they think they would result in expansion, but simply because such rules enabled those groups who observed them to procreate more successfully and to absorb outsiders (Hayek 1988, p. 16).[5] Besides the differential growth effect of the group selection mechanism on the collective level the importance of individual actions underlying that mechanism should not be neglected. As already explained, part of the interdependency between the two levels consists in the fact that only suitable rules of behaviour lead to an order of actions. And the suitability of a certain rule depends on the specific conditions of a historical situation as well as on the already observed rules of behaviour (Hayek 1967, p. 71). Thus, despite introducing the principle of group selection,

[5] Hayek's theory of cultural evolution is thus an early example of the application of so-called population thinking in the social sciences. Population thinking is an integral element of evolutionary theories and overcomes the problem of exclusively focusing on individuals as units of analysis in social processes (Metcalfe 1989, Boyd and Richerson 1985, p. 292).

which provides a super-individual explanation of social phenomena, an analysis of individual behaviour is not rendered obsolete or meaningless.

The interdependencies between the collective and individual levels represent a central theme in Hayek's evolutionary theory of civilization. The order of actions resulting from the rule-guided behaviour of group members represents an essential part of the individual selection framework. A viable order of actions increases the chances of individual survival by satisfying needs and assuring a minimum degree of cooperation. As long as an efficient overall order is obtained the group will succeed in adapting to its environment (to such external factors as climate, external enemies etc.). One may suppose, therefore, that individuals have at least an implicit self-interest in sustaining an efficient order of actions. Individuals as elements of a group adapt voluntarily to the conditions of a hitherto successful order, and try to maintain it so as to improve their future chances of survival. Most of the time this process of adaptation occurs unconsciously through following and imitating the appropriate rules.

In order to be more specific with respect to how cultural transmission works, Hayek refers to hierarchical group structures which, he thinks, influence the imitation and learning processes. Within a group, not all individuals are in the same position of power. Age and experience enable individuals to gain more influential positions, that is, to have an impact on what tend to be transmitted cultural traits. A new rule of behaviour is imitated more quickly if the innovator holds a prestigious position. This is owing to the confidence which the group members have in the judgement of those who are the most experienced (Hayek 1967, p. 79). The idea of such hierarchies existing within groups and their impact on the dissemination of rules is closely connected to Hayek's subjectivist interpretation of methodological individualism and his theory of population thinking. This includes the general variability of individuals and their skills and prevents typological tendencies in the analysis of social phenomena. To summarize the importance of Hayek's duality approach we simply have to consider that both levels of explanation – the collective and the individual – are necessary for a complete analysis of social phenomena.[6] If one of the two levels is ignored the interdependencies between the levels are lost out of sight. But these inter-level relationships are fundamental in a double sense. They show

[6] A similar methodological strategy was presented by Agassi (1975) with his Institutional Individualism. Both authors, Hayek and Agassi, try to integrate collective elements in an individualistically based approach. For a recent assessment of Agassi's methodology as a middle way between holism and psychological individualism, see Toboso (1995).

that individual actions always have to be analysed in the context of inter-subjective relationships and, additionally, they point to the fact that individual chances depend on what order of actions prevails. A social theory that focuses on the collective level alone would deny the impact of individual actions on the overall order. On the other hand, reductionistic individualistic theories which do not consider social processes at the collective level, such as Hayek's theory of group selection, would fail to account for the important role which super-individual phenomena play in individual thought and behaviour.

6. HAYEK'S DUALITY APPROACH AND THE EXPLANATION OF INSTITUTIONAL TRANSITION

In the preceding section we looked at the duality of collective and individual aspects of cultural evolution and the role of institutional transition as one of its main processes. If we wish to consider the impact of Hayek's approach for the analysis of institutional change then it is exactly these two mentioned directions that we have to investigate. First of all we should recognize that – from Hayek's perspective – the transformation of formal and informal institutions is a process of collective learning. This process requires time because new institutions only acquire relevance as guiding principles for human behaviour if they correspond to certain conditions. New formal rules, for example, must be intelligible and understandable to a minimum number of individuals and additionally they require a certain degree of credibility as beneficial modes of behaviour before they affect the collective order. That means that, even if it is possible to establish appropriate formal rules through governmental activity, a resulting viable order of actions cannot be taken for granted. The adapting of individual behaviour, that is, the adoption of appropriate rules of conduct, is equally necessary. The property rights of a market economy, for example, require some kind of capitalistic spirit to be effective, a free trade regime requires arbitrage and so on. Hayek proposes a further classification of rules of conduct when he talks about the implicit character of many informal rules. This means that in recurrent situations we always behave in a similar manner because we have learnt that this is an appropriate way of acting through observation and imitation without being aware that it is rule-guided behaviour. We act without being able to explicitly describe our way of acting. Implicit rules of behaviour are important because they influence most of our everyday actions.

Analysis of institutional transformation, therefore, requires the recognition of such kinds of rules as a major element influencing the collective order.

Hayek's distinction between formal and informal rules and his further distinction between explicit and implicit knowledge of informal rules become especially important in all attempts at enforcing the process of institutional transition from an external position. The passing of new formal rules in a legal process is only one aspect of the whole task. Another is the information and motivation of a sufficient number of individuals (the critical mass) to force their adaptive activities in the right direction. Only in the case of changing both, the formal and the informal rules, will a new order of actions result and the institutional transition be successful. The most critical phase in the process of institutional transformation occurs in a situation where new formal rules have already been passed as legislation but where the informal and especially the implicit rules of behaviour have not been adapted to them. In such conditions a situation of immense uncertainty arises because the external institutions have changed without any possibility of reacting to them in an appropriate way. Thus, the above mentioned processes of collective learning are a necessary condition in solving this problematic situation.

As evidence of these conclusions we may note the problems of some East European countries which have never possessed a tradition of complex trade or a decentralized economic system. Compared with other members of the former Eastern bloc these countries require much more time and effort to change their position. Analysing the actual situation of these countries with the help of Hayek's approach would highlight additional and sometimes alternative fields of external support in the transition process for political authorities in national and international organizations.

As a second aspect of institutional transformation we have to look at the collective level and Hayek's hypothesis of group selection: the group with the most appropriate rules of behaviour is more successful and therefore grows relatively faster than other groups, whether through a higher rate of procreation or through immigration. Applied to the process of institutional transformation, the group selection hypothesis refers to the idea of institutional competition between different legal and economic systems, offering thus an explanation of the origin of institutional change. Institutions have to be changed if a new situation in the environment demands their adaptation. One of the most important external concerns of a state or population is the economic performance of its neighbours and their institutional systems which may offer better opportunities for the rentability of mobile resources.[7] Institutional transformation may result in this area because the export of mobile resources can jeopardize an existing order of actions in a less successful country and require legal action. The collective order of a certain population acquires an even greater selective advantage if it results from institutions which also attract the mobile resources of its neighbours.

The importance of competition between legal systems became obvious with the exit of thousands of East Germans in 1989 which lead to some far from negligible institutional transformations. This transformation of an entire legal system, that of the former GDR, can also be regarded as one of the most spectacular examples of group selection in this century. Another example of institutional competition can be seen in the growth of direct investments of firms from West European welfare states in Poland, the Czech Republic and so on because of the differences in production costs. This exit of capital has induced far-reaching debates on necessary changes in labour market institutions and a rearrangement of the social security system in the Western countries.

Using Hayek's group selection hypothesis we may conclude that the existing selection pressure of an environment forces every legal system to adapt to changing circumstances. Political attempts to avoid institutional transformation (because it is too costly for subgroups in the population) are doomed to fail. The selection pressure increases as long as there is no adaptation, a process that can sometimes continue for decades, and in the worst cases can lead to the collapse of an entire economic system. Hayek's evolutionary theory of institutional transition does not imply that we can always expect a successful spontaneous order of actions without any planned intervention. He does assert, however, that interventions, in the long run, never succeed if they try to avoid adapting to the necessities of a changing world.

To conclude this final section we can summarize that Hayek's theory involves two propositions when applied to the process of institutional transformation. First, he points out that formal as well as informal rules of conduct are objects of institutional transformation and are equally important for successful attempts at adapting to a changing environment. Whereas planned modifications of formal institutions are possible because they exist as explicit knowledge, informal institutions, being themselves the spontaneous result of individual actions, require a much more complicated process to change them. Second, Hayek's notion of group selection draws our attention to the always existing process

[7] For a comprehensive discussion of institutional competition between states, see Vanberg and Kerber (1994) and Wohlgemuth (1995).

of institutional competition at the collective level. Permanent selection pressure forces each legal system and its elements to adapt to new conditions if a collapse of the collective order is to be avoided. Postponing necessary adaptations is perhaps possible in the short run, but will never be a successful strategy in the longer term. The effective role of policy intervention in the process of institutional transformation, Hayek suggests, lies in the analysis and enforcement of necessary adaptations and not in their prevention.

7. CONCLUSION

As was shown above, Hayek's social philosophy is not one based on reductionist individualism as has erroneously been argued by critics favouring methodological holism. One such example which has been discussed here in more detail is Hodgson's criticism of Hayek's plea for an individualistic perspective in the social sciences which fails to acknowledge Hayek's own arguments against reductionism. Hodgson argues in favour of an approach in which institutions are taken as the ultimate level of analysis. Following Veblen he attributes to the rules of behaviour in cultural evolution a function analogous to that of the genes in biological evolution. Institutions 'tend to sustain and thus 'pass on' their important characteristics through time' (Hodgson 1993a, p. 253). Thus far there is no contradiction existing between Hodgson's holistic perspective and Hayek's individualistic theory of cultural evolution. A difference only emerges in Hodgson's attempt to confine the analysis of social phenomena and processes to the level of institutions and to regard the latter as the most significant units in the scientific process. In other words, he tries to explain socio-cultural events through their invariant elements, the institutions. However, this procedure does not explain the formation and change of the units of analysis themselves.

If the question of institutional development is left open, however, we ourselves will be victims of a kind of reductionism. Although methodological holism can account for the influence of institutions on the behaviour of individuals and inter-individual processes, it cannot explain why institutions emerge, change or disappear. In Hayek's theory of cultural evolution, however, analysis of the interactions between the collective level with its order of actions and the individual level with its occurrence of different rules of conduct offers an explanation of institutional change. Emphasizing the interdependencies between the two levels is a way to integrate both the effects of individual behaviour and the influence of super-individual phenomena in one consistent theory of institutional change. An individualistic theory of institutional change, as proposed by Hayek, solves the problem of reductionism in social science because it includes a multidimensional concept of man as well as dealing with the interdependencies between institutions and individual behaviour.

As shown in this chapter, non-reductionist methodological individualism and holism share several views in common, yet they differ in their explanatory power. If decisions can only be made by individuals and not by other social entities the criticism of individualism as an arbitrary way of preventing all attempts at reducing social phenomena to their elements is invalid. A certain individual decision is determined by a multitude of causes such as emotions, reason, physical constitution and external circumstances. Only if this diversity of determinants is indeed accounted for, can the complexity of the human being be fully understood. All these determinants of human behaviour work together so that the search for final causes does not present a valid strategy of scientific inquiry. As social scientists we are not obliged to explain the genetic or physiological structures of man but we do have to analyse human behaviour and predict its possible collective outcome. Cultural traits are bound to individuals because they are the only entities that adopt those traits. The transmission of cultural characteristics such as rules of conduct, habits and traditions could in principle be based on books, television or other media, but the adoption of a certain trait necessarily depends on individual behaviour. Collective results emerge from these individual cases of adoption. This means that through their conscious or unconscious actions only individuals can be the cause of variation in a population. The frequency distribution of certain cultural traits in a group or population depends on individual behaviour and not on the decisions of an autonomous collective entity. For this reason, explanations of super-individual phenomena can be improved by taking the individual as the starting-point while observing, at the same time, the complexity of human decision-making processes and the interdependencies between the individual and the collective level. Non-reductionistic individualism takes seriously into account the relationships which exist between individuals and institutions, offering thereby an integrated theory of institutional change.

REFERENCES

Agassi, J. (1975) 'Institutional Individualism'. *British Journal of Sociology* 26: 144–55.

Bandura, A. (1977) *Social Learning Theory*. Englewood Cliffs, NJ: Prentice-Hall.
Bandura, A. (1986) *Social Foundations of Thought and Action – A Social Cognitive Theory*. Englewood Cliffs, NJ: Prentice-Hall.
Birner, J. and Zijp, R. van (1994) *Hayek, Co-Ordination and Evolution*. London and New York: Routledge.
Blaug, M. (1992) *The Methodology of Economics – Or How Economists Explain*. Cambridge: Cambridge University Press.
Boland, L.A. (1982) *The Foundations of Economic Method*. London: Allen & Unwin.
Boland, L.A. (1992) *The Principles of Economics – Some Lies My Teachers Told Me*. London and New York: Routledge.
Boyd, R. and Richerson, P.J. (1985) *Culture and the Evolutionary Process*. Chicago and London: University of Chicago Press.
Brodbeck, M. (1973) 'On the Philosophy of the Social Sciences' in J. O'Neill (ed.) *Modes of Individualism and Collectivism*. London: Heinemann.
Commons, J.R. (1934) *Institutional Economics – Its Place in Political Economy*. New York: Macmillan.
Dorman, P. (1991) 'Marxism, Methodological Individualism, and the New Institutional Economics: Further Considerations'. *Journal of Institutional and Theoretical Economics* 147: 364–73.
Douglas, M. (1987) *How Institutions Think*. London: Routledge and Kegan Paul.
Eggertsson, T. (1990) *Economic Behaviour and Institutions*. Cambridge: Cambridge University Press.
Furubotn, E.G. and Richter, R. (1991) *The New Institutional Economics: A Collection of Articles from the Journal of Institutional and Theoretical Economics*. Tübingen: Mohr (Siebeck).
Goldstein, L.J. (1973) 'The Inadequacy of the Principle of Methodological Individualism' in J. O'Neill (ed.) *Modes of Individualism and Collectivism*. London: Heinemann.
Hayek, F.A. (1937) 'Economics and Knowledge'. *Economica* IV: 33–54. Repr. in F.A. von Hayek (1948) *Individualism and Economic Order*. Chicago: University of Chicago Press.
Hayek, F.A. (1946) *Individualism: True and False*. Dublin: Hodges, Figgis & Co. Repr. in F.A. von Hayek (1948) *Individualism and Economic Order*. Chicago: University of Chicago Press.
Hayek, F.A. (1948) *Individualism and Economic Order*. Chicago: University of Chicago Press.
Hayek, F.A. (1952a) *The Sensory Order – An Inquiry into the Foundations of Theoretical Psychology*. London: Routledge and Kegan Paul.
Hayek, F.A. (1952b) *The Counter-Revolution of Science – Studies on the Abuse of Reason*. Glencoe, Ill.: Free Press.
Hayek, F.A. (1967) 'Notes on the Evolution of Systems of Rules of Conduct' in *Philosophy, Politics and Economics*. London: Routledge & Kegan Paul.
Hayek, F.A. (1973) *Law, Legislation and Liberty*, Vol. I. Chicago: University of Chicago Press.
Hayek, F.A. (1978) *New Studies in Philosophy, Politics, Economics and the History of Ideas*. London: Routledge.
Hayek, F.A. (1988) *The Fatal Conceit*. London: Routledge.

Heijdra, B.J., Lowenberg, A.D. and Mallick, R.J. (1988) 'Marxism, Methodological Individualism, and the New Institutional Economics'. *Journal of Institutional and Theoretical Economics* 144: 296–317.
Hodgson, G.M. (1986) 'Behind Methodological Individualism'. *Cambridge Journal of Economics* 10: 211–24.
Hodgson, G.M. (1991) 'Hayek's Theory of Cultural Evolution'. *Economics and Philosophy* 7: 67–82.
Hodgson, G.M. (1993a) *Economics and Evolution – Bringing Life Back into Economics.* Cambridge: Polity Press.
Hodgson, G.M. (1993b) 'Institutional Economics: Surveying The Old and the New'. *Metroeconomica* 44 (1): 1–28.
Hodgson, G.M. and Screpanti, E. (eds) (1991) *Rethinking Economics: Markets, Technology and Economic Evolution.* Aldershot: Edward Elgar.
Mayhew, A. (1987) 'The Beginnings of Institutionalism'. *Journal of Economic Issues* 21 (3): 971–98.
Mayhew, A. (1989) 'Contrasting Origins of the Two Institutionalisms: The Social Science Context'. *Review of Political Economy* 1 (3): 319–33.
Metcalfe, S. (1989) 'Evolution and Economic Change' in Silberston (ed.) *Technology and Economic Progress.* London: Macmillan, pp. 54–85.
Mitchell, W.C. (ed.) (1936) *What Veblen Taught.* New York: Augustus Kelley.
North, D.C. (1981) *Structure and Change in Economic History.* New York: Norton.
North, D.C. (1990) *Institutions, Institutional Change and Economic Performance.* Cambridge: Cambridge University Press.
O'Neill, J. (1973) *Modes of Individualism and Collectivism.* London: Heinemann.
Simon, H. (1957) *Models of Man: Social and Rational.* New York: Wiley.
Toboso, F. (1995) 'Is Institutional Individualism an Adequate Method for Analyzing Institutional Changes?'. Discussion paper presented at the European Association for Evolutionary Political Economy Conference 1995, Cracow.
Vanberg, V. (1975) *Die Zwei Soziologien – Individualismus und Kollektivismus in der Sozialtheorie.* Tübingen: Mohr (Siebeck).
Vanberg, V. (1986) 'Spontaneous Market Order and Social Rules'. *Economics and Philosophy* 2: 75–100.
Vanberg, V. and Kerber, W. (1994) 'Institutional Competition among Jurisdictions: An Evolutionary Approach'. *Constitutional Political Economy* 5 (2): 193–219.
Veblen, T.B. (1899) *The Theory of the Leisure Class: An Economic Study of Institutions.* New York: Macmillan.
Witt, U. (1989) 'The Evolution of Economic Institutions as a Propagation Process'. *Public Choice* 62: 155–72.
Witt, U. (1991) 'Reflections on the Present State of Evolutionary Economics' in G.M. Hodgson and E. Screpanti (eds) (1991) *Rethinking Economics: Markets, Technology and Economic Evolution.* Aldershot: Edward Elgar.
Witt, U. (1992) 'Turning Austrian Economics into an Evolutionary Theory' in B.J. Caldwell and S. Boehm (eds) *Austrian Economics: Tensions and New Directions.* Boston, Dordrecht, London: Kluwer Academic Publishers, pp. 215–43.
Witt, U. (1994) 'The Theory of Societal Evolution: Hayek's Unfinished Legacy'

in J. Birner and R. van Zijp (1994) *Hayek, Co-Ordination and Evolution.* London and New York: Routledge.

Wohlgemuth, M. (1995) 'Economic and Political Competition in Neoclassical and Evolutionary Perspective' in *Constitutional Political Economy* 6: 71–96

5. The governance of complexity and the complexity of governance: preliminary remarks on some problems and limits of economic guidance

Bob Jessop[1]

This chapter addresses the recent discovery of 'governance' as the complex art of steering multiple agencies, institutions and systems which are both operationally autonomous from one another and structurally coupled through various forms of reciprocal interdependence. This discovery could well reflect the dramatic intensification of societal complexity which flows from growing functional differentiation of institutional orders within an increasingly global society, with all that this implies for the widening and deepening of systemic interdependencies across various social, spatial and temporal horizons of action. Indeed, governance appears to have moved up the theoretical and practical agendas because high levels of (increasingly globalized) functional differentiation undermine the basis for hierarchical, top-down coordination under the aegis of a single centre at the peak of a given societal formation – let alone at the peak of a global social system with its continuing territorial division into nation states still jealous of their declining formal sovereignty (Luhmann 1984, Willke 1987, 1992).

This differentiation process particularly affects the two core institutional orders traditionally studied in evolutionary political economy: the economy and polity. In particular, the world economy is being reshaped by a complex dialectic of globalization-regionalization under the dominance of capitalist relations. This process is alleged to make it more difficult for (national) states to control economic activities within their borders – let alone the global dynamic of capital accumulation. At the same time capital accumulation is said to depend on a wide

[1] This paper arises from a research project on local governance financed by the Economic and Social Research Council (grant L311253032).

range of extra-economic factors generated on various spatio-temporal scales through other institutional orders (see, e.g. Boyer 1990, Castells 1989, Chesnais 1987, Nelson 1993, Porter 1990, Reich 1991). Major changes are also occurring in the (global) political system with equally paradoxical effects. Thus, on the one hand, there is a tendential denationalization of the state system through the movement of state power upwards, downwards and sideways as attempts are made by state managers to regain operational autonomy (if not formal sovereignty as such) and thereby enhance the state's own strategic capacities. On the other hand, there is a tendential de-statization of politics (a shift from the primacy of top-down government towards more decentred governance mechanisms) as political capacities are seen to depend on the effective coordination of interdependent forces within and beyond the state (for a review of these and related trends, see Jessop (1995)). It is in this context that governance (or 'partnership') strategies have been strongly advocated as alternatives to market anarchy and organizational hierarchy in the field of economic development.

Whilst recognizing that a governance bandwagon now seems to be rolling, I am reluctant to leap onto it – and certainly not in uncritical fashion. Instead, I argue that governing complexity is far from simple and, indeed, that governance failure is routine. In developing this argument, some abstract claims are presented about 'contingent necessity' in order to problematize the notion of social complexity before considering problems of governance. This first set of remarks has two main purposes. They are intended to show how complexity risks becoming a 'chaotic conception' (Marx 1857) which serves neither as a coherent research object nor as a coherent explanatory principle. And they are meant to correct an unfortunate celebratory tendency in some contributions to debates on governance (e.g., uncritical accounts of the potential of stakeholding, associational democracy or learning regions). For, whilst many contributors allege that unstructured complexity somehow dooms market forces and/or bureaucratic planning to failure in realizing collective goals or goods, they also imply (even if they do not directly claim) that, with skilful institutional design and sufficient goodwill, other forms of governance could succeed in almost any circumstances through their introduction of structure and consensus. They could reduce and structure complexity to such an extent on the basis of negotiated consent that the real world becomes collectively manageable and agencies charged with its governance can be rendered collectively accountable. There are powerful arguments, however, against strong versions of this presumption. These I seek to develop briefly on the basis of some general reflections on 'contingently necessary complexity'. But these remarks will also provide the basis for a more modest account of conditions which might contribute to more localized, provisional, and partial successes for attempts at governance.

I then attempt to reduce the risk of chaotic conceptions of complexity and its governance by distinguishing forms of complexity in interpersonal, inter-organizational and inter-systemic relations; and by linking the resulting problems of complexity to issues of 'requisite variety', adaptability and learning in possible governance mechanisms. This second set of ideas is drawn from recent work on social complexity, self-organization and 'autopoietic' (self-referential, self-reproducing) systems. This work is important for its concern with complexity in social as opposed to natural systems. But it also risks neglecting the specific forms of complexity in different institutional orders and the contrasting problems these pose for governance. Accordingly, by combining these general ideas with principles drawn from institutional and evolutionary economics, a 'strategic-relational' approach[2] to social analysis, and the Marxist critique of capital as a social relation, I hope to cast new light on economic governance.

Institutional and evolutionary analyses emphasize that economic systems are socially embedded and socially regulated;[3] and that they evolve in a complex, uneven manner. Hence an adequate account of economic activity should explore how it is related to the wider social environment; how it is embedded in a wider nexus of social institutions; how its development is coupled to that of environing, embedding institutions; and how the latter assist in the 'reproduction-regulation' of the economy broadly interpreted. A strategic-relational approach is well suited to exploring such issues because of its concern with the complex interrelations of structure, agency and strategy, its insistence that form problematizes rather than guarantees function, and its emphasis on conjunctural analysis. And Marxist analyses highlight basic structural contradictions and strategic dilemmas of the capital relation – features which governance mechanisms may well modify but can never fully escape. This last point is especially important because literature on economic governance often focuses on the modalities rather than the objects of governance and thereby abstracts from the distinctive con-

[2] A 'strategic-relational' approach develops the dialectic of structure and agency in a critical realist manner: it regards 'structures' as strategically selective and regards strategies as being reflexively oriented to opportunities for action in specific strategically selective contexts (Jessop 1990a).

[3] This certainly does not exclude more stylized analyses of economic dynamics that abstract from specific institutional contexts and conjunctures.

straints imposed by the self-organizing dynamic and 'ecological dominance'[4] of capitalism. Work on economic governance thereby underestimates the obstacles confronting attempts to guide capital accumulation. Combining arguments from these three (interrelated) theoretical positions should provide a better account of the complexities confronting attempts to steer socially embedded, socially regularized economic processes in all their contradictory and dilemmatic nature and, *a fortiori*, of likely sources of governance failure.

1. CONTINGENT NECESSITY

My approach to issues of complexity has been shaped by earlier work on the distinctive features of 'contingent necessity'. This term, with its seeming *contradictio in adjecto*, refers to the nature of 'real-concrete' phenomena. It rests on the assumption that everything that happens in the real world must happen, that is, is in some sense 'necessary'. Rejecting this assumption would render much scientific enquiry pointless. It is the precise meaning of necessity, however, that is at stake in 'contingent necessity'. For it need not, does not and cannot mean that whatever happens in the real world is the result of a *single* causal mechanism. Instead the concrete actualization of events results from the *interaction* of diverse causal tendencies and counter-tendencies. Now, whilst it may be tempting to argue that this interaction itself can serve as the single causal mechanism which necessarily generates the necessary happening, this is invalid because such interactions cannot be attributed to the operation of any single causal mechanism, for they too result from interaction among diverse causal tendencies and counter-tendencies. This opens the route to an infinite explanatory regress into the path-dependent past. To avoid this, events are best studied 'genealogically' (Foucault 1975) in terms of their provenance as *necessary* products of *contingent* interactions among different sets of causal mechanisms. Contingent necessity also implies an unbounded surplus of (unmanageable, often mutually exclusive) future possibilities, thereby ensuring that the world has an 'open' structure (Luhmann 1979, pp. 6, 13). Governance mechanisms are one way in and through which this surplus of future possibilities and its resulting social complexity is reduced (see below).

[4] Ecological dominance exists to the extent that other systems are obliged to adapt more to a given system than the latter is to them: in this sense they assume a dominant role in shaping the co-evolution of the ecological system as a whole. It has been argued that the economy is the ecologically dominant system in the modern world.

What do contingent necessity and complexity imply for analyses of the real world? *Ontologically*, complexity refers to the nature of events or phenomena in the real world. As Marx noted, the real-concrete is 'the complex synthesis of multiple determinations' (Marx 1857, p. 101). This excludes any simple algorithm to generate explanations of complex phenomena. Contingent necessity in the real world implies infinite complexity in the real world and this calls in turn for complexity reduction. *Epistemologically*, if 'contingent necessities' really exist, to adequately to explain them requires one to combine concepts, assumptions and principles of analysis from different theoretical domains and to link them to a given, theoretically defined explanendum. Since the real world is infinitely complex, however, it is inevitably analytically inexhaustible. Thus an explanation is only more or less satisfactory relative to a given explanendum that has been isolated (and thus 'constructed') by an observer out of that infinite complexity. *Methodologically*, this requires a 'method of articulation' that respects contingent necessity and complexity. One way to understand this is to see it as based on the dual movement from abstract to concrete along one plane of analysis, and from simple to complex as more analytical planes are introduced in order to produce increasingly adequate explanations (Jessop 1982, pp. 213–19).

All three implications apply to 'observation' of the real world as well as to that which is observed. For observation itself occurs in the real world and is therefore also open to (self-)observation. By applying these principles to their own observational practices, observers can reflect on the contingent necessity (situatedness) of their own concepts and categories. This sort of self-reflexiveness may also help secure the relative success of governance mechanisms in localized contexts and for limited periods. In both cases, of course, such (self-)observation and (self-)reflection generate the paradox that complexity reduction mechanisms and practices add to the complexity of the real world (Poggi 1979, Luhmann 1984).[5]

The general links between contingent necessity, complexity and governance can now be stated. Contingent necessity, as it concerns real world phenomena and events, indicates their *de facto* causal determination (necessity) and their *ex ante* indeterminability (contingency). As a feature of the real world, contingent necessity implies that world's ontological complexity. Indeed, if the development of the real world

[5] Thus 'the reduction of complexity through the formation of ever more numerous, differentiated, and sophisticated systems (is) a phenomenon which necessarily generates ever new complexity, and thus feeds upon itself' (Poggi 1979, p. 12).

involves an infinite succession of contingently interdependent as well as contingently necessary 'contingent necessities', then it must also be infinitely complex. This poses a series of questions about how one can best grasp the 'complexity of complexity' in the real world and simplify it in dealing with that world. Governance can be seen as one way self-reflexively to transform unstructured (because infinite) into structured (because simplified) complexity (Marin 1990, p. 21) – albeit without being able to control the (nth order) effects of such simplification and structuration.

For Hayek, the complexity of the social world rules out effective planning and implies that the only epistemologically sound mode of economic governance is the market mechanism (Hayek 1948, 1972). But, as recent recognition of the plurality of governance mechanisms implies, one's choice in this regard is not restricted to a rigid dichotomy based on market versus hierarchy. Hayek's arguments on contingent necessity and social complexity and his conclusion as to the inevitability of planning failure do not exclude alternative forms of governance additional to pure market forces. This is not just a matter of abstract logic but is also confirmed by the wide range of at least partially successful governance mechanisms in various institutional contexts.

The general links between contingent necessity, complexity and governance can now be stated. In particular, any attempt to build effective governance mechanisms should include:

- simplifying models and practices which reduce the complexity of the world and which are congruent with real world processes as well as relevant to the objectives of the actors concerned;
- developing the capacity for dynamic social learning about various causal processes and forms of interdependence, attributions of responsibility and capacity for actions, and possibilities of coordination in a complex, turbulent environment;
- building methods for coordinating actions across different social forces with different identities, interests and meaning systems, over different spatio-temporal horizons and over different domains of action; and
- establishing both a common world view for individual action and a system of meta-governance to stabilize key players' orientations, expectations and rules of conduct.

The development of these complex conditions and practices is the only way for example, many would argue, in which economic governance can be secured in a complex, globalizing world. The result would be a heterarchic rather than anarchic or hierarchic system of coordinated decision-making and policy implementation, that is, a system based neither on the incremental logic of market forces nor on long-range top-down planning but on interactive learning among a plurality of operationally autonomous but interdependent agencies.

2. GOVERNANCE AS THE ART OF COMPLEXITY

I now review some basic issues in governing complexity in interpersonal, inter-organizational and inter-systemic relations and link them to the requisite variety, adaptability and learning capacities of governance mechanisms. So-called 'governance' mechanisms (as contrasted to markets or hierarchy) have long been widely used in coordinating complex organizations and systems. This makes it all the more curious that they have only recently prompted focused scientific interest. They are especially appropriate for systems that are resistant to top-down internal management and/or direct external control and that also co-evolve with other (complex) sets of social relations with which their various decisions, operations and aims are reciprocally[6] interdependent. As Scharpf notes:

> . . . the advantages of hierarchical coordination are lost in a world that is characterized by increasingly dense, extended, and rapidly changing patterns of reciprocal interdependence, and by increasingly frequent, but ephemeral, interactions across all types of pre-established boundaries, intra- and inter-organizational, intra- and intersectoral, intra- and international. (Scharpf 1994, p. 37)

Such patterns of reciprocal interdependence across multiple boundaries with their basic resistance to hierarchical coordination are usefully labelled 'heterarchic'. Not only do they resist top-down command, they are also ill-suited, contrary to Hayekian claims, to simple, blind co-evolution (the so-called 'invisible hand') with its mutual, *post hoc* adaptation. Such incrementalism is sub-optimal from a governance viewpoint because it is based on short-run, localized, ad hoc responses which ignore the paradox of autonomy and interdependence characteristic of modern societies. This paradox is especially acute when what is at stake is the governance of relations among functionally differentiated

[6] Reciprocal interdependence refers to situations where an overall outcome depends on the combined choices of all participants from among their interdependent options: when there are many such interdependent organizations, this generates an explosive complexity (Scharpf 1994, p. 36).

subsystems which are stretched out over space and time (Jessop 1990b, Offe 1996, Willke 1987, 1992).

However, before examining functionally differentiated subsystems, I identify three levels of 'embedded' social organization relevant to governance. These are:

- the social embeddedness of interpersonal relations (Granovetter 1985);
- the institutional embeddedness of inter-organizational relations (Keohane and Nye 1977, Grabher 1993, Powell and di Maggio 1991); and
- the 'societal' embeddedness of functionally differentiated institutional orders (especially those that can be interpreted as autopoietic subsystems)[7] in a complex, de-centred societal formation (Polanyi 1957, Luhmann 1984, Glagow and Willke 1987).

Each type of embeddedness is linked to a corresponding type of heterarchy and its associated problems of negative and positive coordination. The latter in turn may be resolved, at least in a provisional and partial manner, in and through different patterns of governance.

Interpersonal interdependence is associated with an acute problem of trust owing to the many-sided 'double contingencies' of social interaction (grounded in the fact that ego's behaviour depends on expectations about alter's conduct and vice versa) where many actors are involved. This problem is reinforced on an inter-organizational level by the difficulties in securing the internal cohesion and adaptability of individual organizations; and in making compatible their respective operational unities and independence with their *de facto* material and social interdependence on other organizations. Finally, inter-systemic heterarchy poses the problem of the material and social interdependence of operationally autonomous (or closed) functional systems, each with its own autopoietic codes, programmes, institutional logics and interests in self-reproduction.

The simplest heterarchic governance mechanisms emerge from the formalization of *interpersonal networking*. Individual actors build on their past familiarity with others in the network, share an imagined community of interests and orientation to the future and use selective memories to reinforce trust (Elchedus 1990, pp. 197–8, Luhmann 1979,

[7] Autopoiesis is a condition of radical autonomy secured through self-organization. It emerges when a system defines its own boundaries relative to its environment, develops its own operational code, implements its own programmes, reproduces its own elements in a closed circuit and obeys its own laws of motion.

pp. 16–19). These individuals represent themselves and/or their functional systems but are not mandated to commit specific agencies or organizations.

More complex is heterarchic governance through *inter-organizational negotiation* systems. The most general case for a shift from government hierarchy and pure market exchange in this regard can be made in terms of the evolutionary advantage[8] of the self-organizing logic of inter-organizational relations where a plurality of interdependent but autonomous organizations, each controlling important resources, need to coordinate their actions to produce a joint outcome which is deemed mutually beneficial. Thus Mayntz suggests that the typical logic of networks is *negotiation* directed towards the realization of a joint product, such as 'a specific technical innovation, a city plan, a strategy of collective action, or a problem solution in public policy' (Mayntz 1993, p. 11). In this way common short-term objectives can be identified and their self-interested realization used to promote generalized compliance with inter-organizational expectations and rules (Marin 1990, p. 15, Scharpf 1994). Crucial to the success of such arrangements is the building of inter-organizational capacities that synergetically reinforce those of individual organizational members. These arguments can be illustrated from the emergence and dynamics of the so-called 'negotiated economy' (see Section 5 below Nielsen and Pedersen 1988, 1993).

The most complex form of governance emerges in attempts to facilitate the mutual understanding and co-evolution of different functional systems whose structural coupling and strategic coordination affect the attainment of societal objectives. There are two key mechanisms here:

- *noise reduction*, that is, reducing 'noise' in inter-systemic communication by enhancing mutual sensitivity to the autonomous logics or rationales of complex autonomous systems and thereby promoting mutual understanding; and
- *negative coordination*, that is, encouraging agents/agencies to take account of the possible adverse repercussions of their own actions on third parties or other systems and to exercise self-restraint as appropriate.

Together these mechanisms may help to realize an inter-systemic consensus around visions or missions which provide, within a more general framework of 'decentralized context steering', a basis for more specific

[8] This advantage should be understood in Schumpeterian terms: the capacity to innovate and learn in a changing environment.

inter-organizational partnerships oriented to the *positive coordination*[9] of relevant activities around specific objectives. These arguments can be illustrated from work on national systems of innovation (Lundvall 1992, Nelson 1993).

All three levels of governance have their own particular preconditions, which cannot be discussed here (but see e.g. Luhmann 1979, Gambetta 1988, Granovetter 1990, 1992, Marin 1990, Messner 1994, Scharpf 1994). They also display *tangled hierarchies* in so far as lower levels are constrained by higher levels yet simultaneously help to shape the latter. Different forms of governance can be mutually supportive in coping with reciprocal interdependence and together they can help in the governing of complexity. Thus interpersonal trust often helps to maintain markets and hierarchies (Granovetter 1985). It may also ease inter-organizational negotiation and/or help build less personalized, more 'generalized trust' as collective actors are seen to sacrifice short-term interests and reject opportunism (Luhmann 1979, pp. 20–22, Marin 1990). In turn, inter-organizational dialogue eases inter-systemic communication and thereby permits 'systemic trust' (in the integrity of other systems' codes and operations) by promoting mutual understanding and stabilizing expectations as the basis of self-binding actions in the future. In negotiated economies, for example, a few formal organizations and forums are entrusted to formulate and represent the identities and interests of different subsystems at the same time as they contribute to the definition and promotion of a wider 'societal project'.

3. MODALITIES AND OBJECTS OF GOVERNANCE

Much of the literature on governance assumes that the objects of governance pre-exist their coordination in and through specific governance mechanisms. However, as the preceding remarks indicate, at the very least attempts at governance affect the conduct of agents and their conditions of action. In many cases governance mechanisms are also actively involved in constituting governing agents, identities, interests and strategies. Hence some governance theorists now argue that 'objects of governance are only known through attempts to govern them' (Hunt and Wickham 1994, p. 78).[10] In other words, the very processes of

[9] Positive coordination involves multilateral exploration and concerted strategic action towards a joint goal (Scharpf 1994, pp. 38–9, 48).

[10] For example, Campbell et al., in their work on sectoral governance, note that 'sectors are socially constructed through self-organization and/or through public policy so they can be effectively administered' (1991, p. 9).

governance co-constitute the objects which come to be governed in and through these same processes. Thus, while its objects may indeed pre-exist governance attempts as potential 'raw material', they only become real objects of governance to the extent that they are subject to specific, more or less effective governance mechanisms. Pertinent examples include: Porterian industrial 'clusters'; flexible industrial districts; cross-border regions; and 'negotiated economies'. Such phenomena cannot be adequately understood without reference to their co-constitution through forms of governance which conform neither to pure market or pure hierarchy. In this sense, then, governance reduces the unstructured complexity of the 'raw material' (or elements) of governance and adds to structured complexity (by transforming these elements into 'moments' of the governed object). But the emergence of conflicting attempts at governance and/or of uncoordinated governance mechanisms produces in turn new forms of unstructured complexity. The latter could well become constituted as a 'problem' for attempts at higher order governance (or meta-governance); and so on in an endless spiral of governance/meta-governance strategies. There is no point at which any final instance of meta-governance can be established to coordinate myriad subordinate forms of governance – this would reintroduce the principle of hierarchy which social complexity itself rules out.

One implication is that, to paraphrase Marx, just as there is neither production in general nor general production, there is no governance in general nor general governance. Rather, there is only particular governance and the totality of governance (Marx 1857, p. 99, Jessop 1990a, p. 186). There are only definite objects of governance that are shaped in and through definite modes of governance. It is important to note that this excludes any general theory which would apply to all forms of governance. Hence one should focus instead on the many and varied struggles over the constitution of governance objects, competing strategies and techniques of governance, and the contingently necessary incompleteness or failures of attempts to govern them. It is the failure fully to govern (and so stabilize) potential objects of governance that creates in turn space for competing governance strategies and ensures that the future remains pregnant with a surplus of possibilities.

A strategic-relational approach implies that governance is inherently spatio-temporal. This goes beyond the trite conclusion that, since time and space inevitably serve as external conditions and contexts of action, actions may need to be collocated and/or dislocated at particular points in time-space as well as coordinated over time and space to realize interdependent projects. For it is also important to recognize that time and space *qua* social relations are also key objects and stakes in the organization of governance. In short, governance constitutes its objects in spatio-temporal as well as other respects. The temporal and spatial are not separable here. The choice of time horizon will in part dictate the appropriate spatial scale at which governance is organized. In turn, the choice of spatial scale will in part determine the time horizon over which the object of governance will be constructed and governance objects pursued.

By way of illustration, the discursive constitution of the boundaries and nature of the (local) economy affects the temporal dimension of strategy-making as well as its spatial scale. This is quite explicit in many economic strategy documents – with powerful players seeking to shape both the spatial and temporal horizons to which economic and political decisions are oriented so that the economic and political benefits are 'optimized' (on the case of the East Thames Corridor in Britain, see e.g. Jessop (1996b)). The match between spatial scale and time horizon may be a crucial factor shaping the success or failure of local economic development strategies associated with urban regimes. Stable modes of local economic growth typically involve building a structured complementarity (or coherence) between the local economy and one or more of its encompassing regional, national and supranational accumulation regimes. This structured complementarity can only be secured in time and space. Since capitalism is always marked by uneven development and tendencies towards polarization, the success of some economic spaces (and the success of the spaces whose growth dynamic is complemented by their own) will inevitably be associated with the marginalization of other economic spaces. This is seen in the changing hierarchy of economic spaces as capitalist growth dynamics are affected by the relative exhaustion of some accumulation strategies and modes of growth and/or the dynamic potential of innovations in materials, processes, products, organization or markets. None the less, when space and time horizons are articulated more or less successfully, economic development will occur within relatively stable 'time-space envelopes' (Massey 1994, p. 225, Sum 1996, and – on time-space embeddedness – Sum in this volume).

All of this has major implications for the dynamic of governance mechanisms and their capacities to address challenges. For, in strategic-relational terms, social practices, organizations, institutions and systems typically have specific structurally inscribed temporal and spatial forms and are oriented to distinctive spatial and temporal horizons of action. Thus specific forms of economic and political system privilege some strategies over others, access by some forces over others, some interests over others, some spatial scales of action over others, some time horizons over others, some coalition possibilities over others. Structural constraints always operate selectively: they are not absolute and unconditional but are always temporally, spatially, agency- and strategy-specific. Strategies can be oriented in turn to the transformation of these structurally inscribed (or socially embedded) spatio-temporal selectivities. This also suggests that successful governance may depend on the self-reflexive monitoring and transformation of how these (and other) selectivities impinge on embedded social practices and socially stabilized expectations.

Thus governance mechanisms must provide a framework in which relevant actors can reach agreement over (*albeit possibly differential*) spatial and temporal horizons of action *vis-à-vis* their environment. They must also stabilize the cognitive and normative expectations of these actors by shaping and promoting a common 'world view' as well as developing adequate solutions to sequencing problems, that is, predictably ordering various actions, policies, or processes over time, especially where they have different temporal logics.[11] At stake here is establishing secure bases of coordination with their own structurally inscribed strategic selectivity. This does not exclude (and indeed may well require) a certain ambivalence and real flexibility in governance mechanisms so that an adequate repertoire (requisite variety) of governance routines exists to ensure continued vitality in the face of a turbulent environment through the ability to alter strategies and select those that are successful (Grabher 1994, Willke 1992).

Strategic selectivities frame more specific governance strategies insofar as they privilege some strategies and hinder others. Hence, from a more self-reflexive (or meta-governance) perspective, there are also strategic choices about redrawing borders, altering spatio-temporal horizons and re-ordering temporalities. These choices may be linked to changes in time-space distantiation (the stretching out of governance capacities and horizons of action over space and the binding of 'future presents' into the present through path-shaping activities);[12] and/or to changes in time-space compression (the conquest of space by time and/or the domestication of time through enhanced capacities to discriminate events and so react appropriately within a given time period). Meta-strategies intended to entrench or modify strategic selectivities are analogous to a Gramscian 'war of position'. They allow those in

[11] A good example comes from the speed and sequencing of reforms in and across different social domains in post-communist transition (Hausner et al. 1995).

[12] Time-space distantiation can also anchor present action to the past through the 'politics of memory' and/or organizational techniques such as files, records, etc. (Giddens 1985).

privileged positions to capitalize on acquired advantages, plan ahead and win a certain independence in the face of a turbulent environment (on redundancy see e.g. de Certeau (1985, pp. 36–7), Grabher (1994)).

Metaphorically, in a war of position, space is used to govern time. De Certeau contrasts this strategy (which he equates with strategy in general) with the concept of 'tactics'.[13] This is pursued from outside entrenched positions, resorts to time to disrupt established structures of domination, and is especially effective in crises. For, as Debray notes, 'political time moves faster in periods of crisis . . . In every decisive crisis there is an inevitable hiatus between the need to make a decision and the available information on which to base it rationally' (Debray 1971, pp. 90, 107). Crises are also key moments of temporal compression, that is, decisive moments when much is undecided and when decisive actions can therefore have unusually wide-ranging effects on future developments (Debray 1971). Crises make it harder to govern and this enables forces of resistance to intensify the disorder, turbulence and noise which is always already present in complexity. In de Certeau's useful scheme, 'strategies pin their hopes on the resistance that the *establishment of a place* offers to the erosion of time; tactics on a clever *utilization of time*, of the opportunities it presents and also of the play that it introduces into the foundations of power . . . the two ways of acting can be distinguished according to whether they bet on place or on time' (de Certeau 1985, pp. 38–9, original emphasis). In short, structures do not exist outside of specific spatial and temporal horizons of action pursued by specific actors acting alone or together and in the face of opposition from others. Likewise, actors always act in specific action contexts which depend on the coupling between specific institutional materialities and the interaction of other social actors.

Strategic analysis can be taken further yet if we allow for self-reflection on the part of individual and collective actors about the identities and interests which orient their strategies. Individuals and organizations can be reflexive, can reformulate within limits their own identities, and can engage in strategic calculation regarding the 'objective' interests which flow from these identities in particular conjunctures. A further step in strategic-relational analysis (and sometimes in strategic self-reflection) occurs when one examines (and actors build) the capacity to switch among different modes of governance. Since any particular mode of policy-making, coordination or crisis-resolution contains its

[13] In this regard de Certeau's view is dualist in so far as it mechanically opposes strategy and tactics; Gramsci develops a dialectical approach to war of position and war of manoeuvre whereby a counter-hegemonic war of position can prepare the ground for revolutionary, military-political maneouvres (Gramsci 1971).

own distinctive dilemmas, contradictions and weaknesses, the capacity to switch among them facilitates more effective responses to internal and/or external turbulence (Offe 1975). This requisite variety (with its informational, structural and functional redundancies) plays an important role in the adaptability of intra- and inter-organizational networks (Grabher 1994).

On an inter-systemic level, requisite variety can be secured through the separation of different institutional orders so that it becomes possible to displace the dominant and/or hegemonic role across systems in response to different problems, challenges, or crises. It has often been noted that institutional separation of the economic and political orders in capitalist societies permits more flexibility in crisis-management than does their fusion in state socialism (Kaminski 1991).[14] For this separation offers more possibilities both for a more effective self-regulation and for crisis-displacement. The latter could amount to nothing more than a purely negative displacement (i.e., buck-passing); but it could involve using the resources generated by one complex system to solve problems confronting another (e.g., transforming legal institutions or educational systems in response to institutional changes in the market economy). The latter response may well be explicitly pursued in the case of decentralized context-steering. For noise reduction, negative coordination and joint problem-solving based on horizontal as well as vertical subsidiarity[15] principles are well suited to the flexible control of inter-systemic resources (see below).

4. GUIDANCE AS HETERARCHIC GOVERNANCE

A generic mechanism serving these strategically self-reflexive purposes in both inter-organizational and inter-systemic contexts can be identified in *decentralized, cooperative context-steering* which is oriented to producing controlled structural change. This is often described simply as 'guidance' and will be so labelled below. From a strategic-relational viewpoint, such guidance involves both (a) modifying the structurally inscribed strategic selectivities of different levels of socially embedded,

[14] State-socialist fusion of economic and political systems tends to lead to more authoritarian and repressive attempts at tension- and crisis-management operating on the symptoms rather than causes of system failure.

[15] Subsidiarity normally refers to the principle of devolving power to the lowest possible level in a hierarchical system compatible with effective solutions to defined problems; here I extend the idea, by analogy, to the principle that as few functional systems as possible should be strategically involved in solving a problem.

socially regularized action; and (b) modifying the self-understanding of identities, strategic capacities and interests of individual and collective actors in different strategic contexts and hence their implications for preferred strategies and tactics. Whereas modifying the former serves to alter pay-offs in different strategic contexts, modifying the latter provides both common orientations and a basis for the self-guidance of relevant actors and subsystems within the limits of their respective operational autonomies. A key aspect to this process is the transformation of cognitive expectations within and across systems by generating new information about reciprocal interdependencies among actors, organizations, institutions and systems. This information can then become the basis for self-transformation and self-regulation on the part of relevant actors in the light of their own codes or selection criteria (Willke 1987, pp. 27–8). In this way guidance can create 'concerted', highly predictable environments and stabilize expectations (Marin 1990, pp. 15–16).

In functionally differentiated societies 'context steering' procedures work on an inter-systemic level by encouraging operationally closed systems to take account – even as they try to maintain their operational autonomy – of their resource dependence on their environment, functional interdependence with other such systems and high levels of contextual interpenetration. This sort of learning and mutual understanding can occur in various ways: for example, through developing convergent internal models of how other systems perceive their environments and operate within them; through self-reflexive calculation and concern about how a system's own operations will ultimately react back on its own future development through their mediated impact on other systems; through debates among representatives of various systems in a 'negotiated economy' type of social dialogue to promote self-reflection and strategically coordinated co-evolution; and so on. An important effect of such mechanisms is the emergence of a broad consensus on the 'secondary coding' of individual system codes (e.g. the political code of 'government/opposition') in terms of how appropriately coded activities contribute to the performance of other systems (e.g. choose among activities that help political agents to win or maintain government office those that also support economically profitable activities). In this sense operationally autonomous systems can operate in a broader consensus about the (discursively constituted) interests of a wider 'imagined' community. Such strategic linkages can arise through single agents (whether persons or organizations) with multiple roles; interpersonal networks; dialogue between organizations; or the interfaces which exist between subsystems, whether boundary roles, boundary structures, bi- or multivalent resources such as taxation, or explicit linking procedures (Luhmann 1977, pp. 67–9, 73–4, Teubner 1989, pp. 78, 104, 119, Jessop 1990b).

Such coordination is most likely to occur where conditions are sufficiently stable and the options sufficiently restricted that reflexive monitoring and dynamic social learning can occur and individual systems can refine their own internal 'forecasting' models about the dynamic of other systems. This does not mean that subsystems must abandon their own distinctive codes or undergo de-differentiation – merely that the individual programmes which they use to specify the operational implications of these codes must be modified at the margins to facilitate continued negative and/or positive coordination of their respective operations. Such reflexive monitoring, dynamic learning and incremental change can be seen in evolutionary terms as sources of variation; relatively stable, non-turbulent environments will facilitate the selection of responses that stabilize governance mechanisms to the extent that joint goals are being achieved and/or non-achievement is attributed to temporary difficulties in those mechanisms or their environment. In all cases, however, what is crucial is the structural mediation of these procedures – the self-reflexive use of self-organization (self-structured system complexity) linking limited sets of actors to reduce unstructured complexity (hence uncertainty) and thereby provide a basis for coordinated action. In this sense the retention (institutionalization, stabilization, regularization) of given governance mechanisms is closely linked to their structurally inscribed strategic selectivities and the strategic capacities of their agents to self-reflexively monitor how specific actions affect interdependent individual and collective goals.

Guidance need not exclude a state role but the latter would incline more towards meta-governance than government. Thus, in their account of sectoral governance in the US economy, Lindberg, Campbell and Hollingsworth note that

> the state ... is capable of influencing governance in many complex ways, most of which are not available to organizations in civil society ... other actors cannot behave like the state because they cannot serve as gatekeepers, allocate resources and information, influence and structure property rights, or affect governance and governance transformations in other ways as does the state. (1991, p. 31)

This argument can be rephrased in terms of the need for a meta-governance instance which 'organizes the self-organization of inter-organizational relations', that is, provides the ground rules for governance, ensures the compatibility of different governance mechanisms and regimes, deploys a relative monopoly of organizational intelligence and information with which to shape cognitive expectations, acts as a 'court of appeal' for disputes arising within and over governance, serves to re-balance power differentials by strengthening weaker parties or systems in the interests of system integration and/or social cohesion, and so on. This emerging meta-governance role means that networking, negotiation, noise reduction, and negative coordination take place 'in the shadow of hierarchy' (Scharpf 1994, p. 40, Hodgson 1988, pp. 220–28). The need for such a role is especially acute in the light of the wide dispersion of governance mechanisms and the corresponding need to build appropriate macro-organizational capacities to address far-reaching inter-organizational changes without undermining the basic coherence and integrity of the (national) state. And this role tends to fall to the state because of its heightened paradoxical position as an institutional subsystem which is simultaneously merely part of a wider, more complex society (and thus unable to control the latter from above) and also a part normatively charged (notably in the last resort) with securing the institutional integration and social cohesion of that society (Offe 1987, Jessop 1990b).

I am not arguing here that such forms of strategic context-steering rest on a simple, unconstrained, democratic consensus on the 'common good' of various reciprocally interdependent subsystems. On the contrary, social forces from different systems often compete to stabilize orientations and expectations through multilateral agreement on their own preferred 'joint project' – with each project simplifying social relations, marginalizing some forces, regions, time horizons and so on in their own system interests. A hegemonic project achieves this by resolving the abstract problem of conflicts between particular interests and the general interest. If successful, it stabilizes networks of social relations linking different social domains in real time and space as well as in 'functional' time and space – networks that serve the reproduction interests of their own particular system as well as those of the (imagined) wider community or totality. The emergence of any hegemonic project is uncertain, however; and, even if present, it never rests on total unanimity or blind obedience. Instead it provides a conception of the common good and a framework within which different forces can cooperate and/or co-exist with a relative degree of harmony. None the less, viable hegemonic projects (and, one might add even more forcefully, accumulation strategies) must have some organic connection with the dominant mode of growth. They cannot simply be 'arbitrary, rationalistic, and willed' but must have some prospects of forming and consolidating a specific historical bloc, that is, some structural correspondence between the mode of economic growth and its modes of regulation and governance (Gramsci 1971, pp. 376–7, Jessop 1996). A key role in this regard is played by political parties (or similar forces) which link governance strategies with a broader, national hegemonic project and/or supply political privileges, resources and policies which help to sustain a continuing commitment to inter-organizational negotiation and coordination.

5. FROM CORPORATISM TO THE 'NEGOTIATED ECONOMY'

Inter-systemic concertation is sometimes recommended in this context but it is subject to real, if paradoxical, limitations. On the one hand, entire subsystems (such as the economy, law, politics, education) can never be real acting subjects with capacities for conscious action. Thus, to avoid blind co-evolution based entirely on *post hoc* structural coupling, inter-systemic concertation must be mediated through subjects who can engage in *ex ante* self-regulatory strategic coordination, monitor the effects of that coordination on goal attainment and modify their strategies as appropriate. On the other hand, such bodies can never fully represent the operational logic (let alone fully comprehend the current conjuncture and future direction) of whole subsystems. Indeed, they could even promote their own private interests in maintaining inter-organizational exchanges (or simply their own survival as organizations) at the expense of effective inter-systemic concertation. In short, whereas the complexities of strategic interdependence among systems do require specific forms of inter-organizational concertation, the latter needs regularizing to limit the risks of self-serving 'privatization' and to guide strategic interaction so that it remains in line with the 'public interest'. This depends in turn on an hegemonic consensus or project which provides the various forces involved with common programmatic objectives despite differing codes, identities and so on.

In the Fordist period, such concertation was often expressed in tripartite forms of corporatism involving business associations, trade unions and the national state. In some Atlantic Fordist economies, corporatism was a well-established and dominant feature of the social mode of economic regulation; in France, it played a secondary role under a strong, dirigiste state; and, in other cases, it had an intermittent role as an ad hoc economic crisis-management mechanism in more market-oriented, liberal economic regimes. In all cases corporatism acquired particular significance (if not notoriety) in economic crisis-management efforts in the 1960s and 1970s. Where successful, corporatism helped to stabilize Fordist societies by supporting already existing macroeconomic measures with incomes, labour market and industrial policies. In this context corporatism was not intended to replace the market economy or liberal parliamentary democracy (as had been the case with earlier waves of corporatist movements reacting against massifying nineteenth century industrialization and urbanization and/or of corporatist practices emerging in response to the interwar crisis of 'organized capitalism' in continental Europe). Instead it was meant to supplement and reinforce market forces and liberal parliamentary democracy by guiding and legitimating new forms of state intervention and private interest government – in part by securing more effective representation for producer interests than would be possible through a generalized pluralism or catch-all electoral parties.

Corporatism did not prove effective always and everywhere, however, in helping to stabilize Fordism even during its heyday, for key organizational conditions for effective corporatism were sometimes weak or missing; and, in addition, Fordist crisis tendencies were sometimes aggravated by other economic and political problems. In general the conditions most often cited as favouring corporatist stability during this period include: strong, centralized industrial unions; strong, centralized employers' unions; and a state which had the necessary capacities to intervene in economic management but still depended on cooperation from its social partners to realize them.

Even where the various conditions for effective corporatist representation and policy implementation did once exist, this model has become less stable and effective as the parameters of Fordist accumulation have been weakened. Of particular note here are the internationalization of economies, changed perceptions of competitiveness (which enhance the salience of supply-side conditions and supply-side concertation with extra-economic agents and systems at the expense of macroeconomic demand management and concerns about redistribution between capital and labour) and the development of new core technologies which increase the pressure for permanent innovation, strategic alliances to share Research and Development costs, and technology transfer for rapid amortization of development costs (Jessop 1993).

Small open economies already faced some of these problems even in the heyday of Fordism and made continuing efforts to resolve them. The Scandinavian economies, for example, tended to combine orthodox corporatism with a so-called 'negotiated economy' model of concertation (Jessop et al. 1993, Nielsen and Pedersen 1993). To some extent this model is misnamed since the negotiated economy model always involved a wide range of extra-economic as well as economic forces. It was not confined to industrial capital, blue-collar workers and the central state but extended to rural and urban petty bourgeois sectors, the local state and functional domains such as health, education, welfare and scientific research. Moreover, under the impact of the above-noted shifts in the mode of growth, there is now even greater emphasis on inter-systemic noise reduction and negative coordination to supplement inter-organizational negotiation and interpersonal networking. In this sense one could say that the 'negotiated economy' operates in certain respects in a meta-governance manner by embedding corporatism in a wider strategic learning context. It provides a framework which encourages social partners to respect the operational codes and procedures of other systems and to engage in self-regulating conduct within their own operational spheres in the interests of a wider social project.

A key aspect of the negotiated economy model is its successful reduction of two types of complexity in constituting the economy as an object of economic *and extra-economic* heterarchic coordination. This is an essential feature of accumulation strategies, which define a specific economic 'growth model' for a given economic space, identify its various extra-economic preconditions and outline a general strategy appropriate to its realization (Jessop 1982). In this sense accumulation strategies are premised on two distinctions: the first is that between a given (imagined) economic space and its external economic environment; the second is that between the economy and its extra-economic environment (polity, education system, law, science system, family system, religious institutions, etc.).

The first distinction involves a 'spatial imaginary'. It rests on the idea that, however complex and unmanageable economic development might be on a global scale, it may prove possible to endogenize and control at least some conditions bearing on a smaller economic space over a reasonable spatio-temporal horizon. At stake here is how the boundaries of the economy are discursively constructed and materially instituted and the extent to which this 'spatial imaginary' corresponds in some significant sense to real economic, juridico-political and social processes. It is worth noting here that each of the Nordic economies was deemed, despite their openness, to have a coherent national production system at its core (Mjøset 1987, 1992). It is this structured coherence which provided the material basis for economic development strategies and these in turn helped to consolidate that material basis.

The second distinction refers to the several means-ends relations involved in attempts to develop economic strategies in the light of the material and social interdependence between the economy and extra-economic systems on various spatial scales. Thus it concerns the range of activities that should be heterarchically coordinated to realize a given economic development strategy. The distinctiveness and significance of the 'negotiated economy' model is particularly noticeable in this regard because the scope of negotiations extended beyond direct producer interests to include individual and collective representatives of other functional systems whose performance was judged relevant to and/or conditional on economic prosperity. This trait has become more marked since the crisis of Atlantic Fordism and its specific manifestations in those Nordic economies which combined a relatively strong base in flexible rather than mass production with a highly developed Fordist Keynesian welfare state at central and local levels. In this sense the Nordic economies now provide useful illustrations of an hypothesized neo-corporatist variant of 'Schumpeterian workfare regimes' oriented to permanent innovation and structural competitiveness and the subordination of social welfare to the demands of labour market flexibility and international competitiveness (Jessop 1993, Jessop et al. 1993, Andersen and Kjaer 1993, Amin and Thomas 1996, Torfing 1994).

In this context we should note that the 'negotiated economy' system has long rested on a distinctive set of strategically selective institutions which ease the strategic coordination of the various functional systems involved in decentralized economic context-steering. For complex forms of communication are required here to promote decentralized context steering. This is possible in so far as there is an 'interdiscursive' space for attempts to colonize or hegemonize different fields of activity by providing moral, intellectual and political leadership. Drawing directly on Nielsen and Pedersen, one could say that this 'interdiscursive' space is secured through a distinctive complex of institutions. They describe this institutional ensemble as comprising:

- policy institutions and fora that identify joint problems and recommend solutions;
- campaign institutions set up by various private and public sector interests to promote particular interpretations of these problems and specific solutions;
- discourse institutions which test the consistency of dominant conceptions and refine them into analytically coherent discourses;
- negotiation institutions, such as round tables, which outline frameworks, develop timetables and concretize agreements; and
- private or semi-public arbitration and sanction institutions which

> are available to resolve disputes and impose sanctions if agreements are broken. Through their interconnection and complementarity, these institutions mould an elite (and to some extent a popular) consensus on how best to reconcile particular interests with an (emergent) hegemonic concept of the 'universal' (national) interest (Nielsen and Pedersen 1993, pp. 100–101, Nielsen and Pedersen 1988).

The 'negotiated economy' supplements market exchange and pluralist democracy through the coordination of the behaviour of autonomous functional forces. It does so through institutionalized inter-organizational negotiations within a wider framework for mobilization of consensus and mutual understanding (noise reduction) and the largely self-binding and self-regulating implementation of resulting policies (Pedersen and Nielsen 1991, Nielsen and Pedersen 1993). Negotiation brings all the major economic and political forces together in serial, iterative and collective dialogues and learning processes. Economic forces exchange autonomy in economic decision-making for political influence; and political forces exchange formal sovereignty in political decision-making for enhanced strategic capacity (Marin 1990). Markets and hierarchies still exist, of course; but both operate in a context of negotiated decision-making. Thus, on the one hand, market competition is balanced by cooperation; the invisible hand is combined with a visible handshake.[16] And, on the other hand, the state is no longer the sovereign authority for meta-governance. It becomes but one participant among others in the pluralistic guidance system and contributes its own distinctive resources to the negotiation process. In this context the exchange of information and moral persuasion are key sources of legitimation and the state's influence depends as much on its role as a prime source and mediator of collective intelligence as on its command over economic resources or legitimate coercion (Willke 1992). It is for these reasons that the negotiated economy can be described as 'a third way, between market economics and central planning, capable of combining innovation and flexibility with social democracy and collective consensus' (Thomas and Amin 1996, Amin and Thomas 1996).

[16] I owe this metaphor to Klaus Nielsen (personal communication).

6. THOUGHTS ON GOVERNANCE FAILURE

The growing fascination (bordering on obsession) with governance mechanisms as a solution to market and/or state failure should not lead us to overlook the risks of governing complexity and the likelihood of governance failure. Given contingent necessity, social complexity, structural contradictions,[17] strategic dilemmas,[18] and multiple or, at least ambivalent, goals, failure is a contingently necessary outcome of attempts at governance (on the sociology of failure, see Malpas and Wickham (1995)). What is necessarily contingent about governance attempts are their modalities, sites, forms, temporalities, spatialities, effects and capacities for recuperating or responding to failure. On the last point indeed, Offe notes that, since each and every mode of state policy-making is prone to failure, one must either accept that a stable state apparatus is impossible or that it is possible only to the extent that it has the capacity to flexibly shift modes of policy-making as the failures and contradictions of the dominant mode (or the prevailing policy-making mix) become more evident and threaten the state's rationality and legitimacy. He concludes that the state's long-run survival depends on specific organizational qualities of the state, including what I have elsewhere termed the articulation of government and governance. This is a powerful argument and can be generalized to other forms of (self-reflexive) coordination besides the national state.

For any attempt spatio-temporally to isolate a set of social relations from the complex and continuous web of causal connections and constitute them as an object of governance is inherently fragile and bound to produce unintended consequences. These will be harder to deal with and learn from, the more the environment is turbulent and/or the system more complex. For, although most actors routinely monitor the effects of their actions, turbulence and complexity obviously limit their ability to engage in strategic (including organizational) learning. At the same time different kinds of 'raw material' will be more susceptible to some kinds of governance mechanism than others (for the case of governance of different industrial sectors associated with different long waves of economic expansion, see Kitschelt (1991)).

17 A structural contradiction exists when a system is so constituted that its organization or operation tends to produce antagonistic relations or opposed tendencies (e.g. capital versus labour, socialization of forces of production versus private appropriation of profit).

18 A strategic dilemma (trilemma, etc.) exists when agents are faced with choices such that any action undermines key conditions of their existence and/or their capacities to realize some overall interest (e.g. treating labour power as a cost of production or source of demand).

Governance is not always more efficient than markets or states in resolving problems of economic and/or political coordination. Much depends on the strategic capacities to sustain exchange, negotiation, hierarchy or solidarity as well as the specific nature of the coordination problems. Thus, whilst increasing functional differentiation makes hierarchical coordination increasingly problematic, it does not follow that the structural and strategic conditions for effective governance are sufficiently developed to outperform continued reliance on hierarchy or neo-liberal preferences for marketized solutions. We must examine the self-reflexive, self-diagnosing and self-modifying capacities of governing agents and their institutional capacities to redesign themselves in response to failures. Indeed, second best solutions may be more effective and stable when the costs of best solutions are high.

Heterarchic governance mechanisms are prey to strategic dilemmas which may contribute towards failure. I will briefly comment on some of these.

Cooperation versus competition It is a commonplace that capitalist economies operate through an unstable and mutually implicated balance of cooperation and competition (Piore and Sabel 1985, Hirst and Zeitlin 1991). This poses a series of dilemmas for heterarchic governance. One horn of such dilemmas concerns how to maintain interpersonal trust, secure generalized compliance with negotiated understandings, reduce noise through open communication and engage in negative coordination in the face of the many and varied opportunities such practices create for short-term self-interested competitive behaviour which could soon destroy the governance relationship. The other horn of the dilemma is that an excessive commitment to cooperation and consensus could block the emergence of creative tensions, conflicts or efforts at crisis-resolution which could promote learning and/or learning capacities and thereby enhance adaptability (Messner 1994, pp. 589–93). This second dilemmatic horn is especially acute when the environment is turbulent, speedy action is required, incrementalism is inappropriate and consensus would take time to build (and perhaps be irrelevant when it does emerge). Such dilemmas have been extensively discussed in recent economic analysis of flexible industrial districts, learning regions, innovative milieux and so on. They also affect the political system in the form of the trade-off between partnership and partisanship (with multiple partnerships being linked with differential advantages for political parties, tiers of government or departmental interests).

Openness versus closure Heterarchic governance mechanisms operate in complex, tendentially turbulent, environments. They face problems in remaining open to the environment at the same time as securing the closure needed for effective coordination among a limited number of partners. One dilemma here is that closure may lock in members whose exit would be beneficial (e.g., inefficient firms, underemployed workers, sunset sectors) or block recruitment of new social partners (e.g., new firms, marginalized workers, sunrise sectors); or conversely, that openness may discourage long-term commitments and acceptance of long-term collective time horizons and encourage short-term opportunism in the (potentially self-fulfilling) case where partnerships dissolve or involve high turnover. This dilemma can be seen in networking, negotiation, noise reduction and negative coordination. It is reflected in the choice of maximizing the range of possible actions by expanding relevant bases of membership or favouring the 'small is beautiful' principle for the purpose of focused and timely action; the choice of variable geometries of action versus fixed spatial boundaries for membership of a governance arrangement (an interesting variant of this occurs in the form of the transnationalization versus sovereignty dilemma).

Governability versus flexibility Heterarchic governance mechanisms are neither market-mediated nor hierarchically organized and can be described in terms of the 'self-organization of inter-organizational relations'. One argument for the 'visible handshake' of heterarchy over the 'invisible hand' of the market and the 'visible hand' (if not 'iron fist') of the state is that it can provide longer-term strategic guidance (lacking in markets) whilst retaining flexibility (lacking in bureaucratic organizations with their rule-governed procedures). This poses dilemmas of governability (capacity for guidance) versus flexibility (capacity to adapt to changed circumstances). This is reflected in the problematic balance between simplification as a precondition for governing a complex world and recognizing complexity as a precondition for mobilizing the 'requisite variety' of actors and resources; between avoiding duplication of efforts to limit resource costs or maintaining an adequate repertoire of actions and organizational capacities; between exploiting past organizational and inter-organizational learning by standardizing around 'best practice' or maintaining adaptability in the face of a turbulent environment by avoiding 'lock-in' to outmoded routines. This last problem is particularly associated with efforts to impose 'best practice' from above rather than encourage diversity and allow for horizontal communication and learning among partnerships.

Accountability versus efficiency Some public-private partnerships are expected to serve the public interest as well as deliver private benefits but in attempting to do so they blur the public-private distinction. This poses a familiar dilemma in terms of accountability versus efficiency. Not only are there problems about attributing responsibility in interdependent networks (especially where these are inter-organizational rather than interpersonal) but public-private arrangements run the risk of privatizing politics and/or promoting the statization of the private sphere. This refers to the risk of transforming the public sphere into a domain for the exploitative capture of public resources for private purposes and/or the inverse risk of extending the reach of the state into the market economy and civil society to serve the interests of the state or governing party. A related problem is shrinkage or expansion of the public sphere: this concerns the extent to which information about inter-organizational heterarchies and their operations are governed by issues of confidentiality, including commercial sensitivity, as opposed to becoming a means to open up private activities with public externalities to public scrutiny on behalf of, if not directly by, other stakeholders. Linked to this is the relative primacy of economic performance and social inclusion – how far the maximand in public-private partnerships is marketized economic performance as opposed to addressing problems of social cohesion.

This discussion of several (by no means exhaustive) dilemmas of governance has illustrated them by referring to the complex articulation of the economic and political in capitalist democracies. This is only partly a presentational strategem. It also reflects an important point that is often overlooked in general discussions of governance: that governance mechanisms cannot end the structural contradictions and strategic dilemmas of capitalism. However it is governed, capitalism involves the self-valorization of capital based on the exploitation of labour-power as well as the transformation of nature. What is more, as extra-economic functional domains tend to become more relevant to the dynamic of capital accumulation (reflected in ideas such as structural competitiveness), these too tend to be subsumed under (or subordinated to) the logic of accumulation and this spreads its contradictions, dilemmas and forms of competition into other domains. In this sense the rise of governance may serve to extend and intensify capitalist competition rather than substitute non-capitalist principles for those of the market.[19] This is a major limitation to claims that heterarchic governance can tame the anarchy of the market and render planning apparatuses more accountable. For capitalism has always depended on a contradictory balance between the value-form and non-value forms of organization of the capital relation. Although this was previously understood primarily in terms of market versus hierarchy (rooted in the institutional separation and resulting operational autonomy of economics and politics), the rise of governance has not introduced a neutral third term into this conflict but added another site where this conflict can take place. For new forms of governance provide a new meeting ground (as did tripartism before) for the logics of accumulation and political mobilization. They also introduce new forms of logic related to other functional subsystems (such as education, science and health), and intensify the problems of inter-organizational negotiation, noise reduction and negative coordination. The consequences of this are still being worked out as governance mechanisms undergo their own evolution.

7. CONCLUSION

This chapter has ranged over many issues from abstract aspects of contingent necessity and complexity to quite specific (albeit illustrative) dilemmas in heterarchic governance mechanisms. No firm empirical evidence has been given for any of the arguments above and their plausibility here depends primarily on their consistency with well-established analyses by evolutionary political economists of the negotiated economy (for a recent critique and response, see respectively, Christiansen (1994), Andersen et al. (1996)). Other supporting evidence could have been drawn from the governance of complexity in national innovation systems (Lundvall 1992, Nelson 1993, Bowander and Miyake 1992); from recent work on the fifth generation computer project in Japan or its European equivalent in EUREKA (Willke 1988); and from work on local economic governance (Amin and Thrift 1995, Harvey 1989, Mayer 1994, Peck and Tickell 1994). But it remains the case that these ideas are better (and certainly more prudently) described as items

[19] This could occur in at least three ways: the ecological dominance of the capitalist economy in the structural coupling of different systems, an acknowledged primacy of the economy in (negative and/or positive) strategic coordination, or the secondary coding of autonomous institutional logics through economic values. Such secondary coding leads to questions such as whether it is profitable or unprofitable to apply the distinctions characteristic of other systems: e.g. legal-illegal, true-false, sacred-secular.

for an emerging research agenda on the governance of complexity and the complexity of governance. It is in this spirit that I offer four rather simple conclusions with rather complex implications.

First, contingent necessity and complexity are inevitable features of the real world and face any agent with problems of how to reduce and structure that complexity. This is partly a question of cognition and partly a question of self-organization. To repeat an earlier argument, it involves:

- simplifying models and practices which reduce the complexity of the world and which are congruent with real world processes as well as relevant to the objectives of the actors concerned;
- developing the capacity for dynamic social learning about various causal processes and forms of interdependence, attributions of responsibility and capacity for actions, and possibilities of coordination in a complex, turbulent environment;
- building methods for coordinating actions across different social forces with different identities, interests and meaning systems, over different spatio-temporal horizons and over different domains of action; and
- establishing both a common world view for individual action and a system of meta-governance to stabilize key players' orientations, expectations and rules of conduct.

Second, self-organization and its resulting operational autonomy cannot eliminate social, material and spatio-temporal interdependence with the environment and its ecology of systems. It is the management of reciprocal interdependence that provides the basis for attempts at governance, that is, the heterarchic coordination of operationally autonomous systems. Attempts to establish any particular institutional logic as the dominant principle of societalization (axial principle of social organization, principal source of secondary coding of individual system codes) are conditioned by functional linkages between different systems which work 'behind the backs' of those involved as well as by capacities for strategic coordination. Thus the role of governance mechanisms in securing the subordination of other institutional orders or functional subsystems to capital accumulation is necessarily constrained by the contradictory logic and strategic dilemmas with which the capital relation is associated. Crisis plays a key role in guiding this process but does so by providing turbulence (noise) which must then be interpreted in ways favourable to the reimposition of the logic of capital rather than that of some other institutional order. It is in this context that particular attention must be paid to the strategic selectivity of different governance/meta-governance mechanisms.

Third, although there is no master-subject able to govern the intersection of all possible governance arrangements (if there were, this would reduce contingent to necessary necessity), there is scope for meta-governance attempts to conform and coordinate several sites and objects of governance. The strategic-relational approach adopted here implies that the very processes of governance help to constitute the objects which come to be governed: these objects do not fully pre-exist the process of governance. This highlights the need to study struggles over the constitution of such objects, the necessary failures or incompleteness of their governmentalization and the conditions in which, against all odds, the improbable occurs and attempts at governance succeed (Malpas and Wickham 1995). This improbability is none the less evident in the fact that successful governance is always provisional, localized and partial and always has unintended consequences which operate to the detriment of other subjects, interests and projects and may eventually prove counterproductive even for those who instituted the governance mechanisms and projects in question.

Finally, whilst Hayek is wrong to suggest that the free market based on the price mechanism provides the best long-run solution to many problems of governance (subject to the meta-governance of the market through a liberal constitutional order), there is still a rational kernel to his argument. Since there can be no master meta-governance subject, the evolution of governance mechanisms is subject to an invisible hand. Certain governance mechanisms which emerge from chance discovery or random variation will prove more adaptable than others. But the incompleteness of governance and turbulence in the environment means that no single governance mechanism can be perfectly adapted to its environment. It follows that a plurality of governance mechanisms is needed to ensure requisite variety and flexibility in managing the manifold forms of unstructured complexity. Such plurality cannot be guaranteed from above but depends on the scope for initiative from below.

REFERENCES

Amin, A. and Thomas, D. (1996) 'The Negotiated Economy: State and Civic Institutions in Denmark'. *Economy and Society* 25 (2): 255–81.

Amin, A. and Thrift, N. (1995) 'Globalisation, Institutional "Thickness" and

the Local Economy' in P. Healey et al. (eds) *Managing Cities: The New Urban Context.* London: Wiley.
Andersen, N.A. and Kjaer, P. (1993) 'Private Industrial Policy in the Danish Negotiated Economy' in J. Hausner, B. Jessop and K. Nielsen (eds) *Institutional Frameworks of Market Economies.* Aldershot: Avebury, pp. 195–214.
Andersen, N.A., Kjaer, P. and Pedersen, O.K. (1996) 'On the Critique of Negotiated Economy'. *Scandinavian Political Studies* 19 (2): 167–78.
Bowonder, B. and Miyake, T. (1992) 'Japanese Technological Innovation Strategy: Recent Trends'. *Technology Analysis and Strategic Management* 4 (1): 51–70.
Boyer, R. (1990) *The Regulation School: A Critical Introduction.* New York: Columbia University Press.
Campbell, J., and Lindberg, L.N. (1991) 'The Evolution of Governance Regimes' in J. Campbell, J.R. Hollingsworth and L.N. Lindberg (eds) *Governance of the American Economy.* Cambridge: Cambridge University Press, pp. 319–55.
Castells, M. (1989) *The Informational City: Economic Restructuring and Urban Development.* Oxford: Blackwell.
Chesnais, F. (1987) 'Science, Technology and Competitiveness'. *STI Review* 1: 85–129.
Christiansen, P. (1994) 'A Negotiated Economy? Public Regulation of the Manufacturing Sector in Denmark'. *Scandinavian Political Studies* 17 (4): 305–19
Debray, R. (1971) 'Time and Politics' in R. Debray *Prison Writings.* London: Allen Lane, pp. 87–160.
de Certeau, M. (1985) *The Practice of Everyday Life.* Berkeley: University of California Press.
Elchedus, M. (1990) 'The Temporalities of Exchange: The Case of Self-Organization for Societal Guidance' in B. Marin (ed.) *Generalized Political Exchange: Antagonistic Cooperation and Integrated Policy Circuits.* Boulder: Westview, pp. 192–16.
Foucault, M. (1975) *Discipline and Punish.* Harmondsworth: Penguin.
Gambetta, D. (ed.) (1988) *Trust: Making and Breaking Cooperative Relations.* Oxford: Blackwell.
Giddens, A. (1985) *The Nation-State and Violence.* Cambridge: Polity.
Glagow, M. and Willke, H. (eds) (1987) *Dezentrale Gesellschaftssteuerung: Probleme der Integratin polyzentristischer Gesellschaft.* Pfaffenweiler: Centaurus-Verlagsgesellschaft.
Grabher, G. (ed.) (1993) *The Embedded Firm: On the Socioeconomics of Industrial Networks.* London: Routledge.
Grabher, G. (1994) *Lob der Verschwendung. Redundanz in der Regionalentwicklung: ein socioökonomisches Plädoyer* Berlin: Edition Sigma.
Gramsci, A. (1971) *Selections from Prison Notebooks.* London: Lawrence and Wishart.
Granovetter, M. (1985) 'Economic Action and Social Structure: The Problem of Embeddedness'. *American Journal of Sociology* 91 (3): 481–510.
Granovetter, M. (1992) 'The Old and the New Economic Sociology' in R. Friedland and A.F. Robertson (eds) *Beyond the Marketplace: Rethinking Economy and Society.* New York: Aldine de Gruyter, pp. 89–112.
Harvey, D. (1989) 'From Managerialism to Entrepreneurialism: The Transformation in Urban Governance in Late Capitalism'. *Geografisker Annaler* Series B (Human Geography) 71: 3–17.

Hausner, J., Jessop, B. and Nielsen, K. (1995) 'Institutional Change in Post-Socialism' in J. Hausner, B. Jessop and K. Nielsen (eds) *Strategic Choice and Path-Dependency in Post-Socialism.* Aldershot: Edward Elgar, pp. 3–45.

Hayek, F.A. (1948) *Individualism and Economic Order.* Chicago: University of Chicago Press.

Hayek, F.A. (1972) 'The Theory of Complex Phenomena' in F. Hayek *Studies in Philosophy, Politics and Economics.* London: Routledge and Kegan Paul.

Hirst, P.Q. and Zeitlin, J. (1991) 'Flexible Specialisation vs. Post-Fordism: Theory, Evidence and Policy Implications'. *Economy and Society* 20 (1): 1–56.

Hodgson, G. (1988) *Economics and Institutions,* Cambridge: Polity.

Hunt, A. and Wickham, G. (1994) *Foucault and Law: Towards a Sociology of Governance.* London: Pluto Press.

Jessop, B. (1982) *The Capitalist State: Marxist Theories and Methods.* Oxford: Blackwell.

Jessop, B. (1990a) 'Regulation Theories in Retrospect and Prospect'. *Economy and Society* 19 (2): 153–216.

Jessop, B. (1990b) *State Theory: Putting Capitalist States in their Place.* Cambridge: Polity.

Jessop, B. (1993) 'Towards a Schumpeterian Workfare State? Preliminary Remarks on Post-Fordist Political Economy'. *Studies in Political Economy* 40: 7–39.

Jessop, B. (1995) 'Die Zukunft des Nationalstaats: Erosion oder Reorganization? Grundsätzliche Überlegungen zu Westeuropa' in F. Deppe and W. Burkhardt (eds) *Europäische Integration und politische Regulierung – Aspekte, Dimensionen, Perspektiven.* Marburg an der Lahn: FEG Studie 5: 9–48.

Jessop, B. (1996a) 'A Neo-Gramscian Approach to the Regulation of Urban Regimes: Accumulation Strategies, Hegemonic Projects, and Governance' in M. Lauria (ed.) *Reconstructing Urban Regime Theory.* New York: Sage, 51–73.

Jessop, B. (1996b) 'Managing Uneven Development: Government and Governance in the Thames Gateway'. *Lancaster Regionalism Group Working Paper.*

Jessop, B., Nielsen, K., and Pedersen, O.K. (1993) 'Structural Competitiveness and Strategic Capacities: Rethinking the State and International Capital' in S.E. Sjöstrand (ed.) *Institutional Change: Theory and Empirical Findings.* New York: M.E. Sharpe, pp. 227–62.

Kaminski, B. (1991) *The Collapse of State Socialism: The Case of Poland.* Princeton: Princeton University Press.

Keohane, R. and J.S. Nye (1977) *Power and Interdependence: World Politics in Transition.* Boston: Little, Brown & Co.

Kitschelt, H. (1991) 'Industrial Governance Structures, Innovation Strategies, and the Case of Japan: Sectoral or Cross-National Comparative Analysis?'. *International Organization* 45 (4): 453–93.

Lindberg, L.N., Campbell, J.C., and Hollingsworth, R. (1991) 'Economic Governance and the Analysis of Structural Change in the American Economy' in J.L. Campbell, L.N. Lindberg and R. Hollingsworth (eds) *Governance of the US Economy.* Cambridge: Cambridge University Press, pp. 3–34.

Luhmann, N. (1977) 'Politics as a Social System' in N. Luhmann *The Differentiation of Society.* New York: Columbia University Press, pp. 122–65.

Luhmann, N. (1979) *Trust and Power: Two Essays.* Chichester: John Wiley.

Luhmann, N. (1984) *Soziale Systeme. Grundriss einer allgemeinen Theorie.* Frankfurt: Suhrkamp.

Lundvall, B.-A. (ed.) (1992) *National Systems of Innovation: Towards a Theory of Innovation and Interactive Learning.* London: Pinter.

Malpas, J. and Wickham, G. (1995) 'Governance and Failure: On the Limits of Sociology'. *Australian and New Zealand Journal of Sociology* 31 (3): 37–50.

Marin, B. (1990) *Generalized Political Exchange: Antagonistic Cooperation and Integrated Policy Circuits.* Boulder: Westview, pp. 192–216.

Marin, B. (ed.) (1990) *Governance and Generalized Exchange: Self-Organizing Policy Networks.* Boulder: Westview.

Marx, K. (1857) 'Introduction to the Contribution to the Critique of Political Economy' in K. Marx *Grundrisse.* Harmondsworth: Penguin .

Massey, D. (1994) *Space, Place, and Gender.* Cambridge: Polity.

Mayer, M. (1994) 'Post-Fordist City Politics' in A. Amin (ed.) *Post-Fordism – A Reader.* Oxford: Blackwell, pp. 316–37.

Mayntz, R. (1993) 'Modernization and the Logic of Interorganizational Networks' in J. Child, M. Crozier and R. Mayntz (eds) *Societal Change between Market and Organization.* Aldershot: Avebury, pp. 3–18.

Messner, D. (1994) 'Fallstricke und Grenzen der Netzwerksteuerung'. *Prokla* 97: 549–61.

Mjøset, L. (1987) 'Nordic Economic Policies in the 1970s and 1980s'. *International Organization* 41 (3): 403–56.

Mjøset, L. (1992) 'The Nordic Model never Existed, but does it have a Future?'. *Scandinavian Political Studies* 64 (4): 652–71.

Nelson, R. (ed.) (1993) *National Systems of Innovation.* Oxford: Oxford University Press.

Nielsen, K. and Pedersen, O.K. (1988) 'The Negotiated Economy: Ideal and History'. *Scandinavian Political Studies* 11 (2): 79–101.

Nielsen, K. and Pedersen, O.K. (1993) 'The Negotiated Economy: General Features and Theoretical Perspectives' in J. Hausner, B. Jessop, and K. Nielsen (eds) *Institutional Frameworks of Market Economies.* Aldershot: Avebury, pp. 89–112.

Offe, C. (1975) 'The Theory of the Capitalist State and the Problem of Policy Formation' in L.N. Lindberg, R. Alford, C. Crouch and C. Offe (eds) *Stress and Contradiction in Modern Capitalism.* Lexington: D.C. Heath, pp. 125–44.

Offe, C. (1987) 'Die Staatstheorie auf der Suche nach ihrem Gegenstand. Beobachtungen zur aktuelle Diskussion' in T. Ellwein J.J. Hesse, R. Mayntz and F.W. Scharpf (eds) *Jahrbuch zur Staats und Verwaltungsgewissenschaft.* Baden-Baden: Nomos Verlag, pp. 309–20.

Offe, C. (1996) *Modernity and the State: East, West.* Cambridge: Polity.

Peck, J. and Tickell, A. (1994) 'Too Many Partners . . . the Future for Regeneration Partnerships'. *Local Economy* 9 (3): 251–65.

Piore, M. and Sabel, C.F. (1985) *The Second Industrial Divide.* New York: Basic Books.

Poggi, G. (1979) 'Introduction' in N. Luhmann *Trust and Power: Two Essays.* Chichester: John Wiley.

Polanyi, K. (1957) 'The Economy as Instituted Process' in K. Polanyi, C.M. Arensberg and H.W. Pearson (eds) *Trade and Market in the Early Empires. Economies in History and Theory.* New York: Free Press, pp. 243–70.

Porter, M. (1990) *The Competitive Advantage of Nations*. Basingstoke: Macmillan.

Powell, W.W. and di Maggio, P.J. (eds) (1991) *The New Institutionalism in Organizational Analysis*. Chicago: Chicago University Press.

Reich, R. (1991) *The Work of Nations: A Blueprint for the Future*. New York: Simon and Schuster.

Scharpf, F.W. (1994) 'Games Real Actors Could Play: Positive and Negative Coordination in Embedded Negotiations'. *Journal of Theoretical Politics* 6 (1): 27–53.

Sum, N.-L. (1996) 'Modified Human Rights and Unmodified Liberal Feminism: The "Hegemonic Force" of Hilary Clinton in Beijing'. *New Political Economy* 1 (2): 278–82.

Teubner, G. (1989) *Recht als Autopoietisches System*. Frankfurt: Suhrkamp.

Thomas, D. and Amin, A. (1996) ' "Negotiated" Strategies for Economic Renewal in Denmark'. Newcastle upon Tyne: Centre for Urban and Regional Development Studies – Working Paper.

Torfing, J. (1994) 'A Hegemony Approach to Capitalist Regulation'. Paper presented to EAEPE Annual Conference, Copenhagen, 27–9 October.

Willke, H. (1987) 'Observation, Diagnosis, Guidance. A Systems Theoretical View on Intervention' in K. Hurrelmann, F.X. Kaufmann and F. Lösel (eds) *Social Intervention: Potential and Constraints*. Berlin: W. de Gruyter, pp. 21–35.

Willke, H. (1988) 'Staatliche Intervention als Kontextsteuerung. Am Beispiel EUREKA'. *Kritische Vierteljahresschrift für Gesetzgebung und Rechtswissenschaft* 1 (3): 214–29.

Willke, H. (1992) *Ironie des Staates: Grundlinien einer Staatstheorie polyzentrischer Gesellschaft*. Frankfurt: Suhrkamp.

6. The nature of institutional change: managing rival dependencies[1]

Rob van Tulder and Winfried Ruigrok

1. INTRODUCTION

The importance of institutions for the 'competitiveness' of national economies has become widely acknowledged and is receiving increasing attention in the literature on the subject. In this setting Wolfgang Streeck stresses the importance of 'governance regimes' and social institutions as vehicles for economic performance (1992). Michel Albert (1991) has claimed that Rhineland capitalist institutions are an important foundation of the success of the German economy in international competition. Whitley (1992) points to the relevance of specific national 'business systems' and national business 'recipes' as building blocks of national competitiveness. Some of these approaches take governments as an important constituent (Hart 1992), others (Porter 1990) explicitly leave governments out of their analysis. Researchers stress different ingredients of institutions when trying to delineate the key elements of international economic success. Neo-Schumpeterian authors tend to stress the importance of 'national systems of innovation' (Lundvall 1992, Freeman 1988). Others ascribe vital importance to 'trust' in creating (national) prosperity (Fukuyama 1995) or draw attention to 'culture' (Hampden-Turner and Trompenaars 1993).

According to Peter Hall (1986), institutions can be defined as well-established (implicit or explicit) rules, compliance procedures and standard operating practices. If we take this definition seriously, institutions should be considered the result of bargaining processes. Research on institutional change from this perspective will have to identify the actors

[1] This chapter borrows much of its argumentation from a broader study titled *The Logic of International Restructuring* (Ruigrok and Van Tulder 1995). A follow-up study (forthcoming, to be published by Routledge) is to apply the framework presented to the world car industry.

behind institutions – their creation, their continuation and/or their change.

This chapter focuses on bargaining processes at the meso-level of analysis, searching for a synthesis of various networking approaches. Bargaining processes between actors are influenced heavily by the relative positions of dependency of the actors *vis-à-vis* each other. The meso-level approach proposed in this chapter uses a 'dependency scale' as an analytical tool to situate different types of bargaining arenas developed in different advanced industrial systems. By considering the relative dependencies, we can identify fundamental differences between institutions in various industrial systems. These different institutions have not developed in international isolation. This chapter develops a conceptual framework that facilitates the analysis of institutions and which also makes it possible to assess changes in institutions, for instance, due to the (mutual) interpenetration of institutions. The chapter consist of five parts. In Section 2 the level of analysis is defined: the meso-level of 'industrial complexes' grouped around core firms. The problem of how interaction between actors in industrial complexes can be analysed will be considered in Section 3. This section elaborates on the concept of a dependency scale. This dependency scale can then be used to understand the outcome of the various bargaining processes (Section 4). Section 5 looks at the changes resulting from the international interaction of rival bargaining institutions in the most important carriers of rival industrial systems. Finally, the end result of the process of rivalry between national institutions can also be analysed at the supranational level of analysis. The concluding section (6) will speculate on the regional bargaining regime that is developing in Europe, North America and East Asia.

2. THE INDUSTRIAL COMPLEX: THE CENTRAL BUILDING BLOCK IN THE FORMATION OF INSTITUTIONS

Institutions are the result of bargaining processes in society. The bargaining arena in which the most important societal actors get together can be dubbed an *industrial complex*. The industrial complex is a specific type of network.[2] If it contributes to the creation of economic institutions, it should have at least the following characteristics:

[2] In principle, the term 'industrial complex' also pertains to 'service industries'. During the 1980s, services acquired an increasing share of the GNP in the developed economies,

- it is or has become relatively stable, that is, the actors do not meet accidentally;
- the interaction is aimed at the exchange of goods, capital, technology, information, skills and/or people; and
- is aimed at the allocation of values, for instance, at the way in which the interaction should occur (Galtung 1964, 1971, Wallensteen 1973, p. 32). This third element points to the power relations existing between the constituent parties.

All large firms with major production and technology activities aspire to position themselves at the core of supply and distribution networks, as well as at the centre of political and financial networks, in order to play a leading role in the creation of institutions that may ultimately create added value for their business. This does not necessarily mean that the core firm does all this itself. A core firm aspires to be the spider in an industrial web. A core firm is the principal actor as well as the director of the play. In certain types of networks, a core firm may have to give up its role as the sole director, yet it will always remain the leading actor and if possible will try to regain control. A core firm has direct access to domestic and foreign end-markets and/or customers, and owes its relative independence to its financial strength and to its control over a series of core technologies and other strategic competencies particular to an industry or industrial activity. Most importantly, a core firm has an explicit vision of 1) the organization and management of the value chain, including the internal labour process; and 2) the role that external actors (such as banks and governments) should play in facilitating the creation of added value and the (re)structuring of the network.

An illustration of the significance of core firms can be found in the work of Lundvall and others, who, although using a different terminology, documented how large, technologically leading firms through the 1980s were able to impose a global restructuring trajectory upon other firms. These core firms, which Lundvall and his fellow researchers labelled user-producers, not only produced new products and production technologies, but were also among the leading users of these techno-

particularly in the USA, leading to claims of 'servitization' as the new key to creating competitive advantage (Vandermerwe and Rada 1988). In reality, the distinction between industry and services (as between agriculture and industry) is becoming increasingly blurred (Cohen and Zysman 1987). For instance, owing to outsourcing, services such as bookkeeping or catering that were previously defined as 'industrial jobs' have been *redefined* as 'service jobs', without a change in the content of the work (even if the context, i.e., the dependency *vis-à-vis* the core firm, may have changed substantially). Core firms will often be manufacturing firms but may also be independent service providers (e.g., IBM).

logies. This endowed them with greater power and a better bargaining position than other, particularly smaller firms. In this way, these large firms have reduced the prospects for new entrants and have influenced the creation of substitutes (Lundvall 1988, Andersen and Lundvall 1988).

An *industrial complex* can then be defined as *a bargaining configuration organized around a core firm, consisting of (groups of) actors which are directly or indirectly engaged in the production and distribution of a given product.* An industrial complex is made up of *five types of bargaining relationships* between a core firm and its suppliers, workers, dealers, financiers and government(s). The first three bargaining relationships make up a firm's value chain, the last two bargaining relations constitute the most important variables that directly intervene in the functioning of the value chain.

3. BARGAINING AND POWER IN INDUSTRIAL COMPLEXES

A central element in the bargaining process within an industrial complex is the concept of power. According to a traditional US definition, power represents 'the authoritative allocation of norms and values over society' (Parsons 1957). Dahl (1957) defined power as 'actor A's ability to make B do something he would not have done otherwise'. Political scientists have further distinguished between power and influence. 'Influence is applicable to a situation where A affects individual B, without B subordinating his wishes to those of A. . . . That is to say, A has influence over B, and over the making of a decision, but it is B that has the power finally to decide' (Pateman 1979, pp. 69–70).

The question of how to use these concepts in analysing restructuring and corporate strategies is far from evident. According to Williamson and Ouchi, the 'distribution of power within the firms [is] endogenous and determined by the efficiency needs' (1981, pp. 363–4). Although Williamson admits that regulation regimes are sensitive to bargaining processes and relations between business and government, he is not very impressed by the results of the research conducted by political scientists into firm behaviour. In his view, the notion of power 'is often used in ways that are either tautological or confuse power outcomes with efficiency' (1990, p. 8). In spite of this, 'delimiting the uses of power reasoning and establishing when and how the concept of power adds to rather than confuses our understanding of economic organization would be major contributions' (1990, p. 8).

Several authors have argued in favour of introducing the role of power into economic theory. Rothschild (1971) argued that 'economics is a social science', and that 'the economy is guided not only by the search for gain, but also by that for power' (1971, p. 7), and called upon economists to make up this deficiency in economic theory. Mainstream economic theory seems to have made little progress in this respect. In the literature on management, A. Pettigrew (1973, 1992) and J. Pfeffer (1992) have tried to introduce the concept of power into the analysis of organizational behaviour and decision-making.

Obviously, it is often difficult to point out exactly how and why firms exercise power. The act of doing business does not allow business people to talk openly about their strategies of playing off one supplier against another, or of influencing a local government. This lack of reliable information, however, may be circumvented in a similar manner to that achieved by political scientists in analysing 'pure politics'. It is possible, for instance, to measure decisions involving putting certain issues on a firm's agenda or to measure voting behaviour, even if these only show the *outcome* and not necessarily the actual process of exercising power. Likewise, one may interpret the outcome of a bargaining process between a firm and another actor as an indication that power has been exercised, even if we lack detailed information on the very 'whys' and 'hows' of this process. If we define the core firm as actor A and its bargaining partner as actor B, we may assume (even without detailed information on the respective agendas of A and B) that B does not voluntarily manoeuvre itself into a position in which the core firm largely dictates to B what B is to do, that is, into a position in which B depends on A. If a bargaining process between A and B nevertheless *does* create such a position in which B is dependent on A, this can be attributed to A occupying a stronger bargaining position than B. Such an approach implies an *ex post* reconstruction or 'backward engineering' of the initial positions of A and B.

The next step then is to assess the effects of particular deals between two actors on their respective dependence, and to rank these deals on a scale ranging from 'no effect' on either actor's dependence to 'B becoming entirely dependent on A'. One can distinguish three basic positions *vis-à-vis* the core firm: independent, interdependent, dependent (Wallensteen 1974, p. 32). Power, however, may be used two ways: from A to B and from B to A. Thus, even if B is more dependent on A than vice versa, B may still be able to exert some influence on A. Conversely, if B is independent of A, B may still be able to influence A. The relative positions of actors A and B, therefore, are shaped by their respective influence over each other. Figure 6.1 combines these

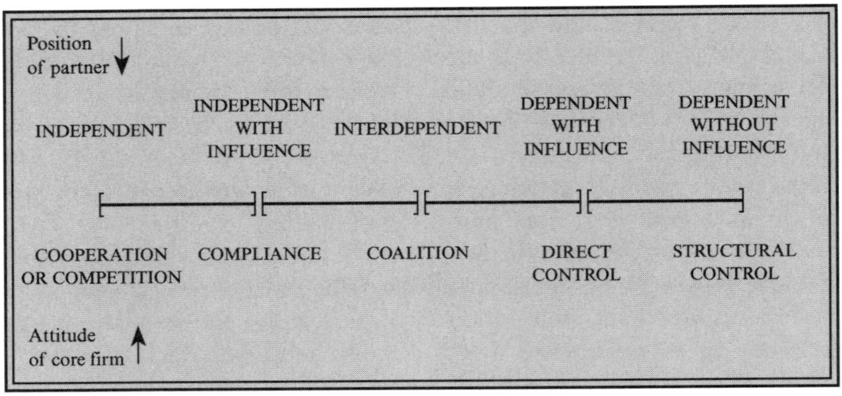

Figure 6.1. A continuum of dependency relations in an industrial complex

two elements in a continuum, which shows the relative bargaining positions of the parties towards each other.

The upper categories in Figure 6.1 refer to the dependency relations in an industrial complex and to B's position in relation to core actor A. The lower categories refer to the attitude or strategy of the core firm. Based on the dimensions of dependency and influence, one can distinguish six basic bargaining attitudes of a core firm *vis-à-vis* the other actors: cooperation or competition; compliance; coalition; direct control; structural control.

The dependency scale shows the relative bargaining position of the two parties at a given instant. Although the scale represents the relative bargaining positions at a particular moment in time, these positions may of course shift over time. Figure 6.2 shows two lines approximating the relative influence of both parties over each other in a qualitative manner. If at a given position one line is further away from the horizontal axis than the other, this should be read as one actor occupying a better bargaining position than the other. The five positions will be briefly discussed below.

- At the extreme left of the scale (*independent*), two actors may choose to interact or not, yet in either case they cannot exert any influence over each other. The distance A–a′ equals the distance A–a″.
- Moving to the right (*independent with influence*), the balance of influence shifts in favour of the partner. This is the only instant

at which the core actor may be driven to act differently than it would have done otherwise, owing to the pressure exerted by the other actor. Thus the distance B–b′ is larger than the distance B–b″.

- In the middle of the scale (*interdependence*), the balance of influence of both partners is restored again. The distance C–c′ again equals the distance C–c″.
- Moving further to the right (*dependent with influence*), the core actor clearly becomes the stronger partner. The line shows that the distance D–d′ is smaller than the distance D–d″. Note, however, that the D position is not simply a reversal of position B. At B, the core actor may have to comply with the other actor's strategies, but it maintains its independence. At D, the partner has arrived at a dependent situation.
- Finally, at the extreme right of the scale (*dependent without influence*), the partner has lost virtually every possibility of

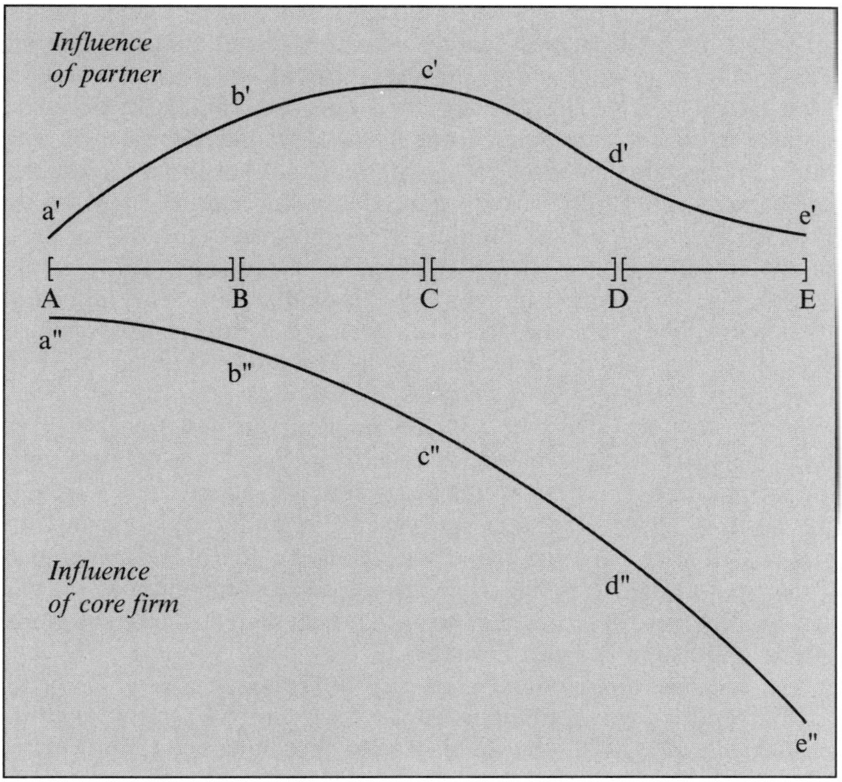

Figure 6.2. Uneven distribution of relative influence

influencing the core actor's behaviour. At this position, the distance E–e′ is infinitely larger than the distance E–e″.

In summary, the upper line of Figure 6.2. depicts what could be seen as an uneven distribution, whereas the lower line shows a progressively downward sloping line. Each position on the dependency scale represents a different mode of conflict management. In case this particular mode of conflict management is reproduced not only between individual actors but also at a societal level, we may consider this an institution.

4. RIVAL INSTITUTIONS: THE HISTORICAL CONSTITUTION OF FIVE DIFFERENT CONCEPTS OF CONTROL

Following the idea of the dependency scale, each of the relationships between the core firm and a bargaining partner can be understood as a dependency relation, representing a control problem for the core firm. The management of each core firm has to decide whether, how and to what extent it is willing and able to control its bargaining partners. Usually, a decision to control one (set of) bargaining partners has direct implications on other bargaining relations. For instance, if many companies decide to limit their dependence on external suppliers by producing essential inputs themselves, this may lead to the 'degradation of work' and to the destruction of crafts (Braverman 1974), while confronting these companies with larger capital requirements (affecting their bargaining relations with financiers) and with organized labour. This is indeed what happened during the rise of *Fordism*: one type of uncertainty was replaced by another. The strength of organized labour exposed the vulnerability of vertically integrated companies to strikes, forcing their top management to enter into direct negotiations with labour unions over higher wages and secondary labour conditions. On the positive side, this mechanism helped to create mass consumption and a customer base for the mass producers. Since the 1930s, this 'productivity-wage' coupling mechanism facilitated the virtuous growth cycles of the Fordist production organization in the USA and with some alterations also in Western Europe.

The dynamics and ultimately the crisis of Fordism can be understood as the result of the continuing efforts to resolve one set of control problems leading to the inevitable rise of another set of control problems. In the medium run, capitalist production and accumulation can only expand after the various control problems have been resolved simultaneously and in an encompassing manner. To this end, the top management of a core firm has to develop a coherent vision on internal company structures and external preconditions for longer-term growth. This requires a comprehensive vision on how to resolve the five control problems, that is, on how a core firm aspires to control its five bargaining partners, including a definition of the 'national' or 'common' interest. Such a view will be dubbed a concept of control.[3]

As the history of Fordism suggests, no resolution of control problems, and therefore no comprehensive concept of control, will function forever. In fact, history suggests that any settlement of control problems will eventually provoke new contradictions and thus lead to new control problems. One can distinguish five rival concepts of control contending for hegemony in modern capitalism.

The first concept of control that has emerged is one based on (networks of) small and medium sized firms which aim at industrial craft-oriented production for small to medium scale markets. This type of industrial organization has been called *'flexible specialization'* (Piore and Sable 1984). Flexible specialization networks may of course also succeed in producing for larger markets. This would only increase the possible hegemonic aspirations of the concept.

The second concept of control that has emerged can be labelled *industrial democracy*. Industrial democracy only emerged as a result of social and political strategies developed by actors other than core firms such as governments or trade unions. On an international scale in the OECD region, some minor attempts have been made towards formulating international codes of conduct for transnationals, while trade union thinking on how to enforce a compliant bargaining attitude among firms has been limited to theories of 'associative democracy' (Mathews 1989). Swedish core firms (in the 1970s) have probably been closest to the concept of industrial democracy. The theoretical notions behind the industrial systems developed in the (former) socialist economies also showed traces of the idea of industrial democracy.

The third concept of control emerged with the purpose of creating mass production in vertically integrated firms, on the basis of formal hierarchies producing for mass markets. This production organization strives for 'economies of scale' and has been called '*Fordism*' (Gramsci

[3] The term concept of control has been borrowed from authors of the so-called 'Amsterdam School' of international relations (Bode 1979, Van der Pijl 1984, Overbeek 1990), who defined a concept of control as 'a coherent set of strategies in the area of labour relations, socio-economic policies and foreign policies' (Overbeek 1990, p. 26) that presents a specific interest in terms of the 'general interest'. For a discussion of their definition of a concept of control and our critique, see Ruigrok and van Tulder (1995).

1980). This has been the concept most clearly associated with the rise of the US system of production. Applying the dependency scale, however, shows that the category 'Fordism' is too broad and multi-interpretative. In order to fine-tune the analysis, this category needs to be divided into two concepts of control. This concept of control can be dubbed *macro-Fordism* (Mjøset 1987) and represents a situation in which core firms are confronted with relatively strong bargaining partners, such as national trade union federations and stronger national governments. Under such a regime, actors share the highest degree of interdependence (in the sense of mutual and equal dependence). The core firm will be forced to strike deals with other actors which most closely resemble a coalition. Under such circumstances it can be relatively attractive for the core firm to transfer its interest representation to a national employers' organization that bargains with governments and trade unions in a national context. In many of the smaller industrial countries this has led to tripartite corporatist bargaining institutions.

The fourth concept of control, then, can be called *micro-Fordism*. It represents the 'ideal typical' Fordism pioneered by Henry Ford. In micro-Fordism, large vertically integrated core firms have been aiming at economies of scale through a company internal division of labour. High levels of vertical integration have led to relatively adversarial bargaining relations with suppliers and distributors/dealers. Deals with workers have been struck at the level of the firm or at most at the level of the relevant industry. The updated version of micro-Fordism in particular could be called '*neo-Fordism*'. The restructuring problems of American industry have often been considered under this heading or under the even more vague heading of 'post-Fordism'. Under neo-Fordism, core firms would also be able to serve medium-sized (and sometimes even small-sized) markets, owing to the use of more flexible technologies and the introduction of less rigid organizational structures.

The fifth concept of control has evolved around large vertically de-integrated firms, overseeing relatively informal hierarchies producing for medium-scale markets at first, but later also for mass markets. When analysing the German shift from Fordism to 'automated Fordism' or 'ultra-Fordism', Dohse (Dohse et al. 1984) observed the rise of an opposing concept which they dubbed '*Toyotism*'. Toyotist firms are aimed at 'economies of scope', which imply shorter production runs than Fordist firms. Toyotism, therefore, is better equipped than Fordism to produce for smaller scale and niche markets. Others have proposed the term 'Japanization' or 'Fujitsuism' (Oliver and Wilkinson 1988,

Kenney and Florida 1988, Jacot 1990). However, Toyotist firms are not necessarily Japanese, and Japanese firms are not necessarily Toyotist. For instance, Japanese companies such as Honda, Canon and Sony are probably closer to the micro-Fordist concept of control, owing to a lack of structural control over their supply and distribution base, and their isolation on the industrial and political scene affected by more established companies.

These five concepts represent ideal types of how – temporarily – to resolve the five basic control problems of capitalist production and accumulation. Each of these ideal types has emerged in a very specific economic, social and political setting, and has flourished in a particular international context. More so, in particular, the craft-oriented production system, based on systems of flexible specialization, was the constituting part of the British economy that reached hegemonic status in the second half of the nineteenth century. The Americans, in response to the economic and military hegemony of the British economy, found a rival solution to some of the control problems and thereby laid the groundwork for micro-Fordism. This rivalry, like the rivalry of the British production system with that of continental Europe in the early nineteenth century, also led to military conflicts (Kennedy 1987).

More importantly, the US core firms in close consultation with the US government started to build trade barriers around the US economy in order to limit the penetration of British producers. From the mid-nineteenth century until the mid-twentieth century, the US economy constituted a virtually closed system. The closed nature of the system created the preconditions for the development of Fordist bargaining relations and the creation of micro-Fordist institutions of high cohesion. The US institutional constellation dominated the world economy from the 1930s until the 1960s. In response to the success of the US Fordist system, the Japanese core producers tried to emulate Fordism, but this failed badly (Cusumano 1985, p. 80). After defeat in the Second World War, Japanese producers began to develop economic relations on the basis of other bargaining institutions. These became known as Toyotist, because it proved impossible to build vertically integrated firms or control suppliers and distributors directly (Ruigrok and van Tulder 1995, p. 41). Instead, over a period of more than 30 years (comparable to the formative periods of British flexible specialization and American Fordism) Toyotist core firms slowly built their 'lean' and hierarchical – but informal – networks. Again, as in the case of Britain and the USA, this could only happen because of high trade barriers which made it possible to build relatively stable bargaining relationships without interference from external parties representing rival concepts of control.

In the interwar period and in the first four decades after the Second World War, socialist states in Central and Eastern Europe tried to develop their own economic systems in isolation. But the cohesion of planned economies – although intended to create industrial democracies – remained rather weak. According to some observers, this weakness was the result of active intervention in the domestic economy by the governments of rival countries, in particular by the US government (Van der Pijl 1984). Whatever the causes, the weak cohesion of the institutions of 'real existing' socialism set the scene for the final breakdown of the planned economies around 1990.

After its emergence, the 'purest' form of a concept of control will long be found in its country of origin. The principles of each concept of control, however, are universally applicable, provided that the proper economic, social and political environment is available or created at the same time. The latter condition is very difficult to realize. Thus, concepts of control are at the same unique in the sense that they require a specific infrastructure and governance structure to emerge, and general in their potential as models for capitalist production and accumulation.

Table 6.1 summarizes the indicators of all five bargaining constellations that can be analysed along the dependency scale (see Figures 6.1, 6.2). The relation between these modes of conflict management and the rival concepts of control is shown in Figure 6.3. As an approximation of the five concepts of control, Table 6.2 mentions some examples of core producers in various industries.

If a core firm has succeeded in organizing its relationships with *all five* domestic bargaining partners at one and the same position on the dependency scale, the bargaining arena of the industrial complex is characterized by a high degree of cohesion. The higher the cohesion of the bargaining arena, the more the outcome of the bargaining processes represents one of the concepts of control. In such a case, the institutional setting, that is, the roles and policies of governments and the bargaining procedures (the 'rules of the game') between the core firm and its bargaining partners, are transparent to all participants (though not necessarily to outsiders). Conversely, the lower the level of cohesion, the more turbulent bargaining patterns within the industrial complex will be, and the more the individual bargaining partners will try to maximize their individual short-term profits.

Since national economies often contain more than one industrial complex, it is useful to distinguish between an industrial complex and the national industrial system (Lundvall 1992, Nelson 1993, De Banville and Chanaron 1991). For instance, the German car system consists of the Volkswagen, Ford, Opel, Mercedes-Benz and BMW complexes. If

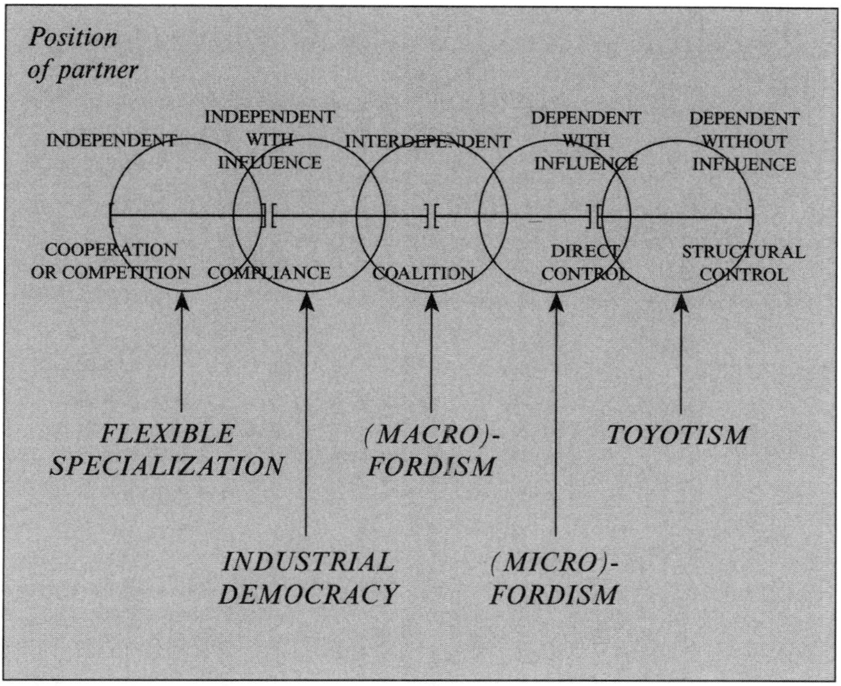

Some general characteristics of the five concepts of control

Performance based on	Cut-throat competition and ad hoc cooperation focused on price and/or quality competition.	Compliance to other partners (depending on the dominant partner in the complex); cost-plus contracts.	Continuous bargaining with all partners in sectoral and national institutions: meso-corporatism.	Direct control; internal efficiency and productivity; profit maximization.	Structural power; quality and flexibility of the supply network; cost-minus relations; market share maximization.
Nature of core firm and customers	Polipsony. Many firms, many buyers/ (closest to perfect market).	Monopsony markets; oligopoly (creating under-capacity with competitors).	Oligopoly; oligopsony.	Oligopoly (striving for monopoly); polipsony.	Oligopoly (creating overcapacity with competitors); polipsony.
Tentative examples of industries in the 1980s	Start-up industries; artisan producers for niche markets: ceramics, textiles, shoes (Italy), machine tools (Germany), service industries, software industries (USA), agricultural specialties (Netherlands); lower-tier subcontractors.	Small nationalized producers; specialized producers in: telecommunications, defence industry, public utilities, civil industries as spin-off from defence industries; Wallenberg consortium.	Large national(ized) producers; industrial conglomerates such as IRI and ENI (Italy), or Daimler-Benz (Germany); large subcontractors: steel, tyres, semiconductors (USA, Japan); resource-based industries (oil).	Mass production, vertically integrated in: cars, consumer electronics, pharmaceuticals, petrochemical industries, food industries, some retailing chains (USA).	Mass production, vertically de-integrated in: cars, consumer electronics, information technologies (vertical keiretsu, Japan).

Figure 6.3. Relation between modes of conflict management and the rival concepts of control

Table 6.1 Five bargaining characteristics related to five concepts of control

POSITION PARTNER→ CORE FIRM TOWARDS ↓	*INDEPENDENT:* ***FLEXIBLE SPECIALIZATION***	*INDEPENDENT WITH INFLUENCE:* ***INDUSTRIAL DEMOCRACY***	*INTERDEPENDENT:* ***MACRO-FORDISM***	*DEPENDENT WITH INFLUENCE:* ***MICRO-FORDISM***	*DEPENDENT WITHOUT INFLUENCE:* ***TOYOTISM***
Suppliers	• division of labour • flexible supply: high degree of substitution between suppliers • local deliveries • competitive and cooperative relations • no clear profit hierarchy	• minority shareholding • supplier of strategic components, longer-term supply contracts favoured • many single-sourcing relations • profit of supplier may surpass that of core firm	• division of labour in which (small number of) suppliers also have relationships with other core firms • local delivery • no clear pattern of profit distribution • single-sourcing relations	• vertical integration • large numbers of competing suppliers • international deliveries (global sourcing) • antagonistic relations • profits tend to diverge, but not in a heirarchy • low level of black box engineering	• vertical de-integration • small number of prime contractors • local deliveries • control hierarchy with coalition between core firm and first tier suppliers • profits: only convergence with first tier suppliers • high level of black box engineering.
Distributors/ dealers	• risk of becoming dominated by distributors is high • limited influence on ultimate price of product	• distributors can hold shares in core firm • core films are confronted with many mega-dealers • dealers can earn larger profit margins than core firms	• converging profit margins • important function for importers • importers 'partners' of the core company: no large price differences around the world	• core firm tries to own the distributors and importers • low price at production site, higher prices abroad (due to higher transport costs)	• control (i.e. via data networks) • single franchise dealers • less importance for importers • higher prices in market of production site, lower prices abroad ('export residual')

Trade unions/ workers	• loose relation with (craft-oriented) unions or no unions • nationally or internationally organized unions	• national union confederations • representation at company council • national productivity coalitions	• (multinational) company council, representing sectoral unions • sectoral productivity coalitions	• firm-oriented or sectoral unions • contrasting interests • country by country productivity coalitions (weak coordination)	• plant/company unions • firm loyalty • decentralized productivity coalitions (centrally coordinated) • rigorous selection
Financiers	• effort to auto-finance • family company • distant relation with (limited number of) banks • cooperatives	• industrial bank with unilateral directorships and considerable shareholding in core firm • institutional investors • commercial bank having financed large part of company's debt	• financial group • relationship with first tier bank issuing bonds or first tier bank issuing stock as head of underwriter syndicate • coalition with bank	• direct control over own finances • large number of small stockholders • high degree of self-financing • underwriter hierarchies • adversarial relations with banks	• collaborative relation with first tier banks • mutual shareholdings in other firms of the same conglomerate • high degree of self-financing without this being used
Governments	• arm's-length relations • government support of 'keep it small' policies • relatively strong supranational governments	• strong national home governments, making use of a variety of instruments curbing the influence of individual firms • nationalizations	• strong regional/ state home governments • loose coalitions • active procurement policies • subsidies sustaining diversity in the industrial structure	• ad hoc coalitions with national/ federal governments • adaptive/ independent from local environment • active 'creation' of local environment in company towns	• local player status preferred • focus primarily on local governments • structurally dominant position • no need to control the region directly

Table 6.2. Five concepts of control and their bargaining institutions

CONCEPT OF CONTROL	*NATURE OF INDUSTRIAL COMPLEX*	*CORE FIRM'S STRATEGY TOWARDS BARGAINING PARTNERS*	*EXAMPLES*
Flexible specialization	changing network of suppliers, different sizes and capabilities, no intervention by government (except in catastrophes)	*cooperation and/or competition*: one core firm is unable to control another	'Italian SME model': clothing, ceramics, shoe and leather industry; ancient 'British model' (Rolls Royce)
Industrial democracy	core firm surrounded by strong and relatively independent suppliers, financiers, labour unions and governments	*compliance*: substantial concessions to bargaining partners	'Swedish model': core players: Volvo, Elektrolux, Enskilda Banken
Macro-Fordism	partial vertical integration, supplemented by strong and relatively interdependent suppliers, financiers, labour unions and governments	*coalition*: established bargaining patterns with strong suppliers, sectoral trade unions and governments	'German model': Volkswagen; Daimler-Benz; Siemens; Mannesmann; Bosch; Deutsche Bank
Micro-Fordism	advanced vertical integration; suppliers, financiers, labour unions and governments unable to exert much influence over core firm	*direct control*: attempt to control bargaining partners via take-overs; play off governments; avert sectoral trade unions	'US model': Ford; IBM
Toyotism	vertical de-integration; vertical supply and distribution pyramid sanctioned by government	*structural control*: attempt to control legally independent bargaining partners via order-portfolio, control over technology, managing their financial room, company unions	'Japanese model': Toyota; NEC

a national system contains more than one industrial complex, different types of bargaining and different concepts of control may co-exist for a transient period. Within national industrial systems, however, bargaining patterns have tended to converge along the lines of the bargaining rules set by the most cohesive complex, at the expense of the weaker complex(es). Core firms with a relatively cohesive industrial complex have usually invested a lot of money and energy in forging well-functioning bargaining practices. Governments tend to favour more cohesive complexes, since they make it not only easier to develop trade and industrial policies (clientelism), but also to implement those policies. Governments always tend to favour non-discriminatory policies over discriminatory policies. The latter is apparent in less transparent bargaining institutions, that is, as the result of less cohesive national industrial systems.

5. CHANGING COHESION, CHANGING NATIONAL INSTITUTIONS

In a closed bargaining arena characterized by high levels of cohesion, that is, in which all major core firms and their bargaining partners are oriented towards the same concept of control, none of the three issues discussed here poses a problem. Tensions emerge only if rival concepts of control are vying for dominance, either because an industrial system becomes penetrated by powerful companies adhering to another concept of control, or because formerly independent industrial systems with different concepts of control are brought together into a larger legal system – such as the EU.

During the 1980s and 1990s, the international restructuring race triggered major changes in most national bargaining arenas. These changes were associated with the internationalization of domestic and foreign firms and thus represented the 'clash' of rival concepts of control on an international scale. Table 6.3 appraises the shifting concepts of control and levels of cohesion in eight industrial systems, plus the former socialist countries as a group.

The cohesion of the German industrial system during the 1960s and 1970s was at an extremely high level. The economic success and international competitiveness of its most important core players helped retain most investments within the national system, fostering the stability of the corporatist bargaining institutions (Grabher 1993). This cohesion has started to fall away since the late 1970s. Inroads by foreign core firms only played a minor role in this process. A more important

Table 6.3. Diverging bargaining arenas and shifting concepts of control in Europe, the USA and Japan

NATIONAL INDUSTRIAL SYSTEM	■ DOMINANT CONCEPT OF CONTROL (c. 1980)* ■ COHESION (indic.)	TRENDS IN DOMESTIC BARGAINING ARENA (1990s)	GOVERNMENT'S BARGAINING POSITION (re industrial/trade policies)
Germany	■ macro-Fordism ■ strong cohesion	cohesion still considerable; East Germany offers new chances: towards renewed macro-Fordism?	sustained, partly owing to need for coordination in East Germany
France	■ macro-Fordism (sometimes leaning towards ind. democr.) ■ strong cohesion	gradual opening up to foreign competition may undermine cohesion (e.g. increasingly weak supply base)	denationalizations reflect gradual decline of govt power; govt may opt for further concentration (e.g. in cars)
UK	■ micro-Fordism ■ weak cohesion	independence of major core firms lost; increasingly becoming extension of Toyotist core firms	increasingly operating in line with Japanese and/or Toyotist interests
Italy	■ flexible specialization/macro-Fordism ■ strong regional cohesion	gradual opening up to foreign competition will undermine cohesion	business response is to seize even more control over govt
Sweden	■ industrial democracy (leaning towards macro-Fordism) ■ strong cohesion	slipping domestic cohesion; independence of core firms under siege (cf. Volvo, Saab), may end up as extension of foreign micro-/macro-Fordist firms	govt faced with inability of banks to play traditional role as financiers; govt power also negatively affected by declining bargaining power of labour
Netherlands	■ macro-Fordism ■ medium cohesion	dominance of distribution interests undermines position of core firms: Toyotism on the rise	relatively weak govt will further undermine manufacturing base and thus promote Toyotism

East European countries	■ industrial democracy (leaning towards macro-Fordism) ■ very weak cohesion	breakdown of (international) institutions owing to sustained weakness; the higher the previous independence of the national systems (in particular Hungary, Czech Republic, Poland) towards the Soviet Union, the bigger the chance that new and relatively cohesive institutions might develop	weak govts will find it difficult to bargain with business on an equal footing; considerable risk of clientism and the seizing of control by most cohesive groups such as (1) former communist partly officials, (2) families, (3) mafia-like organisations
USA	■ micro-Fordism ■ medium cohesion	slipping cohesion owing to runaway US firms (1960s to 1990s) escaping from domestic bargaining arena; cohesion further undermined by massive inroads of Toyotist producers	caught between free market ideology and declining cohesion/competitiveness: relaxes anti-trust regulations, champions 'fair trade', perhaps rehabilitation of defence policy as disguise for industrial policy
Japan	■ Toyotism ■ strong cohesion	cohesion relatively high yet under stress from 'bubble' economy, temporary increase in workers' bargaining power (due to labour shortage) and internationalization; current restructuring aimed at reviving Toyotism appears successful	national govt supports core firms' restructuring agenda: to facilitate restructuring banking system; maintains pressure to save (also to discipline workers) and to reduce pace of internationalization

*The dominant concept of control in this table serves as a point of orientation at the state level. However, a dominant concept of control may not be accomplished by all or even by the majority of core firms in a given industrial system.

factor was that the German institutional setting proved ill adapted to the challenges of the microelectronics revolution. Further, during the 1970s and 1980s many German firms began to search for a regional division of labour within Europe in a modest effort to profit from regional scale economies and in an equally modest effort to escape from domestic bargaining arrangements. After reunification, German firms suddenly faced a potential market of almost 80 million people, representing an increase in potential domestic purchasing power of around 30 per cent. The importance of this new market can hardly be overstated: it could absorb the bulk of German exports, and it could refocus attention on domestic expansion and bargaining. The German federal government channelled hundreds of billions of Deutschmarks to the East, while German core and medium-sized players set up large-scale investment programmes, often aimed at creating a division of labour within Germany instead of within the European region. Consequently, German's international trade dependence is likely to come more into line with the US and Japanese industrial systems (both dedicated around 8 per cent of their GDP to trade in 1993) (*The Economist* 1994, p. 28). Thus there appears to be a reasonable chance of a renewed macro-Fordist growth regime within Germany.

In spite of considerable pressure during the 1980s and 1990s, French bargaining institutions have shown remarkable adaptability in the international restructuring race. The French industrial system has long protected itself from inroads being made by industrial complexes representing alternative concepts of control, while those foreign core firms that have established themselves in France have been forced to adapt to French bargaining institutions. The spirit of Colbert has lived on in France: particular industries with a high public procurement content (defence, aerospace, public utilities, banking and telecommunications) have been able – in close consultation with state agencies – to restructure and remain amongst Europe's most competitive industries. In the car and computer industries, however, it has proven difficult to complement a weak supply base with large national investment projects, aimed at creating a *filière* (chain) of supply activities. Another French government strategy to defend macro-Fordism has been to strengthen bilateral bonds with Germany (home of the renowned *Mittelstand* of small and medium-sized enterprises). At the same time, it has taken a more active (although still ambivalent) approach to the promotion of European integration: over the 1980s, French government and industry bureaucrats have flooded the European bureaucracy.

During the 1980s and 1990s, Dutch companies and financiers have been among the leading sources of foreign direct investment (FDI) in the USA – even outpacing Japanese investors. This enormous investment 'leakage' contributed to a gradual process of de-industrialization, to a lower level of cohesion and to a downward pressure on wages and purchasing power in the Netherlands. Moreover, a rapid decline in trade union membership (from 35 per cent in 1980 to around 20 per cent in 1994) has undermined the traditional tripartite corporatist bargaining structure. The Dutch government has also actively stimulated inward-oriented FDI, and the Dutch economy has become a major target of Japanese distribution centres, accelerating the demise of macro-Fordism and causing a gradual shift towards Toyotism.

During the 1980s, Sweden faced only limited inflows of foreign direct investment (below 5 per cent). However, the Swedish cohesion was undermined by the internationalization of Swedish multinationals in the European continent, stimulated by the industrial banks (in particular the Enskilda Bank). To some extent, this 'hollowed out' the corporatist bargaining institutions and induced the Swedish government to apply for full membership of the European Union. However, while trade union membership declined in all other major industrial systems, membership *increased* in Sweden from 80 per cent in 1980 to 85.3 per cent in 1985 (OECD 1993, p. 49). This created a countermovement from trade unions and large parts of the Swedish population. In this respect, the Swedish application in 1993 for membership of the European Union reflected declining domestic cohesion and posed a test case for the relative bargaining strength of the Swedish trade unions.

By 1980, the Italian industrial system was founded on a mixture of flexible specialization and macro-Fordist institutions. These institutions had materialized in a sub-national, that is, regional context, complemented by weak central state regulation. During the 1970s, this setting spurred economic growth, but it also created an extremely closed system in which two *rival* concepts of control co-existed. This unstable balance of power was undermined by two forces. First, the continued rivalry between regions and related concepts of control could not be resolved owing to the lack of a strong central government. Second, the Single European Act forced the Italian government to gradually open up the Italian economy. On the one hand, traditional core firms such as Fiat, Olivetti, IRI, Feruzzi and ENI became confronted with increasing international competition. On the other hand, new business moguls such as Carlo de Benedetti, Silvio Berlusconi and the Benetton family skilfully profited from the (chaotic) remains of the regionally organized clientelist system. With moderate capital involvement, these family-owned holding companies seized control of a considerable part of the Italian industrial and service economy. In the case of Benetton, the family holding company gradually supplanted networks of flexible specialization into Toyotist networks of informal hierarchical control. Thus a third concept of control joined the battle for dominance in Italy. The presence of Berlusconi, a polititian coming from a non-core part of the industrial system (the media), suggests that the battle for control of the state is likely to continue.

At the beginning of the 1980s, the UK was the only industrial system facing weak cohesion. Bargaining relations between core firms on the one hand, and workers and bankers on the other, had created an unstable domestic setting. Furthermore, the UK had a high number of foreign investors in the national economy. By 1988, the relative level of foreign direct investment stock in the UK economy stood at 15–20 per cent of the whole (UNCTAD 1992, p. 63), a figure only surpassed in the Dutch economy. Although US firms had been the prime investors in the UK economy, and although these shared a micro-Fordist concept of control, US firms regarded their UK activities as an extension of their US home base, and the centre of decision-making processes remained firmly in the USA.

Since the late 1980s, UK cohesion has been further undermined by inward Japanese investments, particularly in manufacturing. In fact, Toyotism may have become the concept of control to which British companies most aspire, even if it is one they cannot implement. On many occasions, the UK government has blocked or frustrated European decision-making, often supporting the interests of Toyotist core firms.[4] Further, it bargained for three provisos in important parts of the 1991 Maastricht Treaty: an exemption from the social charter on workers' rights; a clause preventing more power being given to the European Commission; and an opt-out provision regarding membership of the Monetary Union (Milner 1994, p. 29). The bargaining institution of European Company Councils, for instance, required by the European Commission in companies with more than 1 000 employees, was agreed upon in September 1994 after 20 years of negotiations, but it will not apply to the UK.

[4] Representing the interests of Honda, Nissan and Toyota, the UK government prevented Japanese transplants being included in the EC-Japan Car Trade Agreement 1991 (Ruigrok and van Tulder 1991, p. 197). On behalf of ICL (taken over by Fujitsu), it successfully bargained for ICL's admission to EU collaboration programmes, and pressured the European Commission to open up EU collaborative programmes to companies from non-EU member states (in the USA, by comparison, participation in pre-competitive R&D programmes is restricted to companies that are at least 51% US-owned, while *de facto* restrictions in Japan are even more prohibitive). On behalf of Japanese television makers with UK facilities such as Sony, Matsushita and Sharp, the UK government frustrated the adoption of a European High Definition TV standard.

The former socialist economies made an effort to develop an industrial democracy. Core firms developed forms of vertical integration comparable to the US micro-Fordist core firms. Nevertheless, instead of developing a system of democratic 'checks and balances' to influence core firms – while leaving these firms considerable room to develop autonomous strategies – the 'real existing' socialist system, based on the concept of the planned economy, fixed all power at the state level, also subordinating, for instance, the interests of workers and trade unions to those of the state bureaucracy. The same dependent position was held by many suppliers, distributors and financiers (if they operated at all as independent actors). As a consequence, for example, independent capital markets did not exist, hampering the effective restructuring of institutions in Eastern Europe at any later stage (Cohen and Schwartz 1992). The end of the regional dominance of the Soviet Union has left Eastern European countries with relatively weak industrial systems and equally weak governments. This situation has created the possibility of Eastern Europe becoming the lower end of the supply chain for Western European industrial systems. At the same time, the risk looms large in a weak bargaining arena that more cohesive interest groups (including family businesses, former Communist Party officials, or mafia-like organizations) will take control of the economy and shape the economic institutions to their needs.

Throughout the 1980s, the USA became confronted with an eroded domestic micro-Fordist regime, owing to a combination of factors such as the inroads made by foreign firms using a different concept of control, the flight of US core firms from their own bargaining arena – in particular towards Europe and East Asia – and the priority that consecutive US governments have given to military expenditure over productive investments. In the latter sense the US system suffered from the same disintegrative developments as the Soviet system, but departing from a much stronger and more cohesive position. Of all the industrial systems of the OECD countries, those of the UK and the USA have most adapted to the Japanese concept of control. This can possibly be attributed to the weakened cohesion of both systems, but also to the fact that, on the dependency scale, micro-Fordist bargaining based on direct control is least remote from Toyotist bargaining on the basis of structural control. Japanese firms targeted in particular the UK and the USA when they were forced to expand abroad to circumvent imminent trade barriers.

Finally, during, and particularly after the end of the 'bubble economy', the cohesion of the Japanese industrial system has been under pressure from factors such as road congestion (hindering just-in-time deliveries), pressure on exports (owing to an appreciating Yen and to trade protection in the USA and Europe), labour shortages and problems in Japanese financial institutions (the falling *Nikkei* index, decreasing volume in loans, and the necessity for banks to restructure gigantic 'bad debts'). These problems were partly caused – and further enhanced – by the rivalry between and within ministries. Despite these pressures, the cohesion of the Japanese industrial system has remained relatively high. Adjustment costs, however, have been distributed unevenly throughout society. While Japanese core firms have faced sharply declining profits and occasional losses, many lower-tier suppliers have not survived the post-bubble recession. The Japanese government has remained relatively weak. Under these circumstances, Toyota, which traditionally maintained a low political profile, deemed it necessary to strengthen its direct hold over the Japanese bargaining institutions: for instance by assuming the chair of *Keindanren*, the Japanese employers' federation.

6. RIVALRY CONTAINED OR CONTINUED? REGIONS AS THE PRIME BATTLEGROUND OF RIVAL INSTITUTIONS

As the discussion of institutional change in the preceding section shows, differentiated strategies will continue to be important, even if actors from rival and more cohesive national institutions penetrate less cohesive industrial systems. The national level of analysis, however, does not suffice. At the same time, a growing number of initiatives have matured resulting in the creation of regional bargaining institutions especially in Europe, North America and the East Asian region. Does this process represent a growing convergence of institutions or a continuation of international rivalry between institutions, but now at an intra- and/or interregional level? The concluding part of this contribution appraises the kind of regional institutions that are developing in the three strongest world regions, thereby stretching the proposed dependency analysis to its analytical extreme. The last part of this analysis, therefore, is also the most speculative.[5]

In Europe, it has proved very difficult to formulate common EU policies, owing to the continued rivalry between a number of national institutions. The six European industrial systems which formed the

[5] A more detailed account of these regional regimes or institutions is presented in Ruigrok and van Tulder (1995, p. 289).

cradle of the European Community in 1957 (France, Italy, Germany, Belgium, the Netherlands and Luxembourg) each shared and developed a macro-Fordist environment. In none of the six additional members entering the EEC in 1973 (Britain, Ireland, Denmark, Spain, Portugal and Greece), did macro-Fordism represent the dominant concept of control. The late 1970s and early 1980s became the period of 'Euro-sclerosis', manifested by declining cohesion. The problems were reinforced by Toyotist competition in two carriers of European macro-Fordism – the electronics and the car industries. Next to coal and steel, the electronics and car industries had been well represented in the six original member states of the European Community, but they were either non-existent, poorly developed or had virtually disappeared in the new member states. Thus, while political consensus on steel could still be achieved, the car and electronics industries faced a scattered bargaining arena at the European Community level.

In response to the declining cohesion of their complexes and to Eurosclerosis, some major core firms over the 1980s took initiatives to increase integration and competitiveness, leading to acronyms such as ESPRIT, RACE, AMICE, START and BRITE. 1983 also saw the birth of the European Round Table of Industrialists (ERT), providing European core companies with a European discussion forum as well as a sounding board for the European Commission. Owing to these combined initiatives, European integration gained new impetus, inevitably shifting some bargaining power towards the European Commission. However, the principle of subsidiarity agreed in the Maastricht Treaty implied that the EU institutional setting would remain weak and that the impact of European industrial policies would remain limited.

It can be observed that the shape of major European bargaining institutions has tended to reflect those of the strongest and most cohesive industrial systems, that is, the German and to a lesser extent the French ones. Examples include the areas of competition policy and the creation of a relatively independent European Central Bank. At the same time, however, EU institutions have been unable on fundamental issues to force individual industrial complexes to follow the agreed bargaining rules. The European Union has become the battleground of at least four rival concepts of control: flexible specialization, macro-Fordism, micro-Fordism and Toyotism. This means that it is very difficult to reach consensus on fundamental issues of competitiveness and industrial policy. The European Union's main competitors do not suffer from this weakness: the USA and Japan only have one or at most two concepts of control in their industrial systems competing for dominance. The discussion on a 'multi-speed Europe' (the core industrial systems of Germany, France, the Netherlands, Belgium and Luxembourg are proceeding more rapidly with monetary and political integration than the other member states) may be seen as a desperate attempt to sustain the cohesion of the traditional macro-Fordist European industrial systems, and to limit potentially disruptive competition from other concepts of control.

Since the early 1960s, initiatives have been taken by large micro-Fordist firms in the North American region – backed by the US government – to create formal trade agreements and support their efforts in developing a regional division of labour. Investments by US core firms in Canada and (later) Mexico were part of an effort to evade the national bargaining arena in which they faced strong trade unions, hostile suppliers and often troubled financiers opposing their direct control strategy. When the position of the US industrial system became further undermined owing to the inroads of Japanese and European firms in the 1970s and 1980s, the US government proceeded further towards a regional trade regime. When rival regional institutions developed in particular in Europe and the fear of a 'fortress Europe' matured, the creation of NAFTA (North American Free Trade Agreement) in the early 1990s was a logical step. The creation of a regional trade regime in the North-American region can be understood as a defensive move to sustain American micro-Fordist institutions. However, partly because of the same direct control strategy of the core firms, it has proved almost impossible to transfer regulatory authority to a regional level. In Europe, macro-Fordist complexes were much less opposed to the idea of conveying authority to a regional government because they were already accustomed to bargaining with national governments on an equal footing. Furthermore, the economic gains of NAFTA for the US economy as a whole are much smaller than in the case of the European Union. The enlargement of the market for the USA due to NAFTA is much smaller than the extension of the market for France or Germany due to the formation of the EC/EU. Because of these reasons it seems implausible that NAFTA itself will bring an end to the gradual decline of US cohesion.

Whereas weak institutional arrangements in the North American region can be considered an expression of the relative weakness of the US industrial system and the institutions of micro-Fordism, the opposite seems true for the East Asian region. Because of Japan's dependence on importing food and raw materials, exerting structural control over the South East Asian region may be even more critical to Japanese core firms than securing access to the US and EU markets. After they secured access to the US and EU markets over the 1980s and early

1990s, Japanese core companies changed their investment focus towards the East Asian region. The attraction of the Asian region to Japan is not only based on the region's wealth of mineral fuels waiting to be explored and exploited. Equally important is the fact that none of the economies in the region can match the industrial strength and technological sophistication of Japan. All the newly industrialized economies (Korea, Taiwan, Singapore and Hong Kong) and ASEAN economies are facing a long-term trade deficit with Japan. While many Japanese core firms share a clear interest in gradually extending their ties with the Asia-Pacific region, they do not have a strong interest in forging a formal regional organization at a political level. The Japanese government has not been a catalyst in promoting the Asia-Pacific Economic Cooperation forum (APEC) but instead has tried to follow these developments and play a diplomatic role. It is not in the Japanese interest that Asian and Pacific economies delegate sovereignty to an organization in which Japan is confronted with strong bargaining partners such as the USA, China and Australia (the latter has actively campaigned for Asia-Pacific integration). Moreover, development of APEC as an official bargaining institution rather than a loose federation might accelerate the integration process of the Association of South East Asian Nations (ASEAN) and improve the bargaining position of its member states versus Japan and other regional powers. The potential extension of Toyotist bargaining rules regionally suggests that it is in the interest of the most cohesive industrial complexes in Japan to keep the Asia-Pacific region fragmented and to increase control over the region by supporting only loose political ties.

The logic of institutional change is different in the three most important world regions. There nevertheless remains the question of which of the bargaining institutions creates the best preconditions for the competitiveness of individual firms: the European, the East Asian or the US ones? Europe is struggling to reshape macro-Fordist institutions at a regional scale with some success (but with major challenges ahead). North America is less successful in creating regional micro-Fordist institutions, which probably means that the US government will remain the most important representative of micro-Fordism. Japan seems to some extent successful in creating Toyotist institutions in the East Asian region. Each region in the end seems to be struggling with creating the best preconditions for leading indigenous industrial complexes. International rivalry between Europe, North America and the East Asian region will most likely continue, although it is difficult to define a bargaining arena in which the disputes between these regions can be settled. None of the regional institutions has yet crystallized completely, so the exact nature of institutional rivalry remains unclear. Institutional rivalry is bound to proceed; less between individual countries, but increasingly between regions.

REFERENCES

Albert, M. (1991) *Capitalism versus Capitalism*. New York: Four Walls Eight Windows.

Andersen, E.S. and Lundvall, B.A. (1988) 'Small National Systems of Innovation Facing Technological Revolutions: An Analytical Framework' in C. Freeman and B.A. Lundvall (eds) *Small Countries Facing the Technological Revolution*. London and New York: Pinter, pp. 9–36.

Bachrach, P. and Baratz M. (1969) 'Decisions and Non-Decisions: An Analytical Framework' in R. Bell et al. (eds) *Political Power: A Reader in Theory and Research*. New York: Free Press.

Bode, R. (1979) 'De Nederlandse Bourgeoisie Tussen de Twee Wereldoorlogen'. *Cahiers Voor de Politieke en Sociale Wetenschappen* 2 (4): 9–50.

Braverman, H. (1974) *Labor and Monopoly Capital*. New York: Monthly Review Press.

Burawoy, M. (1985) *The Politics of Production*. London: Verso

Cohen, S. and Schwartz, A. (1992) 'The Tunnel at the End of the Light: Privatization in Eastern Europe'. BRIE Working Paper No. 56, University of California.

Cohen, S. and Zysman, J. (1987) *Manufacturing Matters: The Myth of the Post-Industrial Economy*. New York: Basic Books.

Cusumano, M. (1985) *The Japanese Automobile Industry*. Cambridge, MA: Harvard University Press.

Dahl, R. (1957) 'The Concept of Power'. *Behavioral Science* 2: 201–5.

De Banville, E. and Chanaron, J.J. (1991) *Vers un Système Automobile Européen*. Paris: CPE-Economica.

Dohse, K., Ulrich, J. and Malsch, T. (1984) 'Vom "Fordismus" zum "Toyotismus"? Die Organisation der Industriellen Arbeit in der Japanischen Automobilindustrie'. *Leviathan* 12 (4) (Published in English in *Politics and Society* 14 (2): 115–46).

Freeman, C. (1988) 'Japan: a new national system of innovation', in Dosi, G., Freeman, C., Nelson, R., Silverberg, G. and Soete, L. (eds) *Technical Change and Economic Theory*, London: Pinter Publishers, pp. 330–49.

Fukuyama, F. (1995) *Trust. The Social Virtues and the Creation of Prosperity*. London: Hamish Hamilton.

Galtung, J. (1964) 'A structural theory of aggresion', *Journal of Peace Research* 2: 95–119.

Galtung, J. (1971) 'A Structural Theory of Imperialism'. *Journal of Peace Research* 8 (2): 437–82.

Grabher, G. (ed.) (1993) *The Embedded Firm*. London: Routledge.

Gramsci, A. (1980) *Selections from the Prison Notebooks*, edited by Q. Hoare and G. Nowell Smith. New York/London: Lawrence and Wishart.

Hall, P. (1986) *Governing the Economy: The Politics of State Intervention in Britain and France*. Cambridge, MA: Polity Press.

Hampden-Turner, C. and Trompenaars, A. (1993) *The Seven Cultures of Capitalism.* New York: Currency Doubleday.
Jacot, H. (ed.) (1990) *Du Fordisme au Toyotisme? Les Voies de la Modernisation du Systéme Automobile en France et au Japon.* Paris (La Documentation Francaise): Commisariat General du Plan, February.
Jeffrey Hart (1992) *Rival Capitalists. International Competitiveness in the United States, Japan, and Western Europe.* Ithaca: Cornell University Press.
Junne, G. (1987) 'Automation in the North: Consequences for Developing Countries' Exports' in J. Caporaso *A Changing International Division of Labour.* London: Pinter.
Kenney, M. and Florida, R. (1988) 'Beyond Mass Production: Production and the Labor Process in Japan'. *Politics and Society* 16 (1): 121–58.
Kennedy, P (1987) *The Rise and Fall of the Great Powers: Economic Change and Military Conflict from 1500 to 2000.* New York: Random House.
Lundvall, B.A. (1988) 'Innovation as an Interactive Process: From User-Producer Interaction to the National System of Innovation' in G. Dosi, C. Freeman, R. Nelson, G. Silverberg and L. Soete (eds) *Technical Change and Economic Theory.* London: Pinter, pp. 349–70.
Lundvall, B.A. (1992) *National Systems of Innovation: Towards a Theory of Innovation and Interactive Learning.* London: Pinter.
Mathews, J. (1989) *Age of Democracy: The Politics of Post-Fordism.* Melbourne: Oxford University Press.
Milner, H. (1988) *Resisting Protectionism: Global Industries and the Politics of International Trade.* Princeton, NJ: Princeton University Press.
Mjøset, L. (1987) 'Nordic Economies in the 1970s and 1980s'. *International Organization* 41 (3): 403–56.
Nelson, R. (1993) *National Innovation Systems: A Comparative Analysis.* Oxford: Oxford University Press.
OECD (1993) *Obstacles to Trade and Competition.* Paris: OECD.
Oliver, N. and Wilkinson, B. (1988) *The Japanization of British Industry.* London: Blackwell, p. 188.
Overbeek, H. (1990) *Global Capitalism and National Decline: The Thatcher Decade in Perspective.* London and New York: Unwin Hyman.
Parsons, T. (1957) 'The Distribution of Power in American Society'. *World Politics* 10: 123–43 (October).
Pateman, C. (1979) *Participation and Democratic Theory.* Cambridge: Cambridge University Press.
Petrella, R. (1989) 'La Mondialisation de la Technologie et de l'Economie'. *Futuribles:* 3–25 (September).
Pettigrew, A. (1973) *The Politics of Organizational Decision-Making.* London: Tavistock.
Pettigrew, A. (1992) 'On Studying Managerial Elites'. *Strategic Management Journal* 13: 163–82 (Winter special edition).
Pfeffer, J. (1992) *Managing with Power: Politics and Influence in Organizations.* Boston: Harvard Business School Press.
Piore, M. and Sabel, C. (1984) *The Second Industrial Divide: Possibilities for Prosperity.* New York: Basic Books.
Porter, M. (1990) *The Competitive Advantage of Nations.* New York: Free Press.
Rothschild, K. (ed.) (1971) *Power in Economics: Selected Readings.* Harmondsworth: Penguin, p. 366.

Ruigrok, W. and van Tulder, R. with the assistance of Baven, G. (1991) *Cars and Complexes: Globalization versus Global Localization Strategies in the World Car Industry.* Brussels: Commission of the European Communities/ Monitor-FAST, FOP 285.

Ruigrok, W. and van Tulder, R. (1995) *The Logic of International Restructuring: The Management of Dependencies in Rival Industrial Complexes.* London: Routledge.

Streeck, W. (1992) *Social Institutions and Economic Performance.* London: Sage Publications.

The Economist (1994) *Pocket World in Figures.* London: Penguin and Economist Books.

UNCTAD (1992) *Handbook on International Trade and Development Statistics.* New York: United Nations Conference on Trade and Development.

Vandermerwe, S. and Rada, J. (1988) 'Servitization of Business: Adding Value by Adding Services'. *European Management Journal* 6: 314–24 (Autumn).

Van der Pijl, K. (1984) *The Making of an Atlantic Ruling Class.* London: Verso.

Van Tulder, R. and Junne, G. (1988) *European Multinationals and Core Technologies.* Chichester and London: Wiley, p. 300.

Wallensteen, P. (1973) 'Structure and War: On International Relations 1920–1968'. *Political Sciences Association in Uppsala* 64: 269.

Whitley, R. (ed.) (1992) *European Business Systems. Firms and Markets in their National Contexts.* London: Sage Publications.

Williamson, O. (1990) 'The Firm as a Nexus of Treaties: An Introduction' in M. Aoki, B. Gustafsson and O. Williamson (eds) *The Firm as a Nexus of Treaty.* London: Sage, pp. 9–26.

Williamson, O. and Ouchi, W. (1981) 'The Markets and Hierarchies Perspective: Origins, Implications, Prospects' in A. Francis, J. Turk and P. Willman (1983) *Power, Efficiency and Institutions: A Critical Appraisal of the Markets and Hierarchies Paradigm.* London: Heinemann.

7. 'Time-space embeddedness' and 'geo-governance' of cross-border regional modes of growth: their nature and dynamics in East Asian cases

Ngai-Ling Sum[1]

1. INTRODUCTION AND OVERVIEW

This chapter adopts a neo-institutionalist approach to the development and governance of certain cross-border regional modes of growth[2] clustered around Japan and China. Along with most other approaches in institutional economics, I emphasize the socially embedded and socially regularized nature of economic activity. Among these approaches, my work is closest to the 'regulation school' with its emphasis on the articulation of modes of growth and their social as well as economic modes of regulation;[3] and to the 'innovative milieu' approach associated with GREMI,[4] emphasizing as it does how socially and culturally embedded networks supplement the market and state in contributing to effective economic coordination. Both these schools have recently shown considerable interest in the dynamics of governance and my chapter shares this interest. Likewise, along with at least some approaches in evolutionary economics, I emphasize the spatio-temporal embeddedness (see Section 2.1) of economic activity and its discontinuous expansion and evolution. My approach here is, however, more

[1] I am grateful to Ash Amin and Jerzy Hausner for their advice in revising this chapter and Bob Jessop for his help with editorial refinements.

[2] A mode of growth is an accumulation regime considered in terms of its insertion into the international division of labour and knowledge and with special reference to the relationships between the accumulation regime and the overall dynamics of the world economy (Lipietz 1993, Jessop 1990).

[3] On the regulation approach, see especially: Lipietz (1993), Jessop (1990).

[4] GREMI (the Groupe de Recherche et Etudes sur Milieus Innovatifs) has produced a series of studies on innovative milieus; for a recent summary of its work, see Camagni (1995).

distinctive. For it is concerned with the dependence of effective cross-border regions on the capacity to coordinate the many spatial and temporal dimensions of economic production, circulation and exchange across the public and private divide as well as across territorial borders. Furthermore such regions also depend on the capacity to manage their mutual integration within a nested and tangled hierarchy of local, national, triadic and global spaces. It is in discussing these twin capacities that I introduce the novel concept of 'geo-governance' (see Section 2.2) and, although the latter is illustrated mainly through East Asian cross-border regions, I would claim that it has a wider significance not only for institutional and evolutionary economics but also for other social sciences. A further distinctive feature of my analysis is its concern with electronic space and cybertime and their articulation with other spatio-temporal forms. Building on these ideas I also consider how managing the intersection of the multiple spatial and temporal horizons involved in 'third ways' of economic coordination leads to 'geo-governance tensions' (see Section 2.3).

These are weighty issues and cannot be fully discussed here. Thus my chapter will illustrate the significance of 'geo-governance' through an account of two cross-border regional modes of growth in East Asia. The first of these involves a Japan-centred network organized in part in terms of an imagined 'flying geese' region (see Section 3); the second involves a China-centred network based on the 'Greater China' growth triangle (Hong Kong-Macau, Taiwan and southern China) (see Section 4). I then analyse the gradual opening up of the Japan-centred network, with special reference to its emerging relationship with 'Greater China' (see Section 5). The chapter concludes with observations on three major issues raised by 'geo-governance' as an approach to cross-border regional modes of growth and, more generally, to the institutional embeddedness and evolution of economic systems (see Section 6).

2. 'TIME AND SPACE EMBEDDEDNESS' AND THE GEO-GOVERNANCE OF REGIONAL MODES OF GROWTH

Theoretically, my approach to cross-border regional modes of growth has been influenced by the regulation school, the 'innovative milieu' approach, work on governance, institutional and evolutionary economics, discourse theory and post-modern geography.[5] In particular, I attempt to apply the regulation approach at the regional level by linking it with work on innovative milieus. Moreover, given my concern with cross-border modes of growth, I also stress the spatio-temporal embeddedness of economic activities and the problems of managing (governing) the integration of innovative milieus and broader regions within the global economy. Whilst these concepts are relevant to a wide range of economic regions in different periods and places, recent technological and economic changes have led to the emergence of important and distinctive modes of economic organization. Information and communication technologies have a key role in the globalization of economies (without undermining their place-boundedness in other respects: see Sassen (1996)) and have contributed to new forms of time and space embeddedness – including what one might term 'virtual embeddedness'. These new forms of social relation are coordinated by transnational and translocal actors in 'electronic space' as well as social space and merit special attention in the following analysis of 'geo-governance'.

These socially and 'virtually' embedded networks of actors/organizations are engaged in attempts at regularizing and 'governing' the economic and social time of cross-border trade, technology transfer, labour flows and investment. In so doing they tend to condense global-regional divisions of knowledge as well as labour at specific nodal points and temporal conjunctures. They are also liable to disruption by extra- and intra-network tensions (see Section 2.3). Such strategic networks (often themselves 'networks of networks') provide a basis for regional 'geo-governance' – the governance of social relations qua temporal-spatial practices and relations.[6] In the context of cross-border regional modes of growth, 'geo-governance' involves a new spatially specific structure of social coordination for a more or less coherent mode of growth. This structure typically involves private economic and social agents as well as public authorities; is organized around an imagined community of economic interests at regional level; and is instantiated in, and dependent upon, both material and discursive practices. The resulting (meta-)networks generally aim to promote the competitiveness of the emerging region within the local-global hierarchy; a key feature of such attempts is disciplining and controlling the time-space dimensions of production and exchange in order to secure

[5] In addition to the references in notes 3 and 4 on regulation and GREMI, see Child et al. (1993), Hodgson (1993), Grabher (1993), Kooiman (1993), Amin and Thrift (1994), Fairclough (1992), Massey (1994, 1995).

[6] Strictly speaking, this is a matter of chrono- as well as geo-governance. A desire for conceptual simplicity leads me to write only of geo-governance.

what one might term the reciprocal economies of 'time-space compression and distantiation' (Gereffi and Korzeniewicz 1994, Adam 1994, Giddens 1990, Harvey 1989). Among these time-space dimensions are emerging temporalities and spatialities associated with the reorganization of 'social space' to include 'electronic space', the compression of economic and social time through information and communication technologies as well as new forms of institutional thickness (Amin and Thrift 1994), and the spatio-temporal extension of economic governance through complex social networks. These ideas concerning 'time and space embeddedness' are first presented in general terms and then in relation to my East Asian case studies.

2.1. General Comments on 'Time-Space Embeddedness'

Before considering specific cases, I will comment more generally on the role of embedded time and space in geo-governance. My comments refer to emerging global tendencies which are especially significant in the triad growth poles and their various modes of regional growth. Four aspects are worth highlighting: finance, industry, commerce and culture.

First, the financial time-space moment of a mode of growth is structured by the practices of networks of multinational banks, other financial intermediaries and translocal organizations. Their operations are premised on the denationalization of 'stateless' funds which are pooled and managed in an increasingly 'borderless world' (Ohmae 1990). This has obvious spatio-temporal implications which are often explicitly voiced in the discourses and narratives of the financial intermediaries concerned. Decentralized networks within and beyond the region coordinate their operations and subjectivities virtually instantaneously in and through 'electronic space' and 'cybertime'. In temporal terms, such networks of trans-spatialized actors are oriented to the nanoseconds of computer operations as they coordinate their decision-making units and operations; in turn, speed in time affects profitability and global competitiveness (Adam 1994, pp. 100–103). Spatially, the operations of these networks are mediated in 'electronic space' through telecommunication practices, ranging from the humble fax through electronic data interchange to an ever more mundane Internet and electronic conferencing (Poster 1995, p. 26). In this context, the so-called 'information superhighway' (which is still partial and limited) is coming to play an increasingly important role in transmitting information and knowledge. Share prices, interest rates, stock exchange indices and so on can be exchanged quickly in time and quickly in place in the highly competitive 'global economic village'. This does not mean that social space is unimportant; indeed, it contributes to the institutional thickness and capacities of the region. For global, regional and national actors from the private and public realms usually need to meet face to face to develop trust, establish networks, form partnerships, settle differences, and engage in mutual learning and interaction (Jarillo 1988, Camagni 1991, Conti 1993, Mayntz 1993, Sassen 1996).

Second, industrial and technological time-space moments are shaped by the practices of various global networks of multinational production firms in interaction with regional and more locally based firms which are coinvolved in the evolving regional division of labour and knowledge. Their operations are premised on the exploitation of cost differentials across borders and/or technological complementarities (Simon 1995, p. 4). These networks of strategic firms coordinate industrial/technological times and spaces which they themselves construct through their own planning and managing of time-bound and/or compressed-time production projects oriented to competitiveness in global and regional markets. Temporally, such networks are driven by their aim to produce goods in time, on time and every time to customers wherever they are in the global market. In order to speed up innovation by reducing lead times, and coordinate time-bound schedules, firms within and beyond the region enter strategic partnerships (subcontracting activities, joint ventures, strategic alliances, etc.) in order to produce just in time in 'regional factories'. Likewise, spatially, as production must be closely coordinated in trans-spatial and time-bound or compressed-time schedules, new institutional and technical forms of integrating activities emerge in both social and 'electronic space'. In social space, we find new spatial forms that cut across borders and are mediated by dense networks of private with private and private with public alliances based on complex relations of trust, competition and policy support (Jarillo 1988, Camagni 1991, Conti 1993, Mayntz 1993, Huber 1994). These networks are also cross-cut by strategic calculations of how to produce and reproduce labour across borders in the form of skilled commuter workers, guest and/or migrant labour. Besides social space, these links are reinforced by emerging practices in 'electronic space' which involve the exchange of relevant industrial/technological information concerned with Research and Development (R&D) and stages of the production process from design to manufacturing (Howells 1995).[7] The sites which emerge in this new discourse/identity are 'regional blocs', 'growth triangles', 'growth circles', 'sub-regional

[7] Examples include e-mail, video-conferencing, CAD-CAM data interchange, just-in-time production, simultaneous engineering, etc.

economic zones', 'offshore production sites' and 'learning/technological regions' linking regions with other regional circuits or even global ones (Boisier 1994, Florida 1995).

Third, commercial time-space moments are influenced by the practices of networks of multinational service firms and their regional or local counterparts located in 'global-gateway' cities. Their operations are premised on the provision of producer and distributive services and logistics information (insurance, legal services, consultancies, logistic management, transportation, retail) that 'facilitate all economic transactions, and the driving force that stimulates the production of goods' within the 'regional chain' (Riddle 1986, p. 26). These networks of service firms construct and coordinate the time and space of global-regional and regional-local nodes and nexi of production and distribution chains. In temporal terms, service firms in the 'supply pipeline' manage information flows that balance cost options and lead-and-transit time in time-bound projects. This is increasingly coordinated in 'electronic space' insofar as information is substituted for inventory (virtual inventory) at the centre so that quick responses can be made directly to the replenishment systems through local outsourcing or procurement (Christopher 1992, pp. 108–24). Social space is important here in developing trust, forming liaisons with local subcontractors/management and tapping local information flows that may enhance customer service management

Fourth, cultural time-space is shaped by social practices embedded in intra- and/or cross-cultural networks. Intra-cultural practices and norms are rooted in common traditions such as linguistic, familial, clan and communal ties; and their operations are premised on the need to 'lubricate the functioning of social networks' through practices such as gift exchange and banqueting in order to generate familial/clan/communal loyalty. The resulting intensification of the social space may help speed up the time taken to cross private-public borders. Cross-cultural interaction may involve consolidation of practices and norms that reduce the border-crossing time between cultural spaces (e.g. global entrepreneurship, multiculturalism, and even global post-colonialism).

2.2. Geo-governance Capacities for Cross-border Regional Modes of Growth

These four time-space moments of geo-governance provide the basis for what one might term a 'growth network'. This can be defined as a mode of coordination that is mediated by a multi-layered network of social relations that cuts across global-regional-national, time-space, and private-public dimensions of production and exchange. As a multi-layered network connecting these various dimensions, its capacity for promoting growth and competitiveness is usually influenced by the following components,[8] which may be termed components of geo-governance capacities.[9]

2.2.1. Global-regional-national dimensions

- The (quasi-)hierarchical networks of global, regional and national actors and their specific strategies or mechanisms for coordinating production, finance and trade activities (such as strategic alliances, joint ventures, subcontracting and aid-sponsored links) in the region.
- The strategic selectivity and capacities of this system in consolidating a specific (sub-)regional division of labour and knowledge, either in terms of cost differentials or technological complementarities.
- The condensation, in this structure of social relations, of certain nodal points (such as global-gateway or crossroad cities) providing complex services to bridge time-space gaps between global-regional and cross-border production and exchange.
- The consolidation within this structure of a complementary labour process and labour flow and a mode of social reproduction of labour power in and across borders and generations.[10]

2.2.2. Time-space dimensions

- The condensation of 'electronic space' and social practices that coordinate networks of multinational banks and other financial intermediaries involved in pooling and managing trans-spatialized funds fast in time and fast in space for global competitiveness.
- The consolidation of social and 'electronic space' practices that coordinate networks of production-service firms in planning and managing time-bound and compressed-time projects just in time for global competitiveness.
- The constitution of 'electronic space' and social practices conducive to building networks of service firms in reducing lead and transit times of production and distribution.
- The accumulation and crystallization of cultural/social norms,

[8] This list of components of subregional geo-governance is not exhaustive; it aims at facilitating the formulation of research questions and discussions.

[9] This schema is partly inspired by Clulow and Teague (1993).

[10] This may involve some kind of articulation between Ricardian and Schumpeterian welfare-workfare policies privileging a mix of public expenditure on housing, education, industrial training and infrastructural development.

practices that can reduce the border-crossing time between culture and/or private-public spaces.

2.2.3. Private-public dimensions

- A strong institutional presence and interaction of private-public networks for coordinating economic and political resources (e.g. investment, information, knowledge, aids etc.) at global, (inter-) national, translocal level(s).
- The emergence of new transborder social blocs which accept, support and relay the discourse and practices beyond elites.
- The creation of a unifying discourse around an imagined community of economic interests that ascribes and legitimates common purpose(s) for the region as a whole.

Overall, strategic networks of geo-governance could enhance the following:

- joint decision-making based on information-sharing, trust and commitment;
- the reflexity and creativity of interactive learning among private and public actors and institutions;
- a system of communication and negotiation conducive to societal guidance (steering) in the region;
- the privileging of business and industrial interests in formulating policy;
- capacities to deploy economic and political-bureaucratic resources, such as grants or loans (for infrastructure), authority, organizational intelligence, technology and manufacturing know-how; and
- capacities to engage in time-based competition that is related to shortening the lead time and global competitiveness.

None the less, such networks and structures do not arise simply because they are needed; nor, once they have emerged for whatever reason(s), do they always operate beneficially. They develop in quite specific conditions and cannot be created at will through specific policy initiatives. And, once they have developed, they may have difficulties in coordination and/or face challenges from within and beyond the networks.

2.3. Geo-governance Tensions of a Regional Mode of Growth

Such difficulties may be described as 'geo-governance tensions' which are rooted in the preconditions and dynamic of its structure, strategies and associated identities. In this context we must first note that not all logically possible sets of cross-border or virtual regions are likely to develop into regional modes of growth. In particular, the network of private and public actors might fail to develop a sufficient division of labour and knowledge because the economic spaces in which they are located are too similarly endowed to facilitate the necessary widening and/or deepening of economic complementarities to consolidate a cross-border or virtual region. Moreover, even if conditions are initially favourable, cost differentials in the network may change, for example, a continuous appreciation of the currencies of dominant partners or the rising costs of particular host economies. This could create tensions as attempts are made to improve productivity or cut costs by intensifying or deepening regional production networks. Similarly, if the productive bases of parts of the regional mode of growth converge (e.g. through less developed regions catching up) and/or are otherwise transformed (e.g. through the intensification of other regional linkages), then a relatively successful regional mode of growth may begin to decompose. Analogous arguments can also be developed regarding the conditions for stable modes of growth in particular forms of geo-governance (on the role of governance failure in the limited development of regional modes of growth in post-socialist societies, see e.g Jessop (1995b)).

Other sources of pressure on a regional mode of growth also exist. In today's international technology market, the tendency towards 'techno-globalism', in which global players seek to lower the costs of high-tech investment by proliferating technology transfer and opening cross-border technology flows, is counteracted by the opposing trend towards 'techno-nationalism', in which technologically advanced countries resist transferring technology in strategic fields to subordinate partners (Reich 1988, Ostry and Nelson 1995, Simon 1995). This tension is expressed in the twin dilemmas concerning cooperation-competition and interdependence-dependence. These are especially clear in the strategic behaviour of actors who engage in technological protectionism and/or demand that technology be transferred within a network. This tension could be further complicated if subordinate partners, in building their own techno-nationalist capacities to innovate, learn to compete and even 'leapfrog' the dominant players in the geo-governance network. Thus strategic partnerships may prompt worries about information-sharing, communication, trust and cross-cultural understanding. Such worries need not entail that the partnerships concerned lack the capacities to learn: for they may be able to reorganize and/or combine with other networks around alternative regional projects.

Geo-governance networks based on translocal linkages may involve conflicts over national sovereignty and constitutional issues regarding local autonomy. A further problem is that cross-border 'people-to-people'[11] networks may not be supported by corresponding intergovernmental networks, strategies and collaboration. Moreover, even if the conditions for this type of geo-governance are present, their co-existence with other power geometries could destabilize a region. This could occur through competition arising between different identities cutting through a dense network of economic relations. This can be illustrated from East Asian cross-border regions in terms of conflicts among global and regional hegemons concerning the role of different parts of the region in promoting nationalist or liberal democratic identities, interests and discourses (see Section 4.2).

3. THE GEO-GOVERNANCE OF A JAPAN-CENTRED NETWORK IN EAST ASIA

There are of course many emerging regional networks in East Asia and even more projects to establish such networks. It is impossible within the ambit of this chapter to list, let alone analyse, all these networks. I have therefore chosen to consider two of the most important networks, each of which is associated with a regional hegemon, whether actual or potential. Let us start with the emergence of the Japan-centred network in East Asia since the mid-1980s. Originally, Japanese foreign direct investment (or FDI) was largely concentrated in North-East Asian economies, such as Taiwan and South Korea. Since 1986, Japan's regional production network has also expanded into Hong Kong, Singapore, Malaysia, Indonesia, Thailand and the Philippines. This has occurred against a backdrop of intensifying US moves to correct its trade and employment problems. Under the G5 Plaza Accord in September 1985, the USA has tried to reverse its deteriorating trade relationship with Japan by forcing the appreciation of the yen relative to the dollar.[12] Saddled with uncompetitive prices in its export markets,

[11] On the Taiwanese case, see Clough (1993).

[12] Between September 1985 and December 1987, the yen more than doubled in value against the dollar, from around Y250: US$1.00 to just over Y120: US$1.00. The New Taiwan dollar simultaneously rose around 40% against the US currency, the South Korean won rose about 16%; and the Singapore dollar by a much smaller amount. The Hong Kong dollar remained tied to the US dollar, resulting in an effective 50% devaluation against the yen and, although less pronounced, depreciation against North-Asian NIC currencies.

rising domestic labour costs and fearing greater protectionism in US and European markets, Japan is seeking to reorganize the region through economic and financial means. These include trade, private FDI, official development assistance (ODA) and technology exports. This process is mediated by a strategic network of private-public actors cross-cutting regional-national and time-space dimensions of production and exchange.

Since the mid-1980s, the Plaza Accord has triggered more sector FDI from Japan and re-directed the role of Japanese ODA in the ASEAN region from securing natural resources to promoting export industries (e.g. improving social and economic infrastructures). Between 1988 and 1990, Japanese ODA amounted to US$6.68 billion and US$6.3 billion in South-East Asia and ASEAN respectively. In Asia in general, this amounts to roughly two-thirds of Japanese ODA stretching from India to China. As for Japanese FDI, some US$41 billion went into the East Asian economies between 1985 and 1993 (Bello and Cunningham 1994, p. 453). Unlike Japanese FDI elsewhere in the world, it is largely focused on industry rather than services. In the NICs, manufacturing investments comprised half of all cases of FDI, according to a Toyo Keizai Shimposha survey, and were largely oriented to Japanese innovation in components parts, machinery and sub-assemblies (Bernard and Ravenhill 1995, p. 177). For the EC and North America, the comparable figures were 21.2 and 30.2 per cent respectively (Tokunaga 1992).

The flow of Japanese ODA and FDI to East Asia involves a strategic network of relations embedded in private and public as well as regional and local domains. This multi-layered geo-governance network rests on many institutions of different kinds both in Japan and in the region. On the Japanese front, it involves the presence of Japanese public-private actors and institutions coordinating aid and trade ties in East Asia. This structural network creates certain strategic advantages for Japanese FDI by fostering the regionalization of industrial production centred on Japan. I shall begin with the network in Japan.

3.1. The Japan-centred Network and Flying Geese Region

This is marked by the presence of public-private actors and institutions coordinating aid and trade ties in East Asia.[13] Institutionally, it comprises a vertically segmented bureaucracy of Japanese ministries (e.g.

[13] The emergence of this network can be traced back to 1953 and Japan's urgent postwar attempt to organize its international activities to promote rapid industrial recovery and growth (Arase 1994, p. 173).

Economic Planning Agency, Ministry of Foreign Affairs, Ministry of Finance, Ministry of International Trade and Industry), aid-implementing agencies (e.g. Export-Import Bank, Overseas Economic Cooperation Fund, Japan International Cooperation Agency, Overseas Technical Cooperation Agency), research centres (e.g. Japan External Trade Organization), trade associations and large-scale private multinationals. The strong institutional presence of these bodies is matched by a high level of intra-network interactions, with aid-implementing agencies and trade associations in the middle. Together they constitute a system of communication and negotiation conducive to guiding key Japanese interests in the region. This involves a project-oriented ODA which rests on specific social/bureaucratic practices, thereby privileging certain Japanese economic interests in the overall project cycle. These strategically selective practices may include request-based procedures; decentralized authority; and case-by-case decision-making (Arase 1994, pp. 178–89).

First, the Japanese ministries and agencies act officially only after aid requests have been transmitted by local Japanese embassies. This enables private Japanese actors, such as trading companies, consulting firms and trade associations, to initiate requests in developing countries. Another variant of this system is project-finding missions. Subsidized by JICA and led by prestigious business leaders sponsored by trade associations, they may send delegations to developing countries to discuss preliminary project proposals and aid requests. Second, the local embassy, on receiving aid requests, sends appraisal reports to relevant main ministries and agencies. Informal bureaucratic rules ensure that the substance of the request determines which ministries and agencies are consulted. Since some 16 ministries and agencies share this case-load, this decentralized authority 'is not only important to ensure that the economic ministries retain a central policy-making role, but is also important to the private sector clients of the main ministries and agencies who use bureaucratic sponsorship to gain access to ODA resources' (Arase 1994, p. 178).

Alongside these institutional practices, other informal coordination mechanisms bring together private and public actors by exchanging personnel between the private sector and aid-implementing agencies and informal study groups between official and business leaders (Arase 1994, p. 199). This permits a high level of contacts, cooperation, information exchange which may lead, in time, to a certain mutual isomorphism and strategic positioning of the Japanese aid-trade nexus. Overall this strategic network of coordination can enhance the following:

- the reflexity of interactive learning among private and public actors and institutions;
- a system of cooperation, communication and negotiation conducive to socio-economic guidance in the region;
- the privileging of business and industrial interests in formulating Japanese ODA policy; and
- the capacity to deploy economic and political/bureaucratic resources such as infrastructure funding, political authority, organizational intelligence, technology and manufacturing know-how along lines complementing the Japanese economy. Given the reflexity, selectivity and capacity of this system of geo-governance it could well consolidate an aid-trade nexus in the region.

Parallel to, and capitalizing on, these structural networks and strategic advantages inherent in the private-public partnership, Japanese FDI tends to foster a form of regionalization of industrial production through a layered network in the region. This imagined network is reinforced discursively by the metaphor of a flying geese region. According to these imaginative constructions, 'economic cooperation with countries in Asia' is carried out through private initiatives assisted by government. This policy enables Japan to organize the industrial integration of East Asia in and through the metaphor of a flying geese region. This particular model of development has attained some popularity in the region. Given the diverse stages of economic development achieved in the region, the growth model is compared to the delta-shaped formation of flying geese. It portrays Japan as the spearhead of the flock and the four newly-industrializing countries (hereafter NICs) as following close behind, while the six ASEAN economies[14] are seen as next to have taken off. The post-socialist bloc is expected to join the flight at a later date. This flying geese metaphor represents the NICs' growth trajectory in terms of a movement from traditional to modernized economic orders, with Japan as the pioneer and exemplar of the developmental pattern. This developmental trajectory envisages the latecomers replicating the experience of the countries ahead of them in the formation. Thus, Japan guides the flock of geese in its techno-economic flight to success but each member of the flock follows under its own independent flight power albeit following Japan's staging points.

This image of the flying geese reinforces a synergistic division of

[14] The newly industrializing countries (NICs) comprises South Korea, Taiwan, Hong Kong and Singapore. The ASEAN economies include Singapore, Thailand, Malaysia, Indonesia, the Philippines and Brunei.

labour specializing in component procurement. Basically, domestic Japanese operations produce high-value and high-end-process products; and offshore affiliations produce low-value and low-end-process products/components. In the electronics industry, for example, Japanese companies concentrate on improving technology through indigenous R&D by supplying leading-edge core components such as active matrix LCDs (liquid crystal displays) and large-screen picture tubes. Affiliates in South Korea and Taiwan engage in OEM (original equipment manufacturing) arrangements related to intermediate components, parts and mouldings (Bernard and Ravenhill 1995, p. 191). Low-value products (simple consumer electronics like cassette recorders, headphones, microwave ovens, etc.) come from Malaysia, China and Thailand. The coordination of such production networks is enhanced by complex services offered by global cities that help to discipline the time-space gap between regional-national production and exchange. Thus Hong Kong and Singapore are increasingly condensed as nodal points offering services such as financial settlement, finance, insurance, legal, accounting, data processing, engineering services, market research, cargo handling and so on (Tokunaga 1992, p. 29, Rodan 1993, p. 235).

Although this chapter cannot analyse the time-space moments involved here, both 'social' and 'electronic space' are important arenas for coordinating fast-in-time and fast-in-place financial deals as well as time-bound or compressed-time projects requiring intra-company logistics to link the global, regional and national flows of raw materials, inventories, finished goods and so on. There is an increasing tendency for Japanese FDI to move into the service sectors of Hong Kong and Singapore. In Hong Kong, Japanese FDI has mainly gone into finance, commerce, telecommunication and technical support services – in part to exploit its ready access to, and plentiful knowledge of, China as a cheap production site and consumer market (Steven 1990, pp. 130–31, Sung 1991, pp. 15–26). Conversely, Singapore acts as the regional headquarters of Japanese multinationals (e.g. Sony) as well as providing offshore markets for financing and hedging their FDI in the region (Tokunaga 1992, pp. 181–8). These patterns suggest how Japanese FDI has given rise to a complementary division of labour and knowledge in which Japan is a base for high-tech and R&D development; South Korea and Taiwan engage in OEM arrangements; Hong Kong and Singapore are important for producer services and finance; and other ASEAN countries engage in low-end production.

The Japan-centred network in product/component sourcing is essentially mediated by a constellation of Japanese parent multinationals, their affiliates in East Asia, companies that are part of the parents' group, home suppliers' offshore affiliates and complex service firms. As a mode of social coordination, its production network predominantly consists of the following interactions in component procurement:

- between the parent company and its affiliates in East Asia;
- among the parents' affiliates in East Asia;
- among companies that are part of the parent groups and their East Asian affiliates; and
- those interactions that the parents' East Asian affiliates have established with East Asian subsidiaries of Japanese subcontractors that participate in the parents' domestic subcontracting systems.

The first two interactions constitute intra-firm, the last two intra-group, networks. In other words, interactions are confined within firms or groups with local firms playing a very marginal role. This pattern is sometimes seen as a closed regional production network (Ernst 1995, pp. 11–12).

3.2. The Geo-governance Tensions of the Japan-centred Network

This pattern of closed regional production networks has increasingly been challenged by extra- and intra-network tensions within the flying geese region from around 1992.[15] They have three main sources:

- yen appreciation;
- globalized competition; and
- structural change in East Asian host economies (Ernst 1995, Simon 1995).

First, the continuous yen appreciation since 1992 has substantially increased Japan's export costs. Japanese affiliates based in East Asia must now pay much higher prices for components and production equipment imported from Japan. As most East Asian subsidiaries continue to procure most of their intermediate inputs from Japan, the yen appreciation has wiped out any cost advantages due to the lower costs of labour in the host economies. Moreover, local sourcing costs have declined. Thus, Japan-centred production networks face increasing pressure to reduce their Japanese inputs and source locally. One should not overestimate the importance of yen appreciation. For, while periodic

[15] For a critical evaluation of the flying geese model, see Bernard and Ravenhill (1995).

yen appreciations have acted as catalysts in determining the timing of overseas investment, they are insufficient in explaining Japan's East Asian investment strategies.

A second source of new pressures on the network is the globalization of competition. To remain competitive, Japanese manufacturers, especially so-called flexible or post-Fordist producers, have focused on rapid market share expansion based on shortening the product cycle, developing core components and relying on product variety wars. Constant product differentiation has been the main vehicle of market share expansion. These strategies are now undercut by price wars in the electronics market owing to a shift from sellers' to buyers' markets. During the autumn of 1992, US firms such as Compaq and Dell, followed by Apple and others, started a price war which seriously threatens Japanese producers.

Third, structural changes in the East Asian host economies have also challenged the Japan-centred network. The increasing costs of production and the techno-nationalist drive among latecomer NICs to upgrade their 'national systems of innovation' have complicated the network's synergistic relations.[16] Combined with economic complementarity, they are strengthening their competitive capacities and may even 'leap-frog' Japan. In short, the Japan-NIC relationship involves a dialectic of 'leap-frogging' and dependency. Some latecomers, therefore, are learning to design products independently of foreign buyers (own design manufacture or ODM) and some are even developing and marketing their own brands (own brand manufacture: OBM). Well-known leap-froggers in electronics include Samsung (South Korea) launching its innovation on memory chips (DRAMs), and ACER (Taiwan) licensing its own US-patented Chip Up technology to Intel (Bello and Cunningham 1994, p. 454, Hobday 1995, pp. 86–9, 116–17). Likewise, latecomer multinational service firms such as Singapore Airline and Hong Kong Bank can now compete with their Japanese counterparts in the global market.

However, these examples are exceptions rather than the rule. Developing the capabilities[17] to acquire and operate foreign technology

[16] Hobday (1995) is an excellent study of the NICs' learning strategies and their capacity to constantly narrow the gap between themselves and the market leaders.

[17] Capabilities refer here to the enterprises' relative capacities to react speedily to given incentives within a given institutional setting. Incentives derived from prices are shaped mainly by macroeconomic policy. But it is educational, industrial and technology policies which are crucial for shaping capabilities. The latter represent economic competencies which enable the identification, expansion and exploitation of the opportunity set. In this regard, capabilities can only be built and cannot be transferred or bought. For further discussion, see Radosevic (1994, pp. 89–90).

does not necessarily lead, in each country, to an ability to adapt, innovate or even leap-frog. The ability to foster such activities depends on various other factors, including accumulated technical expertise, a high quality communications infrastructure and good levels of general and technological education. In this regard, most firms in the NICs still depend on Japanese counterparts. Hobday's study of Singapore's electronics industry shows that local firms pursued a long-term, painstaking incremental learning path rather than leaping from one vintage of technology to another. Their development involved a 'hard slog' rather than a 'leap-frog' (Hobday 1995, p. 200). Much of their technological advance in the electronics industry was grounded in OEM arrangements and 'pre-electronic' fields such as machine tooling, plastic moulding and mechanical and precision engineering. This suggests that firms progressed incrementally in response to market growth and depended heavily on international suppliers and overseas experts for advanced technology.

Such geo-governance tensions have created pressure on both Japanese and NIC firms to develop strategies along one or more of the following new lines:

- improving productivity in their production networks;
- developing and consolidating production activities in new locations; and
- opening closed networks and entering new partnerships with other regional actors.

Given limited space, I will consider how the last two strategies are pursued in just two cases. Thus first, I will examine the relocation of the labour-intensive processes of Hong Kong and Taiwan to southern China and the gradual consolidation of a geo-governance network in 'Greater China' (see Section 4). And then I will analyse the gradual opening up of the Japan-centred network as it enters into a new form of partnership with its Chinese counterpart (see Section 5).

4. THE GEO-GOVERNANCE OF A 'GREATER CHINA' NETWORK IN EAST ASIA

The emergence of the Greater China network is related to the strategic articulation of changes in China, Hong Kong, and Taiwan. China's 'open door policy' aims at economic development from local incentives, especially in the two southern coastal provinces (Guangdong and

Fujian) close to Hong Kong and Taiwan. Two strategies for freeing local initiatives from overly top-heavy central control are involved here: decentralization and coastal strategies.

The first strategy was spearheaded by coastal provinces such as Guangdong and Fujian – the two economically most open Chinese provinces. Guangdong, for example, demanded greater autonomy and special policies from the central government. The Party Central Committee responded with the strategic decision to adopt 'special policies and flexible measures' towards both Guangdon and Fujian in 1979. This reformed framework adopted a five-year macro-contracted responsibility system which involves:

- commercial reform allowing enterprises and business units under central control (except those in certain areas) to be transferred to and managed by the province;
- movement from prices set and readjusted by planning agencies to variable prices determined autonomously by buyer and seller;
- fiscal/financial reform enabling Guangdong to retain the surplus portion of foreign currency earnings from exports after it had turned over 30 per cent of the surplus to the central government from 1980;[18] and
- wage reform involves more flexibility in enterprise wage bills, greater wage variation in response to enterprise and individual productivity; reduced employment and welfare guarantees and tightened labour discipline (Cheung 1994, pp. 214–15, Walder 1994, p. 306).

Second, in negotiation with the central government, these reform measures were gradually introduced in coastal provinces such as Guangdong and Fujian. Initially, Guangdong and Fujian were given substantial legal and administrative power in managing the four special economic zones (SEZs), three of which were located in Guangdong (Shenzhen, Zhuhai and Shantou) and one in Fujian (Xiamen). Under administrative bodies that were set up by the provinces, the objectives of the SEZs are:

[18] Other changes involve retaining all above-baseline foreign exchange earned from export processing, joint-ventures and other non-trade sources. To promote infrastructure construction, the province can also exempt taxes and reduce profit remittances from enterprises in relevant sectors. The Guangdong branch of the People's Bank enjoys greater discretion in issuing loans. The centre can still decide on tax laws and international taxation, yet the two provinces can levy and adjust all local taxes and decide on tax reductions.

- to develop economic links between Hong Kong (Shenzhen), Macau (Zhuhai), Taiwan (Xiamen) and overseas Chinese communities (Shantou), with a view to reunifying China; and
- to serve as 'windows' for learning advanced technology and managerial skills as well as attracting foreign investment.

In 1981, the People's Congress in Guangdong was empowered by the National People's Congress to formulate laws and regulations governing economic activities in the SEZs. In 1992, the People's Congress of Shenzhen Municipality was awarded these powers.

During the continual (re-)negotiations between the central and Guangdong (or Fujian) governments, these reform measures for administering FDI have been gradually expanded. In the earlier years (1979–82), only the Ministry of Foreign Economic Relations and Trade (MOFERT) in Beijing was allowed to deal with FDI applications. Given their inexperience with complex joint ventures, provincial governments were later empowered to deal with joint ventures which involved investment of up to US$3 million (extended to US$10 million in 1985 and US$30 million in 1988), although MOFERT still retains the power of veto.

These reforms made Guangdong the most open area for FDI in China. Since the establishment of the four SEZs, China has designated a number of other open areas for FDI. These include: 14 coastal cities (two in Guangdong) and three coastal areas (e.g. the Pearl River Delta in Guangdong). Foreign investment in these different types of open areas enjoy varying incentives, for example, the income tax rate is 15 per cent in SEZs and 24 per cent in coastal areas. Given Guangdong's head start, it has the biggest concentration of open areas in a favourable position for FDI. In addition, the reform programme has offered Guangdong provincial and local governments exclusive fiscal incentives to develop an outward-looking economy. According to a contract between Guangdong and the central government, the former was allowed to retain 70 per cent of export earnings above the 1978 export level (US$1.4 billion), while other provinces (except Fujian) could retain only 30 per cent for centrally managed goods and 40 per cent for locally managed goods. The provincial and local governments in Guangdong and Fujian thus had great incentives to actively attract export-oriented FDI from Hong Kong and Taiwan.

In response to these emerging opportunities within China, the rise of Western protectionism and increases in its own domestic costs for land and labour, Hong Kong's FDI in Guangdong has grown rapidly. It is now by far the biggest investor in the province, supplying 80 per cent of the FDI in Guangdong. Pearl River Delta is now a major production base for its more labour-intensive products. It is estimated that almost 20 000 Hong Kong manufacturing enterprises, mostly in textiles and clothing, toys and consumer electronics, have moved there to take advantage of low labour and rent costs. They directly employ about three million workers.

Unlike Hong Kong, the Taiwanese government in the early 1980s saw few advantages and many serious risks in trade with the mainland. However, the appreciation of the Taiwanese currency since 1986, the rising cost of land and the high standards set by the 1984 Basic Labour Law have all made the Chinese market increasingly attractive to Taiwanese businesses. Some have urged the government to end restrictions on trade and expressed concern that they were losing out in the rapidly growing Chinese market to Japanese and South Korean competitors. The Taiwanese government gave way to growing popular pressure by allowing indirect links with China, beginning with the decision in November 1987 that Taiwanese citizens would be allowed to 'visit relatives' in China. The Central Bank of Taiwan also liberalized the foreign exchange regime in 1987 by allowing free capital outflows of under five million new Taiwanese dollars. The legalization of travel and liberalization of foreign exchange sharply accelerated the growth in trade and FDI between them. In 1988, the Chinese State Council promulgated a set of 22 measures to encourage investment from Taiwan. As a result, some five million Taiwanese have visited China and some 8 000 Taiwanese firms have moved their production facilities there with investment of US$8.6 billion at the end of 1993.

4.1. The China Network and the 'Greater China' Region

Guangdong and Fujian, as FDI hosts, not only possess cheap labour and land, but also have the further advantage of a vast and rapidly growing internal market. These coastal provinces also share a similar cultural background and the use of a common language. The contingent interaction of these cultural traits and economic strategies has brought about the consolidation of a new geo-governance network that cuts across public and private as well as central, provincial and local domains within China and the Greater China bloc.

The decentralization and coastal strategies have created new public, quasi-public and private institutions aiming at expanding foreign economic relations at both the central and lower levels. On the central level, these include MOFERT which manages the introduction of foreign investment, new trading arrangements, and the establishment of joint ventures, and the China International Trust and Investment Company (CITIC)[19] which was to facilitate the establishment of joint ventures. On the provincial level, Guangdong and Fujian followed the centre in setting up the Guangdong (Fujian) province functional and line ministries or state-owned companies to administer, negotiate and finance foreign trade. Further decentralization of the economy in 1984 accelerated this process when branches of foreign and industrial trading corporations controlled by ministries established their own provincial corporations. Guangdong and Fujian, in particular, were allowed to acquire many branches of the public-owned foreign trading corporations, and to set up their own organizations in Hong Kong and Macau for trade promotion and information gathering. By 1987, the number of such corporations had risen to 1900. These strategies/processes have also induced changes at the local level. Here I will concentrate on the emergence of a strategic developmental network in special localities, such as special economic zones or development zones at the county-township-village levels in coastal provinces. At these levels, the network includes:

- county party or government officials and the trading companies they control (which must find foreign investors, export quotas, domestic markets and foreign technology);
- township-village state or party officials and the township-village enterprises (TVEs) they control.

Often, the manager-executives of these new enterprises are drawn from county-, township- or village-level cadres and administrators of precursor activities in the socialist period. For example, agricultural machinery-repair work-shops of a village have often turned into light industrial enterprises and village construction departments into property developers. These companies or enterprises often expand and develop subsidiaries in a largely unregulated way, so that they come to act as conglomerates nominally owned by the village (Zweig 1995, p. 268, Goodman 1995, pp. 136–8). These changes have led to the strong presence of a network made up of a set of new public actors/organizations at central, provincial and local levels as well as a layer of quasi-public actors and enterprises encouraged to be flexible, export- and profit-oriented. These actors and organizations, especially those at local

[19] Shen (1993) estimated that CITIC, a multinational under the direct supervision of the State Council, had an investment portfolio in Hong Kong worth over HK$34 billion.

level, have benefited from the decentralization strategy. The capacities of the local government/enterprise are enhanced by:

- the transfer of the utilization rights of assets (such as taxes, land, labour, loans, power supply, import/export licences, etc.) to the local level, where these rights enable local players to enter into flexible networking practices (such as subcontracting) with Hong Kong or Taiwanese investors;
- a transfer of return rights (the rights to possess some of the fruits of the utilization of assets) to the local level, which could permit a second budget as they creatively shift taxable items away from the central-local budgetary accounts (Oi 1992, p. 100, Wang 1994, p. 99);
- the continual source of fiscal softness permitted by the 'second budget' enabling local governments to experiment with new local projects;
- the granting of additional powers, such as the power to make contracts with foreign firms; and
- the right of local party-state officials to enter into joint ventures or own subsidiaries of state enterprises and become cadre entrepreneurs (Nee 1992, p. 127).

Gaining greater capacity in this way for the localities has changed the patterns of interaction within the network. More specifically, it has changed the nature of bargaining within the polity from a form of paternalism (Kornai 1980, p. 592) to rivalry or partnership. Basically, when the centre and localities are rivals with regard to fiscal issues or decreasing prospects in trade, local government and enterprises become allies; and when the centre and localities are partners in activities such as setting up joint ventures, both of them together with the enterprises form a triple alliance (Zhang and Zou 1994, p. 168).

Let us start with the central-local rivalry especially regarding fiscal issues. Decentralization has changed these relations because:

- it weakens the fiscal leverage of central-level government over local government by making the latter less dependent on the former for revenue and investment funds;
- it heightens the importance of local investment and economic growth in generating revenue; and
- it reorients local party-state officials from compliance with superiors toward economic activities enlarging their revenue (Walder 1994, p. 306).

This weakening of the centre is far from being one-sided because the central government still controls 're-centralization' levers, such as tightening macroeconomic control, reorienting national economic policy, renegotiating the sharing of resources and controlling personnel appointments. Similarly, local authorities have devised various coping strategies to deal with the centre, such as lobbying for central support, creatively interpreting central policies, flexibly implementing central measures and withholding as many funds as possible from central extraction. The use of these bargaining instruments in the tug of war between central and local government is interpreted by Howell (1993) in terms of cycles of decentralization and re-centralization that have been occurring in China since 1978. This rivalry is especially intense when the size of the fiscal and economic 'pie' is shrinking.

Despite the tug of war between central and local political forces over fiscal issues (Wong 1991, pp. 691–3), central and local governments also cooperate as partners. Successful cooperation occurs when participants anticipate rapid expansion in foreign trade. In such cases, localities encourage local enterprises to accept the centre's rules of the game in order to achieve their mutual goal of expanding exports. Thus, in the case of trade, if the goal is to build export bases for raw material production, both sides would work together to set up a joint venture. Here the central-local relationship is reciprocal and mutually dependent. Often enterprises also join such projects, forming triple alliances. For example, the three parties put a certain proportion of funds into constructing a raw material base, or two sides contribute funds while the third contributes technicians.

Capitalizing on these new capacities and opportunities, Taiwan and Hong Kong capitalists have been drawing on their linguistic affinities and kinship ties. They have begun building socio-economic connections in the region. They enter into networking activities with local Chinese officials and quasi-public agencies in the region. These networking activities can be enhanced/deepened in and through cultural practices of '*quanxi*' (relationship). When such pre-existing relationships are absent, it may take time to cultivate new linkages and this will often involve exchanging material/informational gifts (Yang 1989, 1994, Smart and Smart 1991), taking potential partners out for dinner, karaoke or entertainment, and making donations to the community. These practices are often symbolized as signs of friendship, mutual trust and loyalty. It is through the active exchange of these gifts and favours that boundaries and significance are given to *quanxi* networks. A reliable and effective network can speed up the border-crossing time between the private-public space because the latter can choose to adopt a permeable boundary for the needs of the private. For example, pre-existing *quanxi* can expedite the time needed in obtaining licences, loans and raw materials from the cadre entrepreneurs and their organizations.

The above description of the cultural time-space moment within the 'Greater China' region reveals the condensation of a loosely hierarchical network of relations that cuts across private-public and (trans)-local domains. This draws on pre-existing *quanxi* to build networks. Here I examine such networks by reference to international subcontracting. The commodity chain in international subcontracting in the region is mediated by a more complex network of relations within the 'Greater China' bloc that comprises: foreign buyers, Hong Kong and/or Taiwan-owned firms, China's quasi-state trading firms in Hong Kong, state- or privately owned firms in China, and provincial, municipal or local governments and their subsidiaries, as well as county-level cadre entrepreneurs. This network involves the presence of public and private actors and institutions organized in a loosely hierarchical network of relations that cuts across private and public as well as local and cross-border domains. At the local level, this network involves provincial, county and township governments and their subsidiaries, local branches of ministries and their affiliates encouraging investors coming from Hong Kong and Taiwan. This China-centred network also involves small- and medium-sized firms drawing on the informal kinship system. In this sense, it is a more flexible and open system in which small- to medium-sized investors negotiate with local-level governments and/or quasi-public enterprises for contracts and, it is hoped, profits. The resulting structure of cross-border social coordination is less hierarchical than its Japanese counterpart and tends to interlink central and local, public and private, and regional and local domains. The form of interaction tends to be group- and not firm-based: local state or party officials, semi-public enterprises, and incoming firms from Hong Kong and Taiwan all play important roles. This is not a horizontal market connection because the link is not one between legally equal individuals but rather involves power asymmetries between actors and institutions. Nor do these networks resemble hierarchical command-economy linkages because exchanges are not mediated through authority relations between superiors and subordinates: instead, they involve informal material and administrative exchanges from which both actors can exit when desired. For example, local party and state officials still control resources such as land, labour, capital and regulations; semi-public enterprises command information and contacts; and private firms control capital, managerial skills and market outlets. Given the above interdependent relations, there is a tendency for this public-private network to form clientelist alliances and be consolidated in the pattern of an open regional collaborative network when compared with the Japanese counterpart.

This structural network creates strategic advantages and enjoys the support of a cross-border coalition or alliance of local officials, their entrepreneurial affiliates and Hong Kong and Taiwanese capital. This provides social support for the regionalized division of labour in relation to export processing in the 'Greater China' bloc. Hong Kong and Taiwan are moving up the industrial technology ladder by shifting their labour-intensive industries to low-wage and cheap-land regions in southern China.[20] These include 80 per cent of Hong Kong's manufacturing industries such as simple electronics, toys, leather, shoemaking and watches. Because Hong Kong's manufacture is largely oriented to export-processing, the transfer of the industry to southern China promotes entrepôt trade between the two regions. Taiwan's transfer of manufacture lags behind Hong Kong but the transfer of labour-intensive industries is moving quickly. It is reported that Taiwan's traditional industries, for instance, 80 per cent of handbag production, 90 per cent of shoemaking and most of umbrella-making have been transferred to southern China; but a large part of raw materials, components and production equipment still comes from Taiwan. Given the lack of direct links between Taiwan and China, most of the flow of material, people and money targeted on Fujian Province pass through Hong Kong.

The shifting of labour-intensive processes to the Pearl River Delta not only consolidates Hong Kong's entrepôt role but also enhances its capacity, as a gateway city, to coordinate investment, trade and services in the 'Greater China' region. Elsewhere I have termed this 'subcontracting management', to highlight its role in spanning the time and space dimensions of cross-border production, trade and finance. Subcontracting management involves sourcing, production, authority and distribution management. First, Hong Kong or Taiwan producers seek Chinese partners through formal and informal contacts and ties. This involves coordination in the social space embedded in family, kinship and village relationships. On establishing these social ties, they enter agreements with quasi-public corporations/TVEs (Township-village enterprises (Weitzman and Xu 1994)) in China. This may consolidate into longer-lasting ties such as subcontracting partners and joint

[20] In the case of sports shoes such as Nike, most of the raw materials and skills come from Taiwan through Hong Kong to southern China. Hong Kong staff deal with designs, make sure the sample and raw materials reach the factory on time, and ship the finished products out of China through Hong Kong to their destined markets, mainly the USA (Chen 1993, p 102).

ventures. Sourcing and consolidating such alliances requires more complex services related to business consultancy, legal services on production-sharing contracts, licensing, accounting expertise on mergers, take-overs and franchising in Hong Kong. After establishing sourcing networks, the Hong Kong or Taiwanese firms engage in cross-border production management. Essential to this cross-border production is the building and maintaining of good relations with local and/or central officials in China. This kind of institutionalized networking with state officials is important because state authorities still control enormous resources such as land, labour, capital and regulations. In addition to production and authority management in a multi-spatial production process, business services are needed for distribution management. Finished goods need to be exported and distributed to overseas markets to meet consumer demand. This involves the management of information flow that balances cost options and lead and transit time in time-bound projects. This is increasingly being coordinated in the electronic space by synchronizing export procedures of import/export licensing, customs liaison and arranging shipments and so on, so that goods can be delivered just in time and just in place for overseas buyers. Again, this involves a network of service-based firms in Hong Kong and China as well as the trading and customs authorities in China and elsewhere.

In essence, this cross-border private-public network can be cemented through the time-space coordination of production and exchange and this phenomenon was defined by one Hong Kong managing director of a multinational in terms of the three Ts: time, trust and truth. They form the basic ingredients, in the ideal case, for the production and reproduction of this private-public network. It is through the production and reproduction of this strategic network, both in the social and electronic space, that Hong Kong is crystallizing its position as a global-gateway city in providing business and financial services (e.g. legal, banking and accounting expertise) and Taiwan as the source of investment and technology. In the case of Taiwan, it concentrates on the manufacturing of higher-end products such as personal computers (PCs). Taiwan's total PC-related industries have grown by an average annual rate of 25 per cent since 1981. In 1993, it was the fifth largest PC exporter in the world after Japan, the USA, Germany and Singapore. Among Taiwan's major export items are computer monitors, desk-top and portable PCs, motherboards, keyboards and PC mice.

These material developments are reinforced by the discursive construction of an imagined identity of 'Greater China'. An increasing body of literature uses 'Greater China' to summarize the vibrancy of economic interactions in the economically, culturally and linguistically compatible area of Taiwan, Hong Kong, Macau and the mainland's Guangdong and Fujian provinces. Most studies forecast an optimistic future for economic growth in this region (Cheng 1992, Fang 1992, Fu 1992). Ethnic Chinese business people and interested Chinese intellectuals envision a 'Greater China' of a much larger territorial scope and maintain that the formation of an economic 'Greater China' of sorts is the first step towards national reunification. This 'pragmatic nationalism' (Sum 1995, p. 70) is used to redefine and coordinate the internal complementarity of the region in relation to China and to promote its competitiveness in the changing global economy.

According to China, Hong Kong can be defined as a strategic gateway for Beijing in the implementation of its policies of attracting '*huaqiao*' (patriotic) investments in the Chinese 'motherland'. This interpellation of 'patriotic ethnic Chinese investors' links nationalism to economics rather than politics. It thereby enables China to gain Taiwanese and Hong Kong investment/technology without directly addressing, at least in the short term, the thorny problem of the relation between nationalism and politics. As for Hong Kong and Taiwan, the new economic relationship with China is a new source both of economic opportunity and political tension which will be discussed in the next section.

4.2. Geo-governance Tensions of the 'Greater China' Network

This discussion of the 'Greater China' network would be incomplete without examining its intra- and extra-network tensions. As a strategic network of public-private partnerships, it may involve conflict with the centre and/or asymmetric relations between party officials and company executives at the local level. For those TVEs that have turned into joint ventures, there is tension involving technology transfer between the local enterprises and their counterparts in Hong Kong, Taiwan and overseas. In addition, joint ventures strengthen the power of the local state (party or state officials are often 'chairman of the board' of enterprises) to tighten discipline of the workforce. This is especially true of 'guest workers' hired as cheap labour in nearby provinces, living in dormitories, and working for the local community. Income gaps between such outsiders and community insiders living in two and three storey homes remain points of tension.

Looking at the 'Greater China' region, translocal linkages and people-to-people diplomacy between China and Taiwan have given rise to new intra-bloc tensions (Clough 1993). Economic development and the network of coordination is unmatched by official networks and strategies linking the two entities. In response to Taiwan's recent attempts to build a stronger international identity through reapplying for entry into the United Nations and Lee's unofficial visit to the USA, China halted most semi-official talks across the Strait and even threatened Taiwan with missiles during the presidential election (Sum 1996b).

A related tension concerns conflicting economic and political objectives in the region. For example, Hong Kong's geo-economic role as a global gateway for Beijing and Taiwan to pursue their policies of attracting *huaqiao* investments to the motherland coexists with the Anglo-American geopolitical strategy of contrasting Hong Kong as a 'democratic hub' with the possible 'risks' posed by China in the region (Pollock 1993, p. 76, Sum 1996b). The intersection of these two strategies has created a moment of identity struggle in Hong Kong. This struggle is further complicated by the emergence of a democracy movement in Taiwan as well as the USA's geopolitical linkages with that island. This is seen in the continued lease or sale of arms to Taiwan, open support by some senators for the Taiwanese democracy movement, and welcoming the President's unofficial visit to USA (Sum 1996b). These geopolitical partnerships between the USA, UK, Hong Kong and Taiwanese democrats and the geo-economic network centred on China have clearly confronted social forces, whether located within or outside this economic network, with crucial tensions and dilemmas regarding what interests to pursue and how to act (Sum 1995).

5. THE OPENING OF THE JAPAN-CENTRED NETWORK AND THE 'GREATER CHINA' REGION

Thus far, the geo-governance capacities of the two East Asian cases have been treated separately. With the continuous appreciation of the yen, the pressure of global competition and the structural changes in the NICs, the opening of the Japanese network has led to the transfer of more advanced technology to East Asia. The private-public network and investment promoted by Japan's ODA have moved into infrastructural projects as well as industrial and commercial ventures, especially in parts of north-east China such as Shanghai and Dalian. Apart from sourcing and targeting China as a future market, some are beginning to seek non-Japanese suppliers, contracting manufacturers for an increasing number of their components and developing R&D facilities overseas in Asia (Ernst 1995, Simon 1995). In the case of the electronics, automobile and car component industries, they are experimenting with linkages with Taiwanese counterparts to set up joint ventures in China via Hong Kong. This tendential coupling of the two networks is helping to upgrade the regional technological regime and even consolidate a new regional division of knowledge and experiences. Among possible paths here are:

- Japanese technology, high-tech components, global market experience and management system;
- Taiwanese applied technology, Japanese-substitutable components, manufacturing practices in China and contacts in Japan;
- Hong Kong's production and financial services specializing in China (e.g. entrepôt services, capital for infrastructural projects, pre-existing *quanxi* with Chinese local leaders and municipal authorities, market information, business contacts, logistic management and risk-bearing in the case of non-payments by Chinese firms), and;
- China's raw material, cheap technical personnel (e.g. high-quality engineers and computer programmers) and skilled labour.

An analysis of the tendential coupling of the geo-governance networks and the tensions associated with them is beyond the scope of this chapter. However, one can try to map out the trends involved:

- a hybridized network of social relations that may become consolidated in a more sophisticated division of knowledge within the region;
- a denser system of social and time-space coordination which involves a multi-layered network organized in terms of public-private as well as regional, national, provincial and county levels;
- a more complex system of interactive learning in a deeper network;
- the deepening of the 'Greater China' network through technological upgrading;
- the integration of the 'Greater China' network of the southern provinces with the techno-economic heartland of the north (e.g. Shanghai alone has 50 000 more scientists and engineers than Singapore, and 30 000 more researchers than South Korea);
- China emerges as a major participant in the techno-economic affairs of the region;
- Japan can use such developments to build extensive social net-

works that would help them not only set up future production plants but also gain control of distribution channels;
- there may be growing competitive tensions between China and Japan (e.g. they are already beginning to compete in the Middle Eastern car market);
- a reconfigured labour market/process pertinent to the deepening regional division of knowledge; and
- the emergence of multi-cultural discourses that may engender intercultural cooperation.

6. CONCLUSION

This chapter has developed three main themes. First, in the strategic context of changes in the global economy, the concept of geo-governance could offer new insights into competitive-collaborative initiatives of regional economic groupings. As modes of growth, the latter involve the coordination of a multi-layered network of social relations that cuts across the various global-regional-national, time-space and private-public dimensions of production and exchange. In applying the concept of geo-governance to regional modes of growth, I have highlighted the spatio-temporal aspects of economic governance as well as its more familiar (at least conceptually, if not substantively) context of social embeddedness, for the embeddedness of regional modes of growth nowadays involves a complex articulation of real and virtual space across multiple temporal and spatial horizons.

Second, this chapter attempts to apply, in a preliminary way, the concept of geo-governance to two major cross-border networks in East Asia. It argues that the relative success of such networks involves far more than spontaneous market forces or simple, top-down-initiatives coordination by the state. A wide variety of inter-organizational mechanisms are involved with a strong emphasis on the self-organization of such links based on flexible ground rules which are themselves organized by governments acting alone or in cooperation to ensure a modicum of complementarity or consistency among the governance mechanisms. The latter operate in a complex situation marked by the social embeddedness of economic relations: the role of kinship, the Chinese diaspora, the role of trusting interpersonal relationships (*guanxi*), the absence of strong acquisitive individualism and a general inclination towards collectivism on a variety of social and spatial scales. They also operate in a specific climate where shared identities (often contested) provide a provisional framework of trust so that economic relations can be extended and consolidated.

These issues illustrate how the concept of geo-governance can be deployed to overcome the binary demarcation of state-society, private-public, internal-external, and centre-periphery relations which dominate popular approaches on East Asia (e.g. Amsden's and Wade's developmental state; So's centre-periphery analysis; Koo's internal-external interactions). More recently, Evans has developed the concept of embedded autonomy by suggesting that the developmental state (vertical state-society relations) is enclosed by organic networks (horizontal ties formed through formal and informal networks); he concludes with a vague notion of 'internationalization and state involvement' (1995, pp. 203–206). Although there is no doubt that Evans's approach adds sophistication to Wade's 'developmental state' argument it can still be criticized on the following grounds:

- Evan's conception is still embedded in the Euro-centric binary of state-society relations with an ad hoc addition of network ties and
- it is still concerned with trying to explain East Asian success through a national-state perspective and fails to take account of regionalization and regional modes of growth that are pertinent to East Asian growth in the global age.

In contrast, this chapter has sought to transcend these perspectives by addressing global-regional-national, private-public as well as time-space dimensions of growth and competitiveness. It has sought to apply concepts such as networks, societal steering, geo-governance, mode of growth, organizational learning, time-space controls and imagined identities, and to overcome the Euro-centricity of popular approaches in analysing East Asia.

Third, in examining these networks, my chapter adopts an evolutionary approach. Much of the literature on networks considers them either from a purely typological viewpoint or in terms of their specific dynamic features at a particular point in time. The above analysis is more concerned with:

- the dynamic of networks, that is, their development over time, in the context of the emerging global-regional-local network;
- the learning process of actors in mobilizing resources tailored to the new situation; and

- the coupling of networks searching for a new regional division of knowledge and labour.

Clearly my comments here are still provisional. The empirical materials on several issues need further considerations and development. Among these are cross-border social reproduction of labour and the role of trade organizations in building cross-border networks. None the less, this chapter marks an initial attempt to chart a more complex approach to cross-border modes of growth on the basis of geo-governance and the latter's time and space embeddedness in regularizing cross-border production and exchange.

REFERENCES

Adam, B. (1994) *Timewatch*. Cambridge: Polity.
Akamatsu, K. (1962) 'A Historical Pattern of Economic Growth'. *The Developing Economies*. Preliminary Issue 1.
Amin, A. and Thrift, N. (eds) (1994) *Globalization, Institutions, and Regional Development in Europe*. Oxford: Oxford University Press.
Amsden, A. (1989) *Asia's Next Giant*. New York: Oxford University Press.
Anderson, B. (1991) *Imagined Communities: Reflection on the Origin and Spread of Nationalism*. London: Verso.
Arase, D. (1994) 'Public-Private Sector Interest Coordination in Japan's ODA'. *Pacific Affairs* 67 (2): 171–99 (Summer).
Bello, W. and Cunningham, S. (1994) 'Trade Warfare and Regional Integration in the Pacifics: The USA, Japan and the Asian NICs'. *Third World Quarterly* 15 (3):445–58.
Bernard, M. and Ravenhill, J. (1995) 'Beyond Product Cycles and Flying Geese: Regionalization, Hierarchy and the Industrialization of East Asia'. *World Politics* 47 (2): 171–209.
Boisier, S. (1994) 'Regionalization Process: Past Crises and Current Options'. *CEPAL Review* 52: 177–88.
Borrus, M. (1995) 'Punctuated Equilibria in Electronics: Microsystems, Standards' Competitions, and Asian Production Networks'. Paper presented to the IGCC conference 'China Circle: Evolving Relations between China, Taiwan, and Hong Kong-Macao'. Hong Kong, 8–10 December.
Calder, K.E. (1991) 'Japan and the NIEs: The Political Economy of Rising Interdependence' in H.H. Kendall and C. Joewono (eds) *Japan*, ASEAN, *and the United States*. Berkeley: Institute of East Asian Studies, University of California at Berkeley, pp. 222–46.
Camagni, R. (ed.) (1991) *Innovation Networks: Spatial Perspectives*. London: Belhaven Press.
Camagni, R. (1995) 'The Concept of Innovative Milieu and its Relevance for Public Policies in European Lagging Regions'. *Papers in Regional Science* 74 (4): 317–40.
Chai, S.Y. and Lee, T.Y. (1993) 'Subregional Economic Zones: A New Force in

Asia-Pacific Development' in C.F. Bergsten and M. Noland (eds) *Pacific Dynamism and the International Economic System*. Washington: Institute for International Economics, pp. 225–72.

Chan, J.C.M., Sculli, D. and Si, K. (1991) 'The Cost of Manufacturing Toys in the Shenzhen Special Economic Zone in China'. *International Journal of Production Economics* 25: 181–90.

Chen, E. (1993) 'Foreign Direct Investment in East Asia'. *Asian Development Review* 11 (3): 24–59.

Cheng, C.-Y. (1992) 'Greater China Common Market'. *World Journal* 26: C2–4 (July) (in Chinese).

Cheung, P.Y.-Y. (1994) 'The Case of Guangdong in Central-Provincial Relations' in H. Jia and Z. Lin (eds) *Changing Central-Local Relations in China: Reform and State Capacity*. Boulder: Westview, pp. 207–38.

Child, J., Crozier, M. and Mayntz, R. (eds) (1993) *Societal Change between Market and Organization*. Aldershot: Avebury.

Christopher, M. (1992) *Logistics and Supply Chain Management*. London: Pitman Publishing.

Chung, C. (1995) 'The Changing Pattern of Division of Labour Across the Strait: Macro Overview and Sectoral Analysis of the Electronics Industry'. Paper presented to the IGCC conference 'China Circle: Evolving Relations between China, Taiwan, and Hong Kong-Macao'. Hong Kong, 8–10 December.

Clark, C. (1993) 'Taiwan in Post-Cold War Asia Pacific' in J.C. Hsiung (ed.) *Asia Pacific in the New World Politics*. Boulder: Lynne Rienner Publishers, pp. 113–34.

Clough, R.N. (1993) *Reaching Across the Taiwan Strait: People-to-People Diplomacy*. Boulder: Westview Press.

Clulow, R., and Teague, P. (1993) 'Governance Structure and Economic Performance' in P. Teague (ed.) *The Economy of Northern Ireland*. London: Lawrence and Wishart, pp. 60–120.

Conti, S. (1993) 'The Network Perspective in Industrial Geography'. *Geografiska Annualer* 75 B: 115–30.

Courlet, C. and Soulage, B. (1995) 'Industrial Dynamics and Territorial Space'. *Entrepreneurial and Regional Development* 7 (4): 287–307.

Cronin, R.P. (1992) *Japan, the United States, and Prospects for the Asian-Pacific Century: 3 Scenarios for the Future*. New York: St. Martin's Press.

Dicken, P. (1994) 'Global-Local Tensions: Firms and States in Global Space-Economy '. *Economic Geography* 79 (2): 101–28.

Domingues, J.M. (1995) 'Sociological Theory and the Space-Time Dimension of Social Systems'. *Time and Society* 4 (2): 233–50.

Ernst, D. (1995) 'Partners for the China Circle? The East Asian Production Networks of Japanese Electronics Firms'. Paper presented to the IGCC conference 'China Circle: Evolving Relations between China, Taiwan, and Hong Kong-Macao'. Hong Kong, 8–10 December.

Evans, P. (1995) *Embedded Autonomy*. Princeton: Princeton University Press.

Fairclough, N. (1992) *Discourse and Social Change*. Cambridge: Polity.

Fang, S. (1992) 'A Proposal for Establishing a Mainland-Taiwan-Hong Kong Economic Commission'. Jingji Ribao, Beijing, 24 June, 1992: 4 (in Chinese).

Florida, R. (1995) 'Toward the Learning Region'. *Futures* 27 (5): 527–36.

Fu, L. (1992) 'Hong Kong-Macao and Both Sides of the Taiwan Strait: A

Chinese Economic Sphere'. *Journal of Beijing University*, Social Science Edition 5: 85–92 (in Chinese).

Gereffi, G. and Korzeniewicz, M. (eds) (1994) *Commodity Chains and Global Capitalism*. London: Praeger.

Giddens, A. (1990) *The Consequences of Modernity*. Cambridge: Polity.

Goodman, D. (1995) 'New Economic Elites' in R. Benewick and P. Wingrove *China in the 1990s*. Basingstoke: Macmillan.

Grabher, G. (ed.) (1993) *Embedded Firms: On the Socio-economics of Industrial Networks*. London: Routledge.

Harvey, D. (1989) *The Condition of Postmodernity*. Oxford: Blackwell.

Harvey, D. (1994) 'Social Construction of Space and Time'. *Geographical Review of Japan* 67 (2): 126–35.

Hay, C. and Jessop, B. (1995) 'The Governance of Local Economic Development and the Development of Local Economic Governance: A Strategic-Relational Approach'. Paper presented at the annual conference of the American Political Science Association, Chicago, 30 August–2 September.

Henderson, J. (1993) 'Against the Economic Orthodoxy: On the Making of the East Asian Miracle'. *Economy and Society* 22 (2): 200–217.

Herzog, L.A. (1991) 'Cross-National Urban Structure in the Era of Global Cities: The US-Mexico Transfrontier Metropolis'. *Urban Studies* 28 (4): 519–33.

Higgott, R. (1994) 'Asia-Pacific Economic Co-operation: Theoretical Opportunities and Practical Constraints'. *Pacific Review* 7 (4): 103–18.

Higgott, R., Leaver, R. and Ravenhill, J. (eds) (1993) *Pacific Economic Relations in the 1990s: Cooperation or Conflict?*. St Leonards, NSW: Allen Unwin.

Hobday, M. (1994) 'Technological Learning in Singapore: a Test Case of Leapfrogging'. *Journal of Development Studies* 30 (3): 831–58.

Hobday, M. (1995) *Innovation in East Asia*. Aldershot: Edward Elgar.

Hodgson, G.M. (1993) *Economics and Evolution: Bringing Life Back into Economics*. Cambridge: Polity.

Howell, J. (1993) *China Opens its Doors: The Politics of Economic Transition*. Hemel Hempstead: Harvester Wheatsheaf.

Howells, J.R. (1995) 'Going Global: The Use of ICT Networks in Research and Development'. *Research Policy* 24 (2): 169–84.

Huber, T.M. (1994) *Strategic Economy in Japan*. Boulder: Westview Press.

Jarillo, J.C. (1988) 'On Strategic Networks'. *Strategic Management Journal* 9: 31–41.

Jessop, B. (1990) *State Theory*. Cambridge: Polity Press.

Jessop, B. (1995a) 'The Nation-State: Erosion or Reorganization?'. *Lancaster Regionalism Group Working Papers* (Governance Series) No. 50.

Jessop, B. (1995b) 'The Regulation Approach, Governance and Post-Fordism: Alternative Perspectives on Economic and Political Change?'. *Economy and Society*. 24 (2): 334–56.

Jia, H. and Lin, Z. (eds) (1994) *Changing Central-Local Relations in China: Reform and State Capacity*. Boulder: Westview.

Jordan, A.A. and Khanna, J. (1995) 'Economic Interdependence and Challenges to the Nation-State: The Emergence of Natural Economic Territories in the Asia-Pacific' *Journal of International Affairs*, Winter, 48 (2): 433–62.

Kendall, H.H. and Joewono, C. (eds) (1991) *Japan, ASEAN, and the United*

States. Berkeley: Institute of East Asian Studies, University of California at Berkeley.

Kim, S.S. (1994) *China and the World: Chinese Foreign Relations in the Post-Cold War Era.* Boulder: Westview Press.

Klintworth, G. (1994) *Taiwan in the Asia-Pacific in the 1990s.* St Leonards: Allen and Unwin.

Knox, P.L. and Taylor, P.J. (eds) (1995) *World Cities in a World-System.* Cambridge: Cambridge University Press.

Koo, H. (1984) 'World System, Class and State in the Third World Development'. *Sociological Perspectives* 27: 33–52.

Kooiman, J. (ed.) (1993) *Modern Governance: New Government-Society Interactions.* London: Sage.

Kornai, J. (1980) *Economies of Shortage.* New York: Elsevier North-Holland.

Kwan, C.H. (1994) *Economic Interdependence in the Asia-Pacific Region: Towards a Yen Bloc.* London: Routledge.

Lim, H. (1991) 'Japan and the Asian Newly Industrializing Economies' in H.H Kendall and C. Joewono (eds) *Japan,* ASEAN, *and the United States.* Berkeley: Institute of East Asian Studies, University of California at Berkeley, pp. 215–21.

Lin, C.-P. (1993) 'Beijing and Taipei: Interactions in the Post-Tiananmen Period'. *The China Quarterly* 136: 770–804.

Lin, N. (1995) 'Local Market Socialism'. *Theory and Society* 24 (3): 301–54.

Lipietz, A. (1993) 'The Local and the Global: Regional Individuality or Interregionalism'. *Transactions of the Institute of British Geographers* 18:8–18.

Lyons, T.P. and Nee, V. (eds) (1994) *The Economic Transformation of South China: Reform and Development in the Post-Mao Era.* Ithaca: Cornell University.

Martinos, H. and Humphreys, E. (1992) 'Transnational Networks: Evolution and Future Issues'. *Ekistics* 352: 13–19.

Massey, D. (1994) *Time, Place and Gender.* Cambridge: Polity.

Massey, D. (1995) 'Places and their Pasts'. *History Workshop Journal* 39: 182–92.

Mayntz, R. (1993) 'Modernization and the Logic of Inter-organization Networks' in J. Child, M. Crozier and R. Mayntz (eds) *Societal Change Between Market and Organization.* Aldershot: Avebury, pp. 1–17.

Nee, V. (1992) 'Organizational Dynamics of Market Transitions: Hybrid Forms, Property Rights, and Mixed Economy in China'. *Administrative Science Quarterly* 37: 1–27.

Ohmae, K. (1990) *Borderless World.* New York: Harper Perennial.

Ohmae, K. (1993) 'The Rise of Region State'. *Foreign Affairs* 72: 78–87.

Oi, J.C. (1992) 'Fiscal Reform and the Economic Foundations of Local State Corporatism in China'. *World Politics* 45 (1): 99–126.

Okita, S. (1991) 'Japan's Role in Asia-Pacific Cooperation'. *Annals of American Academy of Political and Social Sciences* 513: 25–37.

Oman, C. (1994) *Globalization and Regionalization: The Challenge for Developing Countries.* Paris: OECD.

Ostry, S. and R.R. Nelson (1995) *Techno-Nationalism and Techno-Globalism: Conflict and Cooperation.* Washington: Brookings Institution.

Paasi, A. (1986) 'The Institutionalization of Regions: A Theoretical Framework for Understanding the Emergence of Regions and the Constitution of Regional Identity'. *Fennia* 164: 105–46.

Petri, P.A. (1993) 'The East Asian Trading Bloc: An Analytical History ' in J.A. Frankel and M. Kahler (eds) *Regionalism and Rivalry: Japan and the United States in Pacific Asia*. Chicago: University of Chicago Press, pp. 21–52.

Pollock, J. (1993) 'The United States in East Asia: Holding the Ring' in Conference Papers on Asia's International Role in the Post-Cold War Era, Part I, *Adelphi Paper* 275. London: International Institute of Strategic Studies, pp. 69–82.

Poster, M. (1995) *The Second Media Age*. Cambridge: Polity.

Radosevic, S. (1994) 'Strategic Technology Policy for Eastern Europe'. *Economic Systems* 18 (2): 87–116.

Ravenhill, J. (1993) 'The "Japan Problem" in Pacific Trade' in R. Higgott, R. Leaver, and J. Ravenhill (eds) *Pacific Economic Relations in the 1990s: Cooperation or Conflict?*. St Leonards, NSW: Allen Unwin, pp. 106–32.

Reich, R. (1988) 'Technological Barriers Won't Help Us'. *Japan Economic Journal* 27 (February).

Riddle, D.I. (1986) *Service-Led Growth: The Role of Service Sector in World Development*. New York: Praeger.

Riedel, J. (1991) 'Intra-Asian Trade and Foreign Direct Investment'. *Asian Development Review* 9 (1): 111–46.

Rix, A. (1993) 'Japan and the Region: Leading from Behind' in R. Higgott, R. Leaver, and J. Ravenhill (eds) *Pacific Economic Relations in the 1990s: Cooperation or Conflict?*. St Leonards, NSW: Allen Unwin, pp. 62–82.

Rodan, G. (1993) 'Reconstructing Division of Labour: Singapore's New Regional Emphasis' in R. Higgott, R. Leaver and J. Ravenhill (eds) *Pacific Economic Relations in the 1990s: Cooperation or Conflict?*. St Leonards, NSW: Allen Unwin, pp. 223–49.

Sassen, S. (1991) *The Global City: New York, London, Tokyo*. Princeton: Princeton University Press.

Sassen, S. (1996) 'The State and the Global City: Notes towards a Conception of Place-Centred Governance'. *Competition and Change* 1 (1): 31–50.

Segal, G. (1994) 'China Changes Shape: Regionalism and Foreign Policy'. *Adelphi Paper* No. 287, London: The International Institute for Strategic Studies (March).

Shen, G. (1993) 'China's Investment in Hong Kong' in P.-K. Choi and L.-S., Ho *The Other Hong Kong Report* Hong Kong: Chinese University Press.

Simon, D.F. (ed.) (1995). *The Emerging Technological Trajectory of the Pacific Rim*. Armonk: M.E. Sharpe Inc.

Sit, V.F.S. (1989) 'Industrial Out-Processing – Hong Kong's New Relationship with the Pearl River Delta'. *Asian Profile* 17 (1): 1–13.

Smart, J. and Smart, A. (1991) 'Personal Relations and Divergent Economies: A Case Study of Hong Kong Investment in South China'. *International Journal of Urban and Regional Research* 15 (2): 216–33.

Steven, R. (1990) *Japan's New Imperialism*. London: Macmillan.

Sum, N.-L. (1995) 'More than a "War of Words": Identity Politics and the Struggle for Dominance during the Recent "Political Reform" Period in Hong Kong'. *Economy and Society* 24 (1): 69–100 (February).

Sum, N.-L. (1996a) 'Strategies for East Asia Regionalism and the Construction of NIC Identities in the Post-Cold War Era' in A. Gamble and A. Payne (eds) *Regionalism and World Order* Basingstoke: Macmillan, pp. 207–246.

Sum, N.-L. (1996b) ' "Greater China" and the Global-Regional-Local

Dynamics' in I. Cook and R. Li (eds) *Fragmented Asia*. London: Avebury, pp. 53–74.
Sung, Y.W. (1991) *The China-Hong Kong Connection*. Cambridge: Cambridge University Press.
Tokunaga, S. (ed.) (1992) *Japan's Foreign Investment and Asian Economic Interdependence: Production, Trade and Financial Systems*. Tokyo: University of Tokyo Press.
Unger, D. (1993) 'Japan's Capital Exports: Molding East Asia' in D. Unger and P. Blackburn (eds) *Japan's Emerging Global Role*. Boulder: Lynne Rienner Publishers, pp. 155–70.
Wade, R. (1990) *Governing the Market*. New Jersey: Princeton University Press.
Walder, A.G. (1994) 'The Decline of Communist Power: Elements of a Theory of Institutional Change'. *Theory and Society* 23 (2): 297–324 (April).
Wall, D. (1993) 'Special Economic Zones in China: The Administrative and Regulatory Framework'. *Journal of East Asian Affairs* VII (1) Winter/Spring: 226–60.
Wang, S. (1994) 'Central-Local Fiscal Politics in China' in H. Jia and Z. Lin (eds) *Changing Central-Local Relations in China: Reform and State Capacity*. Boulder: Westview, pp. 91–112.
Wang, Z. (1994) 'Reform and Opening to the Outside World and Economic Development in Guangdong Province'. *Social Sciences in China* 3: 33–44 (Autumn).
Wank, D.L. (1995) 'Private Business, Bureaucracy and Political Alliance in a Chinese City'. *Australian Journal of Chinese Affairs* 33: 55–74 (January).
Weitzman M. and Xu, C. (1994) 'Chinese Township-Village Enterprises as Vaguely Defined Cooperatives', *Journal of Comparative Economics*, 18 (2): 121–45.
Wong, C.P.W. (1991) 'Central-Local Relations in an Era of Fiscal Decline: The Paradox of Fiscal Decentralization in Post-Mao China'. *China Quarterly* 128: 691–715.
Yahuda, M. (1993) 'The Foreign Relations of Greater China'. *The China Quarterly* 136: 687–710.
Yang, M. (1989) 'The Gift Economy and State Power in China'. *Comparative Study of Society and History* 31: 25–54.
Yang, M. (1994) *Gifts, Favours, and Banquets: The Art of Social Relationships in China*. Ithaca: Cornell University Press.
Yi, X. (1994) 'China's US Policy Conundrum in the 1990s: Balancing Autonomy and Interdependence'. *Asian Survey* 34 (8): 675–91.
Zhang, A. and Zou, G. (1994) 'Foreign Trade Decentralization and its Impacts on Central-Local Relations' in H. Jia and Z. Lin (eds) *Changing Central-Local Relations in China: Reform and State Capacity*. Boulder: Westview, pp. 153–80.
Zweig, D. (1995) ' "Developmental Communities" on China's Coast: The Impact on Trade, Investment, and Transnational Alliances'. *Comparative Politics* 27 (3): 253–74.

8. Emergence of path-dependent mixed economies in Central Europe

Bernard Chavance and Eric Magnin

1. CAPITALISM AND THE MIXED ECONOMY

The notion of the 'mixed economy' has been the target of wide criticism. In the 1980s, the negative Hayekian assessment of interventionist policies in general and of mixed economy tendencies was revived, as part of the general questioning of the 'Keynesian' consensus that had dominated for years. When the post-socialist transformation began in Eastern Europe there was a strong free-market orientation by new governments (often with the active participation of economists who had been until the late 1980s proponents of a radical reform of the socialist economy). International influence too pushed in this direction – especially the IMF, whose leaders strongly and repeatedly asserted that a mixed economy model should be avoided in order to guide the 'transition'. The shift of focus, from a reform of socialism to a 'transition to a market economy' had in some countries, such as Poland, either been tacitly accepted in public opinion in the late 1980s, or it took place during the big political change of 1989–90. The rejection of the 'mixed economy' was at that time part of the struggle of new pro-market forces against neo-communist or social-democratic tendencies in these societies (both trends being often confused in political debates).

Economic liberalism opposing or criticizing in principle the notion of the mixed economy has obscured both the real nature and variety of Western capitalism, and the specific problems of systemic change in the post-socialist world. The concept of a 'market economy' understood as a kind of pure or simple system reducible to a single universal coordination mode is misleading. Capitalist systems, in their historical and national diversity, have all been characterized by a high degree of institutional and organizational variety, and by a complex repertoire of coordination modes or governance forms (Boyer 1992, Hollingsworth et al. 1994, Zysman 1994). Such diversity can be understood both as a result and as a cause of the system's dynamics. In place of a mono-causal pure system, we find in the family of capitalist systems combined or mixed economies in which various forms are present and different principles are at work. This is one of many reasons why important theoreticians such as Marx, Keynes or Schumpeter contrasted 'capitalism' in different ways with the model of a 'market economy' – with its weak or oversimplified institutional content and its static equilibrium implications. Post-socialist transformation has produced complex developments in the economy which cannot be reduced either to marketization and privatization as general trends, or to simple obstacles and delays in this direction. Specific and evolving configurations of post-socialist economies are characterized by their composite, combined or mixed features. Such heterogeneity does not boil down to the simple 'transitory' nature of economies moving from one alleged pure system to another. It depends on the historical and path-dependent character of systemic change and on the complex nature of capitalism in general.[1] In this chapter we try to analyse the emergence of various specific post-socialist mixed economies, with reference to the Czech, Hungarian and Polish cases, concentrating particularly on ownership and coordination aspects of systemic change.

2. PATH-DEPENDENCE IN ECONOMIC TRANSFORMATION

The concept of path-dependency refers to evolutionary features of system trajectories characterized by out-of-equilibrium self-organization. Among the different possible patterns of long-term behaviour, one is somehow selected through the cumulation of various events or disturbances that have occurred in the previous evolution of the system. The expression 'history matters' is a frequent way of summarizing the concept. Applied to the problem of systemic change

[1] The contemporary transformation of advanced capitalist economies has been characterized as a shift from one mixed economy regime to another mixed constellation. 'In fact, the last two decades have exhibited a chaotic and rather myopic transition out of one mixed economy regime, which the regulation approach calls Fordist, Beveridgian and Keynesian. This label characterizes respectively the capital-labour compromise, the welfare system deriving from a citizen-state compromise inherited from the great depression of the inter-war years, and finally the counter-cyclical use of monetary and fiscal instruments to smooth economic fluctuations. The rather likely outcome will be another configuration of mixed economies. Tentatively, these regimes have been labelled Toyotist for Japan, Uddevalist for Sweden, or nostalgic and Fordist for US and France. If true, such a diagnosis strongly contradicts any institutional convergence, be it among the Western world, or for East European countries' (Boyer 1991).

in post-socialist economies, a path-dependency approach focuses on the duality of heritage and creation.

Different levels of analysis should be distinguished when discussing path-dependency in post-socialist countries. First, the general level of the family of systems that went from socialism to post-socialist transformation; second, the individual level of given countries in the family. An intermediary level may be considered, namely subgroups of individual countries with similar paths within the family (e.g. reformed economies in the late socialist period). Time-scales should be differentiated too. In a long-term perspective on path-dependency, it is necessary to push the analysis back to pre-socialist times; in a middle-term perspective, the evolution since socialism (or late socialism) should be focused upon; in a short-term one, the trajectory observed since the big change (1989) will be the main concern.

At the time of the former socialist countries embarking upon post-socialist transformation, they had followed diverse paths of change since the early common imitation or imposition of the Soviet-type model. In the conventional approach that dominated the first years of change, such diversity in initial conditions was underestimated. Moreover, the notion of a future convergence towards a single model – a standard view of a 'market economy' of the West European flavour – was dominant. In the following years, a variety of national paths could be observed where some common trends coexisted with divergent tendencies (see Table 8.1). It is too early to reach conclusions about the similarity or the divergence of future stabilized systems in Central Europe. Only comparative analysis of historical paths, as opposed to wishful thinking about convergence, will provide a clue to such a complex question, but strong national specificities are likely to remain or to expand in the middle term.[2]

The last decade of socialist systems in central Europe saw the emergence of a 'socialist mixed economy'. The term was coined by institutional sociologists (Nee and Stark 1989) discussing mainly the Hungarian and Chinese cases, but it can be extended to the Polish case in that period. The role of the developing private sector in these countries was stressed, as was the move away from the organizational homogeneity of the traditional socialist economies. By contrast, Czechoslovakia, where

[2] Discussing the shift from autocratic to democratic regimes in a comparative perspective, P. Schmitter and T. Lynn Karl (1994) observe that 'national differences in consolidation are likely to be greater than national differences in transition'. As for the debate on convergence in the West, see Boyer (1993), Hollingsworth et al. (1994), Zysman (1995).

Table 8.1. Forces of identity and difference

Factors of Similarity

- Post-socialist common features (systemic family path-dependency)
- Institutional mimetism towards the West, desire to join the European Union
- Influence of international organizations (IMF) and of their conditions
- Globalization trends

Factors of Dissimilarity

- Diversity in initial conditions resulting from the past evolution of socialist economies
- National specific paths, after 1989 (unique political, social and economic conditions and events: individual path-dependency)
- Variety of institutional external influences (e.g. Anglo-Saxon vs West European, or German vs British or French)
- Idiosyncratic institutional bricolage, spontaneous adaptation and transformation of imitated institutions according to nationally specific societal contexts

the reform attempts of 1968 had been radically suppressed, was still close to this traditional model when the regime collapsed in 1989.

The radical systemic transformation was initiated by an unexpected and somewhat new historical form of political change, which was neither a reform nor a revolution but a 'refolution' (Garton-Ash), a 'regime change' (Kiss) or a 'gentle demise' (Hausner). This change, although almost simultaneous, took different forms in accordance with national socio-political conditions. While in Czechoslovakia there was a 'capitulation' by the communist leaders, a 'negotiated demise' was observed in the two other countries, a 'compromise' in Poland and an 'electoral competition' in Hungary. Stark (1992) has insisted upon the influence of these different 'extrication paths' on the variety of later national evolutions and of privatization strategies. In the post-socialist period, common trends and national specificities appeared, both among state or government strategies and in the spontaneous evolution of different economies and societies. Klaus (1994) has argued, in a neo-Hayekian spirit, that the systemic change should be seen as a 'delicate mixture of intentions and spontaneity'. Such a mixture is actually typical of the evolution of modern economic systems in general; it is not only a temporary feature of specifically post-socialist conditions – even though the particular content of the mixture is, to be sure, dictated by such conditions.

Following the 'structural adjustment' philosophy of international organizations, all governments of the region proclaimed stabilization and institutional change, especially privatization, as the most important and immediate means of reaching the target model of a market economy based on private ownership. Differences in initial conditions and in policy orientations resulted in various paths: in Poland 'shock therapy' was applied early, but political conditions constantly delayed the mass privatization envisaged, and the actual change in ownership of the previous state sector was rather slow. In Czechoslovakia shock therapy was adopted but after a longer preparation and under better initial conditions than in Poland. Mass 'voucher' privatization was organized successfully, starting in 1992. Hungary adopted from the beginning a more gradual approach to stabilization and privatization, opting for conventional (Western) methods. In the three countries 'small privatization' of small state or 'cooperative' enterprises, notably in the retail trade, proceeded quite fast and successfully, while an impressive development of newly created private firms, generally small, was seen especially in the service sector. Another common feature was the almost immediate disruption of the vertical dependence of firms linked to previous 'bureaucratic coordination' (Kornai 1992), either in its direct (Czechoslovakia) or indirect form (Hungary, Poland). An unexpected development affected all three countries (similar to others undergoing transition): the post-socialist 'great depression' (Chavance 1994c) or 'transformational recession' (Kornai 1994), with important path-dependent effects such as a growth of arrears (inter-enterprise debts, bad loans of banks, delays in tax payments), a fiscal crisis of the state, and a slow or rather defensive restructuring of the productive system linked to the collapse of investment. Some peculiarities in the development of hybrid forms of ownership discussed below are linked to adaptation to the consequences of the depression (Stark 1994).

In all countries a wide array of continuities became manifest in the process of global systemic mutation. A 'self-reorganization' of the economic system is at work, where rearrangements or recombinations of inherited organizational or institutional forms are combined with the genuine creation of new forms.[3] Among the latter, some bear close resemblance to their Western capitalist counterparts, but others have peculiar post-socialist features.

3. AN ORIGINAL COMBINATION OF OWNERSHIP FORMS

The 'transition' process in Eastern Europe is marked by the transformation of the national mixed configurations of ownership forms under the reformed socialist system into new complex transitional configurations. The mixed reformed socialist ownership regimes of the 1980s are themselves the outcome of the traditional Soviet-type system evolution. The transformation of property relations is a complex process characterized by the spontaneous creation of a newly private sector, the privatization of state enterprises by various methods implemented by the state, and the interaction between institutional (systemic and national) legacies and state strategies in an uncertain environment leading to the emergence of new organizational forms.

The post-socialist combined economy is characterized by an *original diversity* of capital ownership forms and owner-manager relations: a continuum of forms, ranging from private forms to public ones (see Table 8.2). Moreover, no clear correlation appears in the first years between ownership forms and the hardening of budget constraints. Finally, many enterprises are themselves of a composite nature; for example, they may combine within a single organizational form employee ownership, managerial ownership, bank participation, foreign participation and public ownership. The common institutional legacy of Central European countries makes this new configuration typical of transforming economies, as can be observed in various fields: the persistence of some socialist economy-type behaviours (more or less soft budgetary constraints, risk aversion, 'good contacts' with the state, state resources pumping, cheating), the presence of intertwined or blurred ownership forms, and the importance of public ownership (although decreasing) and of employee ownership in some countries. From the

[3] Stark (1994), in his remarkable work on the emerging new forms of property and corporate structures in the former state sector, has insisted on 'recombination' in organizational innovation, as 'reconfiguration and rearrangements of existing institutional elements'. The term 'recombination' may carry some ambiguity in so far as it seems to understate the role of new institutions or organizational forms that are not reducible to rearrangements. Recombined and brand new forms emerge from both intentional and spontaneous processes. Transformative systemic 'bricolage' (Stark 1994) is thus at work.

Table 8.2. Emerging configuration of ownership forms

OWNERSHIP FORMS/CAPITAL MANAGEMENT AND BUDGET CONSTRAINT	*OWNERSHIP SEPARATED FROM MANAGEMENT*	*OWNERSHIP NOT SEPARATED FROM MANAGEMENT*
Newly created private ownership • Hard budget constraint	Foreign companies' subsidiaries (strong management control)	Small and medium-sized enterprises (SMEs) with low tax evasion (honest taxpayers) and a difficult credit access
• ± Soft budget constraint	Foreign companies' subsidiaries benefiting from tax preferences	Small and medium-sized enterprises with high tax evasion (grey actors, half-entrepreneurs, multiple ventures) or good relations with the financial sector
Illegal private ownership • ± Soft budget constraint	Underground businesses working for an outside owner	Growing second economy (small individual businesses)
Legal private ownership without any economic activities	• 'Dummy firms' (figurehead in the privatization process)	• 'Shell companies' (small units created only to obtain tax or credit preferences) • 'Phantom firms' (false business ventures created for swindling)
Employees' privatized ownership	Employee buy-outs ESOP scheme	Cooperatives
Private ownership stemming from the privatization process • Hard budget constraint	Large profitable enterprises sold through public tender, straight auctions, invitation to tender, direct sales (mainly joint ventures)	• SMEs from the 'small-scale' privatization programme
	Of which quasi-private enterprises (Polish conglomerates)	• SMEs bought by managers (with low tax evasion)
• ± Soft budget constraint	Joint ventures entering governmental bargaining in search of state protection (tax preferences, access to preferential credits, privileged competitive positions)	SMEs from the 'hidden' form of 'spontaneous privatization', i.e., set up as suppliers or customers of a large state-owned enterprise (SOE) to strip it of part of its assets

Table 8.2 Continued

OWNERSHIP FORMS/CAPITAL MANAGEMENT AND BUDGET CONSTRAINT	*OWNERSHIP SEPARATED FROM MANAGEMENT*	*OWNERSHIP NOT SEPARATED FROM MANAGEMENT*
Emerging interwoven privatized ownership	*Institutional quasi-public cross-ownership*	
• ± Hard budget constraint	Large SOEs after corporatization in Hungary. Important role of banks. Multiple owners. Weak management control *Attenuated interwoven ownership* Large SOEs under mass privatization in Poland. Multiple private owners (various investment funds (NIFs), employees) and state. Complex governance structure.	Private cross-ownership between small and medium limited liability companies in Hungary, with a majority stake of the capital held by the manager, other stocks being distributed among various shareholders (mid-level managers, professional staff, quasi-public holding)
• Soft budget constraint	*Institutional quasi-private cross-ownership* Large SOEs after denationalization through the 'voucher privatization' in the Czech Republic. Dominant role of banks. Multiple owners. Weak management control	
Public ownership (state permanently holding controlling shares, or temporarily before privatization in the short term)	Non-profitable companies surviving for social reasons in regions dependent on a single economic activity (e.g. mining, iron and steel production)	
• ± Soft budget constraint	± profitable large SOEs (diversified situations, weak management control)	
• ± Hard budget constraint	Banks (Renationalization as a result of debt consolidation)	

Note Kornai's concept of soft budget constraint includes here a fiscal side (tax rate bargaining but also tax evasion) and a credit side (credit access, subsidies). The expression 'more or less (±) soft' refers to more or less important softenings on the credit and fiscal sides.

table, two salient features can be noted. On the one hand, small and medium-sized private enterprises[4] (SMEs) have mushroomed in all countries in a similar way since 1989. On the other hand, peculiar interwoven ownership forms are emerging in Central European countries.

3.1. The Proliferation of Diversified Small and Medium-sized Private Enterprises

The impressive increase in the number of private SMEs in all Central European countries is accompanied by a proliferation of company forms: limited liability companies, joint ventures, joint stock companies, individual business units, partnerships, illegal entities and so on (Earle et al. 1994). The diversity of organizational forms is another feature of the small private sector development and the rise in the number of economic actors. Many factors are at work, related to: the separation or otherwise of ownership from management, the size of firms, sector (services, industry, agriculture), capital intensity, the links with large domestic state-owned enterprises – SOEs (sub-contracting firms for example) – the presence of foreign investors (joint venture or 100 per cent subsidiary).

The similarity of the expansion of private SMEs in transitional countries is the result of three groups of factors. First, it was caused by the same combination of various privatization methods implemented in most countries: small-scale privatization programmes, management/employee buy-outs, sale of all or part of the capital to a foreign or a domestic investor. The creation of new small and medium-sized private firms through privatization sometimes involves the break-up of larger units; in other cases only a transformation of ownership occurs.

Second, it can be explained by the 'conversion' of small private businesses, illegal or semi-legal units of the former second economy, and the few legal forms of the reformed socialist system, into legal (or illegal) entities on the model of the Western capitalist mixed economies. Economists expected that the transformation process would result in the 'whitening' of the 'black' economy. On the contrary, the hidden economy has been growing since 1989, but its nature has changed. In the socialist economy, people entered the black economy in order to compensate for the failures of the system and to add a little to the kitty.

[4] Most new small and medium-sized enterprises are small businesses (up to 20 employees), among which a high number of individual enterprises can be observed. Medium-sized enterprises essentially stem from the break-up of large units.

In the transitional economy, people go underground to avoid paying tax and to win the price competition against 'honest taxpaying' businessmen.

In Hungary, the development of the small-scale private sector began in 1982, with the government entitlement to set up quasi-private businesses. The most important of the newly permitted business forms was the so-called Enterprise Contract Work Association (VGMK), which made it possible to form a contract relationship between groups of employees in a state enterprise and allowed the enterprise itself to work independently within the firm in their spare time. The other important form was the Economic Contract Work Association (GMK), which was essentially a private business that could be formed outside the state enterprise. Other business forms which could be established included industrial and service cooperative groups (VGMK in the cooperative sector), small cooperatives and civil law associations (associations of private professional people who could use the assets of a large SOE under a leasing arrangement or be hired by an enterprise under a contractual agreement) (Stark 1986, Neumann 1993). The development of this sector served as a basis for the subsequent development of the small private sector in Hungary (with small limited liability companies entangled in the 'corporate satellite' organizational form mentioned below) and provided the first entrepreneurial knowledge, not born, however, under market conditions.[5]

The diversity of private organizational forms broadened from the early 1980s onwards in Poland too, and the Polish private sector experienced a period of rapid expansion. Direct investment was encouraged through small-scale 'Polonia' firms, theoretically owned by Poles living abroad. After a period of rapid expansion during 1982–4, the growth of the 'Polonia' firms slowed down. Private individuals were also authorized to lease shops, restaurants and kiosks and to manage them privately from the 1970s onwards. After 1987, leasing spread to other activities.[6] Economic Working Groups, which were contractual arrangements between workers and the management of a state enterprise, similar in principle to the Hungarian VGMKs, were also permitted but did not expand much. The existence of small private or quasi-private enterprises in the reformed socialist system may explain why entrepreneurship in Poland has taken off more quickly than in, say, the Czech Republic. However, in the Czech Republic, the limited exist-

[5] The OECD assesses that prosperous small private enterprises had generally been founded before 1989 (OECD 1993b).

[6] In early 1989, for example, the state-owned electronics firm Omig in Warsaw was entirely leased to its manager (Patterson 1993).

Table 8.3. Estimates of the relative importance of ownership forms

OWNERSHIP FORMS	HUNGARY	POLAND	CZECH REPUBLIC
Official share of the private sector (% of GDP, mid-1995)	60%	60%	70%
Large and medium-sized SOEs (book value)	2 200 units in 1990 2 000 billion HUF	8 450 units in 1990	4 300 units in 1991 1 200 billion Ke
Small registered private enterprises			
• Individual entrepreneurs	700 000 (1994) (20% of the labour force)	1.7 million (end 1993) (12% of the labour force) (814 000 in 1989)	> 1.1 million (1993) (22% of the labour force)
• Legal personalities	64 000 in September 1993 40% of small units could be 'false entrepreneurs' (shell, dummy, phantom firms, half and multiple entrepreneurs)	n.a.	n.a. Estimates of registered half-time entrepreneurs range from 60–80% of the total; 33% could be inactive
Illegal private ownership. Second economy (% of GDP) (various estimates)	30% (1993)	20% (1994)	10–15% (1994)
Employee privatized ownership	n.a.	700 workers' buy-outs by October 1993 (220 000 employees) 15% of shares of entreprises involved in mass privatization	0.9% of shares of firms involved in voucher privatization (first wave)
Cooperatives (1992)	> 8 000 units	17 000 units	5 879 units
Private ownership stemming from the privatization process			
• Small-scale privatization	10 300 units	30 000 to 80 000 according to sources	26 000 units
• Joint ventures (1993)	21 500 operational units	16 000 registered units	5 000 registered projects

Table 8.3 Continued

OWNERSHIP FORMS	HUNGARY	POLAND	CZECH REPUBLIC
• Trade sales (medium and large-sized enterprises)	114 (1992) 6 initial public offerings	119 (mid-1994) of which 99 sold to a domestic foreign core investor and 17 public offerings	n.a.
Interwoven ownership	40% of all state enterprises and 10% of their assets before mid-1990	6 big conglomerates	Voucher privatization (two waves): 1 619 enterprises (56% of the labour force in 1991)
	40% of the 220 largest companies in 1994	512 enterprises involved in the mass privatization programme	80% of assets involved in the large privatization (the rest having been privatized by non-voucher methods)
Public ownership	50% of assets still in state hands in mid-1995	6 000 firms still in state hands in early 1994 (60% of industrial output)	580 units not to be privatized before five years
	of which 140 companies in which the state will remain majority owner		The state has a significant stake in 75 enterprises (more than 50% of equity) after the two waves of voucher privatization

Note These datas are complied from various sources: UNO, OECD, *The Economist* National Statistical Offices, Bouin (1995), EBRD (1995), Gabor (1994), Stark (1996). They must be treated cautiously. The aim of the table is to provide a rough estimate of the relative importance of ownership forms.

ence of private activities before 1989 resulted in a dramatic growth in the number of small entrepreneurs in the first years of the transition process.

The third factor explaining the similar expansion of SMEs is the spontaneous creation of national (legal or illegal) SMEs or of foreign group subsidiaries. It should be noted that some of the newly created small private enterprises do not represent the same thing as their Western counterparts (Szabo 1994). Some businesses are 'forced individual enterprise' founded in order to avoid unemployment.

their aim is survival, not profit. Other registered business ventures are 'spare-time enterprises', that is, the entrepreneur is a full-time employee in another enterprise and works overtime for his business. It should be remembered that many people had a second job in the socialist reformed economy. Another version is the 'multiple business venture', namely, the creation of several small enterprises, which are only partly active, essentially in order to limit the tax burden. Newly privatized SMEs may in fact also behave in a non-entrepreneurial way for systemic legacy reasons such as the lack of market culture.

It is not possible to determine precisely the relative importance of privatization and of newly created private businesses in the development of the private sector. SMEs represent a numerical majority, but the above remarks incline us to qualify their importance in terms of economic activity measures in spite of the official share of the private sector in GDP (see Table 8.3). The small private sector output is in fact concentrated in the retail trade, construction and agriculture, that is, low capital-intensive activities. Its share in industry – though increasing – is generally much lower.

3.2. The Emergence of Interwoven Ownership

In the countries of Central Europe, various forms of interwoven ownership are emerging as a consequence of the transformation of the former state sector (privatization and changes in organizational forms). Interwoven ownership has three main characteristics: a multiplicity of heterogeneous owners, a fuzzy border between public and private forms with the development of hybrid types, and cross-ownership ties involving banks in industrial property. In the three countries under study, while emergence paths were different, interwoven ownership has been developing (with the partial exception of Poland as far as the cross-ownership aspect is concerned: see Table 8.4). But it can be found in most post-socialist economies.[7] It represents a significant share of national assets and economic activity (see Table 8.3).

[7] Interwoven ownership is a striking feature of recent evolution in Russia, following mass voucher privatization, but also in China, as a result of the ongoing corporatization of large state enterprises: the capital of an enterprise is usually distributed initially among various other state enterprises (leading to cross-ownership ties), local or regional government, the management, less often the employees, while a part of the capital may be simultaneously sold for participation by foreign investors. The Chinese authorities,

The emergence of an interwoven ownership form in Hungary is linked to the 'spontaneous privatization' process which started in 1988, in the last two years of the former reformed socialist system, as a result of new pieces of legislation facilitating property transformation. In some cases, a large state enterprise contributes some of its assets in kind, which are pooled together with other capital from foreign investors in new companies, and the remaining part of the state enterprise continues to operate. But the basic form of 'spontaneous privatization' is the 'transformation' of a large state enterprise into a group of new companies (most often limited-liability companies), set up on the basis of each of its factories, plants and even administrative departments, which then distribute the assets of the public firm among themselves. The former public enterprise centre (a joint-stock company) keeps the controlling shares of the new companies (called 'corporate satellites' by Stark). In these public holding companies, foreign investors, state-owned organizations, such as banks and other enterprises (joint-stock or limited-liability companies, mainly business partners: suppliers and customers) also participate in share ownership. Thus, it is not privatization in the strict sense of the word (hence our expression 'quasi-public') even if some private investors buy shares in the new companies (mainly SOE managers, who can also establish their own private firms and integrate them in the holding as suppliers or customers). The fastest growing new property form is 'a limited liability company owned by private persons, by private ventures, and by other limited liability companies owned by joint stock companies, banks, and large public enterprises owned by the state' (Stark 1996, p. 1007) (see Figure 8.1). The changing economic and political environment at the end of the 1980s directly triggered the transformation of SOEs. Firms were about to become insolvent and needed additional capital because of a restrictive economic policy, including the cut-back of budgetary subsidies (UNO 1994). After 1989, the post-socialist 'great depression' made the

wishing to avoid a perverse relationship between indebted enterprises and banks, have explicitly forbidden bank participation in industrial (public) ownership. Let us remark here that China has entered the post-socialist transformation too, but by a different route than Eastern Europe. While in the latter the institutional base of the socialist system was broken down by the dismantling of its first political pillar, the one-party regime, in the former it has been gradually eroded by the extension of the 'non-state' sector, modifying the second pillar, the dominance of state ownership (since the beginning of the 1990s the non-state sector has overtaken the state sector in industrial production, while agriculture has been decollectivized since the beginning of the 1980s). China can now be considered as an example of the 'post-socialist mixed economy', with diverse intertwined, fuzzy and hybrid ownership forms and a composite evolving coordination set-up. We believe that extending the comparative analysis to this important experience would strengthen the case for this notion.

Table 8.4. National privatization trajectories

OWNERSHIP FORMS AND DYNAMIC FEATURES	HUNGARY	POLAND	CZECH REPUBLIC
Interwoven ownership	Institutional quasi-public cross-ownership Spontaneous privatization initiated from 1988 onwards ± hard budget constraint Important role of banks: debt equity swap 'Corporate satellites': legacy of the conglomerates dissolved in the early 1980s: more relative independence between units (loose network relations) Shareholders: State Property Agency, banks, cross-ownership between domestic enterprises (suppliers, customers), foreign companies, local authorities, employees, managers. Weak management control	Attenuated interwoven ownership Multiple owners, private and public partners, not yet developed cross-ownership ties. Diversity of ownership transformation processes with uncertain consequences, which might involve a marginal development of cross-ownership ties: • debt-equity swaps between banks and industrial companies, • expansion of conglomerates, • mass privatization programme	Institutional quasi-private cross-ownership Voucher privatization Began in 1992 ± soft budget constraint Dominating role of banks: founders of Investment Privatization Fund (IPF) Holdings: Legacy of the industrial associations (VHJs): strong technical and financial links (tight network relations) Shareholders: citizens, Fund of National Property, cross-ownership between banks via IPFs, domestic enterprises (suppliers, customers), foreign companies, local authorities, employees, managers. Weak management control.
Employees' privatized ownership	Limited participation by employees (preferential shares) Employee Stock Ownership Plan and preferential credits: uncertain results	SME bought after leasing of the firm's assets by its workers, workers' buy-outs Legacy of the Workers' Councils 15% of shares reserved for firms' workers in the mass privatization programme	Weak participations of employees Pre-war legacy of cooperatives

Table 8.4. Continued

OWNERSHIP FORMS AND DYNAMIC FEATURES	HUNGARY	POLAND	CZECH REPUBLIC
'Creative destruction'	Effective bankruptcy law but overburdened courts	Privatization by liquidation under the law on SOEs	Limited number of bankruptcies
Lock-in?	State-bank-industry links Marginalization of the small private sector	Pronounced dualism between large public enterprises and small private businesses	State-bank-industry links

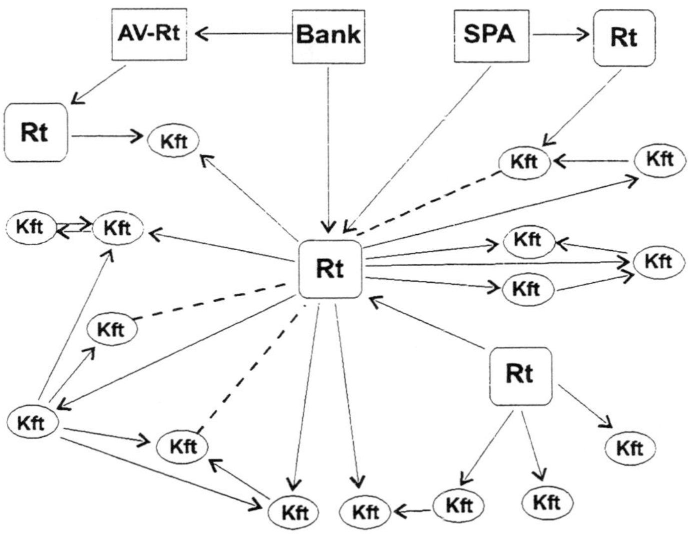

Figure 8.1. A Hungarian metamorphic network

Note
AV-Rt = State Holding Corporation
SPA = State Property Agency
Rt = Shareholding Company
Kft = Limited Liability

Source: Stark (1996).

insolvency problem more acute. In the case of enterprises in a difficult financial situation, corporatization (the transformation of an enterprise into a corporate company with a legal personality) offered the possibility of a debt-to-equity swap with banks or other creditors (state, local authority, suppliers). Quasi-public holdings are then linked to each other by ownership ties (what Stark calls a 'recombinet', see Figure 8.1), often via their numerous limited liability companies. Thus in Hungary, property relations are complex and interwoven between public (for the major part) and private organizations. The hardening of the budget constraint was the precondition for spontaneous 'privatization'.

In the Czech Republic, the emergence of an interwoven ownership form is the unexpected result of the voucher mass privatization organized by the government from 1991 onwards. During the first wave of privatization, 72 per cent of all available voucher points for citizens were collected by the Investment Privatization Funds (IPFs) spontaneously created in the process. The 'average Czech firm' is now controlled by a group of IPFs (see Figure 8.2). The largest IPFs are controlled by major banks (via investment companies) which were also privatized within the voucher scheme; the state remaining however their biggest shareholder with about 40 per cent of shares. Moreover, the state – through the National Property Fund – holds majority participations in 75 companies on a permanent or temporary basis. Thus since the first wave, the major commercial banks, controlled by the state, are the co-owners

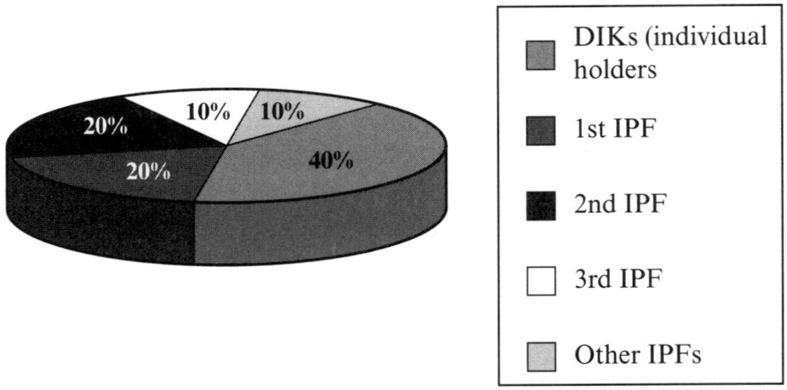

Figure 8.2. The typical structure of a Czech enterprise's capital after distribution through the voucher method

Source: Bouin (1995).

of many Czech companies through their IPFs; they mutually hold some shares in other banks' capital, and in some cases banks indirectly own their own shares. For example, the Czech Investicni Banka owns 17 per cent of its own shares and many shares of other banks (Mladek 1993). In the second wave, funds collected fewer points and the latter were more dispersed than in the first wave, but the general framework of property relations at the end of the first wave was not challenged.

Thus in the Czech Republic, a highly interwoven set of property relations between banks, enterprises, the state and IPFs (on behalf of citizens) can be observed (see Figure 8.3). The close relations between state banks and industry seem to be slowing down the hardening of the SOEs' budgetary constraint.

In Poland, the transformation of property relations requires a more qualified assessment. Indeed to date only a small part of the SOE sector has been truly privatized. Liquidation under the Privatization Law has been the main method of privatization. The most common technique has been the leasing of the liquidated firm's assets by its workers. However, an attenuated interwoven ownership is emerging, characterized by a multiplicity of owners, a mixture of public and private partners, but without complex cross-ownership relations. While it seems difficult to draw any conclusion for the time being, three simultaneous but separate processes seem to open the possibility of some crossed configuration by different routes. First, the *mass privatization* programme set up in 1991, but implemented only since 1994, which concerns about 512 enterprises, involves the participation of new actors, the National Investment Funds (NIFs), established by the state. Sixty per cent of the shares of enterprises included in the programme will be distributed to the NIFs, while the state will keep 25 per cent and workers will receive 15 per cent free of charge. Each of the 15 NIFs is to hold 33 per cent of the capital of nearly 30 firms and about 2 per cent of the stocks in the remaining firms. Citizens will be able to exchange their property certificates for one tradable share in each of the 15 NIFs in 1997. After the programme's implementation, the enterprises concerned will have an initial distribution of their capital of 33 per cent for the main NIF, 2 per cent for each of the 14 other NIFs, 25 per cent for the state and 15 per cent for their employees (Nivet 1994, Slay 1995). Second, the development of *debt-equity swaps* within the framework of the Law on Financial Restructuring of Enterprises and Banks (March 1993) is likely to increase the share of industrial equity holdings in the banks' portfolios, in spite of the initial reluctance of banks to invest in industrial firms. The Łódź-based Powszechny Bank Gospodarczy (PBG), for example, planned to take a 70 per cent stake in 23 troubled state

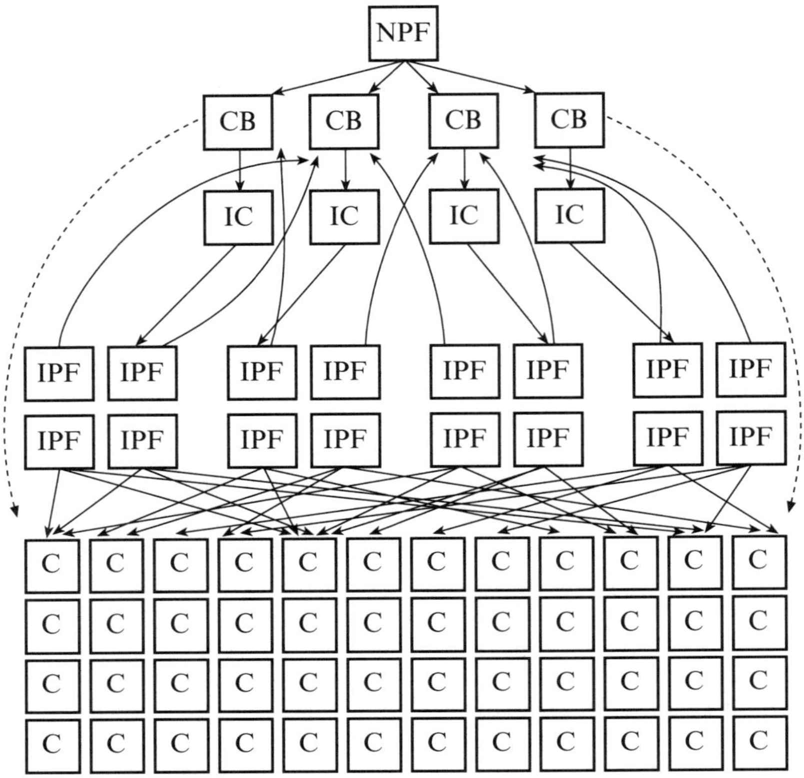

Note
NPF = National Property Fund
CB = Commercial bank
IC = Investment company
IPF = Investment privatization fund
C = Company
—> Ownership control
---> Credits

Source: Mertlik (1995).

Figure 8.3. Ownership structure of the Czech economy after mass privatization

firms (*The Economist* 1994). Third, the transformation of most former socialist state foreign trade organizations into big *conglomerates* contributes to an attenuated interwoven configuration of property rights. These represented in 1995 a third of the value of the Polish stock market.

They used their large foreign currency receipts earned in the first transformation period to buy not only the companies they had represented abroad but also banks and other firms far from their core businesses. Moreover, the state owns a large stake in several conglomerates along with domestic and foreign investors. Bad debts and scarce finance facilitate this process, as well as the breaking up of big monopolies by the government which created firms that were too weak to survive, that became prey to foreign and domestic investors. Elektrim, a former state-trading monopoly for electrical goods, was Poland's biggest domestic investor in 1993. At the end of 1993, it had stakes in 87 companies, including banks, put up for sale by the privatization ministry (*The Economist* 1995b). The state owns 16 per cent of Elektrim's equity but two-thirds of the voting shares. Universal holds large stakes in 50 companies and Mostostal has bought shares in financial companies.

Thus in Poland, a multiple ownership configuration and a diversity of organizational forms (quasi-private conglomerates, public holdings as in the mining industry, private holdings (NIFs)) has emerged, while opening the door to a lesser extent to crossed ownership links.

4. THE EMERGING REPERTOIRE OF COORDINATION MODES

The classical problem of the coordination of the division of labour in capitalism has been approached in various ways. An extreme position sees the market as the single existing or desirable coordination mode. Other theories refer to dual models: state and market, or markets and hierarchies (firms). Recent views stress the importance of other types of coordination modes in economic and social life, such as networks (Thompson et al. 1991). Considering coordination at a general level, and including the coordination of both the *social* and *technical* division of labour, a complex – but still simplified – scheme of coordination modes can be proposed by considering the articulation of state, networks, hierarchies and markets.[8] A distinction has been introduced in relation to the traditional socialist system between the mega-hierarchy or general control hierarchy above the enterprise and the micro-hierarchy within the enterprise (see the discussion of the concept of hierarchy in transaction cost economics in Chavance (1995b)). The

[8] Some authors would rather insist on the *interpenetration* of different modes (Bradach and Eccles 1989). Even though this is an important topic for post-socialist transformation as well, for the sake of simplicity we have only dealt with the *articulation* of various modes.

three categories of traditional socialist system, reformed socialist system and post-socialist transforming economy are used as ideal-types based on stylized historical facts.

In the proposed evolutionary approach, the complexity of the coordination set-up is stressed in order to show the importance of previous endogenous changes in the socialist period, and to localize essential qualitative changes in the 'mix' of various modes in the post-socialist phase. While in the ownership sphere we witnessed a growing diversity of forms, in the coordination sphere we mainly see a transformation of different modes and changes in their articulation and interaction.

The standard view of 'marketization' of the economy is too reductionist. Let us define markets abstractly by the mediation of monetary exchange between production and consumption, as a result of both immediate independence and general interdependence of producers and consumers, depending on the division of labour. On this view the determination of prices and quantities, and the question of market power, depend on different *forms* of markets. Consequently, post-socialist transformation should not be understood as simple *marketization* following the abolition of central planning, but as a process of radical change in market forms, along with modified relations between markets and other coordination modes (state, networks and micro-hierarchies (firms)).

Table 8.5 illustrates both the breaks and the continuities in the field of coordination modes before and after the collapse of socialist regimes. The most important changes are the abolition of the Communist Party and of its coordinating function through its links with the state hierarchy, the shift to state macro-management, the high diversification of the corporate types and of their internal arrangements, and the transformations concerning markets. The latter include modifications of the institutional set-up in which markets are embedded (legal provisions and codes, including property rights, role of the transforming or emerging banking and financial system, etc.), transformation in the behaviour of different agents, and changes in market's processes and forms (modes of determination of prices and quantities, switch from seller's to buyer's markets, forms of competition).

The relative spheres of coordination modes are transformed. 'Destatization' and 'depaternalization' are at work through a contraction of the state's fields of intervention, notably at the micro-level and in the sphere of foreign trade. 'Marketization' is under way not in the sense of changes to price formation mechanisms or in the types of competition – which depend, as observed, on radical modifications in market forms – but in the sense that markets extend their scope to new products and services

Table 8.5. A changing mix of coordination modes

	TRADITIONAL SOCIALIST SYSTEM	REFORMED SOCIALIST SYSTEM	POST-SOCIALIST TRANSFORMATIONAL ECONOMY
State	• Party-state direct micro-regulation based on a mega-hierarchical web (petty tutelage and coordination through priorities plus bargaining within centralized planning)	• Limited disentangling of state and party hierarchies. Abolition or strong weakening of direct micro-regulation and of mega-hierarchy. Attempts at indirect planning, fragmented vertical bargaining with enterprises, shifting to monetary factors (as opposed to physical targets)	• Abolition of party and related hierarchies, abolition of mega-hierarchy leading to early coordination disruption on this level. Emergence of state indirect macro-management, intensive legislative work and institutional transformation policies. Tendency to 'state desertion' in some spheres but maintained involvement in others; legitimacy and credibility problems. Fuzzy border between public and private spheres
Networks	• Stable forward and backward linkages between enterprises in the first and second economies. Clientelist and clan-like relations in the economy and society	• Reproduction and sometimes activation of sectoral or regional networks, in the first and second economy	• Reproduction of some ancient networks; emergence of a few networks inherited from the abolished mega-hierarchy; creation of new networks through ownership transformation (as in cross-ownership ties or in relations between enterprises and banks or investment funds)

Table 8.5. Continued

ITEM	TRADITIONAL SOCIALIST SYSTEM	REFORMED SOCIALIST SYSTEM	POST-SOCIALIST TRANSFORMATIONAL ECONOMY
Micro-hierarchies (enterprises)	• One-man management. Hard hierarchical constraint, mitigated by workers' pressure helped by macro labour shortage	• Weakened hierarchical constraint (introduction of self-management forms; weak activation of unions; or limited introduction of quasi-private contracting within large enterprises)	• Development of a great variety of forms of micro-hierarchies, according to ownership changes, transformation of unions, multiplication of new domestic or foreign enterprises, reorganization of corporate arrangements. Dominant tendency to hardening of the hierarchical constraint
Markets for consumption goods	• Choice of consumers mainly constrained by quantities (shortages). • Dominance of seller's markets. Active money. Prices fixed by mega-hierarchy	• Choice of consumers constrained by quantities or by prices according to the type of goods or services • A variety of seller's and buyer's markets. Active money. Prices fixed by price administration, with some bargaining	• Choice of consumers mainly constrained by prices • Dominance of buyer's markets. Active money. Free prices for most goods and services

Markets for production goods	• Vertical mediation in horizontal relations between enterprises (centralized material supply). Passive money	• Partial de-mediation of horizontal links between enterprises (extension of 'wholesale trade' with dominance of seller's markets). Passive money weakly activated	• Total de-mediation of horizontal links
	• Prices fixed by mega-hierarchy	• Prices fixed by price administration, with some bargaining	• Dominance of buyer's markets. Active money. Free prices for most goods
'Labour market'	• Relatively free labour mobility helped by macro labour shortage. No formal bargaining (but informal pressure from below) for wages, mainly regulated by mega-hierarchy	• Relatively free labour mobility helped by macro labour shortage. Increasing space for informal pressure for higher wages at the enterprise level	• Switch from labour shortage to mass unemployment, with some continuation of labour hoarding. State gradual retirement from wage regulation (except for minimum wage policy). Introduction of weak wage bargaining at the enterprise and at the national level (tripartite commissions).
		• Segmentation between first and second economy	• Segmentation between small and large enterprises, between public sector, legal private and illegal private sectors.

such as, for instance, education, health and culture, and some new markets emerge gradually (e.g. financial markets, housing markets). The so-called 'labour market' is not created *ex nihilo* either, but undergoes deep changes in the mechanisms determining the employment level and structure and level of wages. The hierarchical constraint in enterprises is generally hardened by the mentioned changes in state and market coordination.

In reformed socialist economies, such as Hungary or Poland in the 1980s, the mix of coordination modes had moved from the traditional system to evolve in the direction of the future post-socialist configuration. The weakening of micro-regulation, increased polycentrism in the state administration and the partial activation of money in the state sector had stimulated changes in various markets, but in a context of increased macroeconomic (and sometimes social) tensions. Nevertheless, the importance of the break after 1989 should not be underestimated. In the (almost) non-reformed Czechoslovakia, no transition through a reform period took place, so the elements of continuity in coordination were less important. They are not totally absent though, as can be seen in late-socialist emergence of macroeconomic policy (notably monetary policy (Klaus 1990)), and in the importance of industrial networks in the post-socialist period.

4.1. Coordination and Ownership

The link between ownership forms and coordination mechanisms, suggested by Mises from 1920 onwards, has been stressed in a neo-Misesian perspective by Kornai (1990, 1992), who has asserted a strong 'affinity' between private ownership and market coordination on the one hand, and state ownership and bureaucratic coordination on the other, with other combinations such as state ownership plus market coordination ('market socialism') displaying a weak affinity. While there appears to be wide consensus on this topic, it can be observed that such a reasonable but very general view is not based on a rigorously developed theoretical argument. If the negative systemic consequences of dominant public ownership can be inferred from many historical experiences, it remains the case that various economic theories have not yet given a satisfactory answer to the question of 'why private ownership is important' (Grosfeld 1993). The Misesian approach, the theory of property rights or the theory of corporate control are confronted with difficulties when dealing with managerial forms of capitalism, and with the great variety of relations between ownership and management of capital observed in economic history – as well as with their coordination and dynamic efficiency consequences (Lazonick 1992). An institutional and evolutionary comparative analysis at an intermediate level of abstraction of the various patterns in the links between capital ownership/management and coordination modes in the history of Western capitalism, of socialist and of post-socialist economies, remains to be done.

In the post-socialist mixed economies, where the 'blurring of frontiers' is a widespread tendency,[9] no clear affinity between ownership and coordination changes can be asserted until now. While some clarification can be expected as time goes by (Korsun and Murrell 1995), it remains difficult to find unequivocal relations between developments in the ownership and coordination spheres in a middle-term perspective. Destatization and marketization in the above sense have developed much quicker than privatization. In reformed socialist economies such as Poland and Hungary in the 1980s, or China in the 1980s and 1990s, changes in the coordination mix were significant while changes in the formal ownership structure were mainly confined to the private or 'collective' spheres outside the state sector. The primary importance of the clarification of property rights in view of the shift to a 'market economy', stressed by the theory of property rights as opposed for instance to the extension of competition, is questioned by the experience of post-socialist Central Europe and reformed socialist China. This should not lead to the conclusion that privatization could be neglected in the shift to a modern form of capitalism, but it should lead to a qualification of the widespread idea of the first years of transformation that it was the solution for most problems.

Some 'affinity' can nevertheless be observed in some fields. For instance, the emergence of interwoven forms of ownership points to the role of new network modes of coordination, or of the 'hybrid forms' that are neither market nor hierarchy, stressed in recent versions of transaction cost economics.

5. THE UNCERTAIN CONSEQUENCES OF THE POST-SOCIALIST COMPOSITE ECONOMY

5.1. Possible Lock-in

The ownership transformations in the three Central European countries have presented one remarkable feature. On the one hand, a similar

[9] Stark (1996) writes about a 'triple boundary blurring': between property forms (public/private), between organizational boundaries, and between justificatory principles.

process leads to similar effects in most countries, that is, the proliferation of small and medium-sized private enterprises; on the other hand, different processes result in a quite similar outcome, namely the emergence of new complex interwoven ownership forms. This non-linear evolution is the result of complex interactions between different levels – national (different national legacies) and family-systemic – of path-dependency effects and various state-organized privatization strategies, in a rather uncertain environment where unexpected events spontaneously occur. These interactions trigger off the emergence of new hybrid forms within the range of possibilities determined by a common systemic legacy. The lack of fresh capital at the beginning of the transformation process and the decapitalization of public firms during the 'transformational recession' is one of the features which may explain the importance of the role of the banks in the privatization processes. But the diversity of interwoven ownership forms is related to different national trajectories: a process of corporatization begun in the late 1980s in Hungary, an original mass privatization programme implemented in 1992 in the Czech Republic, the development of industrial giants and debt/equity swaps in Poland and maybe the result of the ongoing Polish version of the mass privatization programme.

Institutional and organizational transformation trajectories in Eastern Europe may become locked into inferior paths of development (Arthur 1989, 1990, Hodgson 1994) or, conversely, atypical capitalist forms may become institutionalized and then may prove to be somehow efficient.[10]

One question facing transition countries now is whether small private enterprises will be able to grow and evolve into medium and large-sized enterprises. SMEs stemming from large SOEs (subcontracting firms) tend to face growth difficulties owing to narrow specialization related to enterprise needs. But scarce finance is the most serious problem. Tight credit access and self-financing out of gross savings may be a major barrier to SME growth, especially in capital-intensive industrial activities.

Moreover, we have noted that some of the small private enterprises,

[10] It is amusing to find in *The Economist* (1995a), in which the concept of mixed economy has been so often criticized in the first years of post-socialism and where peremptory assertions can often be read about the necessary convergence of 'market economies' towards an idealized Anglo-Saxon model, the apt observation that 'to speak about "mutant" capitalism is to imply that "proper" capitalism must always take a constant form. Yet the share-based capitalism of America and Britain clearly differs from the bank-based capitalism of most of Western Europe. The "mutant" corporate structures emerging in Eastern Europe borrow elements from each of these models and mix in novelties of their own. It would be a funny sort of evolution in which at least some of the mutations did not turn out to be thoroughly robust.'

supposedly the best guarantee of a shift to the market economy, are not really market actors but hybrid actors sometimes still pervaded by the socialist heritage. Some of them will become real market actors, others will disappear, but certain survivors may tend to direct private sector evolution towards inferior development paths. Scarce finance and hybrid actors may lead to a marginalization of the small private sector in Hungary (Gabor 1994).

In Poland, conflicting interests between the political actors, management and workers' collective have considerably slowed down the privatization process and led the Polish authorities in the first years to place much of the policy emphasis on the growth of the new private sector. More than in any other Central European country, a dualism can be observed in Poland between large state-owned firms, some of which have been corporatized but not yet privatized and which are in an uncertain situation under the formal control of the state treasury, and a dynamic and prolific small private sector. However, the share of the private sector in total investment has been relatively less dynamic, and the gross profitability ratio seems to have been lower in the private than in the state sector for most branches of the economy (UNO 1994).[11]

5.2. Ownership and Control

The Czech trajectory seems to be now locked in by the role of banks, which exert important control on the country's economy. Some problems may result from the links observed between the state, banks and industrial enterprises, the 'permissive' banking attitude, the artificial survival of non-profitable enterprises, collusion risks, the limited entry of new firms and exit of outdated ones (Grosfeld 1994). An unexpected conflict may arise between a bank's will to initiate the bankruptcy of firms and the interests of its investment fund which has shares in these firms (Svejnar 1994), or between different IPFs holding shares in the same enterprise but with different strategies and interests (Mertlik 1995). The intertwined property relations make managers' control by shareholders rather uneasy. Similar risks could be conjectured in the emerging Hungarian institutional framework.

It should be noted, however, that standard theories of corporate governance stressing the importance of direct or indirect control of owners (shareholders) on managers, mainly based on the US case, have limited explanatory power when applied to the history of European

[11] This information is to be treated with caution because small private firms tend to overstate their costs and understate their profits in order to avoid tax payments.

latecomers, such as France, Germany or Italy (Tamborini and Targetti 1995), or to other national capitalist institutions such as those in the Japanese or Asian economies (Schaede 1994). Managerial capitalism or the 'corporate economy' (Marris 1987) is more frequent in the contemporary world than 'proprietary capitalism' – a model inherited from the nineteenth century, which has remained a hidden reference in more sophisticated theories of agency or of corporate governance (Lazonick 1991, Nuti 1995).

In other words, if some disturbing consequences arise in the relations between owners and managers of capital, they will result from the specific conditions of these transforming economies, rather than from their distance from the questionable normative model of efficient corporate governance. One source of concern might be the weak initial capacities and competencies of banks on the one hand, and of 'inherited' managers on the other hand. Co-learning will remain crucial in this respect.

In recent years, the relation between ownership changes and enterprise behaviour has appeared quite indeterminate – except in the positive case of foreign involvement. While a diversification of managerial attitudes had been observed, for instance, in Poland in the 1980s within the then prevalent state-owned sector (Beksiak 1989), the variety of behavioural responses to the new context has not been clearly connected with privatization. Active restructuring can be observed in a number of still public enterprises, while the behaviour of many privatized (or formally privatized) ones has undergone little change. Firms 'afloat' or 'adrift' (Brada et al. 1994) can be found in various property rights configurations. In a period of weak systemic coherence and of institutional uncertainty, enterprise-specific factors such as the personality of managers confronted with many new constraints or the form of coalitions built within or around the firm, can be decisive, along with increased competitive pressures.

5.3. Future Selection and Evolution Processes

Systemic change is by nature a complex process as elements, subsystems, the whole system and its environment are all changing at the same time (England 1994). Moreover, institutions are both the objects of change and the agents of change. The co-learning of agents and co-evolution of organizations and institutions takes place in a context of weak systemic coherence with partial rigidities and emerging irreversibilities. Given such a complexity of systemic change, the beneficial or detrimental macro-social effects of such crystallized tendencies cannot be predicted in advance.

The transformation of ownership in transition countries is an evolutionary process. The implementation of privatization programmes does not put an end to the process. On the contrary, a post-privatization redistribution of property is likely to result, reinforcing the ownership structure (lock-in), or leading to new post-socialist path-dependent configurations. Such a process is already under way in the Czech Republic, where IPFs are reselling their corporate shares to other owners anxious to increase their equity stake (other IPFs, beneficiaries of restitution, foreign investors) or privatized (quasi-private) companies are buying back restituted plants, reselling others (sometimes to clear debts), and so on. (Mertlik 1995). In Poland, given the size of the conglomerates, a slimming reorganization of property is likely to occur.

Evolutionary authors have underlined that macroeconomic growth requires not only microeconomic diversity and instability, but also processes of harmonization, regulation, standardization and routinization 'to avoid chaotic instability and to reap the benefits of scale economies' (Freeman 1994). Post-socialist transformation is associated with a great increase in the degree of organizational and institutional diversity. A large number of new small enterprises coexist dynamically with a more restricted number of large firms undergoing various types of adaptation, innovation or survival strategies.[12] Some of the big old firms are fragmented or gradually reduced in scale, while some small or medium ones grow or try to expand. This change in the enterprise population takes place in the context of a rapidly evolving institutional and legal environment, and in a period of initial economic depression with large shifts in the structure of global demand (and rather quick opening up to foreign competition). When the population structure (in terms of enterprises, scale, legal types, ownership forms) stabilizes or comes to evolve more gradually, the problem of 'harmonization, regulation and routinization' will inevitably come to the fore. The increase in diversity is also an increase in complexity. Which type of stabilized order will emerge, with which growth properties, remains to be seen. A dynamic and competitive economy, although possible, cannot be expected as an automatic product of 'transition'.

Selection processes taking place in Central Europe are not unambiguous either. They have taken place mainly through differential

[12] The danger of a detrimental segmentation of firms exists in Central Europe: once formed, many private firms do not expand, so that 'a shrinking large firm sector combined with an insider-dominated, small-firm sector could leave many in long-term unemployment' (Busse 1994).

growth and decay of enterprises and industries rather than by bankruptcies proper. The number of bankruptcies is still limited, even if the situation varies among countries. In the Czech Republic, the number of bankruptcies is very low (the government suspended the law in 1992 for a year) and has essentially affected private enterprises. In 1993, 2 000 bankruptcy requests were filed and only 60 effectively pronounced. In Hungary, the new Bankruptcy Law of 1 January 1992 resulted in debtors and creditors reaching agreements, including state-owned commercial banks and other state or central institutions (tax office, customs, social security). Up to August 1993, some 5 000 bankruptcies and more than 15 000 liquidation requests were filed, but only 4 300 bankruptcies and 4 000 liquidation proceedings were actually started (UNO 1994). In Poland, privatization under the law on SOEs (real bankruptcy and the subsequent sale of assets) led to the actual liquidation of 1 171 firms by mid-1994 (OECD 1994). The balance sheet of the destructive and creative aspects of the ongoing change remains unclear in a middle-term perspective. Moreover, even in a stabilized Western capitalist competitive context, it is dubious whether the selection process simply favours the 'fittest' enterprises (Hodgson 1993).

More generally, selective processes of internal and external competition have not abolished country-specific enduring features in institutional arrangements and organizational forms, as the history of capitalist economies shows. Path-dependency is linked with 'locality of learning, opaqueness of environment, embeddedness of organizations within particular institutional contexts', which explains the persistence of national forms of corporate and industrial organization 'even when ex post they lead to different competitive performance' (Dosi 1994). This remark can easily be extended to the present and the future of post-socialist national economies.

6. POST-SOCIALIST FORMS OF CAPITALISM

In place of a (difficult but) simplistic 'transition to a market economy', we see in Central Europe the emergence of various path-dependent mixed economies. The common features of these post-socialist mixed economies, beyond the very high number of small enterprises, are interwoven ownership forms and a composite coordination set-up.

Capital ownership in medium and large enterprises is characterized by a great multiplicity of owners, including the state – still present to a greater or lesser extent, by specific mixtures of public and private forms including numerous hybrids,[13] and by complex cross-ownership ties between enterprises, various institutional investors and banks. The relations between ownership and management of capital are very diversified, and although they are likely to be modified in a middle-term perspective, a common characteristic remains the relative power of managers *vis-à-vis* frequently dispersed, inexperienced, absentee or dependent owners. These economies can thus be defined as a type of managerial capitalism, or a peculiar corporate economy.

The coordination set-up includes different modes or governance types, as in advanced capitalist economies in general, but the nature of the mix has strong post-socialist characteristics. The content of each mode has undergone important changes, and the articulation of various modes has consequently changed. Markets have shifted from the dominance of sellers to the dominance of buyers, and competition forms are coming closer to the imperfect, Western types (Kornai 1995). State intervention has shrunk considerably and has shifted to macro-management and management of institutional change. It is marked by limited initial competencies in the new context, reduced legitimacy and often budgetary crisis, but the presence and importance of the state remain great, because of a still extensive public sector, the state's role in privatization and institution-building processes, and more generally because of the scale of societal tasks and problems. Economic networks, sometimes inherited from the socialist period, sometimes new, play a significant role in coordination, often related to developing cross-ownership ties. Corporate hierarchies in large enterprises are reorganized following competitive pressure and imitation of Western models, with authority being strengthened in general but remnants of paternalist or 'corporatist' relations not disappearing altogether.

The banking sector, which in most cases seems to be evolving towards a model of universal banking, appears crucial in the future evolution of these economies, but it is still concentrated, unsophisticated, with limited competencies, sometimes potentially fragile. The representation of interests, especially for wage earners, is still poorly organized following the crisis of the trade unions in the different countries. More generally, the structure of civil society is evolving only slowly.

While an evolutionary approach stressing path-dependency gives some clues as to the emerging shape of post-socialist capitalisms and

13 Sticking to the questionable division between the private and the public sector, it can be observed that the former has become important everywhere, with a proportion of nearly half of national production. It is imbricated with the public sector (Hungary), or in a dualistic relation with it (Poland), or has itself a dualistic structure (large privatized enterprises/small greenfield or privatized ones – Czech Republic).

the formation of systemic irreversibilities, the middle- and long-term dynamic perspectives of these economies remain partially uncertain and relatively open.

REFERENCES

Anderson, P.W., Arrow, K.J. and Pines, D. (eds) (1988) *The Economy as an Evolving Complex System*. Reading MA: Addison-Wesley.

Andreff, W. (ed.) (1995) *Le Secteur Public à l'Est: Restructuration Industrielle et Financière*. Paris: L'Harmattan.

Arthur, W.B. (1989) 'Competing Technologies, Increasing Returns, and Lock-in by Historical Events'. *Economic Journal* 99 (1): 116–31 (March).

Arthur, W.B. (1990) 'Positive Feedbacks in the Economy'. *Scientific American* 262 (2): 81–5 (February).

Beksiak, J. (1989) 'Role and Functioning of the Enterprise in Poland' in *Economic Reforms in the European Centrally Planned Economies*. New York: Economic Commission for Europe (UN).

Blaas, W. and Foster, J. (1992) *Mixed Economies in Europe: An Evolutionary Perspective on their Emergence, Transition and Regulation*. Aldershot: Edward Elgar.

Bouin, O. (1995) 'Privatisation et Transformation Economique en Europe Centrale et Orientale: L'Exemple de la République Tchèque'. PhD dissertation, EHESS, May.

Bouin, O., and Grosfeld, I. (1994) 'Crédibilité des Réformes et Ajustement des Enterprises en Pologne et en République Tchèque'. Paris: Delta, Document No. 94–24.

Boyer, R. (1991) 'Markets within Alternative Coordinating Mechanisms', mimeo, CEPREMAP (April).

Boyer, R. (1992) 'Markets: History, Theory and Policy'. Paper presented to the EAEPE Conference, Paris, November.

Boyer, R. (1993) 'The Convergence Hypothesis Revisited: Globalization but still the Century of Nations?'. Paper to the Conference 'Domestic Institutions, Trade and Pressures for National Convergence', Bellagio, February.

Brada J., Singh I. and Török, A. (1994) 'Firms Afloat and Firms Adrift: Hungarian Industry and the Economic Transition'. *Eastern European Economics* 32 (1): 3–101 (January–February).

Bradach, J. and Eccles, R. (1989) 'Price, Authority and Trust: From Ideal Types to Plural Forms'. *Annual Review of Sociology* 15: 97–118.

Busse, M. (1994) 'Restructuring and Recovery of Output in Russia'. IIASA, Laxenburg, Working Paper, September.

Chavance, B. (1994a) *The Transformation of Communist Systems: Economic Reforms since the 1950s*. Boulder: Westview Press.

Chavance, B. (1994b) *La Fin des Systèmes Socialistes: Crise, Réforme et Transformation*. Paris: L'Harmattan.

Chavance, B. (1994c) 'Transition et Dépression' in Chavance (1994b).

Chavance, B. (1994d) 'L'Economie Mixte de Transition Post-Socialiste' in Chavance (1994b).

Chavance, B. (1995a) 'Réforme du Socialisme et Conversion au Marché: Les

Voies Centre-Européennes' in R. Boyer and Y. Saillard (eds) *Théorie de la Régulation: Etat des Savoirs.* Paris: La Découverte.

Chavance, B. (1995b) 'Hierarchical Forms and Coordination Problems in Socialist Economies'. *Industrial and Corporate Change* 4 (1): 271–91.

Delorme, R. (1993) 'A Theoretical Frame for the State and Market Issue in the Process of Socio-economic Transformation in the Central and Eastern Europe'. Seminar on Transformation in CEEC, MSH, Paris, December.

Delorme, R. (1994) 'Economic Diversity as Cement and as a Challenge to Evolutionary Perspectives' in R. Delorme and K. Dopfer (eds) *Political Economy of Diversity: Evolutionary Perspectives on Economic Order and Disorder.* Aldershot: Edward Elgar.

Dosi, G. (1994) 'Microfoundations of Macroeconomic Competitiveness' in G. Hodgson, W. Samuels and M. Tool (eds) *The Elgar Companion to Institutional and Evolutionary Economics*, Vol. 2. Aldershot: Edward Elgar.

Earle J.S., Frydman R. and Rapaczyński A. (eds) (1993) *The Privatization Process in Central Europe.* Budapest: Central European University Press.

Earle J.S., Frydman R., Rapaczyński A. and Turkewitz J. (eds) (1994) *Small Privatization: The Transformation of Retail Trade and Consumer Services in the Czech Republic, Hungary and Poland.* Budapest: Central European University Press.

EBRD (1995) *Transition Report 1995.* London: EBRD.

Ellman, M. (1994) 'Transformation, Depression and Economics: Some Lessons'. *Journal of Comparative Economics* 19 (1): 1–21 August.

England, R. (1994) *Evolutionary Concepts in Contemporary Economics.* Ann Arbor: University of Michigan Press.

Estrin, S., Gelb, A. and Singh, I. (eds) (1993) 'East European Enterprises in Transition (I, II)'. *Eastern European Economics* 31 (5, 6): 3–97, 3–113 (Fall and Winter).

Fratellini, N. and Lowit, T. (1994) 'La Survie du Socialisme Réel dans L'Entreprise Post-Soviétique'. *Esprit* 2: 40–51 (February).

Freeman, C. (1994) 'The Economics of Technical Change'. *Cambridge Journal of Economics* 18 (5): 31–65.

Frydman, R. and Rapaczyński, A. (1994) 'Ambiguity of Privatization and the Paths of Transition to a Private Property Regime' in R. Frydman and A. Rapaczyński *Privatization in Eastern Europe: Is the State Withering Away?* Budapest: Central European University Press.

Gabor, R.I. (1994) 'Small Entrepreneurship in Hungary: Ailing or Prospering?' *Acta Œconomica* 46 (3, 4): 333–46.

Grosfeld, I. (1993) 'J. Kornai: The Socialist System, Book Review'. *Economics of Transition* 1 (2): 227–81 (June).

Grosfeld, I. (1994) 'Financial Systems in Transition: Is there a Case for a Bank Based System?' Discussion paper No. 1062, CEPR, November.

Grosfeld, I. and Roland, G. (1995) 'Defensive and Strategic Restructuring in Central European Enterprises'. Discussion Paper No. 1135, CEPR, March.

Hodgson, G. (1993) *Economics and Evolution. Bringing Life Back into Economics.* Cambridge: Polity.

Hodgson, G. (1994) 'Lock-in and Chreodic Development' in G. Hodgson, W. Samuels and M. Tool (eds) *The Elgar Companion to Institutional and Evolutionary Economics*, Vol. 2. Aldershot: Edward Elgar.

Hollingsworth, J., Schmitter P. and Streeck, W. (eds) (1994) *Governing Capitalist*

Economies: Performance and Control of Economic Sectors. New York and Oxford: Oxford University Press.

Keizer, W. (1994) 'Hayek's Critique of Socialism' in J. Birner and R. van Zijp (eds) *Hayek, Co-ordination and Evolution.* London: Routledge.

Klacek, J. (1995) 'The Role of Banks in the Czech Republic and Ownership Structures'. Fifth EACES Workshop 'Privatization and Distribution', Trento, March.

Klaus, V. (1990) 'Monetary Policy in Czechoslovakia in the 1970s and 1980s and the Nature and Problems of the Current Economic Reform'. *Communist Economies* 2 (1): 61–71.

Klaus, V. (1994) 'Systemic Change: The Delicate Mixture of Intentions and Spontaneity'. Address to the Mont Pélerin General Meeting, Cannes, 26 September.

Kochevrin Y., Filatochev, I. and Bradshaw, R. (1994) 'Institutional Transformation in Russia: A Transaction Costs Approach'. *Economics of Transition* 2 (3): 373–90.

Kornai, J. (1990) 'The Affinity between Ownership Forms and Coordination Mechanisms: The Common Experience of Reform in Socialist Countries'. *Journal of Economic Perspectives* 4 (3): 131–47.

Kornai, J. (1992) *The Socialist System: The Political Economy of Communism.* Oxford: Clarendon Press.

Kornai, J. (1994) 'Transformational Recession: The Main Causes'. *Journal of Comparative Economics* 19 (1): 39–63 (August).

Kornai, J. (1995) 'Eliminating the Shortage Economy: A General Analysis and Examination of the Developments in Hungary'. *Economics of Transition* 3 (1, 2): 13–37, 149–68.

Korsun, G. and Murrell, P. (1995) 'History versus Policy: How Much Does Enterprise Governance Change Affect Mass Privatization'. IRIS Working Paper No. 147, University of Maryland, June.

Lavigne, M. (1995) *The Economics of Transition: From Socialist Economy to Market Economy.* Houndmills: Macmillan.

Lazonick, W. (1991) *Business Organizations and the Myth of the Market Economy.* Cambridge: Cambridge University Press.

Lazonick, W. (1992) 'Controlling the Market for Corporate Control: The Historical Significance of Managerial Capitalism'. *Industrial and Corporate Change* 1 (3): 445–88.

Magnin, E. (1996) 'Complexité et Trajectoire Tchèque de Transformation Economique Post-Socialiste'. *Revue d'Etudes Comparatives Est-Ouest* 27 (1): 39–80.

Marris, R. (1987) 'Corporate Economy' in *The New Palgrave Dictionary of Economics*, Vol. 1. London: Macmillan.

McDermott, G.A. (1993) 'Rethinking the Ties that Bind: The Limits of Privatization in the Czech Republic'. Paper presented to the conference 'Economic Transformation in Central and Eastern Europe', WZB, Berlin, September.

Mertlik P. (1995) 'Legal and Organizational Restructuring of Czech Enterprises'. Paper presented to the conference 'Enterprise Restructuring at Different Stages of Ownership Transformation: the Czech Republic and Poland', MSH, Paris, 3–4 July.

Mihalyi, P. (1994) 'Common Patterns and Particularities in Privatization: A

Progress Report on the Transition Economies'. *Acta Œconomica* 46 (1–2): 27–62.

Mink, G. and Szurek, J.C. (eds) (1994) '1989: Une Révolution Sociale? Acteurs, Structures et Représentations à l'Est', *Revue d'Etudes Comparatives Est-Ouest* 25 (4): 5–162 (December).

Mladek, J. (1993) 'Czech Privatization Process: Time for Corporate Governance'. Paper for the conference 'Output Decline in Eastern Europe: Prospects for Recovery?', 18–20 November, IIASA, Laxenburg, Austria.

Morin, F. (1994) 'Liaisons Financières et Coopération des Acteurs-Systèmes'. *Revue Economique* 45 (6): 459–1470 (November).

Mujżel, J. (1994) 'State Enterprises in Transition: Prospects Amidst Crisis' *Emergo* 1 (1): 78–90 (Summer).

Nee, V. (1992) 'Organizational Dynamics of Market Transition: Hybrid Forms Property Rights and Mixed Economy in China'. *Administrative Science Quarterly* 37 (1): 1–27 (March).

Nee, V. and Stark, D. (eds) (1989) *Remaking the Economic Institutions of Socialism: China and Eastern Europe.* Stanford, CA: Stanford University Press.

Nelson, R. (1981) 'Assessing Private Enterprise: An Exegesis of Tangled Doctrine'. *The Bell Journal of Economics* 12 (1): 93–111 (Spring).

Neumann, L. (1993) 'Decentralization and Privatization in Hungary: Towards Supplier Networks' in G. Grabher (ed.) *The Embedded Firm: On the Socio-economics of Industrial Networks.* London and New York: Routledge.

Nivet, J.F. (1994) 'La Privatisation en Pologne: D'une Approche Plurielle aux Difficultés de la Privatisation de Masse'. *Economie et Statistique* 279–80: 121–33.

Nolan, P. (1995) 'Large Firms and Industrial Reform in Former Planned Economies: the Case of China'. DAE Working Paper No. 9516, University of Cambridge.

Nuti, D.M. (1995) 'Corporate Governance et Actionnariat des Salariés'. *Economie Internationale* 62: 13–34 (2 trimestre).

OECD (1993a) *Hongrie.* Etudes Economiques de l'OCDE. CCET, Paris: OECD.

OECD (1993b) *Trends and Policies in Privatization.* CEET, Paris: OECD.

OECD (1994) *Pologne.* Etudes Economiques de l'OCDE. CCET, Paris: OECD.

OECD (1996) *République tchèque.* Etudes Economiques de l'OECD. CCET, Paris, OECD.

Patterson, P. (ed.) (1993) *Capitalist Goals, Socialist Past: The Rise of the Private Sector in Command Economies.* Boulder: Westview Press.

Rizopoulos, Y. (1994) 'Etat et Marché dans l'Est Européen: Une Approche en Termes de Réseaux' in Bellon, B., Caire, G., Cartelier, L., Faugère, J.-P. and Voisin, C. *L'État et le Marché.* Paris: Economica.

Robertson, P. and Langlois, R. (1994) 'Institutions, Inertia and Changing Industrial Leadership'. *Industrial and Corporate Change* 3 (2): 359–78.

Schaede, U. (1994) 'Understanding Corporate Governance in Japan: Do Classical Concepts Apply?'. *Industrial and Corporate Change* 3 (2): 285–323.

Schmitter, P. and Lynn Karl, T. (1994) 'The Conceptual Travels of Transitologists and Consolidologists: How Far East Should They Attempt to Go?' *Slavic Review* 53 (1): 63–82 (Spring).

Sgard, J. (1995) 'Recapitalisation des Banques et Aléa Moral en Hongrie et Pologne'. *Revue Economique*: 481–500 (March).
Slay, B. (1995) 'Mass Privatization (in Poland): Better Late Than Never?'. *Transition* OMRI 1 (14): 16–22 (11 August).
Stark, D. (1986) 'Rethinking Internal Labour Markets: New Insights from a Comparative Perspective'. *American Sociological Review* 51 (4).
Stark, D. (1992) 'Path Dependence and Privatization Strategies in East Central Europe'. *East European Politics and Societies* 6 (1) (Winter).
Stark, D. (1994) 'Not By Design: Recombinant Property in East European Capitalism', Document de Travail, IRSES, MSH, Paris.
Stark, D. (1996) 'Recombinant Property in East European Capitalism'. *American Journal of Sociology* 101 (4): 993–1027 (January).
Stark, D. and Bruszt, L. (1995) 'Networks Properties of Assets and Liabilities: Patterns of Inter-Enterprise Ownership in the Post-socialist Transformation', 'Dynamics of Industrial Transformation: East Central European and East Asian Comparisons' Workshop, Budapest University of Economic Sciences, May.
Svejnar, J. (1994) 'Obstacles to Restructuration Post Privatization' in P. Aghion and N. Stern (eds) 'Obstacles to Enterprise Restructuring in Transition', EBRD, Working Paper No. 16, December.
Swaan, W. (1994) 'Behavioral Constraints and the Creation of Markets in Post-Socialist Economies', EACES Workshop, Trento, February.
Szabo, K. (1994) 'From the Privatization to the Marketization: Schizophrenic Actors in the Transitory Economies'. Paper presented to the third EACES conference, 8–10 September, Budapest.
Tamborini, R. and Targetti, F. (1995) 'Privatisation, Intermédiation Financière et Système Bancaire dans les Economies en Transition' in Andreff (1995).
The Economist (1994) 'A Survey of Poland', 16 April.
The Economist (1995a) 'Eastern Europe Capitalism: Who's Boss Now?', 20 May.
The Economist (1995b) 'Polish Companies: The Accidental Conglomerates', 5 August.
Thompson, G., Frances, J., Levacio, R. and Mitchell, J. (1991) *Markets, Hierarchies and Networks: The Coordination of Social Life*. London: Sage Publications.
UNO (1994) *Economic Survey of Europe in 1993–94*. New York: ECE, United Nations.
UNO (1995) *Economic Survey of Europe in 1994–95*. New York: ECE, United Nations.
UNO (1996) *Economic Survey of Europe in 1995–96*. New York: ECE, United Nations.
Voszka, E. (1994a) 'Centralization, Re-nationalization, Redistribution. The Role of the Government in Changing the Ownership Structure in Hungary, 1989–93', CEPR, London, Discussion Paper No. 916, February.
Voszka, E. (1994b) 'The Revival of Redistribution in Hungary'. *Acta Œconomica* 46 (1–2): 63–78.
Zysman, J. (1994) 'How Institutions Create Historically Rooted Trajectories of Growth'. *Industrial and Corporate Change* 3 (1): 243–83.
Zysman, J. (1995) 'National Roots of a "Global" Economy'. *Revue d'Economie Industrielle* 71: 107–21 (1 trimestre).

9. From patient to active agent: an institutional analysis of the Russian border town of Vyborg[1]

Riitta Kosonen

The collapse of socialism in the Soviet Union wrecked the socialist 'regime of accumulation' (Aglietta 1979). This has forced Russia to search for new avenues to organize production. Concurrently with the domestic transition, Russia is knocking at the door of the European Union with the aim of reintegrating into the international division of labour. From the point of view of local economies in Russia, the situation can be regarded both as a potential threat and as a new possibility. To avoid the threat of isolation or damage to the economy and to secure sustained local development, localities need to work out strategies that link domestic restructuring with a smooth process of reintegration into the international division of labour. Such strategies would equip localities with the independent capacity to participate in the establishment of their own economic course, that is, to become *agents* shaping the development trajectory (to 'hold down the global' as indicated by Amin and Thrift (1994)). The opposite – and the least favourable alternative – would be to transform a locality into a *patient* passively absorbing the reverberations from national and international economic evolution[2].

The key to sustaining local transition lies in the successful implementation of institutional remodelling. This means that a new 'mode of regulation' (Aglietta 1979) needs to be formulated – a new set of implicit and explicit institutions which would enable individual agents to observe the logic of the emerging macroeconomic realignment in production. The total collapse of state-centred socialism implies that a revised institutional structure cannot be brought into existence by the authority of the state. On the other hand, the 'shock therapy' suggested by neo-

[1] Grateful thanks are due to Päivi Oinas, Malla Paajanen, Elja Pitkänen and Arja Saari for their very helpful comments on this paper.

[2] The idea of 'patients' and 'agents' was originally introduced by Oinas (1995a) to categorize the relations of dependency between enterprises and localities.

liberal Western experts has proved to be too rash and has failed to produce sustained growth. This has eroded trust in institutions that promote pure market mechanisms as the basis of transition. As a compromise, a model of 'interactive transition' (Hausner 1994, Nielsen et al. 1995, p. 27) has been proposed to redefine the division of labour between the public and the private sectors. The interactive model of transition is supposed to build on 'powers of association' (Amin and Thrift 1995) and reconcile social justice and democratic representation of economic interests with the increasing demand for competence and productivity at the enterprise level.

The institutional challenges of transition are most explicit on the frontiers where the post-socialist turmoil meets head-on the repercussions of the new integrating Europe. The latter predominantly takes the form of selective development programmes. This chapter studies the question of institutions in local transition in the context of the Russian border town of Vyborg. Vyborg is located in an emerging transborder region between Russia and an EU member state, Finland. A series of questions can be raised about future development in Vyborg. What kind of development trajectory will Vyborg adopt in the emerging European spatial order? To what extent can Vyborg determine this trajectory and thus be an agent of its own development? How will the balance between the public and the private sectors be defined in the context of changes taking place in various spatial dimensions? And finally: what role does an enterprise play in the shaping of local development?

Institutions in economic geography incorporate intangible features dealing with historically and geographically defined forms of action, that is, the habits and values constructing the framework of action – sometimes embodied in rules (Storper 1995). Institutions ensure that production practices are incidental to a regional economy. Accordingly, an institutional spatial analysis puts special emphasis on cultural factors shaping regional economies. The perspective on formal institutions regulating economies has largely concentrated on examining the role of the state, and on making policy suggestions (Aglietta 1979, Lipietz 1994, Peck and Tickell 1994). This chapter makes an attempt towards an integrated institutional analysis linking together, both empirically and theoretically, the geographically defined cultural institutions and the formal aspects of institutions. The endeavour is to understand *how* these two categories of institutions work together to regulate the outcome of local economies. The idea of 'formal and informal institutions', introduced by the institutionalist economic historian Douglass North (1981), is employed for this purpose. The notions of formal and informal institutions are translated here into spatial analysis by treating them as categories of local resources. The formal institutional resources constitute those public regulations constraining the local economy; the informal institutional resources cover the locally specific cultural characteristics (Oinas 1995b).

1. WHY STUDY VYBORG?

The Russian border town of Vyborg is a formerly Finnish town ceded to the Soviet Union during the Second World War in 1944 (see Figure 9.1). Shortly before the Soviet take-over, the entire population (86 000) of Vyborg was evacuated and the town was repopulated by Soviet immigrants. Before the war, Vyborg was an important centre with a high economic, cultural and political status. The Northern conifer belt furnished Vyborg with the asset of a 'staple economy' (Innis 1929) that was dependent on the export of a staple product harvested from the forest. In the event of declining foreign demand for one staple product Vyborg was able to replace the product with another (furs in the Middle Ages, tar in the 1600s and the saw mill industry beginning in the 1700s) Gradually, domestic markets emerged, production diversified and self-generated growth was inaugurated. By the advent of the Second World War, Vyborg had become the second largest town in Finland. Finland's largest export harbour, Uuras, was located in Vyborg (Lakio 1978, p. 170). Such progress was abruptly interrupted in 1944.

As a Soviet town, Vyborg declined into a peripheral frontier town. The exploitation and cultivation of local resources were seriously neglected. A good case in point was the outer port of Vyborg which had only been reopened in 1938 (Veretennikov 1984). Vyborg was regarded as a part of Finnish-Soviet border-trade, but the local production units did not make use of the promising markets in Eastern Finland (Strashuk 1995, Fedorenko 1995). Furthermore, demand in the local consumer markets was only feebly met: in 1975 no more than 90 retail shops (Suraegina 1995, Vasilev and Zakatilov 1975, p. 126) supplied a population of approximately 70 000 inhabitants (compared to 500 outlets for approximately the same level of population in 1939 (see Lakio 1978, p. 1974)). Today, Vyborg is in post-socialist transition and is seeking to re-establish its pre-war status as a centre of international trade.

Vyborg forms an ideal laboratory for an institutional spatial analysis for a number of reasons. First, the story of Vyborg shows that institutional resources matter in local development. The advantages of location (e.g. the availability of or access to markets and raw material)

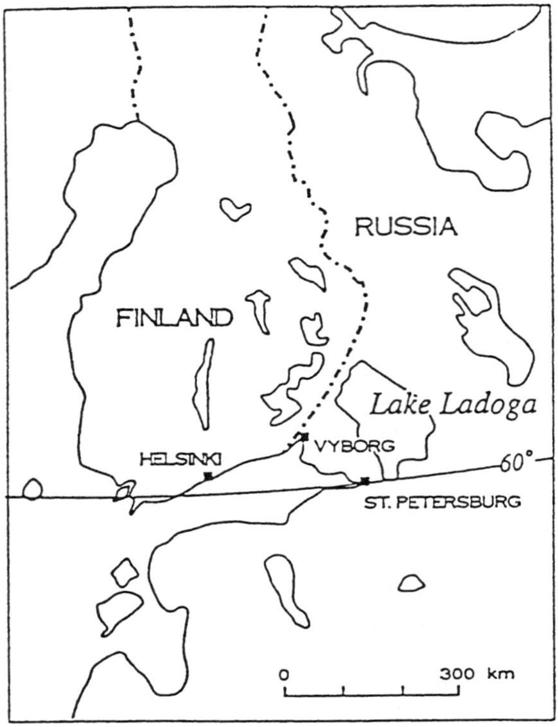

Figure 9.1. Location of the Russian town of Vyborg

remained on site in 1944, but new waves of economic success failed to take off.

Second, a further analysis of Vyborg indicates that an array of institutional features that are currently regarded as safeguards for sustained local development were, in fact, in force during the earlier phases in the evolution of capitalism. A study of the lucrative development of Vyborg before the Second World War shows how the local institutions were fashioned by successive waves of absolutism, mercantilism, the ideas of the enlightenment and liberalism that paved the way for capitalism. The story of post-war Soviet Vyborg, in contrast, reveals how the institutional structure of socialism replaced the capitalist framework. Vyborg exposes not only the quality of institutions supporting the two different ideologies in a local economy, but also allows us to analyse the *mechanisms* that institutions adopt while producing different economic results (Sayer 1992). Two different models of institutional mechanisms can be constructed. The first illustrates a model in which a locality functions as an agent. In the model, the public and the private sectors are linked together in interaction to produce progressive core area development. The other model illustrates the institutional structure of a locality as a patient incapable of making a contribution to the course of local development. Conceptually, the current transition process of post-socialist localities combines these two institutional principles. The issue is one of turning a patient into an agent. It is therefore inviting to review the current process in the light of the historical context.

Third, the views concerning foreign direct investments in transition economies are controversial. On the one hand, investors are praised for inducing wealth and industrial learning. On the other, they are seen as potential colonialists myopically pauperizing the transition economies by exploiting cheap resources. Vyborg provides an insight into the issue of foreign investors as contributors to sustained local development. A characteristic of the pre-war Vyborgian economy was the domination of investors of German, Dutch, Swedish and Russian origin, who gradually became attached to the town and induced indigenous local development. The originally non-local enterprises became rooted by establishing economic, cultural and social networks in the locality.

Fourth, an institutionalist view is evolutionary and path-dependent, which means that the trajectory of each economy is unique and therefore difficult, or even impossible, to replicate (Crevoisier 1990, Amin and Malmberg 1994). The story of Vyborg supports these remarks. Analysis of socialist Vyborg unmasks the institutional heritage upon which the contemporary transition is constituted. It shows that the resuscitation of once abandoned ideas is problematic even within the same locality.

The structure of this chapter is as follows: first, notes on cultural (informal) institutions in the spatial analysis of economic development will be elaborated with empirical reference to Vyborg. Then the analysis will be extended to cover formal institutions, and the principles of institutional interaction will be outlined both theoretically and empirically. Finally, the contemporary post-socialist transition in Vyborg will be extrapolated from these conceptual inferences

2. INSTITUTIONS, NETWORKS AND A LOCAL ECONOMY AS A COMMON PROJECT

It is acknowledged that entrepreneurial activities tend to agglomerate to form geographically defined industrial networks (Cooke and Morgan

1993). The formation of networks is not a novel phenomenon. Hirschman (1958) and later Watkins (1963) proposed that the ability of an economy to generate sustained indigenous growth depends on the power of the economy to form links backwards (to the supporting industries), links forward (towards refinement) and links with industries satisfying increasing local demand. Contemporary spatial analysis has disengaged itself from the economic motivations of networks and emphasizes the significance of socio-cultural aspects, that is, the institutional atmosphere in the creation and maintenance of networked agglomerations. The new approach focuses on territorial 'embeddedness' (Granovetter 1985), that is the inter-organizational relations in networks which transmit information, values and rules of conduct between enterprises, between enterprises and labour markets, and between enterprises and public organizations (Cooke and Morgan 1993, Amin and Thrift 1994, p. 12, Storper 1995 on 'untraded interdependencies'). Networks that link enterprises, labour and public organizations into an integrated economic system, may permeate the economic, social and cultural domains of a society. Besides acknowledging the significance of the existence of diversified networks, observers have also recognized the benefits of dynamic elements in networks supporting economic success. The dynamic features have been amassed together to form the notion of 'institutional thickness' (Amin and Thrift 1993). The theory deals with the benefits derived from the active interaction among institutions in a locality. As a result of interaction, a tradition of collective, rather than sectional or individual, representation is created in a locality. Local actors become aware of being involved in a common enterprise, and the local economy integrates into a common project. The stage is set for an 'associationist model' of development (Amin and Thrift 1995) to make its entrance in a locality. The associationist model puts emphasis on institution-building, interactive governance and civic empowerment. The model was formulated as a suggestion to equip regions with agency in formulating goals in the development trajectory.

But how does an individual enterprise contribute to institutional thickness and to the constitution of agency? Networks form the key factor in the process, as they provide a means of attaching enterprises to a local economy so as to generate indigenous processes. Increasing attachment through participation in many-sided local networks may give rise to a sense of local identity among the economic actors. The logic runs both ways: local identification may provide further impetus to multiply the links between an enterprise and the local community. This way, local identification may prove an indispensable and intangible local asset that produces tangible returns for the economy (as Bolton's notion of 'sense of place' (1989) indicates). Economic actors who most actively contribute to the network formation by encouraging the formation of local firms, by propagating useful information, and by cooperation, have been referred to as 'community entrepreneurs' (Johannisson and Nilsson 1989). In addition to the community entrepreneurs, who try to improve institutions backing local industries directly, 'cultural entrepreneurs' (Spilling 1991) have been identified who believe that all forms of culture provide potential sources of creativity. There are empirical grounds for a view of this kind, as the compound effect of aesthetic values and local traditional skills, wedded to an understanding of technology, has been recognized in many cases as making economies proficient in the area of 'technical culture' (Sweeney (1991) – the furniture industry in northern Italy, the traditions backing precision industry in Stuttgart and the economy of Catalonia backed by a minority language).

The manifestation of a corporatist movement has been recorded in various examples of capitalist development (Lipietz (1994) – on 'organicism' in post-Fordist development, Putnam (1993) – on the impact of what he calls 'civic culture' in northern Italy, Adams (1992) – on the town of Siena, Martinez and Nueño (1988) – on Catalonia, Sweeney (1985) – on Ireland). Some historical data on Vyborg indicate a similar orientation. Accounts of Vyborg in the early 1300s highlight problems caused by illegal visiting Hanseatic merchants who virtually colonized the town, exporting trade revenues across the Finnish Gulf, and depriving Vyborg of the potential to generate multiplier effects (Suutari 1981, p. 15). Not until merchants arriving from Germany, Sweden and Russia settled down to establish social, economic and cultural networks, was Vyborg able to generate indigenous growth. At first, lacking trading facilities, the early networks took on a social guise: the immigrating entrepreneurs secured businesses and married daughters of well-established local merchants. Gradually, genuine Vyborgian business families were established with traditions going back centuries. The local networks emerged in parallel. Side by side with the individual and collective measures to improve transport (e.g. shipping, canal construction etc.), financial institutions (the foundation of banks), insurance and vocational education (e.g., the School of Trade and Navigation), the local entrepreneurs established industrial associations and leisure clubs to ensure the flow of first-hand information (e.g. gambling clubs, industry-specific guilds, including the association of saw mill enterprises, inter-industry coalitions including the Pamaus Association of Vyborgian entrepreneurs named after a local legend (Enbom and Sandelin 1991, pp. 10, 239, Ora 1958, p. 353, Lakio 1981, p. 372). From these organizations, community entrepreneurs and cultural entrepreneurs emerged to take responsibility in shaping the local environment (e.g. the German immigrant Hackmann family between 1777–1944 and the Karelian Lallukka family beginning from the early 1900s). These entrepreneurs expanded their activities in all spheres of society. They were involved in the town administration, in financing local theatres, libraries, hospitals and orphanages; they established folk high schools and basic education for children, constructed housing facilities, organized gas lighting in the town, and much more besides (Enbom and Sandelin pp. 199, 362, Markkanen 1976, pp. 88–129). All things considered, it was largely owing to local enterprises cultivating local institutional resources that Vyborg matured into a distinguished economic centre with no equal in Finland. The flagship of local integration and collaboration, the Torkkeli Society, named after the founder of the town, was established in the early 1900s to bring together local entrepreneurs, journalists, military officers and priests. The main purpose of the society was to restore the former glory of the town (Ilanko 1956, pp. 7–8). A statement given by a German descendant of the Thesleff family characterizes well the significance of local identity: he said he did not feel he was a Finn or a German, but rather a Vyborgian.

In 1944, the whole multitude of the Finnish enterprises abandoned Vyborg and retreated into Finland. The new Soviet Vyborg reassumed the shape of an industrial centre, but it was not able to generate an integrated network body consisting of producers, wholesalers and retailers backed by a complexity of supporting services. The ingredients for such a network were missing from the very beginning. The first Soviet immigrants came mainly from the surrounding districts of Leningrad and from the badly bombed areas of Ukraine and Byelorussia (Adaskina et al. 1961, p. 38, Vasilev and Zakatilov 1975, p. 91, Hämäläinen-Forslund and Hämäläinen 1989, p. 21). They faced in Vyborg an established – although partly badly damaged – infrastructure, which echoed the past of an alien nation: the street names were in Finnish, the statues were of strange heroes and even the books in the abandoned homes were in a foreign language. To solve the dilemma, the local history was thoroughly destroyed and replaced by symbolism cherishing All-Union solidarity. The street names were slavicised and statues were pulled down and replaced by those of Lenin and other socialist heroes. The local press dominated by *Vyborgski Kommunist* (The Vyborgian Communist) was monolithic. The population base was kept heterogeneous. Students were sent to Leningrad and other larger centres for vocational and higher education. After graduation, job applicants received appointments and postings that seldom took into account their place of birth. As a consequence, the local society remained incoherent.

Two major industrial enterprises, the shipyard and the electromechanical plant, were established to supplement the Vyborgian economy. Local links around these enterprises were modest and limited mainly to basic social and cultural commitments to employees. Territorially organized input-output relations between enterprises did not materialize, and shortages of resources were a frequent problem (Zakharov 1995, Kiselev 1986). Supporting services, such as transport, finance and insurance, did not appear on a territorial basis. Vocational education was almost entirely concentrated in Leningrad (Strashuk 1995, Fedorenko 1995). Signs of the new regime were soon evident on the surface of town life: the former School of Trade and Navigation was refurbished to serve as the headquarters of the frontier guards, the former magnificent banking mansions were taken over for the purposes of the town administration, party officials and housing. Networks established by local enterprises were used only to a minimum, which resulted in qualitative failures. The fate of the magnificent former headquarters of the Finnish Lallukka company is significant in this case. The mansions were converted to accommodate employees of the local electromechanical plant. Owing to little attention being paid to housing maintenance, the residents were later moved out and the ramshackle facilities started to collapse. Because of the incoherence of the local society, no active individuals sprang up from the stratum of local industrial plant managers to take the initiative in enriching the local business environment. Potential for indigenous growth was lacking.

Taken as a whole, the story of Vyborg supports the main theoretical and conceptual conclusions made by contemporary institutional spatial analysis. The prosperity of Vyborg before the Second World War leaned on features that are still regarded as instrumental in sustained local development. Respectively, the transformation of Vyborg from an agent managing its own development into a patient incapable of generating self-sustained economic processes concurs with the absence of these critical institutions.

3. HOW DO INSTITUTIONS OPERATE? THE INSTITUTIONAL MECHANISMS

The earlier arguments stress the significance of local cultural characteristics (the informal institutions dealing with skills, values and habits) for the cultivation of local physical resources. Such characteristics define the *ability* and the *will* of the local actors to take advantage of the local opportunities. A comprehensive institutional analysis, however, should include the formal institutions, as the formal regulation of economies embodies a critical institutional dimension: the *possibility* of exploitation. Formal institutions matter in shaping the local development trajectory as they define the profile of incentives to exploit and cultivate the local economic potential. Furthermore, formal institutions are critical in regulating local distinctiveness and the resulting potential for attachment to a locality. What we arrive at is an integrated institutional model in which the formal and informal institutions (covering the ability, the will and the possibility) combine to construct the institutional framework controlling the development of local economy.

This inevitably implies that an institutional analysis of Vyborg has more to offer than merely a qualitative analysis of local institutions constituting the local transition. Vyborg offers the possibility of recording the *mechanisms* underlying the transformation of a local economy into a local economic community, capable of controlling its own development trajectory. Using this information, a model of the institutional structure of the Soviet Vyborg representing a locality as a patient, can be constructed. The information provided by the models of pre-war and postwar Vyborg reveals the *interaction* between the formal and informal institutions and the strategy involved in this interaction in determining the local economic course. The models suggest that institutional interaction is generated by local enterprises and manifests itself through the use of local networks. Three kinds of mechanisms can be identified in the interaction: *adaptation, reinforcement* and *resistance.* In the following section, these mechanisms are first examined as theoretical categories and then empirically put into operation in Vyborg.

3.1. Adaptation

The local orientation of industrial traditions and practices in Finnish Vyborg evolved in a very different form compared to the Vyborg of the Soviet period, while the pool of physical resources remained largely intact. This chapter suggests that the informal institutions, which involve the ability and willingness of the population to take advantage of local economic potential, can be seen as an outcome of one of the mechanisms of institutional interaction: the adaptation of the informal institutions to formal regulation. In the process of adaptation, the constraints and the potential provided by formal regulation fashion the evolution of the local cultural characteristics. Formal institutions affect the local industrial code in two ways. First, incentives anchored in the prevailing property rights structure shape the industrial traditions (Eggertsson 1990, p. 143, Campbell and Lindberg 1990, p. 635). Second, legislation regulates the potential for local identification to develop and attach enterprises to the locality.

Private property regimes create incentives to cultivate entrepreneurial aspirations and encourage individual exploitation of local resources. Once set in motion, the process is cumulative, as the previous enterprises shape local attitudes towards private enterprise (Shapero 1984, p. 31) and thereby establish a sound footing for the emergence of an entrepreneurial culture, defined as a 'life mode of entrepreneurship' by Hjalager (1989). In contrast, property rights regimes with decision-making eliminated at the local level give birth to strict hierarchical systems and the loss of cross-sectoral contacts, which retards the formation of enterprises (Winiecki 1994, p. 67, Kent 1984, p. 173) and may push profit-seeking underground where it will take illegal forms. If a total ban on private enterprise is instigated, the downgrading and gradual abolishment of entrepreneurial skills may be expected (Shapero 1984, p. 34). In the long run, the absence of an entrepreneurial tradition forms an obstacle to the emergence of indigenous economic activity in a locality, as indicated in the experiences of branch plant economies and centrally planned economies (Watts 1981, pp. 54–5, Sweeney 1990, p. 275).

Legislative measures that create and remould local distinctiveness control the gestation of regional aspirations. Formal regulation may plug the building blocks of local distinctiveness from any angle, and may have an impact on the symbolic domain of a locality and its reproduction in education, literature, newspapers, political speeches and individual activity. A strong case has been made, on the other hand, that the features of local administrative and educational organizations, if they deviate from those of the rest of the country, may provide the potential for an increase in local cohesive mentality (Orridge and Williams 1982, Paasi 1986, p. 130).

Vyborg is a good source for recording the adaptation processes involving two dramatically different frameworks of formal institutional resources. In the centuries preceding the Second World War, economic practices taking advantage of the economic potential of the locality matured under legislation that supported private enterprise. Medieval laws and decrees improved entrepreneurial facilities, for example by concentrating trade and handicrafts in urban areas and by regulating competition between rival towns (Ylikangas 1983, p. 122). Skilled merchants from other towns in Finland – in those days a part of Sweden – were compelled under threat of the death penalty to find new premises in Vyborg (Ruuth and Halila 1974). Competition between local enterprises was regulated by organizing trade and industries in dedicated guilds (Suutari 1981, p. 15, Riimala 1991, p. 23). The period of absolutism in the 1600s paved the way for mercantile trade policies (Kaukiainen 1993, p. 21). Vyborg, in conjunction with a few other coastal towns, was declared a 'staple town' with exclusive rights to deal in foreign trade. The privilege was, however, somewhat undermined by a system of quotas and by ordering the merchants to submit to Stockholm-run companies with a monopoly of the tar and tobacco trade (Kuisma 1993, p. 34). The period of the Enlightenment brought about a relaxation of the guild system which had restricted the setting up of new companies. Interest-free credits and tax exemptions were introduced, and everyone with capital was allowed to set up business (Ruuth and Kuujo 1975, pp. 110, 128, Kuisma 1993, p. 64). On the other hand, a few short hostile periods involving decrees restricting forest harvesting, forbidding construction of steam-driven mills, and imposing quotas or temporary bans on foreign trade, negatively affected the balance of the Vyborgian economy (Enbom and Sandelin 1991, p. 12, Kekkonen 1986, p. 86). Liberal policies in the 1800s normalized and consolidated the legislative environment. A liberal customs regulation (1859) abolished export and import restrictions, a decree of free enterprise was established in 1879 and a law of free enterprise was introduced in 1896. These measures stripped the well-established local enterprises of the apparatus to block the entry of newcomers into local business life.

Broadly speaking, legislation was fairly tolerant towards regionalist ideas throughout the pre-war history of Vyborg. Vyborg was granted outright special privileges on many occasions, beginning with a high degree of independence and authority for the medieval lords of the castle. After the incorporation of Vyborg into Tsarist Russia in 1721, the town was considered equal in status to the Baltic regions and was distinguished by an array of special rights and privileges, including the right to use the German language in courts of law (Ruuth and Halila 1974, pp. 165–9). Furthermore, Vyborg was annexed to the rest of Finland in 1812, in those days a Grand Duchy in Russia endowed with special rights. Tolerance towards regionalism is perhaps best conveyed by the variety of languages used in Vyborg (Finnish, Swedish, Russian and German), ranging from the information given in street signs to the provision of basic education. A short period of severe suppression of regionalism occurred in the form of 'Russification' only shortly before Finland gained independence in 1917. In general, the ambience of the formal regulations encouraged risk-taking and profit-seeking in business life. Furthermore, public tolerance towards regionalism facilitated the appearance of local loyalty and identity in Vyborg.

The Soviet regime, in contrast, abolished the risk-bearing and profit-seeking entrepreneur as the key actor in the economy. Instead, a new property rights structure leaning on state-owned enterprises (Butler 1988, p. 147) was introduced. The subordination of Vyborgian plants to outside organizations took place. In the 1960s, local light industries were designed to operate as subsidiaries of industrial corporations in Leningrad (Adaskina et al. 1961, p. 39, Strashuk 1995, Fedorenko 1995). Virtually all important decisions were assumed to be made outside the local plants. State organizations (e.g. Gosplan, Gossnab, industrial ministries etc.) regulated the line and scale of local production, allocated resources and named the end-users of finished products (Strashuk 1995, Fedorenko 1995, Sutela 1983, p. 42, Katila 1985, p. 97). The main task of the local plants was to fulfil the five-year plans and the more detailed one-year plans of production (Zakharov 1995, Strashuk 1995, Nove 1986, pp. 77, 97). Foreign trade, including the barter-based border trade between Finland and the Soviet Union, was a state monopoly run by organizations in Moscow and Leningrad. Consequently, export production was anchored to the annual plans drawn up by the central authority, and the local producers hardly ever consulted the end-user.

The retail system was controlled by Soviet, national and regional organizations, which dictated the number, type and structure of retail outlets, as well as the method of payment used in the shops (*Vyborgski Kommunist*, 19 June 1966). Even the typology of the customers was predetermined; exclusive shops were designed for railway professionals, military people and hard currency tourists (Suraegina 1995).

Legislative measures suffocating regional aspirations included the control of migration and the banning of local symbols of identity. A frontier mentality, a selective type of mentality typical of border areas (Muir 1975, p. 125), did not evolve in Vyborg. The emergence was blocked by administrative measures which curtailed influences from abroad (Relander 1992, Sholmov 1995). For decades, Vyborg was a closed town for foreign visitors. Later, Vyborg was used as a transit area for final tourist destinations such as Leningrad or Moscow. Even in this case contact with tourists was strictly forbidden (Relander 1992). The key factor, however, undermining the emergence of a local identity was harboured in the local residents themselves. Being of Soviet origin, the citizens were already accustomed to an All-Union orientation.

3.2. Reinforcement

Once fashioned by formal regulation, informal institutions are amenable to consolidation and reinforcement. Networks in regional economies mediate the flow of information, values and codes of conduct (Cooke and Morgan 1993, Storper 1995, Amin and Thrift 1994). This way, the local networks serve both as a means of attaching an enterprise to a locality, and as a medium for institutional reinforcement.

Here again, the property rights structure and the legislation fashioning local distinctiveness serve as critical regulators. Property rights with incentives for the long-term expansion of businesses encourage enterprises to invest in a wide range of networks. Furthermore, legislation controlling the growth of regionalism may also affect the direction of investments and the balance of the investment rate between industrial centres. In Vyborg before the war, the property rights structure encouraged long-term investments, as the following record illustrates. The tradition of forming industrial interest groups surfaced as early as the Middle Ages when the control of all trade and industry was legally granted to dedicated guilds. The system of 'dedicated housing' regulated relations between merchants and suppliers, as each Vyborgian tar trader was to accommodate provincial deliverers of supply material, give them credits and even pay their taxes. The expenses were covered by a provision of tar (Ruuth and Halila 1974, p. 115, Kuisma 1993, p. 29). The mercantilist 1600s, granting merchants in staple towns a monopoly of foreign trade, encouraged businesses to expand and collaborate in shipping. The shipping industry lost momentum for a period when the regime abandoned protectionist rules (Ahvenainen 1991, p. 143). The liberal trade policy of the 1800s spurred investment in all forms of transport, and the local merchants embarked on the construction of railways and a canal connecting the sea with lake transport via Vyborg (Ora 1958, p. 353). Tolerance towards regionalism formed the cradle for emerging local identification and encouraged the local entrepreneurs to expand their networks into the social and cultural spheres of Vyborg society. Investments made in health care, education and cultural activities stood as monuments to the evolving local identity. Taken all together, the prevailing atmosphere promoting entrepreneurship and local identity encouraged the local entrepreneurs to operate as Vyborgian entrepreneurs.

In state property regimes, in contrast, the loyalty of local managers is measured using compliance, rather than efficiency, as the yardstick. Local initiatives to rationalize inputs or to enrich the local resource base may not appear (Winiecki 1990, p. 199, Eggertsson 1990, p. 127).

The implications were evident in Vyborg, where the networks panned out according to the resolutions of the centralized planning organizations in Moscow. Decisions made outside the local plants covered virtually everything ranging from the assignment of production tasks and the allocation of resources, to resolutions dealing with sales, transport, finance and insurance. Consequently, enterprises were not confronted with the necessity to make spontaneous investments. In fact, investments spent on efforts to reach production levels 'above the plans' were seen as jeopardizing the main duty of an enterprise, the implementation of the plan (Strashuk 1995, Fedorenko 1995, Zakharov 1995). The example of the electromechanical plant is noteworthy: the dialogue between the electromechanical plant and the neighbouring research unit was minimal and was conducted through Moscow. Fortunately, collaboration between the two units was later made obligatory by state decree (Fedorenko 1995). The fact that the local enterprises were not responsible for the local implications of their operation was highlighted in the infrastructure. The chain of events experienced by the electromechanical assembly plant is an eloquent example. The plant was assigned to move to other facilities three times during the socialist period. After each move the abandoned facilities remained idle and now stand derelict in the town centre (Sholmov 1995).

As the totalitarian society was marked by its low tolerance towards regional aspirations, the platform for the voluntary constitution of a local cultural network remained vague in Soviet Vyborg. Networks cropped up according to centrally designed projects which disregarded the economic potential of a plant. These shortcomings were conspicuous, as indicated by the low quality of housing supplied by the local enterprises. In response to the problems caused by the weak integration of local industries in Vyborg, the local enterprises established networks outside the town. These links covered lobbying in the offices in Moscow. As another solution, a *tolkach* system was developed. *A tolkach* was a person whose function was to travel across the territory of the Soviet Union in search of missing parts which were to be acquired on a barter trade basis (Strashuk 1995, Fedorenko 1995, Nove 1986, p. 106). In general, the property rights structure, biased toward vertical Moscow-based industrial decision-making, and associated with the suppression of local identity, hindered local plant managers from forming local networks.

3.3. Passive and Active Resistance

Adaptation and reinforcement are institutional mechanisms that prevail in an atmosphere of relatively stable formal regulation. When formal institutions change, the third mechanism of institutional interaction, resistance, comes to the fore. Resistance has its roots in the different rates of change between the formal and informal institutions. This entails economic practices, values and codes of conduct that have been established in a locality only gradually to adjust to the changes in the formal institutions, thereby retarding institutional change. A period prevails when the formal and informal rules do not correspond and an institutional lag emerges in an economy. The emergence of an institutional lag can be interpreted as a passive form of resistance. This type of resistance is against the implementation of the intended changes. Resistance becomes active when actors deliberately take measures to reinforce the established practices and actively resist change. Here again, local networks are the key forum for institutional interaction. Resistance may manifest itself via collective action mediated by the local network of industrial and cultural activities (Olson 1965). Formal regulation can be critical in determining the possibilities for resistance: formal institutions may weaken the local collective potential and make it incapable of creating resistance. Societies in totalitarian systems are said by many to lack the coherency necessary for voluntary interest groups to be able to take shape (Koslowski 1992, p. 693).

Institutional resistance was prominent in Vyborg from an early stage. The early start of the local economy was triggered by passive resistance, as the lords of the castle disobeyed the trading embargoes of the Hanseatic League against Russia. Later, having adapted to the entrepreneurial system, the local merchants *cum* industrialists endeavoured to maintain their businesses by resisting unfavourable formal changes, either passively or actively. For example, the failure of the local mercantilist tar and tobacco companies to operate was due to the disobedience and complaints of the Vyborgian shareholders (Ruuth and Halila 1974, p. 130). A large share of the credit for the special privileges granted to Vyborg in Tsarist Russia, had to be given to the delegations of Vyborgian businessmen that solicited the Tsar with their claims (Ranta 1985, pp. 388–91). Again, when the Tsar in the 1700s placed restrictions on the saw mill industry, the local entrepreneurs pressed ahead and disregarded the new rules. Counter-tactics were engineered behind closed doors. The overzealous officers fining the lawbreakers were disposed of using such pretexts, if necessary, as '*trelimiuns tremens alcoholicum*' (Kuisma 1993, p. 132). Successful resistance was, furthermore, to be credited for moderating the curbs on logging, custom tariffs and canal fees. Resistance expanded in non-economic spheres. The Vyborgian entrepreneurs were active in opposing the Russification of Finland in the late 1800s and early 1900s (Markkanen 1976, pp. 88–129, Ora 1958, p. 355).

Once again, the Vyborg of the Soviet period stands out in stark contrast. The formal system ensured that Vyborgian society remained atomistic and was incapable of nurturing regionally based organizations among the local production units. Active resistance remained dormant. Instead, once adapted to the centrally organized system, any endeavour of the central organ to relax the centralized strategies was undermined by passive local resistance. Economic liberalization programmes including the Liberman and Kosygin reforms and the reform aimed at creating larger production units were launched during the decades of socialism. All these reforms failed in Vyborg for the same reason that they failed in other parts of the Soviet Union: the plans were not put into action at the local level (Strashuk 1995, Fedorenko 1995, Sutela 1983, pp. 139–150). Changes in production were considered a threat to the established ways of conducting local production.

3.4. Designing the Institutional Models

The record of Vyborg suggests that the three mechanisms of institutional interaction (adaptation, reinforcement and resistance) were manifest in the institutional structure supporting the capacity of the local economy to master its own development path. General legislation ensured that Vyborg matured into an effective territorial unit with well-established entrepreneurial traditions. Changes in property rights were restricted to laws and decrees regulating the financial transactions of private investors; the right of private enterprise remained intact. The formal institutional framework encouraged the locally operating enterprises to adapt to risk-taking and profit-seeking and to identify themselves as Vyborgian ventures. Once adapted to the system, the local entrepreneurs reinforced their established ways of operating, and networks developed in every area of Vyborg society. In the event of an unfavourable institutional modification, the local network system was used as a medium for institutional resistance.

Postwar Vyborg was marked by its inability to determine its own local economic, social and cultural course. Clearly, such a situation was reinforced by the fact that adaptation was the dominant institutional mechanism shaping the local economy. Adaptation to formal Soviet standards both in industrial decision-making and in local orientation resulted in an inefficient local network formation. This, in turn, eroded the potential for collective institutional resistance. The institutional structure was capable merely of generating passive resistance, which was tuned to appear even when full rationalization of industrial decision-making was attempted. The two different institutional structures are illustrated in see Figure 9.2.

The preceding sections outlined the institutional structures underlying the state of paralysis of the socialist local economy, and the contrast offered by an economy of self-sustaining growth, local initiative-taking and local control of the development path. It is tempting to use these observations as a backdrop to an analysis of the contemporary post-socialist transition.

4. PROJECTING THE INSTITUTIONAL MECHANISMS IN THE CURRENT TRANSITION

Vyborg is currently witnessing a process of profound institutional restructuring promoted by the economic reforms of *perestroika*. Proximity to the Finnish-Russian border makes the post-socialist transition subject to pressures from four different spatial dimensions: the local, the regional, the national, and the international. At the local level, a power game is going on between private enterprise and the public administration to redefine the rights and responsibilities of each party. Another conflict over authority and monetary flow is currently taking place between the local and the regional (Leningrad *oblast*) domains. Vyborg has used various weapons in the struggle, culminating in the plans for a special economic zone (Remeniuk 1995). After the nationwide decentralization of administrative procedures, the local level has achieved greater autonomy in industrial and social decision-making. On the other hand, the system of automatic fiscal support has been blocked, and Vyborg is now charged with responsibility for its own economy. Localities must define their own economic profiles and find a new genre of local identities to fill the void left over by the dissolution of the centralized Soviet system. The disharmony at the national level adds to the political turmoil, depression and the resulting legislative instability. This causes ambiguity in the institutional environment. Finally, Vyborg is situated in the emerging transborder region between Russia and the EU member state, Finland, and has access both to EU development programmes, and to Finnish development programmes aimed at boosting border regions.

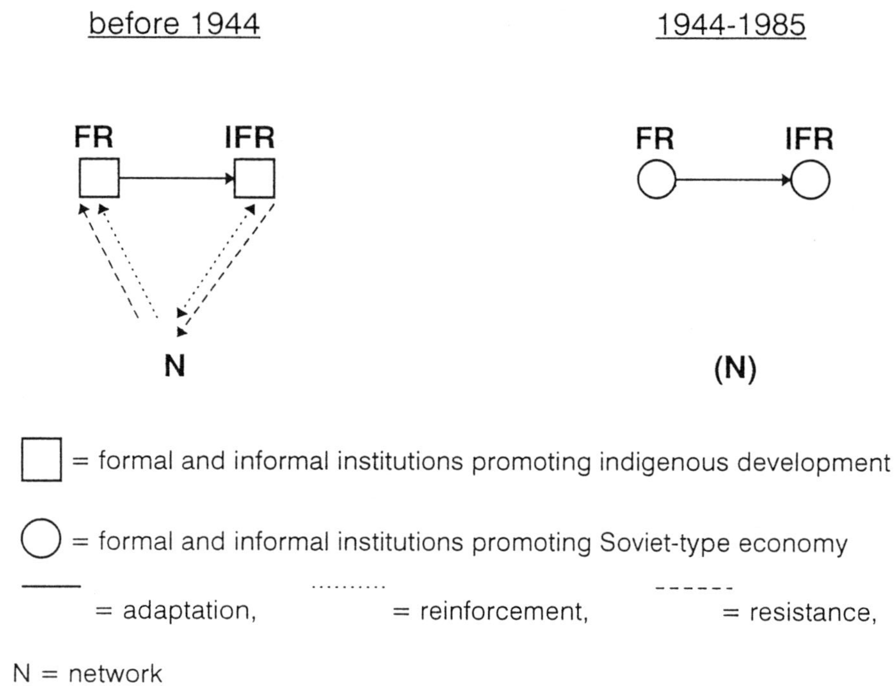

Figure 9.2. The institutional structure of Vyborg before and after the Second World War

It is interesting to examine how the local enterprises in Vyborg operate in this multi-level institutional turmoil. What is the present record of the institutional interaction and the mechanisms revealed in the local networks? The new formal institutions acknowledge private enterprise as the dominant form of business. Most of the old state-owned enterprises in Vyborg have been privatized and are now owned by employee collectives, or (to a lesser degree) by local and non-local investors, including foreign ones. The rate of progress has, so far, been quite modest. The number of local enterprises has not increased satisfactorily, and most of the new enterprises have been established in the area of small-scale retailing (Sholmov 1995).

The profiles of the institutional mechanisms existing between the Russian-owned companies and those owned by foreign investors are disparate. The vast majority of Russian enterprises are owned by worker collectives and suffer from an institutional lag. The labour code dating from the Soviet period is still in existence and will cause resistance until adaptation to the new system takes place through a gradual process of learning. In addition, enterprises purchased by worker collectives are faced with specific problems. Preference for short-term gains inherent in labour-managed enterprises and a low incentive to invest or hire labour are among the handicaps (Sutela 1994, Pejovich 1992). The slow procedure of adapting to the new formal regulations has eroded the financial stability of Vyborgian enterprises and undermined local network formation. Enterprises are unable to invest in supporting facilities and have given up most of their social and cultural tasks (Strashuk 1995, Fedorenko 1995, Zakharov 1995). Local institutional reinforcement is, nevertheless, slowly making progress. The most successful enterprises participate in the town's administration and make collective appearances in newspapers in attempts to boost the developing institutional structure.

Among the foreign investors, Finns have been most active. Finnish enterprises have brought with them the principles of institutional mechanisms that originate in an economy based on Western property rights. However, the importing of Western models into Vyborg has been undermined by the prevailing institutional lag, and several potentially profitable ventures have gone bust because of the opportunistic behaviour of local partners (Narinen 1994). Foreign investors, confronted with a shortage of supporting facilities, recognize that investments in basic infrastructure would be highly desirable. Sophisticated economic networks (collective action, finance etc.) have not yet sufficiently emerged. Residing in Finland, the investors are not personally attached to the town and their contributions to the social and cultural spheres have been modest. Finnish investors are attracted to Vyborg primarily by the relatively inexpensive labour force (Liuhto 1993). Bearing the Finnish past of the town in mind, however, it will be interesting to find out whether the utopia of 'good old Vyborg' will prove an attraction for Finns operating in the town, and if so, whether the dream will find concrete form in the formation of cultural activities around the Finnish-owned companies, for example, in sponsoring the reinvention of Finnish history in Vyborg.

Both Russian and foreign investors are suffering from the ambiguous division existing between private and public rights and responsibilities. Facing severe financial problems, the public sphere has taken tax short cuts and is overtaxing local enterprises – jeopardizing the future of business ventures. Under the unstable institutional framework the main party taking advantage of the situation is the local Mafia operating outside the law.

Overall, the path of indigenous local processes towards an independent and effective local economy based on the agency model of development, may be separated into two phases – the second of which, perhaps, may never be realized. In the first phase, provided that the reform of formal structures maintains its course towards free enterprise and that an acceptable balance in the division of labour between the private and the public sectors on the local, regional, and national levels is achieved, the soil remains fertile for local enterprises trying to adapt to the new system. A gradual up scaling of production would be inaugurated to guarantee at least zero growth. Such an economic course comes close to an 'inward-oriented indigenous development strategy' (Brugger 1992, p. 162). The strategy recommends that a locality sets its goals at such a low level that it is of limited interest to the rest of the world. Gradually, in conjunction with an increasing confidence in the future, local enterprises would consolidate their businesses and the formation of local networks would be boosted. In parallel with an increasing number of enterprises attaching themselves to the locality, the process becomes cumulative, and the many-sided investments made in the economic, and perhaps the social and cultural spheres, increase the attractiveness of the locality for economic investments. Effective institutional resistance would add to the list of potential institutional mechanisms. At this stage, the private and the public sectors would find a balance through an institutional dialogue. This may further activate Russian and foreign investors and result in a favourable impact on the level of production. Vyborg would then be capable of generating an 'outward-oriented indigenous development' (Brugger 1992). This entails that the local economy attracts greater international interest, yet the control of the development path would remain in local hands. The Mafia, which flourishes only in atomistic societies incapable of developing associationist models, would be the potential 'loser' in the game. The quality of institutions and the structure of institutional mechanisms emerging in post-socialist Vyborg might be illustrated as in Figure 9.3.

5. CONCLUSION

The longitudinal analysis of Vyborg showed that the institutional features critical for sustained local development in the contemporary economic, social and political restructuring find their counterparts in the previous phases of capitalistic evolution. It also illustrated how the lack of these features characterized the socialist local economy. The historical analysis illustrated in this chapter presents an attempt to categorize the processes and problems that are taking place in the contemporary transition. Locally operating enterprises form the cornerstone in the analysis. The story of Vyborg suggests that there are several potential avenues for a local enterprise to generate local prosperity. The avenues chosen depend on the division of labour between the private and public sectors. Whatever the outcome of the choices made, the ultimate goal – the increasing embeddedness of local enterprises – can be achieved by bringing the local enterprises into institutional interaction with the public sphere at the local, regional and national levels. It has been argued in this paper that such a dialogue forms the underlying mechanism behind the creation of an associationist interactive model where the local economy is seen as a common project. Unfortunately, experience from elsewhere in Europe (Putnam (1993) – on Southern Italy with its lack of associationist capacities, or, as he terms it, lack of 'civic culture', and Storper (1995, p. 213) – on the 'French desert' in the shadow of Paris) indicates that an associationist transition is a complicated process for atomistic societies that have long suffered from the deprivation of their autonomous capacities. The town of Vyborg is a classic blueprint for this scenario.

The case of Vyborg suggests that the potential negative implications of foreign capital may be avoided by the network formation. Nevertheless, the willingness of foreign, mainly Finnish, investors to become attached to Vyborg by establishing local networks depends on the ability of Vyborg to move towards an outward-oriented indigenous development strategy. With the present shortage of funds and skills in Vyborg, even the few foreign investors, whose attachment to the town

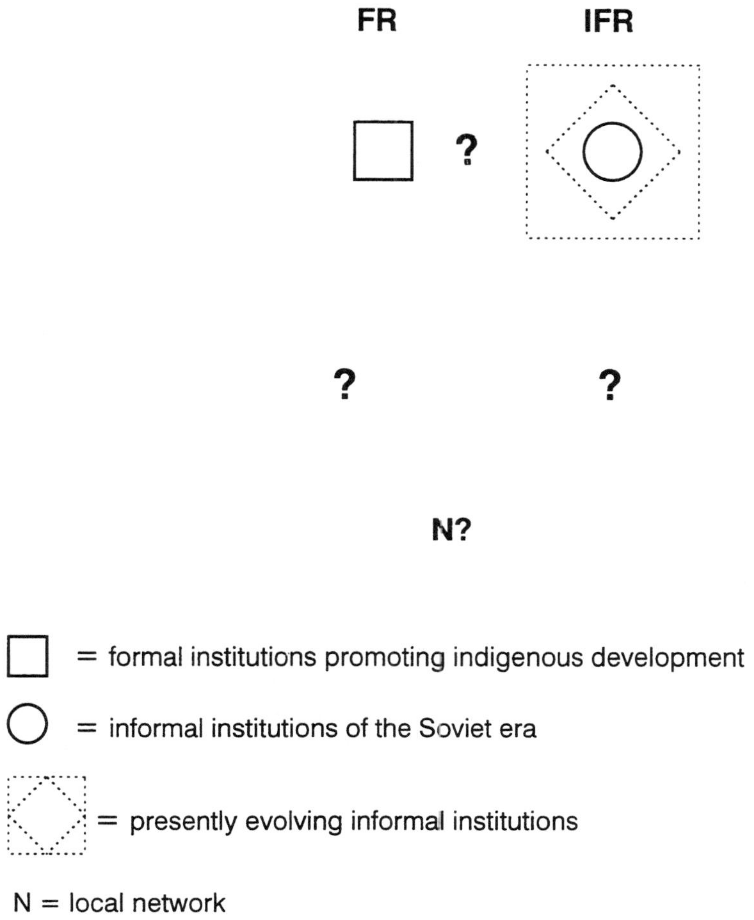

Figure 9.3. The evolving institutional structure of post-socialist Vyborg

remains weak, are of paramount importance to the town, as they provide a model of enterprise and administer a financial injection to the region. Furthermore, the Finns may modify the emerging local identity in two ways: by facilitating the integration of Vyborg into the evolving trans-border region, and by reminding the world of the prosperous past of the town. Whatever the outcome, Vyborg is already exposed to the reverberations of the international economic order. Integration into the transnational economic system is doomed to fail if Vyborg remains a patient incapable of determining its own development course. The fact that Vyborg is a part of a transborder region lying at the crossroads between the Western and the Eastern realms, may facilitate the process of integration.

The case of Vyborg further suggests that the generation of institutional interaction supporting an associationist transition is dependent on two conditions. First, the formal institutions must evoke trust in long-term private enterprise and create incentives to expand local businesses. This is a fundamental precondition for ensuring the formation of local networks. To achieve this, the rights and responsibilities of the private and the public spheres should be defined adequately so as not to suffocate vulnerable fledgling entrepreneurship. Second, the philosophy of regionalism should be tolerated to ensure the local orientation of the emerging networks. An associationist civic culture characterizes only localities with well-established local identity. Accordingly, formal institutions should be designed to encourage risk-taking and long-term profit-seeking on a local basis.

The chapter has endeavoured to place theory and empirical data in a dialectic in order to grasp the institutional mechanisms underlying local evolution. The current post-socialist transition, made more complicated by the problems arising from the new integrating Europe, represents an interesting case for combining the theoretical and empirical worlds in a spatial analysis. A path-dependent institutional analysis provides comprehensive tools for analysing the current transition. Furthermore, the on-going multidimensional changes in the empirical context are reshuffling the cards and may offer new ideas on institutions as determinants in local dynamics.

REFERENCES

Adams, J. (1992) 'Economic Change in the Fourteenth Century: The Case of Siena'. *Journal of Economic Issues* 26 (1): 125–35.

Adaskina, V.I., Vassel, I.P. and Rior, E.M. (1961) *Vyborg i Ego Okrestnosti. Gidrometeorologicheskoe Izdatel'stvo.* [Vyborg and its Surroundings].

Aglietta, M. (1979) *A Theory of Capitalist Regulation: The US Experience.* London: New Left Books.

Ahvenainen, J. (1991) 'Kaupankäyntiä maantieteen ehdoilla' [The Geographical Determination of Trade] in M. Jokipii (ed.) *Suomi Euroopassa. Talous- ja kulttuurisuhteiden historiaa.* Jyväskylä: Gummerus Kirjapaino Oy.

Amin, A. and Malmberg, A. (1994) *Competing Structural and Institutional Influences on the Geography of Production in Europe* in A. Amin (ed.) *Post-Fordism – A Reader.* Oxford: Blackwell, pp. 227–48.

Amin, A. and Thrift, N. (1993) 'Globalization, Institutional Thickness and Local Prospects'. *Revue d'Economie Régionale et Urbaine* 3: 405–27.

Amin, A. and Thrift, N. (1994) 'Living in the Global' in A. Amin and N. Thrift (eds) *Globalization, Institutions, and Regional Development in Europe*. Oxford: Oxford University Press, pp. 1–22.

Amin, A. and Thrift, N. (1995) 'Institutional Issues for the European Regions: From Markets and Plans to Socioeconomics and Powers of Association'. *Economy and Society* 24 (1): 41–66.

Bolton, R. (1989) *An Economic Interpretation of 'Sense of Place'*, mimeo. Williamstown, MA: Department of Economics.

Brugger, E.A. (1992) 'Endogenous Development between Myth and Reality: Pre-Requisites for Endogenous Development Strategies' in H.J. Ewers and J. Allesch (eds) *Innovation and Regional Development. Strategies, Instruments, and Policy Coordination*. Berlin: Walter de Gruyter & Co., pp. 161–6.

Butler, W.E. (1988) *Soviet Law*. London: Butterworths.

Campbell, J.L. and Lindberg, L.N. (1990) 'Property Rights and the Organization of Economic Activity by the State'. *American Sociological Review* 55 (5): 634–47.

Cooke, P. and Morgan, K. (1993) 'The Network Paradigm: New Departures in Corporate and Regional Development'. *Environment and Planning* D 11 (5): 543–64.

Crevoisier, O. (1990) 'Functional Logic and Territorial Logic and How They Interrelate in a Region' in E. Cicciotti, N. Alderman and A. Thwaites (eds) *Technological Change in a Spatial Context*. Berlin: Springer-Verlag, pp. 17–36.

Eggertsson, T. (1990) *Economic Behaviour and Institutions*. Cambridge: Cambridge University Press.

Enbom, S. and Sandelin, C.F. (1991) *Viipurilainen Kauppahuone Hackman & Co. 1880–1925* [History of the Vyborgian Trading House Hackman Ltd 1880–1925]. Helsinki: Oy Hackman Ab.

Granovetter, M. (1985) 'Economic Action and Social Structure: The Problem of Embeddedness'. *American Journal of Sociology* 91 (3): 481–510.

Hämäläinen-Forslund, P. and Hämäläinen, J. (1989) *Lyhyt matka Viipuriin* [A Short Visit to Vyborg]. Porvoo: WSOY.

Hausner, J. (1994) 'Interactive vs Imperative Strategy of Systematic Change in Central and Eastern Europe'. *Review of International Political Economy* 2 (2): 249–66.

Hirschman, A.O. (1958) *The Strategy of Economic Development*. New Haven: Yale University Press.

Hjalager, A.-M. (1989) 'Why No Entrepreneurs? Life Modes, Everyday Life and Unemployment Strategies in an Underdeveloped Region'. *Entrepreneurship and Regional Development* 1 (1): 85–97.

Ilanko, J. (1956) *Teollisuuden- ja liikkeenharjoittajainseura 'Pamaus' 1891–1955* [The Vyborgian Pamaus-Association of Industrialists and Merchants, 1891–1955]. Helsinki: Kauppakirjapaino Oy.

Innis, H.A. (1929) *The Fur Trade in Canada. An Introduction to Canadian Economic History*. Toronto: Toronto University Press, revised edition 1984.

Johannisson, B. and Nilsson, A. (1989) 'Community Entrepreneurs: Networking for Local Development'. *Entrepreneurship and Regional Development* 1 (1): 3–19.

Katila, R. (1985): *Talous- ja ulkomaankauppahallinto Neuvostoliitossa* [The Administration of Industry and Foreign Trade in the USSR]. Porvoo: WSOY.

Kaukiainen, Y. (1993) *The History of Finnish Shipping*. London: Routledge.

Kekkonen, J. (1986) 'Merkantilismista Liberalismiin' ['From Mercantilism to Liberalism'] in J. Kekkonen, K. Korpijaakko and H. Ylikangas (eds) *Oikeudellisen säätelyn kehityslinjoja.* Juva: WSOY, pp. 75–112.

Kent, C.A. (ed.) (1984) *The New Entrepreneurs. In The Environment for Entrepreneurship.* Lexington, MA: Lexington Books, pp. 173–82.

Kiselev, P. (1986) 'Piatiletka: Itogi i Zadachi. Poteriannye Milliony' ['The Five Year Period: Results and Tasks. The Lost Millions']. *Vyborgski Kommunist* 9 January.

Koslowski, R. (1992) 'Market Institutions, East European Reform, and Economic Theory'. *Journal of Economic Issues* 26 (3): 673–705.

Kuisma, M. (1993) *Metsäteollisuuden maa. Suomi, metsät ja kansainvälinen järjestelmä, 1620–1920* [The Country of Forest Industry. Finland, Forests and the International System, 1620–1920]. Helsinki: Societas Historica Finlandiae.

Lakio, M. (1978) *Talouselämä. In Viipurin kaupungin historia V osa, Vuodet, 1917–1944* [The Economy of Vyborg, 1917–1944]. Lappeenranta: Karjalan Kirjapaino Osakeyhtiö, pp. 151–201.

Lakio, M. (1981) *Talouselämä. In Viipurin kaupungin historia IV osa, Vuodet, 1840–1917* [The Economy of Vyborg, 1840–1917]. Lappeenranta: Etelä-Saimaan Kustannus Oy, pp. 363–423.

Lipietz, A. (1994) 'Post-Fordism and Democracy' in A. Amin (ed.) *Post-Fordism – A Reader.* Oxford: Blackwell, pp. 338–57.

Liuhto, K. (1993) *Viipuri – Pietarin talousalueen länsiportti. Suomalaisyritysten kokemuksia ja koettelemuksia nyky-Viipurissa* [Vyborg – Gateway to St Petersburg. Experiences of Finnish Enterprises in Vyborg Today]. Turku: Turku School of Economics and Business Administration. Business Research Centre and Institute for East-West Trade.

Markkanen, E. (1976) *Juho Lallukka. Karjalainen elämäntarina* [The life of Juho Lallukka, a Karelian Businessman]. Jyväskylä: Gummerus Oy.

Martinez, N. and Nueño, P. (1988) 'Catalan Regional Business Culture, Entrepreneurship, and Management Behaviour: An Explanatory Study' in J.W. Weiss (ed.) *Regional Cultures, Managerial Behaviour and Entrepreneurship. An International Perspective.* New York, Westport, CT and London: Quorom Books, pp. 61–77.

Muir, R. (1975) *Modern Political Geography.* London: Macmillan.

Nielsen, K., Jessop, B. and Hausner, J. (1995) 'Institutional Change in Post-Socialism, Strategic Choice and Path-Dependency' in J. Hausner, B. Jessop and K. Nielsen (eds) *Post-Socialism: Institutional Dynamics in the Transformation Process.* Aldershot: Edward Elgar, pp. 3–44.

North, D. (1981) *Structure and Change in Economic History.* USA: W.W. Norton & Company.

Nove, A. (1986) *The Soviet Economic System*, third edition. Boston: Unwin Hyman.

Oinas, P. (1995a) 'Types of Enterprise and Local Relations' in B. van der Knaap and R. Le Heron *Human Resources and Industrial Spaces: A Perspective on Globalization and Localization.* UK: John Wiley & Sons, pp. 177–95.

Oinas, P. (1995b) 'Organizations and Environments: Linking Industrial Geography and Organization Theory' in S. Conti, E.J. Malecki and P. Oinas (eds) *The Industrial Enterprise and its Environment. Spatial Perspectives.* Aldershot: Avebury, pp. 143–67.

Olson, M. (1965) *The Logic of Collective Action.* Cambridge, MA: Harvard University Press.
Ora, Y. (1958) 'Liike-Elämä' ['Business in Vyborg'] in J. Kivi-Koskinen, J.I. Koivu, A. Tuurna and T. Valtavuo (eds) *Viipurin kirja.* Pieksämäki: Torkkelin Säätiö, pp. 299–357.
Orridge, A.W. and Williams, C.H. (1982) 'Autonomist Nationalism: A Theoretical Framework for Spatial Variations in its Genesis and Development'. *The Political Geography Quarterly* 1 (1): 19–39.
Paasi, A. (1986) 'The Institutionalization of Regions: A Theoretical Framework for the Understanding of the Emergence of Regions and the Constitutions of Regional Identity'. *Fennia* 164 (1): 105–46.
Peck, J. and Tickell, A. (1994) 'Searching for a New Institutional Fix: the After-Fordist Crisis and the Global-Local Disorder' in A. Amin (ed.) *Post-Fordism – A Reader.* Oxford: Blackwell, pp. 280–315.
Pejovich, S. (1992) 'A Property Rights Analysis of the Inefficiency of Investment Decisions by Labour-Managed Firms'. *Journal of Institutional and Theoretical Economics* 148 (1): 30–41.
Putnam, R.D. (1993) *Making Democracy Work. Civic Traditions in Modern Italy.* Princeton, NJ: Princeton University Press.
Ranta, R. (1985) *Vanhan Suomen talouselämä vuosina, 1721–43.* [The Economy of the Old Finland, 1721–43]. Helsinki: Societas Historica Finlandiae. Historiallisia Tutkimuksia 130. SHS.
Riimala, E. (1991) *Meren, kanavan ja laivojen Viipuri* [The Vyborg of the Sea, the Canal and the Ships]. Helsinki: Suomen Laivahistoriallinen Yhdistys Ry.
Ruuth, J.W. and A. Halila (1974) *Viipurin kaupungin historia II osa, vuodet 1617–1710* [The History of Vyborg, 1617–1710]. Lappeenranta: Karjalan Kirjapaino Osakeyhtiö.
Ruuth, J.W., and E. Kuujo (1975) *Viipurin Kaupungin Historia III Osa, Vuodet 1710–1812* [The History of Vyborg, 1710–1812]. Lappeenranta: Karjalan Kirjapaino Osakeyhtiö.
Sayer, A. (1992) *Method in Social Science. A Realist Approach*, second edition. London and New York: Routledge.
Shapero, A. (1984) 'The Entrepreneurial Event' in C.A. Kent (ed.) *The Environment for Entrepreneurship.* Lexington, MA: Lexington Books, pp. 21–41.
Spilling, O.R. (1991) 'Entrepreneurship in a Cultural Perspective'. *Entrepreneurship and Regional Development* 3 (1): 33–48.
Storper, M. (1995) 'The Resurgence of Regional Economies, Ten Years Later. The Region as a Nexus of Untraded Interdependencies'. *European Urban and Regional Studies* 2 (3): 191–221.
Sutela, P. (1983) *Neuvostotalouden periaatteet* [The Principles of the Soviet Economic System]. Porvoo: WSOY.
Sutela, P. (1994) 'Insider Privatization in Russia: Speculations on Systemic Change'. *Europe-Asia Studies* 46 (3): 417–35.
Suutari, V. (1981) *Taakankantajat. Luokkataistelu satamissa lastauksista* [The Border Carriers. Class War in the Harbours]. Helsinki: Kustannus Oy Cossus.
Sweeney, G.P. (1985) 'Innovation is Entrepreneur-led' in G.P. Sweeney (ed.) *Innovation Policies: An International Perspective.* London: Pinter, pp. 80–114.
Sweeney, G.P. (1990) 'Endogenous Development Strategies in Peripheral Regions: The Example of Ireland' in H.J. Ewers and J. Allesch *Innovation*

and Regional Development: Strategies, Instruments, and Policy Coordination. Berlin: Walter de Gruyter, pp. 265–85.
Sweeney, G.P. (1991) 'Technical Culture and the Local Dimension of Entrepreneurial Vitality'. *Entrepreneurship and Regional Development* 3 (4): 363–78.
Vasilev, E.N. and Zakatilov, N.I. (1975) *Vyborg.* Lenizdat
Veretennikov, G. (1984) 'Gody Rosta, Gody Stanovleniia' ('The Years of Growth, the Years of Modification'). *Vyborgski Kommunist*, 20 June.
Vyborgski Kommunist, 19 June 1966.
Watkins, M.H. (1963) 'A Staple Theory of Economic Growth'. *The Canadian Journal of Economics and Political Sciences* 29 (2): 141–58.
Watts, H.D. (1981) *The Branch Plant Economy: A Study of External Control.* New York: Longman.
Winiecki, J. (1990) 'Why Economic Reforms Fail in the Soviet System – a Property Rights Based Approach'. *Economic Inquiry* 28 (2): 195–221.
Winiecki, J. (1994) 'Shaping the Institutional Infrastructure'. *Economic Inquiry* 32 (1): 66–78.
Ylikangas, H. (1983) *Miksi oikeus muuttuu? Laki ja oikeus historiallisen kehityksen osana* [Why does the Law Change? Law and Justice in Historical Development]. Porvoo: WSOY.

INTERVIEWS

Fedorenko, Gennadi Nikolaevich (1995). General Director, JSC Vyborg Electronic Equipment Making Plant. 27 April, Vyborg.
Narinen, Juha (1994): Managing Director, East West Trade and Consulting. 17 April, Helsinki.
Relander, Olga (1992). Archivist, resident in Vyborg 1960–1978. 16 June, Helsinki.
Remeniak, Valeri Adolfovich (1995): Councillor for External Economic Cooperation. The Administration of the Vyborg District, Leningrad Region. The Administration of the Vyborg Free Economic Zone. 28 April, 1995.
Sholmov, Konstantin Evgenevich (1995): Correspondent, *Vyborgskie Vedomosti.* 27–28 April, Vyborg.
Strashuk, Anatoli Martynovich (1995): Chief of Export and Import Department. Joint Stock Company Vyborg Shipyard. 27 April, Vyborg.
Suraegina, Vera Vasilevna (1995): Vice Head. The Administration of the Vyborg District, Leningrad Region. The Administration of the Vyborg Free Enterprise Zone. 28 April, Vyborg.
Zakharov, Sergei (1995): Director of the Bakery TOO Marlen. 27 April, Vyborg.

10. Transition problems in the Russian agriculture sector: a historical-institutional perspective[1]

Silke Stahl

1. INTRODUCTION

The first years after the breakdown of the socialist socio-economic order in Central and Eastern Europe were characterized by a rather optimistic view of the feasibility of reform programmes. There was no doubt that the transition towards a Western-style market economy and democracy would in principle be possible. Accordingly, scientific interest was mainly directed towards the question of whether a 'shock therapy' (a prominent approach is Shatalin's 500-days programme) or a more gradualist approach would be appropriate. Assuming that each country of the former Soviet block would need the same 'remedy' it was generally acknowledged that an initial period of decentralization and privatization should be followed by macroeconomic stabilization. Within this framework privatization is considered to be a prerequisite for the functioning of market forces and the further success of the transition (Blanchard et al. 1991, Lipton and Sachs 1990). These contributions, nevertheless, take it for granted that there exist strong forces in the population which are ready to move unambiguously towards a market economy based on private property. Not included in the analysis are certain other behaviourial patterns such as the fundamental opposition to private entrepreneurship which is rooted in the history of the transition states, an attitude which varies from state to state, even from region to region.

Recent developments in the countries in transition have given support to the thesis that there exist country-specific features: the success of the reforms varies enormously in the different countries. While Poland and the Czech Republic are Europe's fastest growing regions today, Russia

[1] I am grateful to Ulrich Witt, Thomas Brenner, Burkhard Flieth, Alison Franke Riita Kosonen, and Jürgen Lange-von Kulessa for helpful comments and discussion.

is plagued by output decline, inflation and political instability. Indeed, it seems as if there are some country-specific factors such as underlying socio-political norms (or informal rules) which further expedite the reforms, especially the establishment of private property rights, in some countries while discouraging them in others. In this chapter the problem of the Russian agricultural sector will be examined.

One may ask, considering the minor role and influence of agriculture in Western Europe, why the agricultural sector should be of importance in the transition process. First of all, agriculture plays a much more important role in Russian everyday life today than it does in Europe. Russians are more sensitive to the agricultural situation because until recently they had experienced shortages in their food supply. In the last decades, chronic food shortages forced the Russian urban population to maintain contact with the countryside, usually by cultivating a private plot (their 'dacha') on a subsistence level. The population's sensitivity concerning questions of food supply renders the success of agricultural policy a crucial reference point in the overall assessment of the success of the reforms. Food supply is therefore a major factor in determining political stability, a precondition for the further success of efforts to transform the economy and society.

Furthermore, the Russian rural population itself can be expected to play an important role during the transition process and the following stabilization of the country. In contrast to the successful businessmen of the larger cities, private farmers own fixed capital. Therefore one should expect them to have an interest in well-defined private property rights and protection against state confiscations or theft by jealous neighbours. Private farmers should be an interest group involved in, and publicly supporting, a democratic and stable state.

The country-specific factors mentioned above can be described as the informal rules of a society. Any argument which takes them into consideration, usually refers to the ideas first introduced by Hayek who described how in different societies in the course of history not only formal rules of law but also informal rules have developed which influence human interaction and therefore also the way formal law is implemented in a society (Hayek 1988, pp. 11–28). This means that identical laws or constitutional rules can shape two societies in totally different ways.[2] In this chapter I will investigate the influence on the

[2] One example of this phenomenon, often referred to in literature on the subject, is the similarity of the written constitutions of the USA and many Latin American countries which has not prevented significant differences in the political stability of these

structure of property rights in the Russian countryside of culture and tradition as well as the costs due to different informal institutions. In the literature on economic transition in Central and Eastern Europe institutional problems in the agricultural sector have received little attention. There are several contributions to institutional problems, especially concerning the property rights structure, in development economics (Hoff 1993, Bardhan 1989), though the transfer of these findings into a theory of transition has not taken place so far. Approaches in this direction have been made by Wegren (1994) and a number of Russian scholars (Ol'sevich 1994, Goricheva 1994). Wegren describes how culture, that is, informal institutions, contradicts the direction of reform attempts. Yet he does not explain how the informal rules influence the reform attempts and why this particular culture emerged. One possible explanation is the historical analysis as used by the New Institutionalists (North and Thomas 1973) which will be applied here.

It will be argued that, in Russia, a tradition of property rights and thus a structure of costs can be found which differs from the tradition in Western Europe even up to the present day. It will be claimed that this tradition influences the rules of social organization in the countryside and leads to a privatization outcome which differs substantially from the target postulated by the Russian government. An overview of the attempts to transform Russian agriculture will be given in Section 3. The conjecture will be that Russian agriculture has apparently been so difficult to organize because during its history Russian rural organization developed forms which never existed in Western European rural societies. These different underlying organizational principles had already found expression in Russia during the reform attempts of the nineteenth and early twentieth centuries. These reform attempts will be described in Section 4. In Section 5 they will be compared to the agrarian history of Western Europe, especially England, and Section 6 will delineate in detail some of the reasons, generally speaking, for the differing costs structures and shared values and for the varying developments. Section 7 offers some tentative conclusions.

countries. In Europe such a phenomenon can also be found: the political constitutions of the Federal Republic of Germany and the Russian Federation are quite similar – in both countries two houses of parliament exist, one directly elected by the citizens, the other as a representation of the federal states. Likewise the system of voting – a majority vote system with two votes for each voter – is very much the same. Yet the everyday political life of the two societies is quite different.

2. THEORETICAL REMARKS: PROPERTY RIGHTS, RELATED COST STRUCTURES AND SHARED VALUES

In view of the preceding considerations, a change in the property rights structure should play a decisive role in the transition of agriculture. To recapitulate, property rights represent the bundle of rights of an individual concerning the use of an economic asset in the framework of a social system. Property rights define 'the position of each individual with respect to the utilization of scarce resources' (Furubotn and Pejovich 1972, p. 1139). Utilization rights can appear in four different forms:

- *usus* – the right to use the hand itself, for example the right to till land;
- *usus fructus* – the right to use the product of the land;
- *abusus* – the freedom not to use the resource even though one has the right to do so; and
- transfer – the right to sell the land to somebody else.

To what extent these rights can actually be used depends on the degree to which the exclusion of others is possible. These others, individuals as well as collectives, are excluded if they cannot claim a right to the same resource or have no possibility of interfering with the individual's sovereignty over the resource. Interference is present if some rights, for example the right to transfer, are not allotted to the individual or the community is allowed a say in the use of the resource, that is, the individual does not have an undiluted *usus* right.

Using this taxonomy, one can differentiate between three main forms of property: there is a so-called open access regime if other individuals are not excluded from the use of the resource. All individuals have the rights *usus* and *usus fructus*, but there is no transfer right. If the use of a resource is limited to a group of people, say a tribe or a village community, we speak of common property. Finally, there are private property rights, characterized by the allocation of (in most cases) all four rights to a single individual who is allowed to exclude all other individuals from the resource. Under private property rights the individual is free to make decisions about the resource.

Of course these are descriptions of ideal types. In practice, a watertight distinction between the three general forms of property is often difficult and mixed forms can be observed. For instance, the form of common property may vary, depending on the degree of community interference in the individuals' decisions. In the course of time, changes in the property rights structure of a society can occur. In the course of economic development, a movement from an open access regime to a system of common property and then to a system of private property rights has often been observed, namely, the gradual abandoning of features of communal organization. Yet this direction of development is by no means a necessary one: as will be discussed in this chapter, a dilution of private property rights and a transition to forms of communal property rights also occurs in history.

Which factors influence the movement from one system of property rights to another and why does a transition towards a system of comparatively weaker property rights appear to be possible? In principle, two interlinked explanations are offered: first, changing net costs[3] related to a certain structure of property rights, which are envisaged as the force inducing the search for new property rights structures; second, the concept of shared values which determine the way the environment (and the set of alternative choices) is perceived and explain the spectrum from which alternative property rights structures are chosen. The actual choice between the known alternatives can be traced back to these net cost structures and shared values.

Let us first discuss the concept and the role of net costs. These costs include the costs of enforcing the property rights (either by the individual or a state authority) or the decision costs related to the administration of the economic asset. To a large extent the amount of the net costs an individual faces is not dependent on certain external factors but on the property rights structure itself. For example, if property rights are well defined it is not difficult to identify the owner in order to negotiate a possible transfer. If rights are to be enforced against others this is much less costly if ownership structures are unambiguous. Otherwise, if costs due to a certain property rights structure are excessive, it may happen that individuals will be unwilling to exchange rights, that is, engage in market transactions. As mentioned above, considerable changes in the cost structure, for example owing to the enhanced possibilities for internalizing externalities, induce a search for alternative property rights structures.

Property rights theory usually assumes that the system of property rights which implies lower net costs will gain acceptance (Witt 1991, p. 23). Nevertheless, without any limitations, this holds only if

[3] Net costs are the difference between gains and costs of a given property rights structure. In this chapter I will focus on the cost side, being aware that, as long as gains are not equal, costs and gains have to be compared. Therefore in the last section of this chapter I will also look at the gain side.

individuals are perfectly informed about the institutional alternatives. Realistically, it has to be assumed that, owing to the limited capacity of the human mind and the complexity of the environment, people are only partly aware of the choice alternatives their environment offers. As information has to be filtered somehow, information concerning alternatives, in this case concerning different institutional settings, is not processed impartially, but within a framework of former experiences, personal convictions and the society's norms and traditions (for a detailed discussion, see Denzau and North (1994)). The latter factors namely, shared values which amount to a large part of a society's culture, are of considerable importance, as they are reinforced in the process of social interaction and are therefore hard to alter. As they influence the information processing by a group's members in a very similar way, they are a prerequisite for the formation of institutions in general. At the same time, right from the beginning, they prevent certain kinds of information, possibly regarding more favourable institutional settings, being taken into account because this information is not compatible with the values which are predominant in the group under consideration. This means that the set of alternative choices might be limited and an alternative with a much more favourable cost structure is not chosen as it is not taken into account at all. An analysis based on cost structures, therefore, as is usually applied in institutional economics, does not suffice and has to be supplemented by an analysis of norms and values.

Nevertheless, even if an alternative institutional set-up is compatible with a group's system of values and it has become evident to the members of the group that it is more efficient, such a set-up may not be established: the design of a new system of property rights itself imposes costs which may turn out to be a major obstacle to the transition from one system of property rights to another. Though this kind of correlation is certainly important, the investigation here will mainly be confined to the question of how costs and shared values influence the development of property rights regimes.

3. RUSSIAN AGRICULTURE IN TRANSITION: THE DOUBTFUL SUCCESS OF THE REFORMS

In general, the aim of recent reforms in the Russian agricultural sector has been the transition from a common property rights structure to a system of private property rights. Until a few years ago, private property rights for land would have been unthinkable in the Soviet Union. Since the collectivization policy of the 1930s, peasants have been organized in either *kolkhozy* or *sovchozy*. With the exception of small private plots, land was tilled collectively according to the directives of a central planning authority. The collective had the rights of *usus* and *usus fructus*, but there was strong interference from the outside. Thus, the individual farmer was under the control of the collective and the central planning authority. Owing to the strong interference of the central planning authority even the notion of communal property was weak, though it is by no means possible to speak of the existence of an open access regime. Usually the form of collective ownership described above is held responsible for the permanent crisis of Russian agriculture. The organizational form misdirected incentives so that productivity was low and the environmental situation deteriorated in an alarming way in many parts of the country. At the end of the last decade, the situation was as follows (van Atta 1993, p. 72): since 1920 there had been no significant increases in potato yields. The productivity of a Russian collective farm had reached just about one-fifth of the productivity of a US farm and harvest losses during storage and transport accounted for up to 50 per cent of the total harvest. At the same time, 20 per cent of total investments were directed into the agricultural sector. Low productivity notwithstanding, agricultural production had an extremely negative ecological impact which, due to deteriorating soil conditions, led to further diminishing productivity (Bobyliev 1995, pp. 97–100).

With the beginning of Glasnost and Perestroika in about 1985, it had already been widely accepted that these conditions were a consequence of organizational failure in agricultural production. None the less, until the beginning of the 1990s undiluted private property rights in land was something unthinkable. As a substitute, the newly created super-ministry Gosagroprom developed leasing models. Even this policy, however, faced massive resistance on the part of conservative communists. According to these models, people gained the possibility of leasing land for a lifetime, to bequeath and even to sell the right to lease land (Smith 1991, pp. 229–47). As long as there was no real ownership of land, however, there was always the possibility of state interference in the decision-making of the landowner. One can only speak, therefore, of very weak private property rights and it seems as if not a lot of potential private farmers could be attracted by this structure. It was not until 1990 that it became accepted opinion that this policy had not led to satisfactory results and Gosagroprom was dissolved. Alexander Rutskoi was given the task of reforming the rural property structure. In order to prevent social turmoil he had to enhance agricultural productivity although the socio-economic transformation of the countryside and its institutions was not greatly appreciated (van Atta 1993, p. 85). The legalization of private agricultural enterprises (*fermerskoe khoziaiztvo*) was considered a means of enhancing productivity in the agricultural sector. These 'family farms' were given the right to private property of land and other factors of production. Their farmers could decide independently on production and sales without any interference from the state or neighbouring collective farms (van Atta 1993, p. 75).

During the ensuing legislation process a whole range of possible forms of private agriculture was developed (Wegren 1994, p. 222). First of all, those forms of private ownership which had already existed before privatization (private plots) could be maintained and enlarged by leasing additional land from the collective farm. In fact this is collective farming under even worse preconditions for the individual peasant, as he or she still remains part of the collective organizational structure as far as the supply of inputs is concerned but has to bear the risk of harvest losses. Moreover, the peasant's position with regard to the managers of the collective farm is very weak. In fact, this form does not differ from the leasing models developed by Gosagroprom.

Nevertheless, the central element of the reforms in the countryside has been the reorganization of the collective farms themselves. The procedure is as follows: each member of the collective farm receives shares in the collective farm. They can either be reinvested so that after restructuring a joint-stock company (*aktionernoe obshchestvo*) will result, or the former members of the collective farm can leave and claim property in land equivalent to his or her share. Since the management of the collective farm can decide the size and quality of land considered equivalent to the share and since the manager has no interest in giving away the better land of the former collective farm, compensation in land has usually led to an unsatisfactory outcome for the prospective private farmer.

Under the latest legislation, land may also be bought privately, provided that the buyer can prove that he or she has sufficient agrotechnical knowledge and is genuinely willing to till the land. Land can either be bought from the state land fund or from an already existing farm. Theoretically, farmers who take this option have nearly undiluted private property rights. There are, however, several problems. As a land register does not so far exist, exclusion is difficult and costly. Furthermore, the right of transfer is not allotted to the individual farmer because of fear of speculation. Finally, the position of the law is still very weak. As a result, potential private farmers have no faith in the law or its protection of their property.

Partly owing to these problems, legislation did not lead to the expected development of private family farming. Instead, collective farmers as well as their managers resisted the measures (van Atta 1993, p. 79). A rural social system based on family farms could not be established. Usually the collective farms reorganized themselves into joint-stock companies with the members not taking any private initiative and responsibility. As a consequence, of the 90 per cent of all former collective farms which had been reorganized by 1992, as many as 92 per cent continued to exist as heavily subsidized joint-stock companies (Sutela 1994, p. 428). This means that they kept some form of common property, differing from the old *sovchozy* and *kolkhozy* only by the lower degree of state interference since the system of central planning had been abandoned. Seventy-five per cent of the newly created private farms were owned by the urban population which tilled the land mainly for the supply of their own families. Owing to the fear of speculative land acquisition, the size of their land is so small that production for the market is hardly feasible.[4]

The lack of secure and undiluted private property rights in land, however, is only one reason for the so far disappointing privatization results. The other, which itself influences the property rights structure, is an organizational tradition in the Russian countryside which differs from the one which can be found in Western Europe. It impedes privatization as it raises the costs of private farming. Today it finds its expression in the strong public opposition to the introduction of 'capitalist production principles'. A considerable number of Russian scholars support this opposition, arguing that the 'countryside is a special social community' (Petrikov 1994, p. 25) which should not be destroyed. Arguing that the market for agricultural products is characterized by market failure, these scholars hold that the introduction of market-oriented principles would aggravate the crisis in the countryside further. Rather than initiating such a development, the existing social institutions in the countryside should be strengthened (Aleksandrov 1994, p. 15). Such reasoning is not only a legacy of 70 years of socialism but also stems from a collectivist property-rights tradition which has deep roots in Russian history.

[4] There is a code which protects private property, but public discussion during the last few years has shown that the value of this code as a guideline for political action is very weak.

4. AGRICULTURAL REFORMS IN RUSSIA IN THE NINETEENTH AND EARLY TWENTIETH CENTURIES

Russian history of the last 150 years is also a history of repeated attempts at modernizing the countryside in order to increase productivity and to modernize the country as a whole. If, as claimed here, the Russian property rights tradition is a collectivist one, we should either find in all the modernization attempts that state legislation favoured collectivist organizational models or that all legal efforts aimed at creating individualistic societal norms were rejected by the Russian people. Following this conjecture, in this section three periods of Russian history will be investigated: the emancipation of the serfs, the dissolution of the *mir* system in the course of the Stolypin reforms and the reintroduction of the *mir* during the first years of Soviet Russia. These periods have been chosen because all three were directed towards reforming the social organization and the property rights structure of the countryside.

In the middle of the nineteenth century, Russia was the last European country where the peasants were living in bondage. In the central Russian region their dues were not, as for example in most Prussian provinces, limited to paying rent but they had to perform services for their landlords. The economies of the demesne and the village were closely interlinked, the social structure basically unshaken. In many respects the internal village organization resembled that which had prevailed in other European regions until industrialization, that is, the three-field system with scattered strips and strong communal regulation. Land redistribution, however, stands out as a peculiar feature especially in central Russia. Land was redistributed on a more or less regular basis among peasant households according to the (changing) size of a household, in order to equalize landholding. This system had always existed in some villages, but developed into a widespread practice during the nineteenth century, first in central Russia and later among the settlers in western Siberia and the Cossacks in the southern steppes (Atkinson 1983, p. 9). While the traditional property structure in Europe can be described as a system of private property rights (see Section 5), even if those rights were weak, the property rights structure of these redistributive villages was communal: land did not belong to the individual but to the village commune which allocated it to the peasant households according to their needs. Thus the spread of the redistributive village commune in the nineteenth century constituted a general development in the larger movement of communalism in the Russian countryside.

This movement was reflected in the administrative treatment of the village commune: the main problem that had to be solved in the course of the emancipation of the serfs was the dissolution of an economy in which lord and peasant were mutually dependent. The peasant had to be supplied with land while the lord had to be compensated for the loss of serf labour. A characteristic of the reform was that legislation did not focus on the single peasant but on his village community. All peasants, therefore, became members of the *mir*, the newly created political counterpart of the village community, the *obshchina*, even in regions where the *obshchina* had not existed before, as for example in the Polish and Ukrainian provinces (Grant 1976). The *mir* became responsible for tax payments and organized the so-called repurchase of peasant land from the lord. The repurchase was intended to compensate the lords, but appeared to be a source of peasant unrest as it contradicted peasant expectations: in their view cultivated land belonged to those whose energy had created it from wilderness. They could not understand why they should pay for land which had been in the possession of their village since time immemorial.

During the following years, the institutions which had been created in the course of the reform had to be tested. Almost immediately, the communes faced enormous difficulties in paying their tax obligations and in raising the repurchase payments. The situation deteriorated when a rapid population increase in the countryside led to a drastic reduction in the standard of living as the share of each household on the land of the commune fell. Furthermore, only one-third of the fields was tilled and productivity was only at a quarter of the productivity in English agriculture (Macey 1993, p. 27). In order to reduce social pressure, the *mir* was strengthened in the 1890s. In 1903 all tax arrears and in 1905 all outstanding redemption payments were cancelled. Nevertheless, in 1905–6 the first Russian revolution could not be prevented.

The first Russian revolution induced the government to rethink their policy towards the peasants. It was gradually realized that a main cause of the desperate situation of the rural population were the close ties of the peasants to the (political) village commune, that is, the *mir*. In order to restore law and order, Prime Minister Stolypin introduced the so-called Stolypin reforms. These reforms aimed at significantly reducing the peasants' ties to the commune and thereby strengthening a property rights structure based on private property rights to land. Unfortunately, they could not be implemented sufficiently: only a minority of peasants (in the literature the estimates vary between 10 per cent (Wegren 1994,

p. 237) and 24 per cent (Lyashchenko 1949, p. 747) of all households in European Russia) separated from the village community and started individual farming. Furthermore, this measure lead to social stratification in the countryside, a source of peasant unrest and one reason for the second Russian revolution in 1917.

After the Bolshevist revolution, the first years of Soviet Russia were characterized by war communism. In the countryside this meant the juxtaposition of a comparatively large degree of political freedom with economic compulsion (Weissman 1991, p. 148). Once again the demographic structure changed considerably: the serious food shortages in the cities forced those members of the peasant households who worked in the cities to return to their villages. In addition, the population increased owing to soldiers returning from the Tsarist army (Weiner 1991, p. 148). In this situation the traditional village commune was re-established. It undertook the task of redistributing the land and the means of production – it revived the traditions of the redistributive village commune and its communal property rights structure (Hoffmann 1994, p. 639). In 1922, the old *obshchina* was officially reintroduced as the land society (*selskoe obshchestvo*). Until 1930, the land society and the village soviets coexisted, though the impact of the land society on everyday life in the countryside was much greater than the impact of the soviets. Even after the collectivization in 1930, it took years until the traditional organizational structures in the countryside were eliminated.[5]

At the beginning of the 1920s, therefore, life in the Russian countryside was once again characterized by collective ownership: all land belonged to the village commune and was redistributed in order to meet the needs of the village population. Little, thus, had changed regarding the internal organization of village life since the emancipation of the serfs some 60 years previously.

5. HAS THE 'WEST' DEVELOPED DIFFERENTLY?

As was shown in the last section, Russia's agrarian history of the last two centuries has been characterized by several efforts to modernize a traditional peasant economy. At the turn of the century and on the eve of the Bolshevist revolution, life in the Russian countryside was still

[5] Male reports that in 1934, four years after the collectivization which was followed by enormous political pressure, only 75% of the households were collectivized (Male 1962, p. 242).

shaped by the all-embracing influence of the village commune and a strong notion of communal ownership. After the revolution, the village commune was strengthened until the collectivization of the 1930s. In the twentieth century, Western European agriculture developed very differently from its Russian counterpart. This divergence can of course be traced back to the different underlying political systems. It may be asked, however, whether these different developments would have been possible had there been comparable historical experiences before the revolution. We have to ask ourselves, therefore, whether Western European and Russian development paths already differed before the revolution. If there is a difference we have to consider why these two societies took different development paths at a certain time.

As has been mentioned before, communal village organization could be found in the whole of Europe before industrialization, although it had not always existed in Europe. Rather, in the later part of the Middle Ages communal practices replaced individualistic organizational forms, first in the south-west German Alemannic region, northern France and England, as a response to growing population pressures in economies based on relatively fixed resources and technology (Hoffmann 1975, pp. 33–5). In the following centuries the village community spread across the continent. Communal village organization, though varying with local needs and traditions, had the following key features:

- open fields, that is, large fields which had no visible subdivision and were cultivated as scattered strips by the individual peasants;
- during stubble and fallow these open fields were used collectively for pasture;
- communal regulation of the commons usually used for pasture;
- regulation of cropping and grazing on the open fields by the village commune (Blum 1971, pp. 541–3).

In central Russia,[6] especially in the nineteenth century, an additional feature emerged: arable land was redistributed periodically in order to equalize the landholding of the peasants (Atkinson 1983, p. 11).

Contrary to the redistributive village community in Russia, the ownership structure in most parts of Europe was based on private property rights. The individual households were allocated, though with some reservations, the rights of *usus, usus fructus* and *abusus*, and sometimes

[6] Occasionally redistributional practices could also be found in other parts of Europe. For example in the Swiss cantons of Graubünden and Valais the so called '*Wechselalpen*', rotating periodically among the peasants, existed until the nineteenth century (see Stevenson 1991, p. 112).

also the right of transfer. Land could be attributed to a single peasant household and was safe from being claimed by the commune. Nevertheless, private property rights were not undiluted, because interference by the village commune was considerable, especially during the times when the arable land was used collectively as pasture and exclusion of the other peasants was not possible. During these periods private property rights turned into communal property rights.

In most parts of Europe the disintegration of the village commune began in the eighteenth and early nineteenth centuries (Blum 1971, p. 541). Why this came to happen has been extensively discussed in the relevant literature. One convincing explanation is Carl Dahlman's theory of the enclosure of the commons and the disappearance of open field agro-technology in England (Dahlman 1980). It is instructive to compare Dahlman's findings with Russian development in the eighteenth and early nineteenth centuries.

Dahlman claims that in the late Middle Ages, the European answer to population pressure was the specific form of property rights and decision mechanisms in the village community as described above. Owing to population pressure, land, both plough land as well as pasture, became scarce. In order to maximize output under the agro-technological conditions given, the arable land had temporarily to become pasture. On the one hand, the fertility of the arable land was thus increased because of better fertilizing. On the other hand the amount of land available for pasture rose. Thereby the production of grain and livestock could be increased.

Yet, there was always the threat that farmers considered it more profitable to use their arable land as pasture for their own livestock and abandon communal organizational features as costs of communal organization – for example the costs of decision-making in the assembly or of the joint organization of harvests on the scattered fields, were comparatively high. The threat was particularly problematic where individual fields were so large that the peasants were able to realize increasing returns to scale. Relative to the size of livestock, it paid to erect fences, build shelters and engage a herdsman. This also had adverse effects on the management of the commons which were vital for village life. As an answer to the threat, scattered strips emerged: in this form individual fields were so small that it did not pay to use them as individual pastures. The peasants were dependent on communal regulations. A system of commons on the one hand and scattered fields on the other appeared to be the most efficient under the given conditions.

Nevertheless, enclosures appeared. First came the Tudor enclosures in the sixteenth century, followed by a second wave of enclosures in the seventeenth century and, finally, from the middle of the eighteenth century there were the so-called parliamentary enclosures. By the end of the latter, the traditional communal organization of village life had almost totally disappeared in England. The reason for the last and decisive wave of enclosures was industrialization. Population pressure was absorbed by the rising industrial cities and the development of interregional transport led to interregional markets for the means of production and food. In this situation the production of both grain and livestock was no longer efficient. A process of specialization began. In the English villages either grain or livestock was produced, that is, there was no longer any need to organize grazing on the arable land. Peasants started to enclose the formerly scattered fields and the commons. This led to the dissolution of the traditional communal village structure. In the middle of the nineteenth century, therefore, undiluted private property right structures without any interference from the village commune prevailed almost completely in the English countryside. At about the same time, communal forms of ownership in Russia were being strengthened by supplementing traditional forms of field rotation by repartitions.

6. WHY RUSSIAN AGRICULTURE DID NOT ABANDON COLLECTIVE OWNERSHIP

To give an overview, there are three starting-points for explaining the different Russian development in the nineteenth century: population pressures which emerged before industrialization, backwardness in the development of interregional markets and trade, and popular views and religious beliefs, that is, shared values, disregarding capitalist institutions.

Let us turn to the first point. Like England, Russia experienced a population explosion at the beginning of the nineteenth century. During the early nineteenth century, the population of the Russian empire increased rapidly by about 60 per cent, that is, by a total of almost 70 million by 1863 (Blackwell 1982, p. 16). In contrast to England, Russia experienced this population increase before industrialization could gain a foothold in the country.[7] Industrial structures started to develop in

[7] It has often been claimed that demographic growth is a result of industrialization and accordingly economic growth. That this is not the case has been shown convincingly

the late 1850s (Blackwell 1982, p. 25). Accelerated industrialization began no earlier than the mid-1880s when, with the heavy involvement of the Russian state, railway construction reached its peak (Lyashchenko 1949, p. 502). Even at that time, however, the influx of peasants into the cities was comparatively small. For example, for the period 1870–86 urban migration absorbed less than 6 per cent of the natural demographic growth in the country (Mironov 1985, p. 456). Less than 0.28 per cent of the rural population left the countryside each year during this period. Thus, at the turn of the century, Russia was still more an agricultural than an industrialized country with a ratio of agricultural to industrial production of two to one (Blackwell 1982, p. 24).

Why did the countryside have to bear the heavy burden of population increase which placed enormous pressure on already scarce resources? Apparently a kind of vicious cycle was set in motion in the middle of the nineteenth century when redistributional practices spread in the Russian countryside, a cycle in which an already pauperized peasantry, a low level of industrialization and the misguided stabilization policies of the paternalist state reinforced each other. Poor soil, the loss of pastures and meadows after the emancipation of the serfs, a backward agro-technology, and the population increase which diminished the size of land allotments all combined to cause poverty among a large segment of the rural population (Atkinson 1983, p. 28). The poverty of the peasants was one reason for the low level of industrialization: the limited demand for consumer goods could only nourish a small-scale home industry (*kustar*).

The poverty of the peasants was the cause of social pressure and occasional uprisings. The state, already weakened by the defeat in the Crimean war, feared further destabilization of the country by peasant unrest. In order to protect the central values of the state, autocracy, orthodoxy and nation (Gerschenkron 1968, p. 144), but also motivated by solicitousness towards the rural population (Zakharova 1994, p. 30), the state strengthened, in the way of a paternalist state, the traditional village commune by tying the peasants to their village. They were kept in a state of semi-servitude and immobility. As a result, the formation of a permanent urban factory workforce was impeded while population

by Easterlin (1995). There it is suggested that demographic growth is a result of more favourable living conditions due to increased medical knowledge. Medical innovations can be realized comparatively more cheaply than technological ones with the result that medical progress can be spread more rapidly than technological achievements. Accordingly, demographic growth can occur before industrialization has reached a country.

pressures in the countryside increased (Grant 1976). Thus, poverty increased and industrialization was held back further.

In this situation of evident economic backwardness, the state engaged in fostering industrialization. It made progress with railway construction and tried to attract foreign investors. One decisive impediment for foreign investors was the very unstable and non-convertible paper rouble. Ways of both financing state expenditures and stabilizing the currency had to be found. The measures which were taken, however, laid the burden of stabilizing the financial situation on the shoulders of the peasants: capitation and liquor taxes were imposed on them, and grain was confiscated for sale to Western Europe.[8] The consequences of this policy are evident: poverty in the countryside increased further. As a result of the extreme deterioration of their situation, the peasants tried to find alternative ways of rural organization. In their traditional society, characterized by a spirit of egalitarianism, they searched among social models of the past or those adopted by neighbouring communities, and what they found was the extremely egalitarian practice of regular repartitions of the village's arable land. It made sure that nobody was in possession of more land than he could till. This meant the land available in a village commune was, under the conditions given, used as intensively as possible, and, as there were no differences in the size of landholding, social conflict could not be a threat to the community.

The second factor causing a diverging pattern of development between England and Russia was the state of interregional markets and trade. Even though industrialization and the development of markets are closely interlinked, it seems appropriate to draw a distinction between the two. The reason is that interregional markets can appear without industrialization, but not vice versa. Indeed, interregional trade and commerce in England were deeply rooted before industrialization and paved the way for it. In Russia, by contrast, the preconditions for the development of interregional markets were not at all favourable. Excessive relative costs deterred potential entrepreneurs from engaging in interregional markets. Furthermore, most of the village households existed on a subsistence level. If markets appeared, they were regional (local fairs) and lacked the institutions of a developed money economy such as, for example, credit (Lyashchenko 1949, pp. 498–500).

The cost structure had such a negative impact on the development of interregional markets because average costs were so high. As average costs (e.g. for transporting goods or enforcing standardized contracts)

[8] According to Lyashchenko (1949, p. 518), 46.3% of the overall wheat output was sold for export.

fall with the increase in the number of goods traded, an entrepreneur will be willing to engage in a market if the potential size of that market is sufficiently large. Excessive costs will deter an entrepreneur from engaging in a market if its potential size is only small. In Russia, owing to the lack of purchasing power of the peasant population, a negligible middle class and a nobility orientating its demand towards foreign markets in Western Europe (White 1987, p. 200), the potential size of markets was limited. Thus the influence of the costs was relatively high.

The costs for carrying out transactions and enforcing contracts were particularly considerable. Regarding the costs for carrying out transactions, transport costs should first of all be mentioned. The size of the country, the long distances between the cities and unfavourable geographical features such as the lack of a natural system of waterways which, as in England, could have connected the different regions of the country, raised transport costs (Blackwell 1982, p. 2). Transport over such distances was risky. Owing to the high and incalculable risks, there was no domestic development of insurance (White 1987, p. 161), so that an important means of reducing costs could not be used. Rather than developing a commercial insurance market, therefore, Russians tried to reduce risk by organizing themselves into risk-sharing communities and by avoiding additional risks and costs resulting from the use of the market system.

As a result of an underdeveloped judicial system, a limited sense of justice and a social environment inimical to those who were financially successful, enforcement costs were high. In Tsarist Russia, the legal tradition differed considerably from the one in Western Europe. One reason for this was that Russian law had its roots in the Byzantine and not in the Roman tradition. From the time of Peter the Great, laws were not intended to regulate social interaction but to express the political will of the autocrat: from the passing of the laws it was clear that it would never be implemented (White 1987, p. 119). And even if the law was intended to be translated into action, the influence of the central government was not strong enough to enforce the law in the countryside. Quarrels were regularly solved by the peasant or the lord according to rather insecure customary rights. In the countryside (and often in the cities as well) 'the rule of man rather than the rule of law' was prevalent (Wortmann 1976, p. 12). This meant that merchants could not rely on the rule of law. Bribes had to be paid and, in order to enforce contracts, merchants took the law into their own hands. Accordingly, fraud among merchants was the order of the day; Russian merchants were said to be extremely unreliable and had a tendency to cheat (White 1987, p. 158). Costs were high because enforcement had to be organized privately which in turn led to an underdeveloped sense of justice and notorious fraud. On top of this, general public hostility against those who stood out from the masses, that is, those who had been economically successful, further raised costs. Merchants and traders were not only in danger of being cheated by their market partners but, in addition, they lacked the support of the population and were in danger of being the victim of theft and riots.

As a result of excessive costs relative to the potential market size, interregional markets and trade did not develop spontaneously. Where interregional transfers occurred it was not by voluntary exchange but by expropriation: the state confiscated grain for export purposes and in order to supply the army and the urban population. The nobility took products from their rural demesnes in order to cover the costs of their living in the cities. Owing to the lack of interregional markets and an interregional division of labour, the precondition for specialization,[9] as described by Dahlman, could not be found in Russia.

Up to now my line of argument has paralleled that of Dahlman (1980). There is an additional factor, however, which Dahlman did not account for and which seems to have had a decisive influence: unwritten rules of behaviour, that is, informal institutions or shared values, which originate from deeply rooted popular views and religious beliefs. In Russia these deeply rooted institutions found their expression in egalitarianism and collectivism. Egalitarianism is the psychological disposition of a group of people who consider material equality as the essential basis of social interaction. Collectivism is closely related to egalitarianism. It refers to a societal organizational pattern which centres around the group and not the individual as the basic unit in society. In such societies the well-being of the group is much more important than the well-being of the individual and responsibility does not appear on the level of the individual but rather on the level of the group. The single person is subordinated to the commune.

The reasons for egalitarianism and collectivism can be found in popular views and religious beliefs. Life in the Russian countryside was dominated by two authorities: the village commune and the church. The village commune exerted extreme control over the peasant. Behaviour deviating from the narrow conformism of everyday life in the village was disapproved of by popular opinion and severely punished. Peasants

[9] It is rather doubtful whether the development of interregional markets is a sufficient condition for specialization as specialization requires the existence of relative advantages. In the agricultural sector these advantages mainly stem from geographical differences which could be found in England, but not in the rather uniform plains of central Russia.

occasionally destroyed the fields of those who openly displayed signs of wealth and excluded them from social life inside the community. The village commune itself had a very effective means at its disposal: it could select deviants for recruitment into the army. As a rule this meant never coming back as the duration of military service was 25 years (Mironov 1985, p. 445).

One can find a further reason why entrepreneurial attitudes[10] and a civil ethic of responsibility had little chance to develop in the Russian population given prevailing religious attitudes, if one is prepared to follow Max Weber and his hypothesis about the relationship between religious traditions and capitalist mentalities (Weber 1920/21). According to this hypothesis, it is not a religion's dogma, as for example the Calvinist theory of predestination, but the attitudes and the motivation aroused by a distinct conception of God which is responsible for the development of a capitalist spirit (Buss 1989, p. 50). The Russian Orthodox Church with its strong ritualization, as expressed for example in its liturgy, its worship of withdrawn monks and its strong mystic element, fostered the ideal of a withdrawn existence with no interest or engagement in worldly affairs. Protestantism, by contrast, considered active participation in society as a way to God. The differences between these religions with regard to the development of an entrepreneurial spirit is obvious. Moreover, the mystic and, for large parts of the population, even magic element of orthodox religion discouraged the development of a civil ethic, as it tended to absolve the individual of responsibility. Instead, the church with its anti-rational, anti-scientific and anti-progressive tendency, took responsibility on behalf of the population and left little room for individualism (Blackwell 1982, p. 5).

Thus, to sum up, both egalitarianism and collectivism can be traced back to religious beliefs and the organizational structure of the village. Given these shared values, which greatly influenced the way the rural population perceived its environment, it was highly unlikely that the peasants who, because of economic pressure caused by mass pauperization, were looking for new organizational structures would fall back upon private property rights. Such rights were outside the scope of their world and with the need for formal enforcement mechanisms they would have been relatively costly given the underdeveloped sense of responsibility and the very vague notion of individualism which existed in the Russian countryside. In contrast to this, under a regime of communal property, general acceptance of the village elder and strong

[10] The strategy of enclosure as a way to increase individual profits can be viewed as entrepreneurship.

social control rendered formal enforcement mechanisms of that regime almost unnecessary. In fact, control was decentralized and imposed relatively small costs on society.

7. CONCLUSION

As has been explained in this chapter, socio-economic rules in Russia began to develop systematically differently from those in the West as early as the last century. The reasons for this divergence in development have been discussed in detail. The collectivist tendencies still prevailing at the beginning of the twentieth century were reinforced by Soviet agricultural policy. Russian agrarian history has experienced private property to a very limited degree only and the population has never had the chance to experience the economic spirit upon which private property is based. Not surprisingly, recent opinion polls show that not only formal but also informal capitalist institutions are underdeveloped today (Voigt 1993, pp. 514–28).

The result of such a development is obvious: on the one hand peasants have no concept of private farming and would not risk becoming independent and self-reliant farmers. At the same time, the spirit of egalitarianism and collectivism just described is still alive in the population. Thus, owing to the mechanisms discussed in Section 2, information on private farming is regarded with distrust. The large majority of farmers remain within a collective organizational framework. As during the Stolypin reforms at the beginning of this century, those who separate from collective organizational structures have to deal with the hostility of large parts of the population. Their activities are hindered because of a lack of will for cooperation and a bureaucracy which mainly supports the interests of the former collective farms. The costs of private entrepreneurship are therefore substantial, especially if one considers the low gains which can be realized in the present situation which is characterized by a very unstable system of transport, an insufficient integration of private farmers in existing commercial systems and very low retail prices for basic food due to regulations, while the producers face world market prices for their inputs.

As a consequence of these findings, mainstream economic theory on privatization needs to be supplemented by an interdisciplinary analysis of shared values which may influence the transition process considerably, as comparison of the Polish and Czech success stories with the Russian 'malady' vividly demonstrates. Bearing these findings in mind, a strategy for successful transition in the Russian countryside should not only be focused on changing the costs and gains structure, but should also take into account the possibilities of influencing the informal rules, that is, the shared values, as well. As influencing informal rules involves the implementation of learning processes, this means that a theory of transition has to be supplemented by an appropriate learning theory. Nevertheless, even if learning on the individual level were to be successful there is still the problem of collective transition: under what conditions will there be a critical mass of farmers embarking on private agriculture so that the gains for the individual farmer will rise and a self-enforcing process perhaps be set in motion?

What are the policy implications of these results? Within the limited scope of this contribution only a few suggestions can be offered: in order to induce social learning processes, direct contact between Western European and Russian farmers should be supported. In this way, Russian peasants can become acquainted with private family farming and overcome their inherent resistance to this institutional structure. Furthermore, educational programmes, introducing the agro-technical and economic aspects of private farming, should be supported. In order to cope with the critical mass problem mentioned above, one possibility may be to offer financial aid to the first-comers. Nevertheless, one has to ask whether the establishment of private family farming can take place within a sufficient period of time as the learning process itself is time-consuming and a development trap has to be overcome. One therefore also has to consider whether it is necessary to redefine the aim of the transition: is it possible to establish a Western-type agricultural sector based on family farms at all or will the informal rules be so entrenched that an agrarian system will develop which is based on market principles, but which takes country-specific peculiarities into account as well? The answer to this question, however, lies outside the scope of this chapter and must therefore be left to further research.

REFERENCES

Aleksandrov, I. (1994) 'Agrarian Reform Based on Social Agreement'. *Problems of Economic Transition* 37: 3–18.

Atkinson, D. (1983) *The End of the Russian Land Commune, 1905–1930*. Stanford: Stanford University Press.

Bardhan, P. (1989) *The Economic Theory of Agrarian Institutions*. Oxford: Clarendon Press.

Blackwell, W.L. (1982) *The Industrialization of Russia*. Arlington Heights: Harlan Davidson Inc.

Blanchard, O. et al. (1991) *Reforms in Eastern Europe.* Cambridge MA: MIT Press.

Blum, J. (1971) 'The Internal Structure and Polity of the European Village Community from the Fifteenth to the Nineteenth Century'. *The Journal of Modern History* 43: 541–75.

Bobyliev, S. (1995) 'Prospects for Agricultural and Environmental Policy Integration in Russia' in OECD document *Agriculture and the Environment in the Transition to a Market Economy.* Paris: OECD.

Buss, A. (1989) *Die Wirtschaftsethik des Russisch-Orthodoxen Christentums.* Heidelberg: Carl Winter.

Coase, R. (1960) 'The Problem of Social Cost'. *Journal of Law and Economics* 3: 1–44.

Dahlman, C.J. (1980) *The Open Field System and Beyond.* Cambridge.

Denzau, A.T. and North, D.C. (1994) 'Shared Mental Models: Ideologies and Institutions'. *Kyklos* 47: 3–31.

Easterlin, R.A. (1995) 'Industrial Revolution and Mortality Revolution: Two of a Kind?'. *Journal of Evolutionary Economics* 5: 393–408.

Feder, G. and Feeny, D. (1993) 'The Theory of Land Tenure and Property Rights' in K. Hoff, A. Braverman and J.E. Stiglitz (eds) *The Economics of Rural Organization: Theory, Practice, and Policy.* Oxford, New York, Toronto and Melbourne: Oxford University Press.

Furubotn, E.G. and Pejovich, S. (1972) 'Property Rights and Economic Theory: A Survey of Recent Literature'. *Journal of Economic Literature* 4: 1137–62.

Gerschenkron, A. (1968) 'Russia – Agrarian Policies and Industrialization 1861–1917' in *Continuity in History.* Cambridge, MA: Belknap.

Goricheva, L. (1994) 'Economic Problems and National Self-Awareness'. *Problems of Economic Transition* 37: 78–92.

Grant, S.A. (1976) 'Obshchina and Mir'. *Slavic Review* 35 (4): 636–51.

Hayek, F.A. (1988) *The Fatal Conceit.* London: Routledge.

Herrmann-Pillath, C. (1995) 'Wissenschaft und Kultur als Kräfte gesellschaftlicher Ordnung während der Transformation'. Discussion paper. University of Witten-Herdecke.

Hoff, K. (1993) 'Designing Land Policies – An Overview' in K. Hoff, A. Braverman and J.E. Stiglitz (eds) *The Economics of Rural Organization: Theory, Practice and Policy.* Oxford, New York, Toronto and Melbourne: Oxford University Press.

Hoffmann, D.A.J. (1994) 'Land, Freedom and Discontent: Russian Peasants of the Central Industrial Region Prior to Collectivization'. *Europe-Asia Studies* 46 (4): 637–48.

Hoffmann, R.C. (1975) 'Medieval Origins of the Common Fields' in W.N. Parker and E.L. Jones (eds) *European Peasants and Their Markets.* Princeton: Princeton University Press.

Lipton, D. and Sachs, J. (1990) 'Creating a Market Economy in Eastern Europe'. *Brookings Papers on Economic Activity.*

Lyashchenko, P. (1949) *History of the National Economy of Russia to the 1917 Revolution.* New York: Macmillan.

Macey, D.A.J. (1993) 'Stolypin is Risen! The Ideology of Agrarian Reform in Contemporary Russia' in D. van Atta (ed.) *The 'Farmer Threat': The Political Economy of Agrarian Reform in Post-Soviet Russia.* Boulder, San Francisco and New York: Westview Press.

Male, D.J. (1962) 'The Village Community 1925–30'. *Soviet Studies* 14: 225–48.
McCloskey, D.N. (1975) 'The Persistence of English Common Fields' in W.N. Parker and E.L. Jones (eds) *European Peasants and Their Markets*. Princeton: Princeton University Press.
Mironov, B. (1985) 'The Russian Peasant Commune After the Reforms of the 1860s'. *Slavic Review* 44 (3): 436–67.
North, D.C. and Thomas, R.P. (1973) *The Rise of the Western World: A New Economic History*. Cambridge: Cambridge University Press.
Ol'sevich, I. (1994) 'The Economic System and Ethnic Culture'. *Problems of Economic Transition* 37: 63–77 (June).
Petrikov, A. (1994) 'Rural Society and Agrarian Reform'. *Problems of Economic Transition* 37 (6): 19–28.
Renard, V. (1994) 'Emerging Land Markets in Eastern Europe'. *Economics of Transition* 2 (4): 501–509.
Shatalin, S. (1990) *Transition to the Market*. Moscow.
Smith, H. (1991) *Die Neuen Russen*. Hamburg: Rahwalt.
Sutela, P. (1994) 'Insider Privatization in Russia: Speculations on Systemic Change'. *Europe-Asia Studies* 46 (3): 417–35.
Stevenson, G.G. (1991) *Common Property Economics. A General Theory and Land Use Applications*. Cambridge: Cambridge University Press.
Taranovski, T. (1995) 'The Problem of Reform in Russian and Soviet History' in T. Taranovski (ed.) *Reform in Modern Russian History – Progress or Cycle?* Cambridge.
van Atta, D. (1993) 'The Return of Individual Farming in Russia' in D. van Atta (ed.) *The 'Farmer Threat': The Political Economy of Agrarian Reform in Post-Soviet Russia*. Boulder, San Francisco and New York: Westview Press.
Voigt, S. (1993) 'Values, Norms, Institutions and the Prospects for Economic Growth in Central and Eastern Europe' in *Journal des Economistes et des Etudes Humaines* 4 (4): 495–529.
Weber, M. (1920/21) *Gesammelte Aufsätze zur Religionssoziologie*. Tübingen: Mohr.
Wegren, S.K. (1994) 'Rural Reforms and Political Culture in Russia'. *Europe-Asia Studies* 46 (2): 215–41.
Weiner, D.R. (1991) ' "Razmychka?": Urban Unemployment and Peasant In-Migration as a Source of Social Conflict' in S. Fitzpatrick, A. Rabinowitch and R. Stites (eds) *Russia in the Era of NEP*. Bloomington and Indianapolis: Indiana University Press pp. 144–55.
Weissmann, N. (1991) 'Policing the NEP-Countryside' in S. Fitzpatrick, A. Rabinowitch and R. Stites (eds) *Russia in the Era of NEP*. Bloomington and Indianapolis: Indiana University Press pp. 174–88.
White, C. (1987) *Russia and America – The Roots of Economic Divergence*. London, New York and Sydney: Croom Helm.
Witt, U. (1991) 'On the Emergence of Private Property Rights'. *Archives of Economic History* 1 (2): 19–30.
Wortman, R. (1976) *The Development of Russian Legal Consciousness*. Chicago and London: University of Chicago Press.
Zakharova, L. (1994) 'Autocracy and the Reforms of 1861–1874 – Choosing Paths of Development' in B. Eklof, J. Bushnell and L. Zakharova (eds) *Russia's Great Reforms 1855–1881*. Bloomington and Indianapolis: Indiana University Press.

11. The globalization of European research and technology organizations (RTOs)

Michael Kluth and Jørn Andersen

1. INTRODUCTION

In the course of the 1980s, the term 'globalization' became a 'buzzword' in the social sciences, with numerous connotations across and within disciplines. In the literature on institutional political economy the term is applied to denote both that which was previously simply considered internationalization as well as that which concerns qualitative new dynamics in relation to institutional development.

Particular attention has been devoted to grasping the character and implication of globalization within the context of technological development. An attempt at conceptual clarification has recently been made by Archibugi and Michie who have distinguished three categories of 'techno-globalism' (Archibugi and Michie 1995). These are:

- global *exploitation* of technology;
- global technological *collaboration*;
- global *generation* of technology.

Exploitation of technology is worldwide with diminishing lead times between the market of origin and other markets. While virtually all countries maintain systems underpinning this aspect of globalization, such as patent laws, some countries have adopted a deliberate strategy of enhancing the capacity of national industry to absorb and incorporate international technological advances in production processes and products. This is particularly true of some of the Asian economies, but also of Denmark, Norway and Italy. The latter offer examples of national successes which have relied on the application of externally generated technology. The observed escalation with regard to this aspect of techno-globalism is thus mainly numerical.

Firms increasingly embark on cross-border *collaboration*, not least with respect to research and development (R&D). However, as Archibugi and Michie point out, this phenomenon may not be as recent as is often believed, and the growth which can be recorded in this area 'is confined to a very few, although crucial, fields' (ibid.).

Multinationals are relying on information technology in their effort to create synergy between several national innovation facilities in connection with the *generation* of new technology. If a hierarchy, or some measurement of 'matureness', were to be constructed, this aspect of Archibugi and Michie's taxonomy could be said to constitute the epitomy of what is identified as the globalization process within technology. It is also, however, the aspect which exhibits the most modest growth rates!

Following Archibugi and Michie, techno-globalism is viewed as a 'natural' extension of the internationalization of the economy witnessed throughout the postwar era. The taxonomy summarizes the various usages of techno-globalism within mainstream economic literature. Approaching the question from a political science perspective, however, it is evident that a new dimension needs to be added in order to fully grasp the globalization process in relation to technology. The globalization of technology contains a distinct institutional element.

This chapter will investigate the process of change and adaptation in national Research and Technology Organizations (RTOs) across Europe. The process will be analysed with reference to variations in formal organization and informal institutional features. Three case study countries, Britain, Germany and France, are examined. The variations between national systems with regard to strategies of adaptation will be assessed for each of the countries.

2. GLOBALIZATION AND INSTITUTIONAL CHANGE

Viewed from an institutional angle, globalization can be interpreted as a continuation of the internationalization debate of the 1970s. Although this debate has taken place across the social sciences, a central theme can be identified which holds that a process of institutional convergence is under way as market pressures force national institutions to adjust in ways which most effectively fit the international situation and optimally serve the national economies. In Figure 11.1 the basic contentions of the 'convergence thesis' are illustrated.

The logic implied in the convergence thesis can be linked to that of classical political economists such as Smith and Ricardo, who were

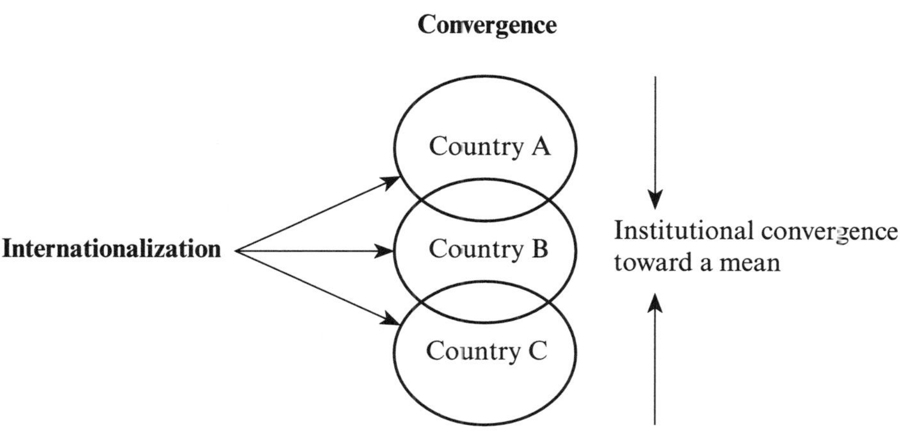

Figure 11.1. Globalization as institutional convergence

mainly preoccupied with the distortive mechanisms of private and public regulatory regimes based on the state and the guild system. In the works of Friedrich List the focus was on the possible positive effects on national economic performance of enhancing and re-engineering the properties of institutions deemed 'obstructive' by the liberals, and employing them in the quest for industrialization.

National economic performance varies from country to country beyond what can merely be attributed to differences in factor endowments. This difference reflects corresponding variations in the character of the dynamics of national and regional market-places. Thus, different patterns in the quality, sophistication and adaptation of goods and services demanded and supplied can be observed between for instance the UK and Japan.

Key national institutions define the character of national political economies which even within the traditional Western economic bloc vary considerably. The most important examples of key national institutions are the financial regime, the labour market and the core elements of the national innovation system such as technological services performed by the RTOs.

Institutions are historically rooted and culturally embedded. As a consequence, their impact on national economic activity extends beyond macro-level economic policy. Institutions can be altered but the degree of alteration cannot be fully determined in advance and, in general, institutional properties exhibit a vast degree of rigidity. As illustrated in Figure 11.2, globalization denotes a process whereby key national

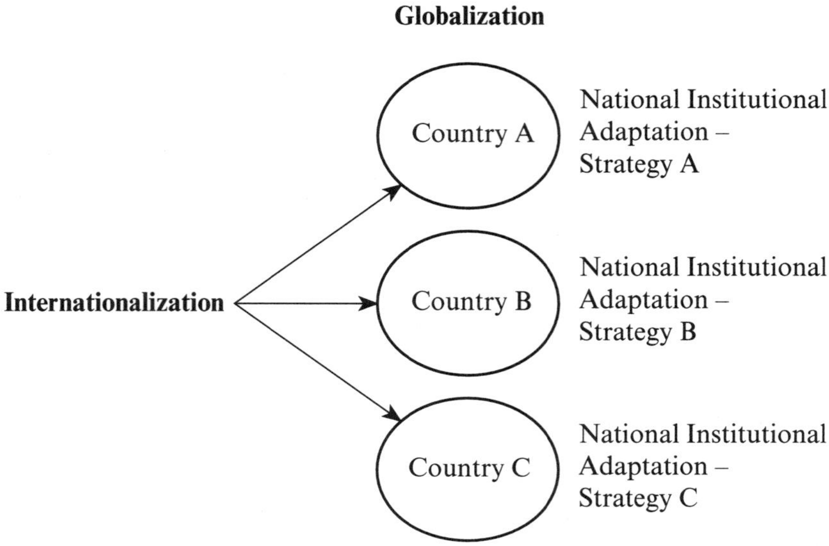

Figure 11.2. Globalization as institutional adaptation

institutions are subject to increased external pressures for change and adaptation. As such, globalization represents a qualitatively different process from internationalization which merely implies an increase in international transactions.

Changes in international banking practices and regulation are good illustrations of the globalization process. National banking systems have been subject to immense pressure owing to the process of deregulation and the prominence of the discourse on free capital movement. The effects of this on individual financial systems have varied as national institutional features have influenced the character of the adaptation process. As a consequence, even after globalization, German banking will not completely resemble US or UK banking despite the fact that the dominant discourse associated with the globalization of banking is biased towards a UK- or US-style banking system.

Financial systems were the first key institutions which became subject to globalization. This event has accelerated and shaped the process as it prompted a reorientation in economic thinking from the macro to the micro level. As a consequence the second round of substantial globalization will take place at levels directly related to the firm. It is likely to influence the organization of firms and the innovation, application and diffusion of new technologies.

The globalization of the economy has been prompted by a dramatic increase in international transactions. In addition to an expansion in the volume of traditional international transactions, the thrust of globalization has been boosted by the growing diversity of transactions. The dimensions of techno-globalism listed by Archibugi and Michie contain elements which point to the impact of globalization on institutions. The genuine level of growth which can be detected in international collaborative R&D, for example, is likely to exert globalization pressures on national institutions. Implied in this line of thinking is the assertion that an upsurge in collaborative R&D is likely to undermine the raison d'être of customized national institutions erected with the sole purpose of disseminating competencies presently acquired directly from collaborating partners.

A comprehensive analysis of the globalization of technology thus needs to take into account the adaptation processes in national systems of innovation caused by global pressures. We believe that this supplementary approach must include a comparative and qualitative study of the changes in the key components of national systems of innovation.

3. NATIONAL SYSTEMS OF INNOVATION AND RTOs

Virtually all OECD countries have RTOs. Germany boasts the world-renowned Fraunhofer Gesellschaft (FhG), the Dutch similarly operate a nationwide system in the form of the TNO, the British system involves a series of mutually independent operators established on the basis of sectors (e.g. ERA Technology Limited and Leatherhead Food Research Association), Denmark has the so-called GTS system, France has ANVAR and so on. Several of these organizations originate from the first half of the century. RTOs play a crucial role as major agents in the diffusion of new R&D results and technology among potential users/firms, thereby enhancing the innovation capacity of firms. As a consequence, RTOs have increasingly become the focus of political scrutiny and attention in the OECD countries. This intermediary role performed by RTOs is often referred to as one of technology transfer, which in turn plays a key role in the distributive power of national systems of innovation (NSI).

The continued generation and exploitation of new technology is a key factor in creating advantages in the competition between nations, regions and firms. The efficient employment of technical advances thus influences the level and distribution of economic growth. Most users of technology are forced to acquire technology from the original innovators, from intermediaries or from other users. This is the essence of technology transfer: 'the transfer of technology from an innovator to a user in a situation where the technique has not already been used' (Clement 1994).

The development of research and technology policies over the past two decades has been characterized by the increasing use of measures designed to enhance collaborative research, joint technological projects and the transfer of technology. From the mid-1970s to the early 1980s, European governments became increasingly concerned with the lack of cooperation between industry and the universities. The general problems of Euro-sclerosis and the apparent backwardness of the information technology sectors were both seen to be partly the result of this lack of cooperation. It was not until the mid-1980s, however, that technology policies gained momentum, introducing national technology programmes and collaborative pre-competitive research projects which focused on firms with high levels of technology. In addition, the internationalization of industrial activity has called into question the efficacy of national RTOs, particularly with regard to their role as 'bridging institutions' and facilitators of international R&D results for domestic users. The following section of the chapter examines current development issues and trends among European RTOs, and in particular their relationship to national governments in the process of internationalization.

2.1. RTOs – Tasks and Rationale

The definition used in this chapter is that given by the Commission of the European Union which defines RTOs as research and technology organizations which support the R&D activities of clients and disseminate new technological innovations, and whose activities include more than one of the following:

- applied research;
- certification, testing, measurement and standards;
- information, consultation and training.

This definition excludes universities and public research centres, which concentrate on research rather than on technology transfer. Similarly, purely private enterprises such as contract research companies are not regarded as RTOs (Kandel 1994). Differences in national practice, however, make the application of a standard definition of RTOs difficult. Hence, we also consider organizations that in a national context are regarded either legally or historically as RTOs.

The policies implemented by European governments for the promotion of technology transfer share certain common characteristics. First, the public sector is encouraged to share and distribute the results of research generated by government R&D laboratories and officially commissioned research programmes. Second, governments assist R&D intensive firms by removing barriers which limit access to finance (especially venture capital).

Thus, at the surface there exist a number of common elements with regard to technology transfer initiatives in different nations, but diverse political, economic, legal and educational systems within countries result in different strategies for the development of RTOs.

As a consequence, the globalization of RTOs cannot simply be understood as a result of the globalization strategies of the clients of RTOs (firms) nor of the globalization of technology. The pace, character and direction of the globalization of the RTOs will be driven just as much by the underpinnings of the national institutional setting from which they originated.

The world of RTOs is far from homogeneous, so even if the questions of globalization are the same, the answers are different. Greater demand for speed in the field of innovation places a considerable strain on the expenditure of RTOs in terms of renewing equipment, providing staff with continuous training and marketing campaigns. Moreover, this is occurring at a time when public funding is drying up, clients are losing confidence and becoming more demanding and competition is increasingly fierce. Choosing a strategy in these conditions is of course essential, but not an easy task. How far should the RTOs go to maintain their own R&D capacity in order to assimilate technological innovations from elsewhere? Should they resign from having their own R&D capacity and make do with using the results of R&D carried out by others? Or should they follow their inherent desire for national independence and maintain their R&D capacity and levels of expenditure, which is expensive for RTOs owing to the fact that their R&D investment capacity is limited and R&D seldom has immediate relevance for their financial future?

The choice between commercial and 'public service' activity is an especially difficult one for many RTOs. Each strategy has its advantages and disadvantages. RTOs operate partly as basic research institutions and partly as purely commercial business – consultancy firms. RTOs thus have a dual role – on the one hand to operate as a firm among firms (when they sell their technology services to other firms in market conditions), and on the other hand to engage in a certain level of R&D. This bridging function is what makes them unique in relation to university laboratories and consultancy firms.

Nevertheless, the services they sell on a commercial basis are essentially a product of their R&D activities. These are activities which to a large extent are financed by 'core grants' from governments. As a consequence, RTOs are vulnerable to cuts in government spending. This suggests that RTOs which originated in nations traditionally founded on free market principles will adopt a globalization strategy which will bring them closer to private consultancy firms, and they might eventually give up their long-term R&D activities as well as their close relationship with their national governments. Similarly, it can be expected that RTOs from more interventionist states will remain bridging institutions with substantial in-house R&D, and be supported financially by their respective governments in the process of globalization.

International experience demonstrates the crucial importance of high-quality technical services that are widely and easily available to all firms, and especially to small and medium-sized enterprises (SMEs). Autarky is impossible in the field of science and technology: all firms need external sources of advice, information and technical collaboration in addition to specialized testing and measurement services as well as advanced equipment and instruments.

As a consequence, technology policies in most OECD countries have recently given far greater emphasis to the role of intermediary organizations such as RTOs. The provision of techno-economic framework conditions that enable companies to be at the forefront of technological innovation, and thereby to remain competitive in the face of increasingly fierce international competition, is thus becoming a key factor in industrial policy.

This change of focus is particularly relevant following the new evolutionary line of thought which has had important implications for the way innovation and economic growth are perceived today. Technology trajectories, creative destruction and imperfect competition have thus become key buzz-words in the new vocabulary of national innovation policies. At present, evolutionary economic thought stands out as an alternative basis for economic policy-making. Its major breakthrough on the policy level was the Technology and Economic Programme –

known as the TEP report – carried out by the OECD in 1992 (OECD 1992).

A company's innovative capacity is not only determined by its investments in R&D. Access to the right sources of knowledge is essential. A nation's technological capacity is determined by its capacity to produce technological knowledge and its ability to transfer technological knowledge to potential users. In short, a country's national system of innovation (NSI) should be assessed on its productive and distributive efficiency. It is within this context that the role assigned to RTOs should be evaluated and understood.

Strengthening the framework conditions of industry has become the new policy paradigm in OECD countries. It is evident, explicitly or implicitly, in the policies and actions of an increasing number of governments. It follows from, and in certain respects complements, the structural adjustment (liberalization, deregulation and competition) policies of the 1980s. The future success of the adjustment reforms initiated in the 1980s may depend on the efficacy of accompanying policies introduced to strengthen the framework conditions of industry.

A critical issue here is that the important role of RTOs – such as in the area of technological knowledge – cannot be exogenous to arguments about growth and trade. The argument presented here is thus close to, for instance, Zysman's argument that:

> at the core of the growth process are ideas, not simply the accumulation of physical or financial capital. The ideas are not just a matter of training workers in existing procedures, or of education that transmits codified knowledge. Rather, economic growth springs from better recipes not just from more cooking . . . economic growth occurs whenever people take resources and rearrange them in ways that are more valuable. (Zysman 1994b)

RTOs belong to the category of institutions within NSIs that import, modify, translate and diffuse new technology. In this light, RTOs can be seen as 'cooks' who provide national firms with new recipes. As there are different technology trajectories, the pace and direction of development is a matter of judgement. In this sense 'innovation policies matter', because they influence the future technology trajectories of countries and firms. Zysman compares this:

> to the covering of the table at the roulette wheel. The multiple bets that technological development requires will not be evenly placed around the table. The 'placer' of bets, be it a company or a nation, will place bets according to past practice and the needs to which technology is being applied will be different. As a consequence, in each national community the tasks

> to be addressed will vary from firm to firm and country to country. (Zysman 1994b).

As the organizing principles of RTOs differ from country to country (e.g. access to knowledge may be based on the firms' willingness or ability to pay the market price for the information) this will affect the firms' strategies for gaining access to information. Institutionally, therefore, RTOs play an important part in what Soskice labels the national framework of incentives and constraints (NFICs) (Soskice 1991). Soskice advocates that NFICs create distinctive national product market and innovation strategies for firms. Or, to use the words of Dosi and Orsengio (1988):

> social rules, inherited norms and attitudes, the laws of organisation of the linkages between and within various groups of economic agents do matter in determining the set of admissible strategies and behaviours, and of observed innovative performances. The specification of the institutional rules constraining individual behaviour becomes therefore a crucial task in the analysis of the patterns of technical change, which accounts for the observed differences across countries within the same technologies.

We argue that the same logic should be applied in analysing the globalization strategies of RTOs – since specific interactions between actors within NSIs, the role of governments and the character of the company base produces distinct strategies.

4. GLOBALIZATION AND NATIONAL RTOs

Divergent national industrial policies in general and different degrees of adherence to the theory of 'the invisible hand' which spurs growth and technological development have created national systems of innovation which vary considerably from country to country. The countries that concern us here are first and foremost the UK, Germany, France and to a lesser extent Holland and Denmark. In assessing different strategies for the globalization of national RTOs we are concerned primarily with the national features of these RTOs, but we also consider more localized bridging institutions such as the German Steinbeis-Stiftung and the UK's Business Link.

4.1. Germany – Between Market and Hierarchy

In comparison with other European states Germany was a latecomer, both in political and economic terms. As was the case in other countries which industrialized relatively late, such as Sweden and Japan, the government played from the beginning a key role in the country's industrial development. The theoretical understanding of Germany's RTOs and the general role played by the government in relation to, for example, the globalization of technology services may essentially be explained with reference to the works of Friedrich List and Joseph Schumpeter. In opposition to the classical political economy of Smith and Ricardo, List and Schumpeter advocated an evolutionary perspective focusing on the long-term development of productive forces and on the relationship between entrepreneurship, innovation and growth (Reinert 1994).

German adherence to the ideas of these two scholars is not only relevant from a theoretical point of view, but also helps explain why, for instance, the German RTO, Fraunhofer Gesellschaft (FhG), adopted a completely different globalization strategy from, for example, British RTOs.

In his later writings, Schumpeter stressed that the entrepreneurial function need not be embodied in a single person. The function of the entrepreneur may be, and often is, performed cooperatively. Even the state can play the role of the entrepreneur and Schumpeter referred to the case of the US Department of Agriculture as an example which had often revolutionized farming by introducing new methods of cultivation (Swedeberg 1991).

Combining this line of thought with that of List provides us to a great extent with a key for understanding the German NSI. According to List, the English economists failed to distinguish between national and global interests. Their political economy was a cosmo-political economy, but nations needed to build a national system of political economy (Reinert 1994).

The institutional arrangements that characterize the national system of innovation in Germany have two distinct features. First, there is the German model of education that puts much emphasis on combining formal education with practical work experience through apprenticeships. The second feature is the existence of a number of semi-public 'bridging institutions' of which the institutions of the Fraunhofer Gesellschaft (FhG) are the most important at the national level, and the Steinbeis Stiftung in Baden-Württemberg the most significant at the länder level.

The FhG was founded in 1949 and specifically designed to secure German industry a strong position internationally. The FhG is the biggest European RTO and consists of 46 institutes with 7 700 employees and has an annual budget of 1 billion DM. Financially the FhG receives one-third of its income from the Federal Government and the länder governments. Another one-third of FhG funds comes from public contract research projects and the final one-third comes from doing contract research for industry. Each of the FhG institutions has close ties with both the academic world and industry. The mechanisms that ensure close links with universities include:

- a common infrastructure shared by the FhGs and their complementary university institutes (e.g. shared measurement and testing equipment);
- the employment by FhG institutions of students as research candidates who often take the opportunity to write their diploma thesis under the guidance of the FhG;
- university faculties complement their teaching programmes by appointing FhG researchers to lecture on their experience in applied research and in new industrial applications and the FhG engages university staff members as consultants in its research projects.

Close links with industry are established by:

- the deployment of researchers from industry to the FhG institutions, partly through the support of federal programmes, and partly at the cost of individual firms;
- representatives from industry play a major role in the supervisory board, which monitors the work and results of the FhG institutions;
- the FhG serves as a stepping-stone to an industrial career for many engineers, with approximately 50 per cent leaving the organization after three to five years to take up positions in industry.

As opposed to, for example, France which has a mission-oriented system, Germany's NSI is predominantly a distribution-oriented system. Technological cooperation among firms is encouraged by the government but the government is not an active matchmaker.

As the commercial use of R&D results has become more important to the international competitiveness of firms, several countries have looked over the fence to the German model. At present, FhG is the role model for countries such as Malaysia, Poland, Spain and Hungary. All countries where the FhG has been an active agent have established RTOs that resemble the FhG. In the USA, the FhG has established an office to survey technological development in the USA, and the FhG is currently negotiating with several states with the aim of setting up FhG institutes on a joint basis. The financing of these FhG establishments is done on a fifty-fifty basis, the costs being shared equally between the FhG and its US partners. The same model for financing applies to the FhG's activities in Poland, and in general the federal government supports the FhG financially in its efforts to become a major international provider of 'bridging' services.

To summarize, the FRG as an RTO institution has exhibited little in the way of adapting to globalization. Instead, Germany confidently appears set on exporting its successful recipe for industrial development. This response may in itself be regarded as being in line with Germany's national trajectory of growth which stresses internationalization by means of export.

4.2. UK – Deregulating the Technology Market

In the postwar era, the 1960s and 1980s stand out as the decades in which the most determined and coherent efforts were made to halt the decline of the British economy. The approaches taken, however, could hardly have been more different (Walker 1993). During the 1960s, the guiding assumption was that the market economy could no longer be left to its own devices. The state had an important role to play in order to ensure that inventions turned into successful innovations. This decade resembles what could be labelled Schumpeterian, with efforts focused on managing and strengthening the British system of innovation by means of allocating more resources to R&D, education and technological activity.

During and after the 1980s, British economic and industrial policy has became heavily biased towards the belief that the market economy *must* be left to its own devices, and that Britain's economic problems stem from the excessive state protection of individuals and firms. The aim has been to restore the 'spirit of free enterprise' and individual responsibility. A guiding assumption was that the government's support for innovation should be constrained in terms of expenditure. During the 1980s, the strategy adopted by British RTOs thus became focused on short-term gains and trading activities rather than on developing R&D capacities for longer-term strategic use.

The case of ERA Technology Limited is illustrative in explaining why

British RTOs, compared to, for example, German RTOs, will pursue a strategy of adaptation which stresses internationalization and places special emphasis on market orientation and independence from government support.

ERA Technology Limited dates back to 1910, when technical directors of UK electrical manufacturing companies began to meet on a monthly basis to discuss pre-competitive collaborative research. In 1919, the government offered 50 per cent funding to industry research associations and the above committee set up the Electrical Research Association to qualify for public funds. In 1969, it was recommended that 25 per cent of funding support for various research associations should be withdrawn over a period of three years. As a result the ERA became a company limited by guarantee in 1974. Today, single client business provides 80 per cent of the income of ERA Technology Limited. Furthermore, income from public contracts is expected to decrease, leaving private contracts as the major source of income.

The main strategic issue for ERA has been the disappearance of its domestic customer base, which has made it imperative for the organization to expand its business overseas. This necessity has been reinforced by the decline in UK public contracts. This has forced ERA not to rely on the Department of Trade and Industry (DTI) as a source of UK public funding. ERA is now looking at the world market and not simply the European market. In addition, ERA has set up an office in Singapore and is considering opening another in Houston, USA (SPRINT/EIMS 1994).

British Maritime Technology (BMT) is another organization that has suffered from the decline in public funding and the *laissez-faire* attitude of central government to RTOs, thereby compelling it to move from R&D to more customer-driven activities. Until 1990, BMT continued to benefit from funding, but since that time has received no direct government grants. Strategically, BMT is keen to operate more as a high-tech consulting agency than as a traditional RTO. It has become necessary to run the organization as a commercial operation and as a result most strategic issues are essentially financial ones. BMT has increased its international operations and has offices in Bangkok, Poland, USA and Hong Kong. Finally, it is noteworthy that BMT considers the lack of political support and the declining infrastructure as strategic market issues. As a consequence, the BMT has declared its support for a European system in which RTOs are subsidized purely on the basis of turnover gained competitively in the market-place – a system of fifty-fifty funding, which in turn will support the regeneration of the technology base (ibid.).

UK government policies towards technology service organizations have remained more pragmatic in practice than the rhetoric suggests. An example of such pragmatism is the regional technology transfer initiative known as 'one-stop-shops' or Business Links, which were established to provide business support services. Business Link was initiated by DTI and inspired both by the German Steinbeis model and the Danish Technology Information Centres (TICs). As such, the networking component plays a significant role in this enterprise. In addition, the British government has set up an assessment panel whose function is to evaluate each new proposal for setting up a business link. The guiding principle of the business link system is that of franchising – meaning that local industrial policy networks which gain the right to call themselves business links will benefit from state support (UK – Department of Trade and Industry 1994).

In general, the business link model has many features in common with the German and Danish network models and implies an orientation towards a more diffusion-oriented technology service system in England. The franchise model, however, is clearly geared more towards a market model than is the case with Denmark's TICs or comparable local organizations such as the Innovation Centres in Holland. In other words, the franchise component of business links adheres ideologically to the 'British flavour' of free market competition.

Until the late 1980s, the majority of European RTOs did not traditionally export their services and most of their clients tended to be domestic. A 1987 study conducted by the EU Commission on RTOs in Europe revealed that this sector was very closed in international terms, except for certain British RTOs, the most export-minded of which drew up to 20 per cent of their resources from foreign clients. Although RTOs, such as Holland's TNO, the Danish Technological Institute and certain FhG institutes can show comparable or higher incomes from foreign clients today, the British RTOs were the first to go international. Generally, international comparative studies on bridging technology service organizations seem to support the view that the UK adheres more to the market model than most other countries and has developed a market-oriented profile at a faster pace than the RTOs of most other countries. Finally, the UK experience should partly be seen as a result of the substantial reduction in the state's role in the national innovation system during the 1980s.

4.3. France – Keeping the State in

The French system of innovation is in many respects one of the clearest examples of a 'mission-oriented' innovation system. Big is seen as beautiful and priority has traditionally been given to large technology-intensive systems (military, electrical power and electrical transport) or to products that are inherently systemic (e.g. aircraft or space products). The market demand for these products has traditionally been created via politically dictated public procurement and sold abroad through political deals made by the French state.

Accordingly, French technology policy has been very much geared towards France's biggest companies, its biggest R&D institutions and 'grand projets'. As early as the beginning of the 1980s, the French government considered technology as the foundation of all economic growth, and has since then worked with the purpose of coordinating economic and technological development (Chesnais 1993).

France's technology services at the national level centre especially around the 'Agence Nationale de la Valorisation de la Recherche' – ANVAR, which is under the control of the Ministry of Industry and Economic Development and the Ministry for Education and R&D. Its legal status is comparable to that of the SNCF – the French railway system.

The French state contributes 66 per cent of ANVAR's annual budget and the rest comes from clients and contract research. Like the RTOs of most other countries, ANVAR was created to strengthen the commercial exploitation of public R&D results, but has in later years broadened its scope to other areas of activity. For example, ANVAR provides financial support for SMEs and tries to enhance network cooperation between SMEs in France.

The interaction of ANVAR with other private and public R&D institutions is guaranteed by its status as the provider of finance for commercial R&D. This financing is mainly channelled through 'high-risk' loans for the development of new products or technologies and through technology transfer. Levy (1994) argues that the attempts made to reform the French banking system in the 1980s did not solve some of the problems of financing innovations in French SMEs. Hence, the French state created a privileged state-lending pool working through ANVAR, which offers a foolproof source of cheap credit.

Another illustrative example of a French RTO and the role of the French government in its development is the Centre Scientifique et Technique du Bâtiment (CSTB) which was founded in 1947 and acquired the status of public establishment. The main reason for the creation of the CSTB was the need for the ministry in charge of reconstruction after the war to gain technical assistance in evaluating reconstruction projects. Initially, the CSTB was almost exclusively financed by state funds and was involved in very little commercial activity. Later, in the 1970s and 1980s, the CSTB was encouraged to work more on a demand–pull basis than on a technology-push basis.

As a result, basic state funds represented approximately 50 per cent of the CSTB budget in 1980. Nevertheless, the CSTB failed to expand its commercial activities at a pace which satisfied the French government and this put pressure on the CSTB to reorganize and to set up a special management department within the organization.

The CSTB has been involved in international activity since its creation – primarily at the European level. In recent years, its international strategy has been particularly focused on the European Community. In this context, the CSTB has played a role on the European stage with regard to the harmonization of standards, the codification of building products and the improvement of European cooperation research. The CSTB has been very active in penetrating EU R&D programmes such as BRITE-EURAM, ESPRIT and SPRINT.

In spite of recent efforts to 'commercialize' the CSTB it is still today a public organization and plays a role as a regulatory body between government, industry and final users.

Compared to the RTOs of other countries, the role of the government has clearly been decisive in the French case. Take for instance the original creation of different RTOs. In countries such as the UK, Germany or for that matter smaller states such as Denmark, RTOs originated as the result of initiatives made by industrialists (sometimes in concert with the authorities) in the first half of the twentieth century. And the role of the state has never taken the same symbiotic character in Germany, Denmark and Britain as it has in France. This situation is further reflected in relation to the globalization process. British RTOs were among the first to go truly international in their activities. The British strategy has been to make RTOs less dependent on public funding, and to rely less on contracts from the national government or from the EU. In stark contrast, the French RTOs seem to have followed a strategy of trying to expand internationally by interacting with the EU in the same way as they did with the French government. Indeed, French officials had earlier turned to European institutions to 'support' emerging industries such as high definition television and semiconductors. French authorities have to a greater extent than most other EU countries looked to Europe to stimulate French industry in a way that their own government no longer could. As such Europe may provide relief for exhausted national dirigiste prescriptions (Levy 1994).

In spite of the moves made towards a more market-oriented approach, the French are basically following a technology-push strategy as opposed to the British market-pull strategy. Somewhere in between these two extremes can be found the strategies of Germany, Holland and Denmark.

5. NATIONAL PATTERNS OF INSTITUTIONAL ADAPTATION

In this study RTOs from various European countries have been examined. Table 11.1 attempts to group the RTOs according to institutional affiliation and level of operation.

In France the state plays a leading and often decisive role. French RTOs have the status of state agencies and their services are provided to other state agencies and individual firms upon request. A major proportion of French RTO funding stems from government or EU funded research programmes. Hence ANVAR and CSTB, the two French RTOs considered in this study, are placed under the 'state' label while at the same time operating at the firm level.

Table 11.1. The institutional affiliation of RTOs

Level	STATE	NETWORK	MARKET
National			British Maritime Technology ERA Research Ltd Business Link (UK)
Sector	Fraunhofer *(FRG)*	Steinbeis Stiftung (Baden-Württemberg)	TNO (Netherlands) GTS-system (Denmark)
Firm	CSTB ANVAR (France)	ERVET (Italy) CNA (Italy)	

There are two development models existing in Germany. At the regional level Baden-Württemberg's Steinbeis Stiftung is the dominant actor and has established strong networks with the Länder government, banks, industry and unions. At the national level the federal government plays a more prominent role, but still with a strong 'networking' component, in relation to, for example, Fraunhofer Gesellschaft (FhG).

The UK shows the clearest example of a market-oriented model, where the role of government has been reduced dramatically during the 1980s. The two smaller countries, the Netherlands and Denmark, resemble a model which can be said to be situated somewhere between Germany and the UK. In both countries there are strong similarities to the German institutionalist model. Both the TNO and the Danish GTS system, on the other hand, are more market oriented than the FhG.

The globalization of R&D and other technology-related fields has prompted some to call into question the notion of specific national institutional and technology trajectories. Nevertheless, as demonstrated above, national patterns of institutional design are repeated and copied in the adaptation strategies of RTOs.

5.1. The Political Economy of National Systems of Innovation

As argued above, strategies of adaptation in the face of pressures for globalization follow distinct national trajectories. When analysing the operation of markets in countries such as France, Germany and the UK, political economists have pointed to the historical 'specificities' of national institutional configurations (Shonfield 1965, Zysman 1983, Katzenstein 1985).

Early contributions to the idea of the institutional shaping of market dynamics took as their point of departure the role of the state. The dichotomy, strong state – weak state, was first introduced into academic debate by Stephen Krasner. According to Krasner, the power and ability of strong states to intervene in industry was a consequence of their late industrialization. A school centred around Kenneth Dyson argued that a state's capacity for industrial restructuring was essentially dependent on the industrial culture of the society in which that state had to operate and recruit its staff. When determining the nature of a given society's 'industrial culture' popular notions of public authority are of central importance (Kluth 1995).

Andrew Shonfield's comparative study of 1965 expanded the focus of interest to include alongside the state the role of institutions such as social partners and the financial system. John Zysman, in his 1983 study of *Governments, Markets and Growth*, identified three roads to political-economic management in industrial countries:

- a state-led path with developmental objectives in which the distri-

bution of costs and gains is imposed by political manipulation of the market;
- a negotiated path with a corporatist tone in which explicit bargains are made between elites representing different segments of society; and,
- a company-led approach in which the political settlement is simply left to the market and the government is reduced to acting principally as a regulator and umpire and providing some compensation for dissatisfied losers.

Zysman argues that the institutional arrangements of the market and the public administration provide the setting in which political conflicts over the economy take place. They provide the form and structure of those conflicts which occur over industrial change and economic policy:

> The institutions, both economic and political, in which those fights occur articulate how groups must organise to achieve their objectives, often who their allies will be, usually what their tactics must be, and certainly what can be obtained from them. (Zysman 1983).

In France, the state apparatus itself appears to be the arena where political conflicts are fought. The main actors in this process are the executive branch of government and the highly skilled central bureaucracy recruited on the basis of an extremely elitist yet transparent set of rules.

In Italy, the state also assumes a critical role in political battles. In the Italian model of clientelism, public enterprises have held a dominant position in industrial and labour market policies. Interest groups do not, to the same extent as for example in northern Europe, constitute permanent and stable power centres in their own right.

Both the French and Italian systems are, in a certain sense, essentially 'etatist'. Nevertheless, while the French state is a highly autonomous actor in its own right, Italian politics is characterized by its focus on battles for control of various branches and levels of government.

France can thus be seen as proponent of a centralized state-management system. Industries have worked directly through government rather than through 'civic' interest groups. Policy outcomes have often been monumental although not always entirely relevant to the problems that needed to be solved. The private nature of interests gaining access to the policy arena has often resulted in solutions based on 'favouritism'. Instead of attempting to find structural solutions which could be jointly adopted and implemented, concerning for example the problems of unemployment and limited economic growth, French policies have been geared towards solutions favouring 'national champions', which have benefited from massive loans, excessive public procurement and generous research grants.

Consequently, the French approach to RTO design places the state at the centre of the stage. The operations of ANVAR and CSTB are thus directly aimed at individual firms as prescribed by the country's industrial policy tradition. With regard to internal organization, both agencies submit to the legacy of state bureaucracy.

Italy's RTOs share certain elements in common with their French counterparts. Notable differences, however, greatly overshadow these common features. First and foremost, the political culture of clientelism acts in parallel with an economic culture featuring strong communal elements which are most evident in the operation of rather close networks between firms. This is reflected in the design of ERVET in Emilia Romagna, which, although geared towards firm-level operation, is placed in the network category of the typology presented in Table 11.1.

The USA and UK in turn can be viewed as examples of decentralized market-managed systems. Governments have preferred to intervene as little as possible in the economic sphere, providing little incentive for the rise of nationwide interest groups. As a rule, groups tend to be more fragmented, issue specific and directly aimed at tangible benefit aggregation than is the case with their northern European counterparts. This has spurred the development of a political system dominated by pluralism.

Both US and UK economic cultures feature a dynamic competitive ideal of firm behaviour. In line with this, British RTOs operate according to a market rationale and display little of the bureaucratic features inherent in ANVAR and CSTB.

Finally, Germany, Scandinavia and Holland have operated a system emphasizing direct negotiations between labour, business and government. This has produced a political climate which encourages complex bargains with long-term consequences.

In his study of German and UK competitiveness, David Soskice (1991) draws attention to the operation of 'institutional infrastructures' which predispose societies towards specific modes of policy making. Soskice points to the duration of, and level of trust in, relations between societal actors and the state as being particularly important in shaping the general political environment.

In polities with advanced institutional infrastructures, no formal institutions are necessarily needed in order to achieve an effective system of private-public sector interaction. The demise of high salience institutional configurations, as found in the neo-corporatist systems of northwestern Europe in the mid-1970s, has not resulted in competitive pluralism but rather in a decentralized yet negotiated polity defined by Soskice as a flexible system of coordination.

As in the writings of Dyson and the negotiated approach, political culture, and what in neo-Gramscian language has been labelled 'discourse setting', assumes a central role in identifying the basic institutional infrastructure of a given polity.

Table 11.2 below summarized the basic characteristics of national political economies. Following Zysman, the overall institutional properties of national polities frame decisions on the future developments of NSIs.

Table 11.2. An institutional typology of political economies

	WEAK FORMAL INSTITUTIONAL STRUCTURES	*STRONG FORMAL INSTITUTIONAL STRUCTURES*
Simple Institutional infrastructures	*Pluralism* Competing elites sectorized governance	*Etatism* Centralized 'dirigiste' governance
Advanced Institutional infrastructures	Clientelism Segmented patron governance	Networking Post-corporatist discourse governance

Formal institutional structures denote mainly the character of the state and the efficiency and operational transparency of other political-economic pillars such as business associations and trade unions. Institutional infrastructures denote the character of relationships between actors (e.g. firms, government agencies and trade unions) in national political economies. Institutional infrastructures to a large extent determine the development of formal structures. Consequently, institutional infrastructures are more firmly socially and culturally embedded than formal structures. The table above illustrates the framework within which national adaptation processes take place.

6. CONCLUSION

Distinct national approaches to the production, diffusion and application of technology can be identified. This is well illustrated by reference to the German, the British and the French models. The differences are reflected in the design and operation of national RTOs and in their response to pressures for globalization. We have illustrated above the differences between national RTOs in relation to institutional dynamics and design.

In order to assess the patterns of adaptation adopted by RTOs, it must be noted that the pressures for change have been channelled through the distinct community of actors in which these organizations are embedded. In addition, the responses of the RTOs dealt with here should be understood in relation to two kinds of development. The first involves the pressure sparked off by global changes. This refers to forces outside the control of each RTO and nation. The second concerns developments arising from internal national responses and pressures caused by political choices made in the course of change. In this respect, the RTOs' communities are national in the same sense as there are distinct national technology trajectories, technological networks and communities. However, networks do not operate along identical patterns across industries or technologies. The dye-stuff industry, for example, emerged as a largely German industry. In this case, the network was clearly determined by common training in German universities, and by the links existing between company laboratories and the universities. In the USA and Denmark, communities concerned with farming and the processing of farm products developed in association with government-supported research programmes and various forms of cooperatives (Nelson 1993).

Looking at other areas of economic and technological activity, 'the national impact hypothesis' is given even further support. The financial systems of the three countries compared here all reflect distinct national characteristics, as do their airline systems or the strategies of telecommunications companies such as British Telecom, Deutsche Telekom or Alcatel in France. In accordance with this argument, British RTOs and companies will most likely adopt a market-oriented approach when going global, whereas the French case will be one of tight cooperation with governments and public authorities at home and abroad. The German and, with some variations, the Danish and Dutch models will be institutionalist in the sense that the free market approach of the British is basically seen as sound but needs – at least initially – a guiding hand. In addition, it should be mentioned that in Germany, Holland and Denmark the different RTOs have created common bodies – in Denmark there is the Advanced Technology Group in cooperation with a newly established Technology Service Council, and in Holland the institutes of the TNOs have established a TNO Marketing Department:

the Bureau for International Coordination and Consultant Services. While being competitors at home, therefore, the RTOs of these countries have more or less pooled their resources in such areas as marketing where it may be possible to create economies of scale without resigning from traditional competition in the market. There does not seem to be a similar model of cooperation in the UK. It is difficult to predict the impact of such 'pooling of resources', but most of the UK's RTOs belong to the medium-sized category (200–300 persons), whereas the pooling of resources among institutes in TNO, FhG and the Danish GTS system increases the number of people involved to 4 200, 7 700 and 3 100 respectively. This is bound to give some advantages of scale on the international level to the latter and give the RTOs of these countries better chances of 'exporting' their individual institutes as 'systems'.

Furthermore, it may be instructive to refer to the legacy of List. According to List, English economists failed to distinguish between national and global interests. Nations need to build a national system of political economy. This seems to be the case in Germany, Holland and Denmark, but not the UK. Finally, the fact that French RTOs are less engaged internationally is mainly due to the historical 'tutelage' of the French government. If or when, however, the French adopt a more global strategy, it can be expected that the government will try to establish advantages of scale for its RTOs similar to those achieved in other strategies of industrial development in France.

The globalization of RTOs, however, also complicates the 'national hypothesis'. In particular, the adaptation strategies of the FhG and British RTOs may serve to blur the central features of NSI. Just as the early story of radio was one of transnational activity, involving inventors and companies in the UK, the USA and Western Europe, all building on the work of each other, German and British-based RTOs may assume a role of bridging institutions, integrating the work of government laboratories, universities, manufacturers and labour force educators of different countries. Likewise, the French way of conducting business within the EU could essentially be interpreted as a way of expanding the French NSI to a European level. If successful, the implication would be that the NSIs of the other member countries would only have to converge in a new model.

Germany, Britain, France, the Netherlands and Denmark are countries featuring a clear national identity and a well-established state apparatus. Evidence in support of a *regional* trajectory argument, however, can be found in countries displaying fragmented national identity and government institutions. The Canadian NSI exhibits profound traits of French influence in the province of Quebec and British influence in most other provinces. Given the guiding hypothesis of this paper, one should expect that Quebec's provincial research organization, the Centre De Recherche Industrielle Du Quebec (CRIQ), would have strong affiliations to the French NSI whereas, for example, the Saskatchewan Research Council (SRC), would resemble the British system. Needless to say, this test of the 'national versus globalization hypothesis' within one country falls outside the scope of this chapter, but there are certainly indications pointing to the fact that the Canadian provinces reveal such institutional biases. The French-speaking province of Quebec has thus signed a memorandum of understanding with France with the aim of creating a centre for the promotion of technological and industrial cooperation, and the French region of Rhône-Alpes has a promotional office in Montreal (NGL 1991). In addition, cooperation between France and Quebec, which accounted for 18.4 per cent of exchanges in 1990, is three times greater than official cooperation between Quebec's other ten main partners in international scientific cooperation (Gouvernement Quebec 1993).

REFERENCES

Archibugi, D. and Michie, J. (1995) 'The Globalization of Technology: A New Taxonomy'. *Cambridge Journal of Economics* 19.

Chesnais, F. (1993) 'The French National System of Innovation' in R. Nelson (ed.) *National Innovation Systems – A Comparative Perspective*. Oxford: Oxford University Press.

Clement, K. (1994) *Regional Policy and Technology Transfer: A Cross National Perspective*. Glasgow: European Research Centre, University of Stratchclyde.

Danmarks Teknologiske Institut (1994) *SPRINT EIMS*. Copenhagen.

Department of Trade and Industry (1994) *Business Link – Prospectus for One Stop Shops for Business*. London: HMSO.

Dosi, G. and Orsengio, L. (1988) 'Industrial Structure and Technical Change' in A. Heertje (ed.) *Innovation, Technology, and Finance*. Oxford: Basil Blackwell.

Dyson, K. (1983) The State Tradition in Western Europe. Oxford: Martin Robertson.

Dyson, K. and Wilks, S. (eds) (1983) *Industrial Crises – A Comparative Study of State and Industry*. Oxford, Martin Robertson.

Ergas, H. (1986) 'Does Technology Policy Matter?'. CEPS Paper No. 29, Centre for European Policy Studies, Brussels.

Francois, C. (1993) 'The French National System of Innovation' in R. Nelson (ed.) *National Innovation Systems – A Comparative Analysis*. Oxford: Oxford University Press.

Gouvernement Quebec, Ministère de l'Enseignement Supérieur et de la Science (1993) *Science Indicators Compendium 1993*. Quebec, Canada.

Kandel, N. (1994) 'RTO Infrastructure in Europe: Analytical Survey' in J.R. Tiscar (ed.) *The Future of Research and Technology Organisations in Europe.* Luxembourg: CEC.

Katzenstein, P. (1985) *Small States in World Markets.* Ithaca, NY: Cornell University Press.

Kluth, M. (1995) 'Why a Social Dimension' FS&P. Roskilde University.

Levy, J. (1994) 'After Etatisme: Dilemmas of Institutional Reform in Post-Dirigiste France' in *De Toqueville's Revenge: Dilemmas of Institution Building in Post-Dirigiste France.* San Francisco: University of California Berkeley.

Ministry of Business and Industry and Danish Agency for Development Trade and Industry (1995) *Teknologisk Service.* Copenhagen.

Nelson, R. (ed.) (1993) *National Innovation Systems – A Comparative Perspective.* Oxford: Oxford University Press.

NGL Consulting Ltd (1991) 'Canada's Science and Technology Relations with Europe'. A Review Prepared for Industry, Science and Technology Canada, Ontario, Canada.

OECD (1992) *TEP – The Technology Economy Programme – Technology and The Economy The Key Relationships.* Paris: OECD.

Reinert, E. (1994) 'Competitiveness and its Predecessors – A 500 Year Cross National Perspective'. Paper presented at the Nordic Innovation Network Conference, Copenhagen.

Shonfield, A. (1965) *Modern Capitalism.* London.

Soskice, D. (1991) 'The Institutional Infrastructure for International Competitiveness: A Comparative analysis of the UK and Germany', Unpublished paper. Berlin: WZB.

SPRINT/EIMS (1994) *Research and Technology Organisations Study to Support Evaluation, Auditing and Benchmarking leading to Strategy Development.* Denmark: Danish Technological Institute.

Swedeberg, R. (1991) *Joseph A. Schumpeter – His Life and Work.* Cambridge: Polity.

Tiscar, J.R. (ed.) (1994) *The Future of Research and Technology Organisations in Europe.* Brussels: EU Commission.

Walker, W. (1993) 'National Innovations Systems – Britain' in R. Nelson (ed.) *National Innovation Systems – A Comparative Perspective.* Oxford: Oxford University Press.

Zysman, J. (1983) *Governments, Markets and Growth.* Cornell: University Press.

Zysman, J. (1993) 'Trade Technology and National Competition'. Restricted paper presented at the first meeting of the Working Group on Innovation and Technology Policy, OECD, Paris.

Zysman, J. (1994a) *How Institutions Create Historically Rooted Trajectories.* Oxford.

Zysman, J. (1994b) 'Nations, Institutions and Technological Development'. BRIE Paper, University of California, Berkeley.

Index